Instructional Computing

An Action Guide for Educators

Instructional Computing

An Action Guide for Educators

J. Richard Dennis
University of Illinois at Urbana-Champaign

Robert J. Kansky
University of Wyoming

Scott, Foresman and Company **Glenview, Illinois**
Dallas, Texas *Oakland, New Jersey* *Palo Alto, California* *Tucker, Georgia* *London*

Library of Congress Cataloging in Publication Data

Dennis, J. Richard
Instructional computing

Includes index
1. Computer-assisted instruction. 2. Computer managed instruction. 3. Education—Computer programs—Purchasing.
I. Kansky, Robert J. II. Title
LB1028.5.D38 1984 371.3'9445 84-1259
ISBN 0-673-16606-6

Printed in the United States of America.

1 2 3 4 5 6 7 - DBH - 89 88 87 86 85 84

Preface

Instructional Computing: An Action Guide for Educators is directed to any educator who is interested in the use of the computer to improve classroom instruction. It is a book about the materials, human factors, and decision-making procedures that comprise the instructional application of computers. Its single goal is to promote educators' thoughtful selection and use of both computerized courseware and the devices needed to deliver it.

For the undergraduate student of education, *Instructional Computing* provides a broad overview of the ideas, materials, and decision-making forces that are shaping the instructional application of computers. In addition, the issues raised with respect to courseware design and the interaction of computers and curricula should generate ideas worthy of further investigation by graduate students who are new to the field of instructional computing. Inservice teachers, administrators, and curriculum developers will find that the book offers practical assistance in planning for and implementing the use of computers as tools of instruction.

To Know the Territory: Chapters 1–14

In *The Music Man,* Meredith Willson's traveling salesmen reduce success to a single principle: "Ya gotta know the territory!" The principle is equally applicable to the development of a successful plan for implementing instructional computing. Like Willson's traveling salesmen, educators seeking to provide leadership in introducing instructional uses of computers must be familiar both with the products to be "sold" and with the concerns and motivations of the persons who will "buy" those products. This book is designed to be a guide to the recently discovered territory of instructional computing.

Chapter 1 takes a brief glance backward at the origins of computers in the classroom. After a Chapter 2 overview of several instructional faces which computers present to the educator, we turn to the critical issue of locating and evaluating computerized instructional materials in Chapter 4. Chapters 3 and 5 through 12 further serve the single issue of courseware evaluation by examining the characteristics, potential, current limitations, and components of each of several types of instructional computer programs. In short, Chapters 2 through 12 seek to make the educator a learned critic of computerized courseware.

In the final chapters, the focus of the discourse moves from the presentation of information to the making of decisions. Chapter 13 seeks to engage the educator in exercising his or her newly acquired in-depth awareness of computerized courseware. The task presented is that of developing and implementing a planned program of instructional computing. That planning, in turn, provides the statements of purpose which are the necessary bases of the purchasing decisions made in Chapter 14.

The ICAC Papers

Each of Chapters 1 through 14 evolved from a "paper" that discussed a topic identified as important to the members of a very special group of professionals: the educators and laypersons who comprise the Instructional Computing Advisory Committee (ICAC) of East Roachmont Independent School District. Originally called "The ICAC Papers" by their authors, these documents have been rewritten and augmented for a broader audience. Augmentation has taken the form of a Study Guide that appears at the end of each chapter. The purpose of each chapter's Study Guide is to look into the discussions of the chapter to assure an understanding of what is written.

A Decision-Making Context

One of the inherent attractions of an autobiography is that it presents decision making within personal and historical contexts. The situations presented have immediate relevance to the reader who can identify with the author or who can see the author's situations as reasonable approximations of current events. By contrast, textbooks often seem removed from, even unaware of, the variety of realities within which their lessons are to be applied.

Since this book makes the claim of being "An Action Guide for Educators," it is obligatory that we somehow address the practical side of introducing instructional computing into a precollege environment. To this end, the considerations of all the chapters are accompanied by a report of the deliberations of the members of ICAC. In fact, the issues discussed throughout are those chosen by the members of ICAC to guide them in their study and decision making. This example of school decision making (called Agenda for Action) begins following Chapter 2. Additional episodes appear following Chapters 4 through 14. The Agenda look outward from the discussions of the chapters to their application.

Appendixes

While the Study Guides and Agenda are add-ons by which "papers" become "chapters," four of the original papers (now Chapters 6, 12, 13, and 14) concluded with "appendixes" which were, in fact, integral parts of the papers. Each appendix is an illustration or instrument that helps to sharpen the reader's vision relative to a major concept discussed in the body of the chapter it accompanies. The decision to place these illustrative materials at the end of chapters as so-called appendixes was consistent with the wish to make them easy to refer to during and after the reading of the chapter. Hence, the appendixes comprise a central feature of the overall text, their physical positions not to be equated with their importance.

A Beginner's Glossary of Computer Terms

The ultimate appendix to *Instructional Computing* is its Glossary of Computerese. Although the authors took care to replace the specialized vocabulary of the field of instructional computing with the more familiar language of the schools and instruction, there were occasions (such as in Chapter 4) in which total avoidance of computing terms would have been foolhardy. While the Beginner's Glossary of Computerese is a modest lexicon by almost any measure of the demands for precise communication among computing enthusiasts, it is sufficient as a handy reference when reading Chapters 1 through 13. In Chapter 14, this beginner's guide to the jargon of the instructional computing journals and the vendors of instructional computing materials is suddenly and emphatically elevated to the role of essential aid (i.e., constant companion).

Realizing that you will meet both computing journals and vendors long before Chapter 14, the glossary has been detached from that chapter and placed at the end of the text. Its entries have been placed on one side of the page in order to provide you with space to extend and personalize this minimal listing with such terms as either answer to your special interests or simply tickle your fancy.

A Cancelled Attraction (and How to Obtain It)

Despite the efforts of this Preface to draw your attention to such unique or salutary features as this book *has*, you will be quick to observe a feature which it *has not:* nowhere upon its pages will you find a single reference to an example of a commercially available item of computerized courseware. This obvious omission is neither an oversight nor an implicit argument that exemplary programs do not exist. The omission is, however, deliberate. You may well ask "Why?"

Why, indeed? Why, as one reviewer put it, do we "avoid a world of computer software"? In fact, we are very much aware of both the dimensions and dynamics of that world. It is a fluid world whose boundaries are undergoing constant redefinition as equipment improves, teachers' expectations are refined, research and experience are brought to bear, and curricula are restructured to make use of this new instructional resource. It is a world that has been heretofore populated mainly by small shopkeepers and which is only loosely governed by tentative standards of development, marketing, and evaluation. Today's best example of a given application is improved, renamed, or superceded by another before the ink is dry on its review. But even at the moment of this writing, the entry of large corporations into the computerized courseware field promises sudden and dramatic reshaping of the software world. Whatever examples we might give would be obsolete before this book is printed, and an obsolete example is worse than no example at all.

However, we will tell you how to locate current examples of courseware (and their reviews). Although such sources also are subject to change, their stability is far greater than the items of the field they survey. In the course of this book, and particularly in Chapter 4, we will direct you to several sources of courseware identification and review. then, fully agreeing with our reviewer's observation that it is utter folly to discuss computer software while avoiding contact with it, we urge you to use our suggested sources to enter and explore the current world of computerized instructional materials. It is there that you will see the latest embodiments of the many faces of instructional computing.

A Matter of Dedication

The organization and substance of this book have evolved during three years of evaluation by students and colleagues. Its present form was significantly influenced by the observations and suggestions of four dedicated reviewers of earlier drafts: Richard Hamlin, Henry Kepner, Charles Lamb, and Deborah Soglin. In addition, our special in-house critics, Charlene and Gretchen, have shared foregone vacations while excising conceptual and grammatical blunders from drafts we thought were perfect.

Special thanks are in order for Bill Heck, Jerry Johnson, and the National Council of Teachers of Mathematics. It is through their cooperation that we are able to bring you the contents of Chapter 4 in the form that has met enthusiastic reception by educators in many subject matter fields.

We bow to the translation skills and nimble fingers of our typists, Betty Ann Absher and Ginny McCarrey. It is their keen eyesight and much-worn spelling guides that have produced recognizable words and sentences from our handscript.

Finally — and although we are obligated to tell you that they do not exist — we are grateful to the educators of East Roachmont School District who have guided us in the development of both style and content. Awards of special merit go to those intrepid members of the Instructional Computing Advisory Committee (ICAC): John, Carrinne, Donna, Gerri, Jeanne, Lolita, Phil, and Ted.

J. Richard Dennis

Robert J. Kansky

Contents

Instructional Computing

An Action Guide for Educators

CHAPTER ONE

Computers in the Classroom: A Historical Perspective

The purpose of the next few pages is to present an informal overview of recent history (since 1950) with respect to the uses of computers in elementary and secondary schools. It is not a scholarly history of educational computing; neither is it an attempt to review the general history of computers.

Our style of writing is also informal. Apart from using footnotes to give credit where credit is due on specific issues and a few headings to help you focus on time periods or issues, we deliberately avoid long lists of references that you probably have neither the time nor interest to pursue at this point. Besides, there is little value in detailing the past; rather, this simple introduction will give you sufficient background to read journals and newsletters dealing with current issues in instructional computing. Cross-references found in those publications will direct you on appropriate trips into the past.

From time to time, we may use a computer-related term which is not part of your current vocabulary. For instance, in this chapter we will refer to *hardware*, *software*, a *high-level computing language*, *memory*, *program*, and *syntax*. Remember that many such terms (these, in particular) are defined in the Beginner's Glossary of Computerese which appears as the appendix to this book.

First Efforts: Instruction as a Function of Computing Hardware

Some of the earliest efforts to utilize computers in instruction took place in the late 1950s and early 1960s. At that time, computers were very large and very expensive. They required lots of electrical power and demanded careful control of the environmental conditions (humidity, dust, temperature, and static) within which they worked. In short, they had expensive tastes and were very fussy about service.

The "Sputnik surprise" of 1957 had a major influence on U.S. education at the very time that computers first were entering the precollege curriculum. American shock at the Russian accomplishment was translated into a concern for the quality of American education in mathematics and the sciences and generated a national effort to improve matters through federally and privately supported curriculum projects (the "new math" and "new science") and associated teacher reeducation programs.

The "new math" and "new science" fervor of the 1950s and 1960s generally ignored the computer due to what was then its extreme cost. Such computer programming as was included in teacher education institutes of the period usually was concerned with the mathematics of digital circuits. The focus was on the mechanics of computing rather than upon its application in instruction. One teacher, exposed to this level of computing and seeking to apply his knowledge within the classroom, discovered that telephone companies often had a surplus supply of operable switching relays and that they would donate some of these relays to schools. Using such equipment, the teacher set about having his students experiment with the construction of circuits that would add numbers (expressed in binary form), make simple branching decisions, etc. The teacher's experience in computing resulted in an instructional use that examined the machine-level operation of the computer. Thus, the computer was an *object of* instruction rather than a *tool for* instruction.

During this period, a project at Stanford University implicitly defined one direction for the design of future computer-based instructional materials. The project, directed by Dr. Patrick Suppes, created a complete, computer-based arithmetic skills practice facility. These arithmetic materials were used in a variety of elementary school settings. The same group of developers then produced skill materials for elementary school language arts. Today, evolved forms of both programs are available for a minicomputer system through the corporation formed by Suppes.[1] Many companies developing materials for the microcomputer market today also are preparing skills packages of the type designed by Suppes.

One important outcome of the work by Suppes was the demonstration that successful use of computers in the schools would require the creation of a large number of articulated programs rather than isolated, topical lessons. Many vendors of computerized instructional materials still have not accepted the need to develop carefully organized and integrated sets of materials (computer programs, texts, laboratory materials, etc.) which are linked to computer programs able to manage and evaluate both instruction and instructional resources. To accomplish such a goal, the computer must be "taught" all the details of what any good teacher knows as a *curriculum*.

Computing Hardware as a Function of Instruction

While the majority of educators of the early 1960s took existing computer equipment as a given and accepted the task of developing instructional applications to fit that equipment, a project at the University of Illinois took a significantly different stance. Just as the automobile of the early 1900s had been recognized as a valuable new general-purpose mode of transportation, so the computer was recognized as a breakthrough in (among other things) the field of communication. On the other hand, the general-purpose automobile was quickly modified to fit a wide variety of specific transportation uses: it made no sense to try to use a touring car to haul crushed rock. Thus, the PLATO® Project[2] set about the tasks of developing computing machinery (hardware) and computer programs (software) which were designed specifically for educational purposes. The PLATO® Project sought to develop a system which could carry on instruction in a wide range of subjects (chemistry, Chinese, veterinary science, elementary school mathematics, etc.) for a large number of persons both simultaneously and inexpensively. Over the years, the project's hardware inventions and software demonstrations have served to illustrate the magnitude of the technological needs of education. Now in use across the United States and in several foreign countries, PLATO® lessons accommodate an audience which includes children, college students, adults needing training in reading and basic mathematics, and highly skilled professionals expanding their knowledge and skill. The system is used to reach persons with different cultural backgrounds, different native languages, or with a variety of special needs such as blindness or orthopedic handicaps.

[1] Computer Curriculum Corporation, 1701 W. Euless Blvd., Suite 139, Euless, Texas 76039.

[2] PLATO® now is a registered trademark of the Control Data Corporation.

GIVING A LOT TO GET A LITTLE STARTED

The impact of computers upon elementary and secondary education was gradual. Classroom applications were scattered physically and were a function of local resources, both human and machine. In the 1960s, for instance, a mathematics or science teacher working near a large city or university might organize a field trip to a computer center. Another teacher, who had encountered programming, might present a short unit to an advanced mathematics class, the unit often being taught without student access to a computer. Since the programs written under such conditions could not be validated by execution on a computer, the teacher would evaluate them in much the same way as an English teacher would evaluate a theme. Such evaluation was a laborious task for the teacher and, understandably, not very rewarding for the student.

A few teachers managed to get access to the computing equipment of nearby businesses or universities for the purpose of running (and obtaining printed feedback on) a few student programs. These programming experiences demanded that the student programs first be converted to a medium readable by the computer. This, in turn, generally required obtaining access to card-punching machines for enough time for the students (or the teacher) to type the programs onto those famous IBM cards. The decks of cards were then taken to the computing facility and left there to be run when time was available. The results of the run would be picked up at some future date (or returned to the teacher by mail). Programs which did not run properly were analyzed for errors in typing or logic, new cards were prepared, and the process was repeated. Clearly, the teacher doing this pioneering work had to display inordinate patience and dedication; hence, the opportunity for students to engage in computing was a function of the academic devotion of individual teachers. (So what's new?)

GETTING DOWN TO BASICS

Another milestone in educational computing occurred at Dartmouth College in 1963, when a high-level computing language for "teaching" (programming) a computer to do specific tasks was invented. The language was called BASIC (for *B*eginners *A*ll-purpose *S*ymbolic *I*nstruction *C*ode). The word *beginners* in the name of this language is significant, since one of its touted attributes is the ease with which it can be learned. This feature has caused BASIC to become overwhelmingly the most common language used at the precollege level, where it has proved to be an easy and relatively efficient medium for students to use in creating problem-solving programs. Teaching *about* computers has become a dominant aspect of computer use in schools since the introduction of BASIC.

Today there are almost as many dialects of BASIC as there are models of computers. Like dialects of a spoken language, all dialects of BASIC share vocabulary, syntax, punctuation, and logic. But because of the literal precision with which a computer interprets language (unlike a human understanding variations in dialect of the mother tongue), a program written in one dialect of BASIC will not be understood by a computer prepared with a different dialect. Humans must intervene at this point and translate a program from one dialect to the other before it can be successfully used on a different model computer. Some limited success has been achieved using a computer even for this dialect-changing task, although the computer's work must be refined through a manual "cleaning up" by a knowledgeable person.

BEYOND TUTORIALS: NEW INSTRUCTIONAL ROLES FOR COMPUTERS

The period 1965–70 showed a gradual change in the instructional computing scene. Realization of the extraordinary effort required to produce effective computerized instructional materials caused educators to take another look at the role of the computer in the classroom. Attempts to develop the computer as a substitute for the teacher were replaced by extensive efforts to teach students to use a computer as a problem-solving tool and by efforts to utilize the computer as a teacher aide. In the latter case, instructional computing enthusiasts turned to the application usually referred to as computer-managed instruction (CMI).

Interest in CMI was, in part, an expression of the great stress placed on individualization of education after the 1960s. Efforts to individualize each student's schooling in such variables as content, time devoted to specific topics, style of presentation, and level of difficulty resulted in dramatic increases in the complexity of management tasks required of the teacher. A variety of next assignments, multiple versions of tests, a schedule of individual consultations with students, and programs of specific remediation had to be easily accessed and frequently updated. While the hiring and training of teacher aides was one method of satisfying these increased management loads, educators soon noted that many of the management tasks were routine and could be described in great detail. Recognition of the mechanical and repetitious nature of many tasks led some school districts to establish projects aimed at instituting computer management of those tasks, projects which restructured certain instructional materials to permit computer-readable student responses. Based upon the responses of an individual student, the computer would conduct a diagnosis, make assignments, and collect/process data about both the student and the instructional materials.

One aspect of instructional management received so much attention that it is now viewed as a separate educational application of computers called *computer-assisted testing* (CAT) or *computer-assisted test construction* (CATC). The computer's role in CAT is to store, organize, and quickly retrieve large numbers of test items associated with some area of subject matter. Given the desired characteristics of an examination, the computer's tasks are to present a set of test questions which fit those characteristics, score the tests, and present an analysis of the performance of either an individual student or group of students. Also, the program can gather and report information about the test questions themselves that can be used to modify and improve them.

THE 1970S: A DECADE OF CHANGE

By the late 1960s, computing machinery was beginning to appear in the schools. The principal function of that machinery, however, was to provide administrative services. Small amounts of computing time were allotted to instruction, and this usually was devoted to teaching computer programming.

Nationwide data gathered in 1970 and again in 1975 revealed considerable growth in the use of computers in secondary education.[3] In 1970, about 31 percent of the nation's secondary schools were making administrative use of computers, and 13 percent used computers in instruction. However, to say that 13 percent of the nation's schools are making instructional uses of computers does not mean that 13 percent of the teachers or students are involved in or benefiting from those uses. On the contrary, the 1970 data of Bukoski and Korotkin showed that the median number of students in computer-using schools was about 1350, while the median number of terminals available was two. The instructional impact of the computer across the curriculum necessarily was severely limited, with classes in mathematics and computer science accounting for 61 percent of all computer utilization. This restricted use was understandable in view of teacher training and of equipment cost and efficiency. Available equipment tended to be very slow; schools simply could not afford the equipment necessary to keep several students actively engaged at the same time or for a sufficient length of time.

The decade of the 1970s saw three major changes in school computing. Two of these involved hardware; the third, instructional materials. The hardware breakthroughs began with the development and aggressive marketing of minicomputers. These machines were much smaller, required fewer environmental controls, and were far less expensive than earlier equipment. School districts (mainly those having several secondary schools) acquired their own minicomputers for shared use among the district's schools. Some districts purchased computer systems devoted wholly to instructional activities, with administrative computing to be done on a separate system. A few schools had a "computers-for-everyone" vision, which was first expressed as a special unit on computers placed within an existing course required of all or most students.

The latter half of the 1970s was marked by the introduction of the microcomputer. Available for the first time in assembled form for a few hundred to a few thousand dollars, the microcomputer (soon to be called the personal computer) promised a sudden and major influence on the future of instructional computing. Retail computer stores appeared in even modest-sized communities; the purchase and servicing of computers became like that of television sets. This latest generation of computers was characterized by compactness, reliability, versatility, and, last but certainly not least, low cost. Technology was making schools an offer that they couldn't refuse.

Before 1975, microcomputers had been available in kit form. The marketing target was the electronic hobbyist who thought that half the fun of computing was getting all the little parts to cooperate. More than a few teachers were to be found in this mother-I'd-rather-do-it-myself group, and it is probably their influence which led schools to believe that significant savings could be had through self-assembly (by students and teachers) of computing equipment. While the few teachers who tried this self-assembly probably would agree that the experience was valuable for all concerned, the practice was soon abandoned for a number of reasons. For one thing, only a few people could participate actively in the project. For those involved, the time required to produce a working unit was great enough to give rise to significant problems of continued motivation. Moreover, the risk of never getting reliable operation was

[3]William J. Bukoski and Arthur L. Korotkin, "Computing Activities in Secondary Education," *Educational Technology* 16, no. 1 (January 1976): 9–23.

high. Thus, while the plan was a good one for the few who wanted to learn a lot about computer design and operation, it was a poor way to equip a school to do instructional computing.

The decade of the 1970s also witnessed important changes in the volume, variety, and quality of educational materials. Established publishing houses began to release books about computers (their history, construction, impact on society, etc.), computer programming, and the application of computers to a variety of fields. A host of small, "mom-and-pop" publishing operations came into being seemingly overnight. These new firms marketed a wide spectrum of different journals, books, and newsletters designed for the computing enthusiast. Many published reviews of computer programs available (at a price, of course) to microcomputer users; some printed the computer programs themselves. Some went so far as to publish programs in a computer-readable form so that the purchaser could immediately use the program on a given machine! By the end of the 1970s, the sale of programs of all kinds for microcomputers had reached sizeable proportions.

The study by Bukoski and Korotkin presented one measure of the changes introduced between 1970 and 1975. In 1975, about 53 percent of the nation's secondary schools were making administrative use of computers, and 27 percent were using computers for instructional purposes. (Of the latter, 5 percent had computer systems devoted entirely to instructional applications.) When compared with the 1970 data, the 1975 figures revealed that administrative use of computers had grown at a rate of about 5 percent per year, whereas instructional use had grown about 3 percent per year. Assuming the same rate of growth over the next ten years, it was estimated that about 51 percent of the schools would be making some instructional application of computers in 1984. It's worth noting, however, that work by Bukoski and Korotkin was completed just before the microcomputer revolution. The current availability of small, powerful, inexpensive computers has accelerated instructional applications far beyond the 1984 projections.

That the growth rate for administrative use was higher than that for instructional use during the period 1970–75 is not surprising. Good support materials (computer programs) for aiding school administration had been made available as modifications of programs developed for other business operations. By contrast, no segment of the economy other than the schools had a vested interest in developing instructional programs in the various precollege subject areas. Also, the monies necessary to purchase administrative computing services could be obtained more readily, since the benefits of computerizing administrative tasks could be clearly identified and expressed in terms of dollars saved or new services performed. It was not possible to identify and ensure similar gains relative to instructional uses. Finally, gains in the administrative environment usually meant training a few people (the administrator and immediate support staff) to change their habits with regard to very specific aspects of their work. The implementation of computing for instruction, on the other hand, posed monumental problems because of the number of persons potentially affected and the variety of changes implied.

Unfortunately, the advances in hardware and software had no immediate effect upon instructional computing in the schools. The scope of school activity in this area in 1975 was little changed from that of 1970. The Bukoski and Korotkin report showed that the principal activity was still the teaching of programming. The focus of such activity was usually introductory; only a few schools offered extended experience (four to six semesters of work) with several computing languages. Also, it was a rare school that attempted the "computers-for-everyone" approach. As in 1970, only a few teachers were involved. It was not surprising that those teachers came from fields in which computing was accepted at face value: mathematics, business, and science. The incidence and scope of instructional computing in other areas of the curriculum was very low. In the absence of readily available instructional materials, what more could be expected?

The 1980s: The Rebirth of Instructional Computing

There is reason to believe that the 1980s will be the decade in which instructional computing will emerge from the chrysalis formed by the hobbyist and the teacher of computer programming. The combination of forces that are creating a new body of instructional computing activity includes the widespread interests of professional educational groups, the rapid development of microcomputer hardware, and a growing financial incentive to produce high-quality computerized instructional materials.

The wholesale production of small computers effected a hardware revolution in the schools in just ten years. In 1970, schools would strive for access to one or two teletypewriter terminals linked by phone lines to a large, centrally located computer. In 1980, the same schools were purchasing dozens of microcomputers with such features as television-like terminals, color, graphics, character sets for several languages, and music-generating capability. The teletype-printing speed of 11 keystrokes per second (about 80 words per minute) was replaced by a television-terminal speed of as much as 960 keystrokes per second (about 7200 words per minute).[4]

By 1982, it was possible to purchase a battery-operated computer as small as a hand calculator and programmable in BASIC for less than $200. Another computer with 4000 keystrokes of memory would use the family TV set as a display screen and an inexpensive cassette tape recorder for storing programs; the computer was available for under $90. The low prices of the new machines allowed school budgets to cover the purchase of more equipment; the high speed of those new machines meant that more students could be accommodated by each unit. The earlier vision of "computers for everyone" was becoming an attainable goal.

Computers no longer are just *accepted* in the schools—they are *desired*. Teacher concerns that computers will replace them in the classroom and/or dehumanize instruction are being replaced by the realization that the computer is just another teaching tool, albeit a very versatile one. Professional organizations such as the Association for Computing Machinery, the National Association of Secondary School Principals, the National Education Association, and the National Council of Teachers of Mathematics have issued policy statements encouraging schools to develop instructional computing throughout the school curriculum.

The efforts of the National Council of Teachers of Mathematics (NCTM) deserve special note because of their dual character. The NCTM not only has spoken to the importance of computers in the teaching of mathematics at all levels but also has urged educators to view instructional computing as an activity which has no subject-matter bounds.

In April of 1980, NCTM released *An Agenda for Action: Recommendations for School Mathematics of the 1980s*. The culmination of years of study (including national surveys of educators and the lay public), the document details eight specific recommendations aimed at shaping educational development in the 1980s. NCTM President Shirley Hill described the recommendations of the agenda as follows:

> These recommendations represent a professional position, and the intended audience goes well beyond our own membership. They are directed to all teachers and the education profession in general, to school administrators and school boards, to government agencies and legislatures, to producers of educational materials and tests, and—perhaps most important—to parents and the public at large.[5]

Within this broad educational context, the third of the eight NCTM recommendations speaks of the need of education to take advantage of the power of computers at all grade levels.[6] Specifically, the recommendation asserts that a course in computer literacy should be included in the education of every student and teacher and that teachers of any school subject in which mathematics is applied should make appropriate use of computers. The literacy charge placed upon the schools is further expanded to include the responsibility to assist all adults in learning to use and understand computers. Taking the point of view that most teachers will be users rather than programmers of computers, the recommendation addresses the need to develop quality software and asserts that this task is the joint responsibility of users and producers. This multidisciplinary, multilevel stand regarding instructional computing was explicitly restated in October 1980 when NCTM announced a position statement on computers in the classroom. It stated that computer programming was but one application of computers in education; a curriculum that wished to take full advantage of the instructional potential of the computer also should include such applications as problem solving, simulations in decision making, tutorial instruction, word processing, data retrieval (as in careeer counseling), evaluation (e.g., test construction, scoring, and analysis), and teacher-support services.[7]

Educators' interests in computers as instructional tools are encouraging the widespread development of computerized instructional materials. A 1980 survey of fourteen major textbook companies found that seven had committed major time and financial resources to software development; only three of the other seven reported no active interest in the field.[8] A variety of other agencies, both nonprofit organizations under governmental or private funding and commercial enterprises, have been established for the purposes of creating, gathering, and/or evaluating computer software. The educational software market that has been created so recently is promising large financial rewards for the producer.

While minicomputers and microcomputers have had a dramatic impact upon instructional computing, one should not infer from the preceding discussion that

---

[4]For this calculation, an average word is defined as one having seven characters and followed by one space.

[5]Shirley Hill, "An Agenda for a Decade of Action," *NCTM Newsletter* (March 1980): 1.

[6]National Council of Teachers of Mathematics, *An Agenda for Action: Recommendations for School Mathematics of the 1980s* (Reston, VA: National Council of Teachers of Mathematics, 1980), pp. 8–11.

[7]National Council of Teachers of Mathematics, *A Position Statement on Computers in the Classroom*, (Reston, VA: National Council of Teachers of Mathematics, October 1980).

[8]Phyllis Caputo, "From Hardbacks to Software," *Classroom Computer News* (November–December, 1980): 6.

large computing systems are out of the educational picture. In fact, the shared use of a single large computer by hundreds of users scattered over a large geographic area is an instructional pattern that has undergone considerable refinement and gained increased acceptance. In 1974, for example, Control Data Corporation assumed marketing rights to PLATO®, the computer-based instructional system developed at the University of Illinois. The event is noteworthy since it has led to the establishment of a worldwide library of evaluated lessons and support programs. This library, which in 1980 contained several thousand lessons in several subject areas and was growing at a rate of several hundred programs per year, is the world's largest single collection of computerized instructional materials. While the majority of the lessons first placed in the PLATO® library were designed for university and postcollege instruction, efforts are now aimed at generating materials for elementary and secondary education. Moreover, lessons written and tested on the PLATO® system are being made available for use on popular microcomputer systems.

As of the start of the 1980s, large instructional computing systems such as PLATO® have had no significant impact upon precollege instruction because the cost of using them is still too high. Nevertheless, the libraries of teaching and support programs being created for and validated by such systems are awesome and cannot be discounted. The history of computing has shown us that what seemed impossible yesterday may be within our reach by tomorrow and obsolete by the beginning of the new year.

Study Guide: Chapter 1

1. Condense the history of educational computing for the period 1950–1980 into no more than 250 words. Identify the main issues which characterize change during that period; don't get bogged down in detail.
2. Writing in 1976, Bukoski and Korotkin predicted that by 1984 just over half the secondary schools in the United States would be using computers in instruction. Gather current data relative to the following questions.
   a. What fraction of secondary schools now use computers for instruction?
   b. What fraction of elementary schools now use computers for instruction?
   c. At each level (elementary and secondary), characterize the instructional use of computers with respect to such general applications as computer programming, computer literacy, and the delivery of instruction in other subjects by using a computer.
3. At this time, what appear to be the barriers to broader implementation of instructional computing in the elementary and secondary schools?
4. Select a professional journal in your field of interest.
   a. Survey the issues of that journal for the past twelve months for articles about computing. What kinds of hardware are discussed? What kinds of software are reviewed? What is said about the use of computers in the classroom? What kinds of applications are included? What attention is given to issues of evaluating software or hardware?
   b. Survey the issues of the same journal for the year 1975 and answer the same questions.
   c. Compare 1975 with the past twelve months.

CHAPTER TWO

A Teacher's Style-Guide to Instructional Computing

Faced with a new venture in schooling, institutions tend to be—shall we say—cautious. Decisions to introduce curricular change must consider more than finances because the change may imply new roles for school personnel or noticeable alterations in students' programs. The speed and correctness of such decisions are, moreover, a function of the level(s) in the educational hierarchy at which they are made. Some districts employ a "bubble up" procedure in which the persons immediately affected by a decision are involved in generating, modifying, and justifying that decision; the decision is then negotiated with administrators at higher levels in the structure. Sometimes changes are introduced at school-building level by administrators who may or may not have carried on an appropriate dialogue with students, parents, or teachers. Alternatively, it is not unusual to find instructional decision making operating through a "trickle down" process in which issues, discussed and resolved at a state or district level, are passed along to the schools to implement. As the gap widens between the level at which a change is approved and the level at which the change is to be implemented, there is bound to be a loss of focus on the major issues associated with that change. When decision makers are not familiar with the details of the proposed venture, potentially good ideas can be destroyed by misdirection, inaccurate claims, unreasonable expectations, or lack of commitment.

The introduction of computers into instruction is a case in point. Given the complexity of such a venture, it's no surprise that things have gone awry in many situations. Consider the problem. After all, few schools have faculty or administrators who have acquired even minimal training in computers and their educational uses. Lacking such training, one is inclined either to do nothing (indeed, the natural inclination is to actively resist doing anything) or to place decision-making power in the hands of "experts." Frequently, schools have turned to vendors of computing equipment with the request: "Tell us what we need and how much it will cost." This approach is doomed to failure since a computer is a *general* tool; its applications are defined by the *user.*

The experiences of the past quarter century suggest at least three stages of study and decision making for the school considering instructional computing:

1. deciding on the use of computers as an instructional medium;
2. obtaining computers appropriate to the proposed instructional uses;
3. keeping instructional computers operating.

The purpose of this chapter is to give an overview of the first of these three stages. Chapters 3–12 will give detailed attention to several of the issues raised here with respect to the many ways in which computers are applied to instruction. Chapters 13 and 14 will address the other two stages listed above.

Deciding on the Use of Computers

Suppose you could peek inside the closets and storage rooms of America's schools. What do you think you'd find (other than a few harried teachers seeking a quiet place to eat lunch)? The question is, of course, rhetorical. It was raised in order to provide a little fun in answering it.

A reasonable guess is that you'd find a lot of terrific solutions to the problems of education, each in mint condition except for a thick layer of dust. There would be stacks of "teaching machines" with their accompanying rolls or boxes of programmed lessons. How about all those neat rows of "new math" books that set out to teach proof to average junior high school students? Where? Over there on top of those large boxes of equipment for the "new science" programs for the elementary schools. Those strange looking brackets are wall mounts for the monitors (still in the boxes) for the instructional television project. I'm not certain, but I think those hundreds of little bags of colored rods had something to do with teaching elementary school mathematics. Then again, maybe they were supposed to be used in teaching the metric system. At any rate, the videotape players and film projectors certainly were great ideas! (Too bad the tapes and films were so poor—and so expensive.) I wonder if there's anyone alive who could identify all that other stuff. . . .

Now suppose that you could peek inside those same closets and storage rooms in, say, ten years. Will there be stacks of computers piled on top of everything else? Will there be printers, disk drives, video monitors, and cables?[1] Will there still be room for those harried teachers looking for a quiet spot for lunch? This time the questions aren't rhetorical. Answers are expected, and the answers depend upon the decisions that you—and other educators like you—make in responding to issues such as the following:

- In what ways can a computer participate in instruction?
- What educationally important things could a school do *with* the aid of computers that it could not do *without* them?
- What aspects of instruction can be performed significantly better with the aid of computers?
- What problems can be expected from using computers in the ways identified?
- Is it likely that we really will do any of the things that computers will make possible?

Clearly, we need to think a bit about how computers might be used in instruction.

Instructional uses of computers can be sorted into two piles. In one case, the uses involve the computer itself as the object of instruction; the focus is upon teaching *about* computers. In the other pile are those uses in which the computer is a medium (or tool) of instruction; these uses focus upon teaching *with* a computer.

Teaching *About* Computers

Possible Justifications

To date, schools usually have made computers the object of instruction. Primary emphasis has been upon teaching students how to make a computer do what it can do. That is, students have been taught how to program a computer using one or more computer languages. Sometimes instruction would include a little information about how a computer is constructed and how it does what it does. These activities are common components of programs which are offered under the popular rubric *computer literacy.*

Computer literacy has been defined as "what every person should know about computers." Since "every person" includes the butcher, baker, doctor, lawyer, elementary school teacher, computer scientist, and ballet artist, it's immediately obvious that the definition leaves much to be desired. Perhaps it would help to think of computer literacy having the same relationship to a computer education as the fundamentals of mathematics (which some call mathematical literacy) have to

[1]If some of these terms are unfamiliar, now's a good time to turn to the Beginner's Glossary of Computerese at the end of this book.

a mathematical education. Each is a body of basic concepts and skills which the learner later builds upon or modifies to meet the requirements of a chosen profession or task.

There is no single, accepted definition of computer literacy. The term is used to describe various blendings of ideas about how a computer is constructed, the ways that computers may be used, how a computer is controlled (i.e., computer programming), and the social issues that arise from the contacts between people and computers (e.g., privacy, career displacement, computerized crime, etc.). In a school—generally speaking, a secondary school—computer literacy might be developed in a unit required of every student as part of a mathematics course or a career education course; instruction might occupy as many as six weeks.

Educators have developed a number of justifications for teaching about computers. At the secondary school level, the most common argument insists that computer literacy is a necessary component of college preparation. Proponents point out that a basic understanding of computers and their uses is required as part of the undergraduate programs of over half of the university courses of study. Precollege computer offerings are promoted as opportunities akin to courses in calculus, a second year of physics, or creative writing. (If you see flaws in this position, you're not alone. However, let's press on to other justifications.)

A second rationale for teaching about computers is that computers provide the concrete experiences needed to teach mathematical thinking in a way that young children can master. This position is stated quite eloquently by Seymour Papert, a professor of mathematics whose work with instructional computing reflects his extended association with Jean Piaget.[2] If Papert is correct, learning about computers (specifically, how to program computers) can be of great value in developing problem-solving skills.

It is also proposed that teaching about computers is important because computers are valuable problem-solving tools. Computers provide the means of solving problems that otherwise might be unmanageable because of the huge amount of time required to check cases or to carry out large numbers of tedious and complex calculations. Computers provide access to large volumes of information and permit it to be quickly recalled and viewed in a variety of ways. Undeniably, the person who has learned how to use a computer has acquired enormous power to execute tasks which require the gathering, organizing, or analyzing of information.

A less frequently proposed justification for teaching about computers is associated with career education. The objective here is to have students graduate from secondary school with the entry-level skills needed for computer-related jobs. But while it may be possible for students to acquire those skills, many such jobs simply are not open to persons with only a high school education. Schools using career education as a primary argument to support teaching about computers should be certain that competent graduates will be accepted for employment without college training. If postsecondary education is to be required, perhaps it would be advisable for students to take additional high-school courses in English or mathematics rather than in computing. Most colleges provide students the opportunity to study about computers; they often do not provide instruction in secondary school subjects which are prerequisites to college studies.

Two Procedures

The teaching of computer programming, a common component of many a computer literacy effort, can be carried out either with or without the use of a computer. Believe it or not, there are universities which offer correspondence courses in computer programming to students who do not have access to any form of computer equipment. Still, one would hope that students of computer programming would be able to interact with a machine. Certainly it is difficult to imagine a person investing six weeks in studying the preparation of French cuisine, while being denied the opportunity to put a single product to the taste test. In a like manner, computer programs are tasty tidbits for the mind—but enthusiasm for their creation may quickly fade if one is denied a valid test of their excellence.

Let's imagine the better of the two possible worlds of teaching computer programming. Assuming, then, that computers will be involved in teaching computer programming, there are two general procedures by which communication between student and machine can be achieved. These two procedures are commonly referred to as *batch* and *interactive*.

The procedure with the longer history is *batch*-style computing. Students engaged in this style of computing communicate with the computer by marking (with a pencil) or punching holes (with a machine) in special computer-readable cards. The computer uses a printer to type its responses, which make perfectly good sense if the program was prepared correctly or amount to so much gibberish or semi-intelligible computer jargon if the program has flaws.

Few of the schools using batch-style computing make use of punched cards. The machine needed to punch the cards is expensive. A poor typist must labor

---

[2]Seymour Papert, *Mindstorms: Children, Computers, and Powerful Ideas* (New York: Basic Books, 1980).

long (while others fume and fuss) and usually must face the frustration of program failure due to typing errors rather than to programming errors. Thus, the punched-card option promises high cost to serve a limited number of students.

Batch-style programming courses now use pencil-marked cards. The letters or numerals of a program are indicated by using a pencil to shade the appropriate boxes of the card. While it takes experience to become proficient at marking the cards, the procedure is superior to the punch-card method for several reasons. Obviously, it is cheaper, since the card-punching machinery is eliminated. All of the students can work on programs simultaneously and independently, because there is no need to stand in line to use the card-punch and typing skill is not a prerequisite to efficient generation of a program. Many errors made in writing programs on pencil-marked cards are corrected quickly with an eraser; again, there is no time wasted in queuing up at the card-punch. Finally, the pencil-marking method has been improved by the appearance of special cards which permit entire words (instructions in the computer language) to be recorded by shading a single block rather than by shading each letter. (Figure 2.1)

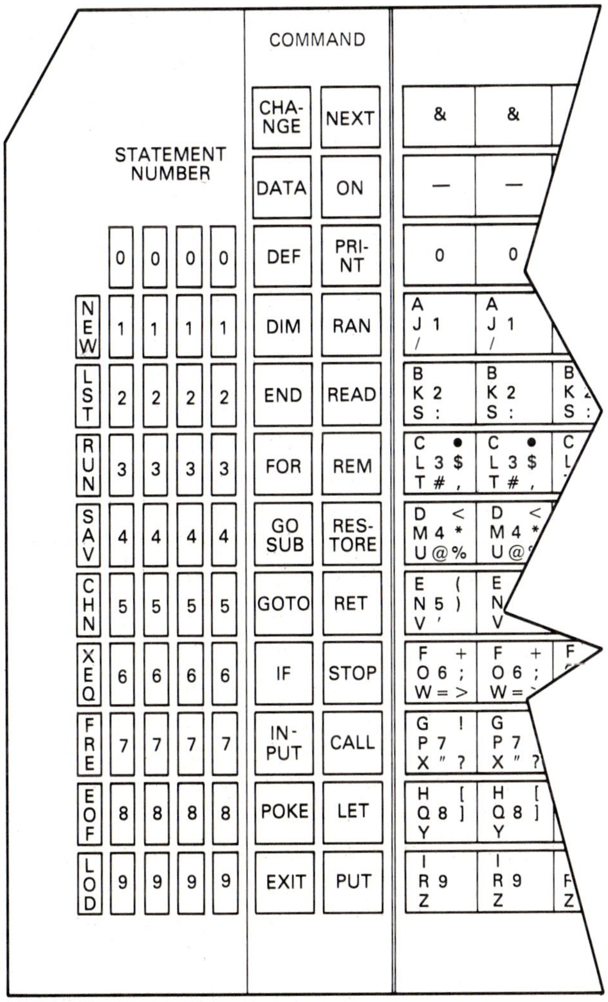

Figure 2.1

When a program has been recorded on the cards—punched or pencil-marked—it is presented to the computer by means of a card-reading device. The computer executes the program or locates errors in it and reports the results using some sort of printing device. Well-designed (not necessarily expensive) batch systems can easily process fifty to sixty different student programs in the course of a class period.

The second style of communication between student and computer permits the student to present the program to the computer directly by typing on a keyboard. The student's typing is displayed immediately on paper or on a television-like screen. Many computer systems will respond to each program line typed by the student, noting errors in spelling, syntax, or logic. When the entire program has been entered, the student instructs the computer to execute it and to present the results on paper or the screen. Because of this constant communication between student and computer, the style is called *interactive*.

From the point of view of the student, interactive programming is much more efficient than batch programming. The student receives feedback from the computer during program writing and editing; many errors are detected and corrected immediately. This gives the student a feeling of direct control of the computing environment. It also can encourage sloppy and inefficient programming habits. Let's face it, errors made in batch programming call for considerable corrective effort by the student; an error might mean finding and deleting cards which caused the error, preparing new cards, and waiting to resubmit the program through the card-reader. The procedure is sufficiently tedious to encourage careful work. When the students work in interactive style, their efforts in correcting errors are greatly reduced since the computer does much of the work. Exit tedium, enter a cavalier attitude toward program preparation.

In large classes, the quantity of equipment required for interactive programming is large. Whereas a single card-reader and printer could handle fifty to sixty student programs per class period in batch style, very careful scheduling and efficient typing might support individual access to the computer by five students during the same period. To get a better feeling for the scheduling and supply problems of interactive programming, let's consider two situations.

School Situation A: You are teaching computer programming to a class of thirty bright and cooperative students who never miss a day of school. You would like each student to complete two programs per week, and experience has shown that each program will require forty minutes of student-computer interaction from inception to completion. The faculty of your school is so thrilled by your computing efforts that it has volunteered to release your students from other classes in order that you may schedule their use of the computer at any time between 8 A.M. and 4 P.M., Monday through Friday. Finally—and, of course—the computer never breaks down.

School Situation A requires forty clock-hours of computer access per week for the class. You can handle the situation with one computer station—at least in theory. Should the station break down, should one of the students happen not to be as bright as advertised, should a member of the faculty decide to abandon the my-time-is-your-time agreement, well . . . . But let's not think about such things. Rather, consider a second situation.

School Situation B: You have the same thirty students and the same course objectives. However, students will have access to the computer only during your daily, sixty-minute class period.

School Situation B requires at least eight computer stations (assuming that no station is ever in need of repair during class time). You must have the class organized in such a way that each of the stations is in use at any given time and that the twenty-two students who are not at the stations are working elsewhere. Under these circumstances, the entire class never could meet for a lecture since eight students will always be engaged with the computer. In fact, during a class period, as many as twenty-four of the thirty students might spend twenty minutes at a station. The situation calls for careful scheduling and flexible teaching by you and for self-discipline by your students. Nothing to it.

Be not discouraged. Lots of folks are teaching with a limited amount of equipment. The point of the examples and discussion is that planning is essential to success and one must be prepared to cope when ideal conditions collapse. Thus, the school or school district needs a Computer Advisory Committee to do some arithmetic in order to approximate resource requirements. The committee's calculations must, of course, follow teachers' decisions regarding the purposes for which the computer is likely to be used, who will use it, and what style of communication—batch or interactive—will be used. Moreover, the two styles should not be viewed as mutually exclusive; rather the committee should consider the mixture of styles which best serves a given set of intended classroom uses.

Should the Computer Advisory Committee contain persons who have some computing experience, some may argue that batch-style computer programming is an inferior, if not detrimental, experience. (The opposite of this position was argued earlier.) The issue is mainly a matter of opinion and teaching style. When all is said and done, interactive computing probably is a better experience, provided that the school budget can support such activity for more than a handful of selected students. Still, our committee should consider giving highest priority to achieving *some* level of computer literacy with as many students as possible. Given that priority, a well-designed, batch-style experience may be the answer.

Teaching *With* Computers

It is not a purpose of this book to explore further the teaching of programming or, generally, those instructional uses in which the computer is the object of instruction. The preceding discussion of teaching *about* computers was intended to define that role of instructional computing and to acquaint the reader with some of the problems associated with implementing instruction about computers.

In the remainder of this chapter, we will give an overview of those teaching activities in which the computer is the *medium* of instruction; teaching is done *with* a computer. Several of the chapters which follow will expand upon aspects of teaching with computers. It is this kind of connection between computers and instruction which offers good things to every classroom teacher regardless of grade level of instruction or subject area interest. One need not be a pilot in order to realize the benefits of air travel. One need not be a computernik with soldering iron in one hand and the latest book on programming in obscure languages in the other in order to realize the benefits of teaching with a computer.

Teaching with a computer reveals that the computer is a many-splendored thing. Each year we discover new applications of its talents. Although a definitive list of its uses may never be written, the use of the computer as a medium of instruction has revealed three important sides to its educational personality.

- **The Computer as Teacher.** In its role as teacher, the computer assumes the task of executing some specific component of the teaching act. Using the instructions it has been given, it exercises principal control of the decision-making process which governs execution of that component.
- **The Computer as Partner.** Here, the bounds of the computer's role in the teaching act are set by the user. Major decisions which control the teaching act are shared by the computer, the teacher, and the student.
- **The Computer as Aide-de-Camp.** In this role, the computer acts like the one and only private in

an army of major generals. Its task is to perform as directed, not to direct or judge.

Although these personalities are not separate and have been described in other ways,[3] they are handy intellectual organizers for studying and planning computer uses in the school.

The Computer as Teacher

Teachers who understand instructional computing might well say, "If your computer can replace me, then it should." It's a safe challenge. Good teaching is ever changing, a complex blend of many skills, emotions, and intuitions. Anyone who has tried to reproduce good teaching by means of a computer has found the task not unlike painting a picture on the surface of a moving stream. For all its high-speed calculating power, unfailing attention to tedious tasks, and prodigious displays of memory, the computer poses no threat to the competent teacher. On the contrary, the computer offers opportunities to teach in new or better ways; it offers release from many of the noncreative tasks of teaching.

The computer can assume responsibility for a specific fragment of the total teaching act. Insofar as it has been programmed to make all of the decisions which guide execution of that fragment, we say that it has assumed the role of teacher. For instance, the computer might be used to prepare a test on a given topic constructed to meet the specifications of the classroom teacher. It could be used to score that test and to present both a summary of student performances and an analysis of the test items. The computer could be used to help the teacher locate resources useful in fitting instruction to the needs of a particular student. It could keep records or generate reports. It might be assigned the task of helping a transfer or an absentee student to catch up by introducing a topic he or she has not studied before. It might provide practice aimed at maintaining or refining some skill. Each of these tasks has two basic characteristics: 1) the execution has a direct effect upon the dialogue between teacher and student; and 2) the decision making which guides execution of the task is wholly the responsibility of the teacher (human or electronic).

There are four types of teaching services which can be carried out by a computer:

1. management of the instructional process;
2. test construction and analysis;
3. instruction in a new topic;
4. reinforcement of instruction in a topic previously introduced.

Teaching includes all of these tasks (and much more). As a result, the excellence with which a given teacher will perform any one of the services listed is dependent upon that teacher's training, experience, interests, "smarts," and dedication. The quality of performance of a computer on the same tasks depends upon how well the computer has been instructed by the teacher (through a programmer) and how well the teacher utilizes the computer's features. The computer brings speed and endless patience to the delivery of these services, but it cannot improve upon the fundamental quality of what is served.

Management of Instruction. The computer can assume major responsibility for the control and direction of an individualized teaching environment. This application of the computer in the role of teacher is called computer-managed instruction (CMI) and covers a myriad of teaching duties. The mechanics of CMI include diagnosis of a student's learning level or of specific gaps in the student's understanding of a given topic. This diagnosis is linked to a prescription which could be placement in a certain study group or assignment of a learning task to be executed with suitable materials and teacher input. If instruction requires the use of limited resources (laboratory stations, machines, etc.), the computer can schedule those resources in a manner which not only optimizes their use but also ensures regular maintenance or repair. CMI can be used to route students through an entire curriculum, the routing of any individual student being adjusted to the student's achievement, interests, and learning style by means of regular evaluation. As individualization within large groups makes increasing demands upon student-teacher and student-student communication, the computer can facilitate that communication by providing "electronic mailboxes" for all participants.[4] The computer can keep track of the academic progress or perils of individuals and groups in ways which the teacher may quickly and regularly use as a basis for modifying instruction, overriding computer decisions, changing the materials of instruction, and working with individuals as individuals. The record-keeping features of CMI also can be used to generate written reports for the student, teacher, parents, or school system.

In performing its CMI duties, the computer may generate some prescriptions which direct students to use the computer in other ways (e.g., to drill on a list of irregular French verbs that have given the student trouble in doing translations). However, the instruction

---

[3]Robert Taylor, ed., *The Computer in the School: Tutor, Tool, Tutee* (New York: Teachers College Press, 1980).

[4]"Mailboxing" is a feature not obviously useful to the conventional classroom teacher. But in more totally individualized environments, groups may meet less often or less regularly. This drastically alters the normal information channels between student and teacher.

called for under CMI need not itself be computer-based. Teaching still may take place in traditional lecture/demonstration, laboratory, or tutorial settings.

The computer's responsibility in all of this is to keep each person—student or teacher—focused upon the most productive task he can perform at a given time. This, as any teacher can tell you, is a nontrivial assignment. How well the computer does the job depends upon at least two things:

1. There must be clearly defined routes through the curriculum being managed. At each decision point encountered along a route, there must be specification of all possible alternatives and ready access to the materials needed to support each of those alternatives.
2. There must be a well-developed computer program which controls student progress through the curriculum. The data and specifications necessary for controlling that progress either must be a permanent part of that program or, where progress is based upon student input, must be entered easily.

If you think that's a lot to ask, just remember that the good teacher does it every day with several subjects and with different groups of students.

Construction and Analysis of Tests. Educators speak of the *garbage-in/garbage-out* error. If the concepts, generalizations, or skills that we attempt to teach a student are presented at the wrong time or in the wrong form (i.e., are *garbage in*), then the best we can hope for are rote echoings (i.e., *garbage out*). The student is a pipe through which ideas have passed without leaving behind an intellectual residue.

One way to prevent garbage-in/garbage-out errors is to use evaluation as the basis for prescribing instruction. As students, we're only too familiar with the use of evaluation *to determine what has been learned.* In prescribing instruction, the role of evaluation is *to determine what should be taught and how it should be taught.* The procedure requires not only a deep understanding of the subject, students, and teaching materials, but also a great deal of time. If you've got the understanding, the computer can provide the time. The result is known as *computer-assisted testing.*

Computer-assisted testing might be part of a fancy CMI system; it also can stand alone. This instructional application includes three services that can be provided by even the most inexpensive computing system: test scoring, test analysis, and test generation.

If you give tests, it follows that somebody must score them. As you move toward the use of many tests (in order to refine instruction), grading and the reporting of results becomes a major task. Enter the computer. . . . Given that the responses are in a form readable by the computer (and that need not mean only a multiple-guess test format), the computer can be used to score the test, point out "classic" errors, summarize class results in tabular or graphical form, report measures of group performance (e.g., means, ranges, standard deviations), and print individual reports for each student. It can use the results to tell you what instructional objectives have been successfully met by whom and which need additional attention. (Really good systems also will heat your hot chocolate while you wait for the above.)

So far, computer-assisted testing has served to prepare evaluations of the students. It can also evaluate the test itself. A well-designed test processing system can give item-by-item information about item difficulty, how well the item discriminates between those who know something and those who do not, and poor choices (on multiple-choice items). It can also detect questions which have been keyed incorrectly or which may have more than one possible correct answer.

The third testing service that a computer can provide is the generation of the test itself (with a key for the teacher). It can efficiently handle the cataloging and retrieval of test items. Using its retrieval skills, it can prepare (arrange and print the items of) a test that is tailored to the teacher's wishes. Although such test-item banking and generating were once features of large computer systems only, practical versions of these services now can be made available to any classroom teacher.

Tutorial Instruction. One view of education pictures the student on one end of a log and the teacher on the other. Teaching takes place as dialogue between teacher and student in which the questions and statements of each are a response to the questions and statements of the other. When not used to the exclusion of other instructional schemas, this is a powerful instructional technique. We call it *tutoring.*

Computers have been shown to be an effective and economical resource for tutoring. The quality of the tutoring, of course, is a function of the computer programs available. The problem for the designer of such programs is to make the computer behave as if it were a very knowledgeable and creative teacher who is engaged in a dialogue with a single student for the purpose of helping that student to develop important new thoughts. The designer must make the dialogue rich enough to account for variations in student achievement, interest, and learning style. In view of the complex nature of such programs, it should come as no surprise that the supply of them is meager. Furthermore, the programs related to any specific subject area (e.g., Algebra I or elementary school language arts) have gaps in content and are disjoint in instructional style. Successful computerized tutorial programs have to be topical in nature. Collectively, the programs now available will not supply tutorial instruction for any complete course.

There are educational situations which are "tutorial-intensive". Among these are programs for the physically or emotionally handicapped, remedial programs for students who have had limited educational opportunities, and individualized programs for homebound students. In situations which demand extensive use of tutorial instruction, the cost of providing skilled personnel to maintain the necessary intensity of tutoring probably will be significantly greater than the cost of computerized tutoring. Moreover, if skilled tutors are not available, computerized tutoring certainly is a cost-effective alternative to the training and employment of humans.

Drill Activities. Every field of knowledge needs an environment designed to promote rapid recall learning. The fact of the matter is that every field has a mass of concepts which must be accessible to the learner at push-button speed. Vocabulary is one example of such a mass of concepts; the so-called basic facts of arithmetic make up another.

In any secondary school English course, there is much that might be learned about the word *sarcophagus*. For instance, one might be interested in the word's etymology or its use in literature. One might want to study the word's referent in terms of its physical characteristics or social significance. Such studies call for complex learning skills. If, however, the purpose were to learn to spell the word, the procedure for doing so would take us back to the basics of *associative learning*.

Associative learning, as required for success in a spelling competition, calls for the services of some kindly soul who will sit for hours pronouncing words and checking your spelling against that of the ruling lexicographer. You can claim success (learning) when spaced presentations of the pronunciation of *sarcophagus* (the stimulus) are met by your unerring verbal dissection *s-a-r-c-o-p-h-a-g-u-s* (the response). The procedure is known as *drill.* It's not a very exciting activity for your partner, so you might want to try shouting in order to ensure his or her consciousness.

Textbooks and teachers are not the most effective resources for drills. Textbooks cannot respond with the flexibility needed to shape the student's learning. Teachers cannot give each individual student the time needed to fix all of the associations that are part of education. Using a teacher to carry out such a tedious, unrewarding task is as unforgivable as using a Ming vase as a paperweight.

The computer has been shown to be an effective drillmaster in promoting associative learning. Students achieve mastery of such associations quickly and show high levels of retention. And for reasons that are anyone's guess, students appear to be highly motivated to engage in drill activity with a computer.

Practice Activities. Beware! Whereas some folks use the words *drill* and *practice* as synonyms, we do not. We use the word *drill* to name the process by which simple associations are fixed. Thus, we *drill* on French-English verb associations, spelling, the one hundred basic addition facts, or the touch location of the keys on a typewriter.

The word *practice* also will be used to name a teaching process; the objects of practice are, however, quite different from those of drill. The objects of practice are processes or procedures. In mathematics, for example, we learn step-by-step procedures (also called algorithms) for doing problems such as the following:

$$\begin{array}{r} 2748 \\ +\ 965 \\ \hline \end{array} \qquad 38\overline{)20368} \qquad \begin{array}{r} 312 \\ -173 \\ \hline \end{array} \qquad \begin{array}{r} 238 \\ \times\ 79 \\ \hline \end{array}$$

In science laboratories, students learn procedures for titrating acids and counting bacteria. Language teachers have tried to teach us procedures for constructing grammatically correct sentences. Outside the classroom, there are procedures for changing a tire on your car, tuning a piano, and planting sod.

Computers have been used successfully to help students practice logical processes or procedures. They provide a carefully monitored environment in which the student may repeatedly execute an ordered sequence of steps which makes up the procedure. The computer can immediately notify the student of any error and suggest a way of correcting it.

The Computer as Partner

There are problems which may be expressed in many ways or solved by taking a number of different routes. Each of the decisions made in any attempt to solve the problem may not only affect the final form of the solution but also alter the nature of the problem itself. Suppose, for instance, that you were given a task of producing a balance of trade between the United States and a certain well-known island nation. It is unlikely that any single decision on import taxes or quotas, factory locations, or new products will realize that balance. One of several possibilities could be negotiated as a first move toward attaining a balance. The specific choice and the effects of its implementation will alter the balance (and, perhaps, the spirit of cooperation among the negotiators). Thus, the general goal may still be the same after the first move, but the problem situation may have been changed significantly.

The computer can be used in learning situations which involve joint decision making. The computer and the user (teacher or student) cooperate or compete to resolve some problem. Whether competing or cooperating, the computer and the user make independent decisions which cause important changes in the learning environment. For this reason, we say that they are partners in instruction. In the paragraphs that follow, we discuss three types of learning situations in which the computer takes that role:

1. situations in which motivation is sorely needed;
2. situations which place the user where decision making is the focus of instruction;
3. situations in which the user needs help maintaining data in search of information and ideas.

Using the Computer to Motivate. The "lyrics" of rock music notwithstanding, the human animal generally is not enthralled by repetition of simpleminded events. Yet the price for mastering a subject seems always to include ways of learning that are most unattractive. The memorization of basic facts of arithmetic must hold the permanent title of *World's Dullest Academic Exercise.* When confronted with the teaching of such homely bits of knowledge, the teacher's biggest chore is to motivate the student to endure the necessary repetition.

Clever teachers long have used instructional games to put a sugarcoating on the drill pill. It has been recognized for some time that game formats can be used to motivate students to stick with the study of concepts or skills which are not interesting of themselves.[5] In such formats, the monitoring of the learning is done by the other player(s); the interaction among the participants provides feedback regarding whether a player's move is correct or, in terms of strategy, wise.

The interaction among players, often in a state of excitement, makes games difficult to incorporate into the activities of some classrooms. The players' display of enjoyment may distract students who are engaged in less stimulating pursuits. Worse yet, some other teacher, parent, or administrator might catch sight of students having a good time and conclude that teaching has been abandoned in favor of fun.

A computer is less obstreperous as a participant in an instructional game. Still, it can provide the monitoring and interaction needed to ensure learning. It can also control its playing skill so as to encourage the novice or to challenge the expert. A computer, then, can provide a nice blend of the learning attributes of play while minimizing the undesirable side effects.

[5]There is a catch-22. The game format can be so attractive that the instructional purpose is overwhelmed by it. The job of the game-maker is to be clever without being *too* clever.

Using the Computer to Teach Decision Making. The problems usually encountered in schooling bear little resemblance to the problems of life. *The* solution to the nastiest high school chemistry problem can, with rare exceptions, be found by reviewing the ten pages which preceded that problem. Solutions to problems in the real worlds of science, politics, business, or personal finance are rarely so tidy. The latter kinds of problems require gathering and analyzing data, making decisions, suffering the consequences of poor decisions, and regrouping to try again. Success in adult vocations, interpersonal relationships, and citizenship activities requires nondisastrous experiences in dealing with such problems.

Learning to make intelligent decisions regarding public behavior, value-laden issues, allocation of time or money, or matters calling for complex skills can be treated in the secondary school. Instructional computing systems can support such learning opportunities through the use of programs which simulate situations from life. The student experiences the necessity to make decisions and will be informed of the results of those decisions without experiencing the real, and possibly devastating, consequences of misjudgment. Computer simulations have been shown to be effective both in teaching decision making in stable environments and in teaching recovery decision-making processes in unstable environments where unexpected events may occur at random.

Facilitating Problem Solving With a Computer. Regardless of field, problem-solving skill certainly is the ultimate goal of any curriculum. Again regardless of field, a problem-solving activity invariably involves the manipulation of data in search of information. In mathematics or the sciences (natural or social), the data is usually in numerical form. Problem solving in other fields may deal with data in forms which are aural (music), graphic (art), verbal (journalism or literature), or olfactory (wine making).

The teaching of problem solving in any of these fields is often handicapped by human inability to process data rapidly and in sophisticated ways. In fields dealing with numerical data, the slide rule and, later, the electronic calculator greatly facilitated problem solving. The programmable calculator was hailed by physicists and real estate brokers alike! And the computer has provided a general means for manipulating both numeric *and nonnumeric data* at incredible speed and in ways formerly impossible due to the brief life span of the human critter.

Procedures for using this new and powerful problem-solving tool are well within the grasp of precollege students. In fact, a few studies have shown that students having marginal understanding of (and general disenchantment with) mathematics will take readily to computer programming and the use of the computer in solving problems. Also, there are indications that students hampered by dexterity problems (e.g., messiness or slowness of pen) when doing written composition are greatly helped by computer text processing systems. The frustrations involved either in thinking much faster than recording or in the revising needed to improve a written product are minimized.

The Computer as Aide-de-Camp

The term *teacher aide* generally is used to refer to students or adults who—motivated by an interest in education, financial considerations, or some form of academic coercion—perform a variety of services which assist teachers in carrying out classroom instruction. You may have heard the term *student aide* applied to students involved in such activity. Whatever they're called, they perform their duties under the direction of teachers.

All teachers invest large blocks of time in tasks which are noninstructional in that they have no direct contact with students. Although these tasks are an important part of the total teaching act, the fact that they do not call upon the teacher's interpersonal skills gives them a peripheral status. For instance, good teaching makes use of a wide variety of books, articles, films, and laboratory supplies. Efficient use of such materials, including the addition of new items and the deletion of outdated materials, demands an inventory system which allows students and teachers to locate resources readily. There is need to locate the addresses of vendors in order to reorder supplies or to obtain maintenance services. Students must be scheduled for conferences and tutorial sessions; equipment must be scheduled for regular examination and repair. Handouts must be prepared, revised, and reproduced in legible form. In short, the conscientious teacher has a complex set of "noninstructional" duties.

The burden of each of the activities described above can be eased markedly through the use of a computer. Computerized inventories, developed to meet the demand of business computer systems, are now available for school applications. Computerized word-processing systems have been designed for the sole purpose of expediting the creation, improvement, and production of printed materials.

In its role as aide—and it may be serving the teacher, the student or both—the computer offers a variety of useful items of software. There are programs designed specifically for teacher-use in demonstrating, by example, complex ideas; the programs allow the teacher to manipulate any of several conditions in order to generate examples which reveal the effects of those manipulations. There are programs which are designed to produce large quantities of data as requested by the user. There are "tool" programs which may be attached to other programs to perform such general tasks as alphabetizing, numerical ordering, spelling, judging of answers, statistical work, and conversion of data to graphical form. There even are programs which make the user aware of the special instructional features (sound, color, flashing displays, etc.) that could be used in planning other instructional applications.

Looking Back

What one can accomplish in teaching with a computer depends in part on the style of computing (batch or interactive) being used. Applications such as CMI, computer-assisted testing, problem solving, and data generation can take place in either environment. On the other hand, interactive computing should be acknowledged as prerequisite to the use of programs classified as simulations, tutorials, instructional games, drill, practice, inventory management, classroom demonstration, or word processing. And there are other considerations . . . but we'll take those up in future chapters.

In closing this chapter, we confess our glibness in the repeated use of the phrases *well-designed* and *well-organized* in referring to computer systems and computer programs. "What," we hear you cry, "is meant by *well-designed* this time?" If you've been annoyed by our lack of specificity on that point, you've taken the first step along the road to making intelligent uses of computers in the schools. The remaining chapters are designed (well-designed?) to help you to state and answer the detailed kinds of questions that must be asked and to find the relevant information that must be gathered in order to ensure a successful experience in instructional computing.

The Agenda for Action

Genesis of the Instructional Computing Advisory Committee (ICAC)

Now we wish to show you how things work—what can go wrong and how you can overcome problems. This is your invitation to participate in a simulated adventure in planning for instructional computing. The opportunity to assume the role of a member of the Instructional Computing Advisory Committee (ICAC) is provided in order that you may achieve special insight into instructional computing. This will be accomplished by having you share the unique learning and planning experiences of a group of educators charged with guiding the implementation of instructional applications of computers into the schools of East Roachmont, New York. Under the direction of East Roachmont's Superintendent of Schools, Josephine Ennis, and in company with eight dedicated professionals, you may participate in the development of a plan to define and implement instructional uses of computers in the East Roachmont schools. The committee will strive to respond to the twofold charge of Superintendent Ennis

1. to become well informed regarding instructional applications of computers in grades K-12 and across all subject matter areas;
2. to develop a plan for implementing the instructional uses of computers in the East Roachmont schools.

To support the committee's work Superintendent Ennis has engaged as consultants two experts in the instructional uses of computers. For purposes of this simulation, the consultants' role is being played by the authors of this book.

Should you choose to join ICAC, you will be given access to the private correspondence file which reports the committee's purposes, activities, problems, and decisions. Through the memoranda and letters, you'll gain insight into the committee's organization and operational decisions; you'll also share with ICAC the reports from representatives of two school systems in which classic errors of inadequate planning brought instructional computing to a standstill.

The evolution of the committee's awareness of the dimensions of instructional computing are revealed in the memoranda appended here and to Chapters 4–14. To the casual student of instructional computing, reading of the Agenda could be reduced to academic eavesdropping—an act of uninvolved interest in the continuing saga of ICAC's struggle to understand and initiate appropriate instructional applications of computers. To the practical scholar, the decisions and committee assignments found in the Agenda will serve as guidelines for personal actions. Those who join the members of ICAC in carrying out the activities suggested by the Agenda make the transition from ICAC observer to ICAC participant and gain access to a higher level of understanding. With that higher level of understanding comes a certain personal involvement with ICAC's accomplishments and future as reported in the Epilogue.

To be honest, we must tell you in advance that the other members of ICAC don't really exist. In apparent contradiction, we then wish to suggest that these composite educators fashioned from our own experiences are *very* real. The task that ICAC faces is now before many educators; the interest, caution, and determination which mark the committee's efforts to do the job correctly are genuine. Whether the committee is alive and well in a town which has been renamed East Roachmont for the purpose of this book, whether it is a literary composite of several groups of computer-using educators, or whether it is a shameless bit of fiction is unimportant. What is important is that the purpose of ICAC is real, the issues addressed by ICAC are real, and the implementation problems faced by ICAC are real. Given those realities, the existence of ICAC can be expressed by parodying the first line of what is perhaps America's best known editorial: "Yes, Virginia, there *is* an Instructional Computing Advisory Committee."

So, the committee, Ms. Ennis, and we—your author-consultants— welcome your involvement with ICAC. We hope that you decide to join us in this endeavor.

AGENDA FOR ACTION

EAST ROACHMONT INDEPENDENT SCHOOL DISTRICT
108 East Avenue
East Roachmont, New York

Dr. Josephine G. Ennis
Superintendent

(716) 568-8804

MEMORANDUM

FROM: Dr. Josephine Ennis

RE: Your Nomination To The Instructional Computing Advisory Committee

DATE: October 26, 1982

At its meetings this year, the East Roachmont Board of Education has given increasing attention to the possible instructional uses of computers. A few schools have obtained one or two small computers through the use of discretionary funds or as gifts of the parents' organization. In one school, the students raised the necessary money through a variety of activities; in another, a teacher has purchased his own computer and is using it in his classes.

If we can believe the popular media and what we're hearing at professional meetings, the impact of computers on education will rank with that of the printing press. The National Council of Teachers of Mathematics in its March, 1981, Newsletter, reported its official position that:

> Computer literacy is an essential outcome of contemporary education. Each student should acquire an understanding of the versatility and limitations of the computer through firsthand experiences with applications in a variety of subject matter fields.

Teaching both with and about computers is being proposed by many professional groups as a component of basic education in the next decade. In November, 1981, the National Council of Teachers of English established a Committee on Instructional Technology to develop and disseminate information and guidelines about appropriate uses of instructional technologies in the precollege language arts curriculum.

The open board meeting last week generated a mixture of enthusiastic support and thoughtful concern regarding the future of computers in the East Roachmont schools. As a result, the board feels it must develop a plan for implementing instructional applications of computers. It must also answer questions regarding the nature of those applications at the various grade levels, the need for retraining teachers and administrators to carry out those applications, the possible loss of teaching positions to computers, the purchase and maintenance costs of computing equipment and materials, and the selection of quality equipment and instructional programs.

Because the proposed task has broad implications, it requires careful study by East Roachmont educators. At the board's direction, therefore, I am inviting you to serve as a member of the Instructional Computing Advisory Committee (ICAC). The charges of ICAC are (1) to become well informed regarding instructional applications of computers in grades K-12 and across all subject matter areas and (2) to develop a plan for implementing the instructional uses of computers in the East Roachmont schools.

The board realizes that instructional computing will be a topic about which little is known by some ICAC members. Indeed, the committee membership has been selected with an eye to ensuring a spectrum of experience in order that we may not overlook the concerns of any of our faculty. Therefore, to assist ICAC in carrying out its charges, the board has agreed to

Memorandum October 26, 1982

allocate funds to provide each committee member from the secondary staff with release from one class (the chairman will be released from two) during the duration of the committee's work. Committee members from the elementary staff will be released one-half day per week for this task. The board also has provided a small budget for travel, communications, and study materials.

I hope that you will accept this assignment. Please advise me of your decision (in writing or by phone) no later than November 5, 1982.

JE:sn

■ ■ ■

EAST ROACHMONT INDEPENDENT SCHOOL DISTRICT
108 East Avenue
East Roachmont, New York

Dr. Josephine G. Ennis
Superintendent

(716) 568-8804

MEMORANDUM

TO: The Instructional Computing Advisory Committee

FROM: Dr. Josephine Ennis

RE: Membership and Initial Activities

DATE: November 8, 1982

Thank you for agreeing to serve on the Instructional Computing Advisory Committee (ICAC). The names, school affiliations and subject-matter specialties of your ICAC colleagues are given on the attachment.

I have asked John Russell to serve as chairman. It was John who brought this issue to the attention of the school board following his sabbatical leave last year. Having given considerable attention to computing during his leave, John forcefully argued that there is an immediate need for a multilevel interdisciplinary study of instructional applications of computers in East Roachmont. The board is convinced of that need.

As I noted in my recent telephone call, I am negotiating your release time for the remainder of the school year. While the exact manner of accomplishing this (direct hiring of substitute, replacement by a department head in exchange for the services of a teacher aide, etc.) will vary according to the specific assignment of an ICAC member, it is now clear that the reassignments are possible.

It is important that the committee have a brief organizational meeting before we dismiss for the holidays. Because of my interest in and commitment to your work, I'm asking that we gather at my home (8 Pittsford Manor Lane) at 4:00 p.m. on Friday, November 12, for preprandial refreshments and an informal discussion of ICAC tasks and operational procedures.

JE:sn

AGENDA FOR ACTION

Instructional Computing Advisory Committee Membership List

NAME AND HOME PHONE	BUSINESS ADDRESS AND PHONE	SUBJECT-AREA(S) OF INTEREST
*Mr. John C. Russell Chairperson 442-5620	Obourn Senior High School Teacher 568-8840	Mathematics
**Ms. Carrinne Calabresi School Board Representative 742-3131	Alf's Supermarket Manager 381-2222	Business
*Ms. Gerri Cilento 331-9147	Roachmont Senior High School Teacher 567-8742	Office Practice Data Management
Mr. Ted Kanaley 442-0288	Conners Middle School Principal 568-8491	Social Studies Physical Education
Ms. Lolita Marino 442-2263	Bird Elementary School Teacher 567-6544	Reading Language Arts
Ms. Jeanne Nenno 331-0055	Verzella Elementary School Special Education Resource Person 568-4739	Speech Pathology Handicapped
Mr. Phil Paris 331-4606	Morgan Junior High School Teacher 567-8147	Science
Ms. Donna Tirabassi 442-4311	McKay Junior High School Teacher 568-4445	Music

* Has some computer programming experience.

** Makes use of computers but does not program them.

AGENDA FOR ACTION

Obourn Senior High School

200 Woodbine Avenue
East Roachmont, New York

M. Jack Stivers
Principal

(716) 568-8840

ICAC Memo #1

TO: Members of ICAC

FROM: John Russell

DATE: November 19, 1982

In keeping with your request at our organizational meeting last Friday, here's the first ICAC memo. I'll number them for ease of possible future reference.

Since Gerri was unable to be with us last Friday (her personal GM transportation gremlin struck again) and to bring everyone up to date on some details, let me begin with a list of our procedural agreements.

1. ICAC meetings will be held at 2:30 P.M. every other Tuesday. Our first regular meeting will be on November 30 (Dr. Ennis has reserved the superintendent's conference room for this purpose). Each meeting will dismiss by 4:00 P.M.
2. There will be no detailed minutes taken at the meetings. It was felt that this would be both time-consuming and unnecessary. Anyone missing a meeting is expected to remain informed by contacting another ICAC member.
3. The chairman will prepare an "ICAC Memo" as a follow-up to each meeting. These memos will provide Superintendent Ennis and the committee with a brief summary of current actions, assignments, and problems.
4. I will serve as the communication link between ICAC and Superintendent Ennis.
5. Ms. Calabresi will make regular reports to the East Roachmont School Board and will transmit ICAC requests for further clarification, direction or support.

Dr. Ennis has good news regarding our request for "grist for the mill." She is making available to us two consultants with considerable expertise in instructional uses of computers. They are J. Richard Dennis of the University of Illinois and Robert J. Kansky of the University of Wyoming. They will be providing us with pertinent information in the form of topical papers.

At the suggestion of the board, I've just completed visits to two schools which have had some experience in implementing instructional uses of computers: LaRamie Middle School (grades 5-9) in Near Santo and Plato Senior High School in Durbanville. The visits were informative, even if not altogether encouraging. Although I'll report on these visits at our November 30 meeting, I thought it important that ICAC should also hear directly from the schools' movers and shakers regarding what they have identified as critical issues. A copy of a letter from Ms. Glena Harris (LaRamie) is attached. Ms. Gretchen Potter (Plato) will write soon.

JR:ms

Attachment

AGENDA FOR ACTION

glena c harris
715 SOUTH TWELFTH
NEAR SANTO, NY

November 13, 1982

Dear John,

Enclosed is a draft of the article that I told you I was writing for Palisades Area Computer-Using Teachers (PACUT) Newsletter. (The excellent typing job is the freewill contribution of our school secretary, Betty Ann.) Our Newsletter is just beginning a "True Confessions" section which will be devoted to reporting the blunders of its members with the hope that new members will learn from the mistakes of the "oldtimers." Experience is a great teacher, but we're trying to put the painful experiences of OTHERS before teachers so they won't have to learn from the duplication of those errors.

The formation of PACUT was a good move for all of us who are participating in it—though why we failed to see that our abbreviated name could provide such an obvious target for teachers and organizations opposed to computers in the schools is beyond me. (Another blunder for "True Confessions.") I hope that East Roachmont will join PACUT and use the Newsletter to share the observations and plans of your committee.

We enjoyed your visit and look forward to seeing you again during the upcoming vacation. The skiing prospects look really good!

Yours truly,

Glena C. Harris

Enclosure

AGENDA FOR ACTION

NOTE TO THE EDITOR: Here's the draft of the first item for our "True Confessions" section in the January issue of the PACUT Newsletter. I'm sorry it's so heavy on problems and devoid of solutions (except by avoidance). Still, it's the way things happened.

A Microcosm of Middle School Microcomputer Misery

Our entry into instructional computing was born of 7 parts enthusiasm, 5 parts opportunity, and 1 part knowledge. It all started when 7 members of the LaRamie Middle School faculty (our principal, guidance counselor, and a teacher from each grade level 5-9) attended the Instructional Technology Fair held at the Adamston Convention Center last October. Representatives of 23 microcomputer dealerships were on hand to display their wares. We were astounded at the capabilities of these small computers to do such things as play word games and conduct arithmetic drills using color graphics (animated) and sound (including music). A couple of us even tried our hand at writing some simple programs with just a little help from one of the exhibitors. It was really easy!

The $3000 Honeymoon

Upon returning from the Fair, the five teachers in the group put together a successful proposal for an "Innovative Project Grant" (maximum budget: $3000) available through the State Department. Through what we felt was some very clever bargaining with a dealer in Pennsylvania, we managed to purchase five (Guess why <u>five?</u>) separate computers, each accompanied by a cassette tape of demonstration programs and a self-instructional book on how to program in the BASIC language. The package price included delivery and a one-day workshop on how to use the equipment. We couldn't afford a maintenance contract, but we have a very capable electronics teacher at the high school who offered to help insofar as he could.

The Morning After

The computers arrived during the second week of school this year. Our awakening took place about one week later. The five cassettes accompanying the machines all contained the same programs: drill on the basic facts of arithmetic, a "hangman" word game, a computerized version of checkers in which the student plays against the computer, a states-and-capitals quiz (15 states—not including New York!), and a program which continually displays some fancy geometric patterns. For a few days, the students fought for a turn at running these programs. (We paired students in order to speed things up.) By the end of the week, everyone had run all of the programs. A few asked for additional chances to play "hangman" or checkers, but most (especially the students in Grades 7-9) were bored by the programs on the cassettes. More programs were needed, but no money was available to purchase them.

AGENDA FOR ACTION

Into the Breach

Having exhausted the library of "lessons" provided, the five of us decided to teach ourselves to program in preparation for producing our own instructional materials. We moved the five units to a vacant room off the auditorium and embarked on a daily 3:30-5:00 p.m. study session. Since not one of us had taken a class in computer programming, the early sessions were characterized by a good bit of fumbling and frustration. With the passing of time, however, the experience has produced a modicum of primitive programming ability and new levels of personal and professional camaraderie among the nine teachers now in the group. (Four "outsiders" have joined us.) On the other hand, we've yet to produce a single program that we can use for instruction with our students. What had appeared so "easy" at the fair wasn't representative of the time and skill required to create useful lessons. We also have discovered further errors of our ways:

1. Our machines have very small memories. Although 4000 bytes (keystrokes) of memory sounded large, we now find that we can write only very simple programs under such a limitation.
2. Students are eager to try programming. The demand has been overwhelming despite our careful scheduling of the machines (all of which are now housed in a single room). In fact, the students are getting ahead of us in the development of programming skills. It's a humbling, if healthy, experience for a ninth-grade mathematics teacher to ask a fifth-grader to debug that teacher's program.
3. Program writing requires a lot of cassette tapes—at least two for each teacher (and, now, student) involved. The first is used to store the program being worked on, and the second is needed for that all-important backup copy just in case the other tape is damaged, lost, or erased. (I'd rather not talk about how we learned this lesson.)
4. We should have used some of our $3000 to buy a printer. Oh, how we wish we had a printer! If it were possible to print a copy of a nonworking (grr!) program, the search for programming errors could be done in the quiet of one's room while the computer is released to another user. As it is, errors must be located by repeatedly searching portions of the program as they flit by on the video screen. One printer could eliminate much inefficient use of the machines and of the programmer's time.

A Few Words About Sharing

It immediately occurred to us that there might be teachers with greater programming talents who would share with us the programs they had written. Indeed, we have used PACUT to develop a "program exchange" which has given us the opportunity to see a large number of programs—both commercially prepared and teacher authored. Most have been useless to us due to copyright protection (commercial programs), incompatibility of machinery (Right—computers are not all alike!), or program size (i.e., the program is too large for our 4000-byte machines). Of greater interest and disappointment, however, has been the quality of the programs. Among the problems we've noted are heavy text (using the program is like reading a book), poor pedagogy (ease of programming takes priority over good instruction), trivial applications (mostly isolated drill exercises), and cutesy graphics (where a "smiley face" lurks behind each and every correct response). Using such programs would fail to recognize the potential of the computer—it would be like using a Rolls Royce limousine to haul garbage.

Now that we've begun to think about the possible classroom applications of our computers, we're learning that it may take time and additional funds to find the programs we need. (Our principal is ecstatic about this!)

Due to Technical Difficulties . . .

Last week one of our computers developed a malady which resulted in total nonresponsiveness. Our volunteer, the electronics teacher from the high school, immediately responded to our distress call, arriving with a box filled with promising electronic cure-alls. Upon preparing to remove the computer's housing, however, he discovered a warning that our warranty would be considered null and void if the housing were removed by anyone other than a factory-authorized repair person. Although he thinks he could correct the difficulty, we're afraid to lose the warranty. Hence, 20 percent of our computing power is sidelined until someone has the time and inclination to haul it 168 miles (one way) to the nearest repair center. Then comes the wait for repair, the sad news of the cost, and a 336-mile round trip to retrieve it. (Note to our future selves: make certain that local maintenance is possible.)

Seeing Ourselves as Others See Us

Last, but certainly not least, we've been startled by the reaction of parents and colleagues. Outside of our little nine-member study group, many LaRamie teachers see computers as a threat to their employment. They fear that they may be replaced by a room full of television screens. While some recognize the financial absurdity of such a situation, few will accept arguments that computers—far from replacing teachers—promise new teaching opportunities and a release from the burden of nonteaching tasks that consume so much of a teacher's time and energy. Both teachers and parents complain of the "dehumanizing" of learning that will occur as students interact "with machines rather than people." Unfortunately, we're not as yet well enough informed to offer intelligent responses to such fears and criticisms.

In Search of Comfort

From what little we've learned, we believe that LaRamie Middle School is a microcosm of one world of instructional computing. Through PACUT we've contacted school systems whose experiences differed from ours only in terms of the magnitude of their investments. All were victims of what I would term "The Hardware Syndrome"—the eager purchase of machinery without knowing what was expected of the application of computers to instruction or of how teachers would acquire the necessary skills once the applications were identified. Through articles such as this, we hope to shape an alternate world in which purchases are guided by educational purposes rather than by bargain (?) prices.

AGENDA FOR ACTION

EAST ROACHMONT INDEPENDENT SCHOOL DISTRICT
108 East Avenue
East Roachmont, New York

Dr. Josephine G. Ennis
Superintendent

(716) 568-8804

MEMORANDUM

TO: The Instructional Computing Advisory Committee

FROM: Dr. Josephine Ennis

RE: Topical Resource Papers

DATE: November 22, 1982

The ICAC consultants phoned this morning to confirm their participation in the committee. They described many topics of possible interest to the committee. Having put them before John Russell, I agree that the breadth and depth of study represented by those topics may be more than the committee would wish to consider. We therefore decided to take two actions in order to get things under way.

(1) The consultants today will rush us copies of two introductory papers:

a. Computers in the Classroom: A Historical Perspective (This is a brief history of the role of computers in education.)

b. A Teacher's Style-Guide to Instructional Computing (This paper presents an overview of the various roles which the computer can assume in an instructional environment.)

These papers will be sent directly to your home addresses. Mr. Russell asks that you read them in preparation for the November 30 meeting.

(2) Dennis or Kansky also will send each of you a description of several "topical papers" of possible interest. The committee, at its November 30 meeting, will select and order those topics that it wishes to consider. The authors then will begin the preparation of those papers so as to meet the committee's every-other-Tuesday schedule. (The papers eventually may be the chapters in an emerging book.)

JE:sn

cc: J. Richard Dennis
Robert J. Kansky

Obourn Senior High School

200 Woodbine Avenue
East Roachmont, New York

M. Jack Stivers
Principal

(716) 568-8840

ICAC Memo #2

TO: Members of ICAC

FROM: John Russell

DATE: November 23, 1982

The attached letter from Gretchen Potter arrived today. Although the computing programs at both Near Santo and Durbanville seem to be in trouble due to errors in planning, the basic situations are quite different. I thought you would want to read and compare the two before our meeting on November 30.

JR:ms

Attachment

■ ■ ■

PLATO SENIOR HIGH SCHOOL
"Where the library is larger than the gymnasium"
2 Stellen Villa
Durbanville, New York
(716) 399-3980

Dr. A.J.L. Sinclair
Principal

Ms. B. Miller
Vice-Principal

19 November 1982

Dear Mr. Russell:

When you presented me with your if-you-had-it-all-to-do-over-again question, I did not realize how little thought I had given to the conditions and decisions behind the present instructional computing program in Durbanville. The preparation of this response for your committee has been for me a useful, if not altogether heartening, experience.

When I applied for a teaching job at Plato High School in September of 1980, I had no idea that I would be involved in teaching with and about computers. True, I did have considerable experience in data processing during my 20 years in the military, especially during the final three years in Washington. I thought, however, that public school teaching would be restricted to instruction in typing, bookkeeping, and general office mangement. I had sent applications to several schools in the area with the expectation of such a teaching assignment.

As it turned out, it was my background in computer work which led Durbanville's school superintendent to contact me. He had been in Durbanville only one year himself, but he was eager to purchase a relatively large computer to handle the district's administrative work. Although the computer was available at half price (the model was being phased out of production in favor of a radically new machine), he felt that he would be unable to convince the Durbanville District School Board to allocate $68,000 to purchase a computer solely for administrative uses. He invited me to take the position at the high school and to help him develop an instructional component to support his proposal. I accepted the position and assisted in drafting the proposal which resulted in the purchase of our present 16-terminal system.

With the background provided by the preceding paragraphs, I'll continue this report by enumerating the decisions and events which followed the Board's acceptance of our proposal.

1. The 16 terminals were to be distributed among eight locations in the school system. The locations and the number of terminals placed in each are as follows:

   2-School District Business Office

   1-District Transportation Pool

   1-Principal's Office, Plato High School

   1-Principal's Office, Lancer Junior High School

   6-High School Business Department

   2-High School Mathematics Department

   1-High School Science Department

   2-Junior High Mathematics Department

   The computer itself is located in the basement of the District Administration Building. Of the 16 terminals, 14 are connected to the computer by phone hook-ups.

2. The entire system was to be operational on 1 September 1981. In fact, the five terminals used for administrative purposes were first in use in November of 1981. I began use of the six terminals for my Data Processing course at the high school in early February of 1982. All 16 terminals were connected by the middle of March.

3. The programs provided by the vendor needed several modifications to fit the specific administrative needs of our district. Although such "tailoring" was promised by the vendor, it was not part of the written contract. Due to the immediate need to get these programs in operation, I've been released from two classes in order to make the required changes.

4. The instructional programs in data processing that I am using in my classes are <u>not</u> the ones that were demonstrated during our prepurchase visit to the vendor's headquarters. What we saw demonstrated were programs designed for the <u>new</u> model of the computer. They will not operate on the model we purchased. The programs we received have many limitations not present in those designed for the new machine. Some of these programs could be improved if I had the time to devote to the task.

5. Although the vendor plans to develop instructional programs in mathematics, science, reading, and English, no such programs exist at present. When developed, they will be designed for the new model and, hence, may not be available to us.

6. For the moment, the only possible use of the terminals in the mathematics and science classrooms is to teach computer programming. Unfortunately, none of the teachers has had the necessary training. Moreover, the number of terminals is sufficient to handle only a few students. As a result, the five terminals are not being used. We may move them into the Business Department.

7. I have been unsuccessful in attempts to convince the administration to do its processing at times which are not in conflict with instructional uses of the computers. As a result, my students often are unable to gain access to the computer during class time. The administrative terminals have a higher priority than ours.

8. All of the terminals used for instruction are connected to the computer by phone lines. The transmission rate for typed characters is 30 characters per second. Compared with a rate of 960 characters per second available on microcomputers, the printing is painfully slow.
9. Although the computer has the potential to handle large quantities of data, the memory capacity included in our "fire-sale" model is taxed by the demands of administrative uses. There is very little memory left for allocation to instructional applications. Hence, the five terminals which have not been in use may not be usable until we can afford to purchase additional memory. Since this machine is now out of production, however, we may have difficulty in getting the service required.

Despite our problems, the experience has not been without its personal rewards. I've learned a great deal. Also, I've been offered a position in the administrative offices of a much larger school district. The salary associated with the new position is tempting, but I'm concerned about what would happen in Durbanville if I were to leave. The superintendent is the only other person who has been centrally involved in the project, and rumor has it that he may accept an attractive position elsewhere.

I hope that this account of our experience in Durbanville will be of value to your committee. Please contact me if you feel I may be of further service.

Sincerely,

M. Gretchen Potter

M. Gretchen Potter

■ ■ ■

University of Illinois
at Urbana-Champaign

**Department of
Secondary Education**

395 Education Building
1310 South Sixth Street
Champaign
Illinois 61820

College of Education

217 333-0227

MEMORANDUM

TO: Members of East Roachmont's Instructional Computing Advisory Committee

FROM: Dick Dennis and Bob Kansky

RE: The Selection of Topical Papers on Instructional Applications of Computers

DATE: 11-29-82

We've prepared the attached list of topical papers dealing with the educational applications of computers. The papers are in various stages of preparation. Your selection and ordering of a list of topics of immediate interest to you will tell us how to focus our developmental energies.

Papers 1 and 2, requested in your behalf by Dr. Ennis, will soon be on their way under separate cover. They should arrive in a few days.

Of the remaining papers, two (Papers 3 and 4) explore topics regarding administrative applications of computers. Papers 5-9 examine instructional applications of computers in which the computer itself is the object of study (i.e., they are papers directed toward teaching about computers). Papers 10-19 consider instructional applications of computers in which the computer is viewed as a tool for facilitating some aspect of the instructional process (i.e., they are papers which address the issues of teaching with computers). Papers 20 and 21 turn to the task of preparing an implementation plan for the use of computers in the classroom and of selecting the computing hardware which will support that plan.

Papers 1-21 are addressed to teachers or administrators who, it is assumed, have no experience in computer programming. (They also speak to the educator who does have programming skills and who wishes to employ those skills in the development of computer programs to be used in instruction.) Papers 22-27, on the other hand, require a firm understanding of computer programming and a willingness to translate from one version of the BASIC language to another.

While there is some logical order to the presentation of specific topics, a great deal of flexibility exists. Our intent is to refine and send only those papers which you identify as meeting your needs. Insofar as possible, we'll produce these papers in the order you indicate.

Some important questions that your committee might consider in selecting the papers are as follows.

* Will the paper help us to meet the tasks set forth for it by Superintendent Ennis?
* Is the topic of the paper one which <u>every</u> member of the committee can and should read?
* Is the total number of papers small enough that the committee can complete reading and discussing them in the time available? (Generally speaking, we'll need two weeks to prepare each paper that you select.)

Please advise us of the committee's decisions. (It also would be very helpful to us if you'd make note of why you selected—or rejected—any group of topics since this would give us further insight into your needs and priorities.)

We look forward to hearing from you soon and to working with you during the next several weeks.

DD:BK:glm

cc: Dr. Jo Ennis

Attachment: List of Suggested Topical Papers

■ ■ ■

SUGGESTED TOPICAL PAPERS ON EDUCATIONAL APPLICATIONS OF COMPUTERS

INTRODUCTORY PAPERS

1. Computers in the Classroom: A Historical Perspective
   A brief history of computers in education.
2. A Teacher's Style-Guide to Instructional Computing
   A broad overview of the ways in which computers can be used in an instructional environment.

PAPERS ON ADMINISTRATIVE APPLICATIONS

3. A Teacher's Introduction to Administrative Computing
   An overview of administrative computing written for the nonadministrator.
4. The School Administrator's Introduction to Computing
   An overview of administrative computing written for the administrator who is not yet using a computer to cope with those tasks.

AGENDA FOR ACTION

PAPERS ON TEACHING ABOUT COMPUTERS

5. Computers in Anytown, USA
   An identification of often overlooked but garden-variety uses of computers in society (i.e., an awareness experience).
6. The Many Faces of Computers
   A nontechnical introduction to the maxi-, mini-, and microcomputer systems: where they are found, what they look like, what kinds of jobs are appropriate for each, and how they do their jobs.
7. The Anatomy of a Microcomputer
   A nontechnical look inside the kind of computer which has put instructional computing within the reach of any school.
8. A New Kind of Literacy
   Some suggestions regarding what every informed citizen should know about computers.
9. Who's in Control?
   A discussion of matters of personal rights, laws, privacy, and moral issues involving computers.

PAPERS ON TEACHING WITH COMPUTERS

10. Questioning Episodes: The Building Blocks of Instructional Computing
    This short paper introduces concepts and vocabulary which are needed for the discussion of computerized instructional materials in Paper 11.
11. Getting Hardnosed About Software: Evaluating Computerized Instructional Materials
    Guidelines for locating and evaluating computerized instructional materials.
12. Questioning Episodes Revisited
    This discussion of questioning techniques builds upon Paper 9. It provides the additional details needed to understand the uses of computers which are presented in Papers 13-19.
13. One-On-One: The Computer as Tutor
    Through tutorial discourse, the computer assumes total responsibility for teaching a new concept, generalization, or skill.
14. Play It Again, Sam: Drill or Practice on the Computer
    The computer is applied to reinforce associations or practice complex procedures for which concepts have been established by previous instruction.
15. An Examination of Computer-Assisted Testing Operations
    The computer is used to construct, score, and analyze objective-referenced tests.
16. Individualization and Instructional Management With a Computer
    The computer supports the flexible and efficient management of both students and instructional resources.
17. Electronic Slices of Reality: The Instructional Role of Computerized Simulations
    The computer provides experiences in decision-making in situations where actual experience is ruled out by extreme expense, danger, or time considerations.
18. In Search of Strategies: Computerized Instructional Games
    The computer is applied to the development of general problem-solving skills within a competitive or cooperative game environment.
19. The Computer as Aide-de-Camp
    The computer is used in a variety of ways to support and improve teaching/learning processes and materials.

PAPERS ON IMPLEMENTATION ISSUES

20. Profiles in Computing: Defining the Role of Computers in Your School

A detailed analysis of the kind of instructional planning needed for thoughtful uses of the computer.

21. Wi$e Buy$: The Purchase as a Function of Purpose
A plan for countering the computerese of the computer salesperson with a list of specifications which meet your instructional computing needs.

TECHNICAL PAPERS

(Note: The reading/use of the following papers requires considerable expertise in computer programming. Each paper presents and discusses a computer program—written in the BASIC language for one of three microcomputer systems. While no one of these is in common use as an instructional microcomputer in precollege classrooms, the flow charts, code listings, and programmer's documentation should make it possible to rewrite the programs for use on other systems.)

22. Documentation of a Computerized Test-Reporting System
23. Documentation of a Small Data-Base Management System for School Applications
24. Documentation of a Small Computer Attendance-Keeping System
25. Documentation of a Computerized Drill Paradigm
26. Documentation of a Small Computer Instructional Management System
27. Documentation of a Computerized Instructional Resource Management System

■ ■ ■

Obourn Senior High School

200 Woodbine Avenue
East Roachmont, New York

M. Jack Stivers
Principal

(716) 568-8840

12-1-82

Professor J. Richard Dennis
University of Illinois
1310 South Sixth Street
Champaign, IL 61820

Professor Robert J. Kansky
University of Wyoming
P.O. Box 3992
Laramie, WY 82070

Dear Professors:

The committee was more than a little overwhelmed by the list of possible topics of study. Although three of us have some computer programming experience, none of us was familiar with the many applications suggested. Moreover, we're not certain how much we can absorb in the time we have available. In fairness to you we don't want to ask you to generate more than we can reasonably expect to read, discuss and (hopefully) understand well enough to translate into practical plans for the East Roachmont schools.

We've selected 14 papers to constitute our course of study. The selections represent compromises but generally are the consequence of six conditions basic to our task and membership: (1) we felt that we could give adequate treatment to 14 topics at most in the time available, (2) we must consider all grade levels and subject matter fields in recommending instructional uses of computers, (3) we presently have access to very little computing equipment and we do not have any purchase commitment from our school board, (4) we have chosen to focus upon teaching with, rather than about, computers, (5) articles on computer literacy issues are readily available, and (6) most members of the ICAC have no training as programmers (or, at present, any interest in acquiring programming skills).

The committee has requested that I expand a bit on its comment regarding "computer literacy issues" (item 5 above). While we have a strong interest in such issues, ICAC is not charged with defining a computer literacy program for the Roachmont schools. Moreover, such general information as we need about computer literacy certainly must be accessible from many journals; we want you to focus your efforts on topics which may not be so easily found. However, we would appreciate your directing us to sources of information and opinion on computer literacy issues.

Based upon the conditions stated, our decisions (selections/rejections) regarding the topical papers are as follows:

1. The committee concurred with the selection of Papers 1 and 2. These should provide some useful general ideas.
2. We rejected Papers 3 and 4 since our interests are in instructional, rather than administrative, uses.
3. Papers 5-9 also were rejected. Our focus is to be upon teaching with computers. As noted, we felt that we could (with your help) find some information about these topics in books or journals devoted to computing.
4. The committee was uncertain regarding the relevance of Papers 10 and 11. While we do have access to a few microcomputers (at schools and computer shops in the area), the detailed job of selecting computerized courseware goes beyond the tasks given us by Superintendent Ennis. Still, some of us argued that the committee should examine examples of such courseware in a critical manner if it is to be able to make realistic recommendations when developing "a plan for implementing the instructional uses of computers." The papers were finally accepted by a vote of 5 to 3.
5. There was strong agreement upon the selection of papers 12-19. These would seem to address the basic question of what computers can do in instruction.
6. Paper 20 was another unanimous choice since it is on a topic that corresponds to one of ICAC's primary charges.
7. While the committee supported the selection of Paper 21, there was considerable debate about how soon it is needed. While we feel some immediate need to know about hardware in case a purchasing opportunity is presented, we also feel that the problems reported in Near Santo and Durbanville are a result of focusing on hardware before deciding what will be done with it. In the end, we were in accord that Paper 21 is necessary and that the timing of its delivery should be left to you, the consultants.
8. Papers 22-27 were rejected on two grounds. First, many ICAC members aren't programmers so the papers would be readable (maybe) by only a few. Secondly, the programming members suspect that these programs might require major rewriting efforts to be used on any equipment that we get. Since we have no teaching time allotted to such a task, we hope to be able to get started by purchasing programs which can be used without time-consuming modification.

As you've probably inferred from our selections, we prefer to have the papers written for readers with no computer programming experience. In addition to our ICAC members, we have the future interests of other East Roachmont teachers in mind.

We think this will be an exciting venture. Certainly, it's been a rare experience to pick the chapters to our own book, so to speak.

Cordially,

John C. Russell

JCR:ms

John C. Russell

cc: ICAC Membership

■ ■ ■

SCIENCE AND MATHEMATICS
TEACHING CENTER

ADDRESS REPLY TO WRITER

THE UNIVERSITY OF WYOMING
UNIVERSITY STATION, BOX 3992
LARAMIE, WYOMING, 82071

December 6, 1982

Mr. John Russell, Chairman: Instructional Computing Advisory Committee
Obourn Senior High School
200 Woodbine Avenue
East Roachmont, NY

Dear Mr. Russell:

Thank you for your quick selection of the papers to be prepared. We have discussed your selections and are impressed with the substantive reasoning behind the committee's decisions.

In response to points 4 and 7 of your letter of December 1, we agree that Papers 10, 11, and 21 are good selections. We also concur with those who would place hardware consideration (Paper 21) after a thorough examination of the possible classroom uses of computers.

We see the papers (which we have renumbered and chosen to call "The ICAC Papers") falling into the five groups indicated on the enclosed listing. We will begin the development of Paper 3 of the list immediately and will attempt to hold to producing a paper every two weeks. This biweekly schedule will keep in mind your committee's meeting dates. To guarantee efficient delivery of the papers, we will mail all copies to you. We'd appreciate your distributing them to the other members of the committee.

We hope you'll keep us informed of the committee's uses of and reactions to the papers and please place us on the distribution list for the "ICAC Memos" that Jo Ennis has mentioned.

Sincerely yours,

Robert J. Kansky

Robert J. Kansky

RJK:baa

Agenda for Action

The ICAC Papers

Introductory Papers

1. Computers in the Classroom: A Historical Perspective
2. A Teacher's Style-Guide to Instructional Computing
3. Questioning Episodes: The Building Blocks of Instructional Computing
4. Getting Hard-Nosed About Software: Evaluating Computerized Instructional Materials
5. Questioning Episodes Revisited

Instructional Applications with the Computer as Teacher

6. One-On-One: The Computer as Tutor
7. Play It Again, Sam: Drill or Practice on the Computer
8. An Examination of Computer-Assisted Testing Operations
9. Individualization and Instructional Management with a Computer

Instructional Applications with the Computer as Partner

10. Electronic Slices of Reality: The Instructional Role of Computerized Simulations
11. In Search of Strategies: Computerized Instructional Games

Instructional Applications with the Computer as Servant

12. The Computer as Aide-de-Camp

Planning the Implementation of Instructional Uses of Computers

13. Profiles in Computing: Defining the Role of Computers in *Your* School
14. Wi$e Buy$: Purchase as a Function of Purpose

■ ■ ■

University of Illinois
at Urbana-Champaign

**Department of
Secondary Education**

395 Education Building
1310 South Sixth Street
Champaign
Illinois 61820

College of Education

217 333-0227

MEMORANDUM

TO: Members of the Instructional Computing Advisory Committee

FROM: Dick Dennis

DATE: December 6, 1982

RE: ICAC Paper 1

The first of the two topical papers requested by Dr. Ennis is enclosed. "Computers in the Classroom" is a rather informal summary of the development of the instructional application of computers since 1950. Bob is completing a companion paper, "A Teacher's Style-Guide to Instructional Computing," which further describes the types of applications which have evolved over the past three decades. (This second paper should be in the mail tomorrow.)

Just a few words about the purpose of ICAC Paper 1. This little history was prepared on the assumption that to appreciate where we are, it helps to know where we've been. On the other hand, it is virtually impossible to write about where we are. Developments in computing equipment and its use are proceeding so rapidly that any statement of where we are is sadly out-of-date before it gets into print. This week's wild predictions often become next week's historical accomplishments.

The enclosed paper provides some "ancient history" on instructional computing. For more recent information, members of the committee should share in the skimming of periodicals such as Classroom Computer News, Educational Computer Magazine, Electronic Education, Electronic Learning, Personal Computing, Popular Computing, and The Computing Teacher. Several of these should be available in your local libraries (school or public), computing shops, or bookstores.

As you know, it's our hope to place these topical papers into book form. At that time the paper undoubtedly will be given some pedestrian designations such as "chapters." For now, however, we prefer to think of them as documents developed specifically to guide the deliberations and actions of your Instructional Computing Advisory Committee (ICAC). Whatever they may someday be called, they are "the ICAC Papers."

DD:glm

Enclosure: ICAC Paper 1

cc: Bob Kansky

■ ■ ■

SCIENCE AND MATHEMATICS
TEACHING CENTER

ADDRESS REPLY TO WRITER

THE UNIVERSITY OF WYOMING
UNIVERSITY STATION, BOX 3992
LARAMIE, WYOMING, 82071

MEMORANDUM

TO: Members of ICAC

FROM: Bob Kansky

DATE: December 7, 1982

RE: ICAC Paper 2

ICAC Paper 1 presented a quick overview of three decades of hardware and software development. Paper 2 complements that effort by presenting a first analysis of the environments in which instructional computing is being done and of the kinds of instructional applications that are being tried.

The discussions of Paper 2 pose one major problem—vocabulary. Dictionaries, even those advertised as "computer dictionaries," are of little or no value. The language of instructional computing is still evolving, and many terms do not have universally accepted definitions as yet. I mention this for two reasons: (1) so you won't be shocked if you see our terms used in slightly different ways by other authors, and (2) so you won't get hung up in the useless task of memorizing definitions. Just be aware that we'll make definitions in order to permit useful distinctions. Take those definitions with a grain of salt and keep moving. Also, keep in mind that future papers will revisit the ideas of Paper 2 in greater detail.

After consultation with Dick, I've also prepared the enclosed "Beginner's Glossary of Computerese" to assist you in overcoming the aforementioned language problem. There are many terms in it that may be of no particular relevance to you at the moment; also, it is probably missing items that you will encounter later and wish to add. It's our suggestion that you keep this glossary at hand as you read the ICAC Papers, referring to it—and expanding it—as needed.

BK:baa

Enclosures: ICAC Paper 2
A Beginner's Glossary of Computerese

cc: Dick Dennis

■ ■ ■

Obourn Senior High School

200 Woodbine Avenue
East Roachmont, New York

M. Jack Stivers
Principal

(716) 568-8840

ICAC Memo #3

TO: Members of ICAC

FROM: John Russell

DATE: December 17, 1982

Although Tuesday's meeting went on until 5:15 p.m., we are resolved to return to our original agreement to disband by 4:00 p.m.! Now that we're better organized, we should be able to accomplish more between meetings and to reserve our time together for taking action on major issues. In this regard, it is agreed that the following should be added to the list of procedural agreements given in ICAC Memo #1.

6. Any request for action by the committee must be submitted in writing. It should be stated as a resolution and must be supported by a brief (written) rationale.
7. Signed resolutions should be distributed to Dr. Ennis and the committee through interschool mail since this guarantees quick delivery. Mailing should be done no later than the Thursday preceding the meeting at which the resolution is to be considered. (This is a bit tight, but we need to keep moving. We are agreed that each of us will take the initiative to make premeeting contact with the person submitting the resolution in order to ask questions, get clarification, etc.)
8. Whenever a resolution calls for "homework" by one or more members of the committee, the substance of the resolution will be noted in the ICAC Memo which is the follow-up to that meeting.
9. Dick Dennis and Bob Kansky will be supplied with a copy of each ICAC Memo (including the memo of 11-19-1982). This action should provide efficient communication between the committee and the consultants.

In keeping with item 8 above, the assignments associated with the resolutions passed at Tuesday's meeting are summarized below. With self-righteous glee, Gerri and I note that our homework is done and that we await your calls.

AGENDA FOR ACTION

COMMITTEE ASSIGNMENTS

1. Gerri and John will prepare an annotated list of no more than 20 journals and newsletters on instructional computing now available at school and public libraries in the Roachmont area. This list will be mailed to all members no later than Thursday.

2. Members of the committee will get themselves some hands-on experience with computers before our first post-holiday meeting (1-4-1983). In addition to such visits to computer shops that folks do themselves, the following group visits will be arranged:

   (A) Donna will contact Gretchen Potter at Durbanville and schedule a two-hour visit which will include experience with appropriate programs.

   (B) John will contact Glena Harris to schedule a visit to LaRamie Middle School.

   It's believed that we'll have no trouble arranging visits during the vacation period. Donna and John will schedule the visits using the list of dates agreed upon by the committee and will report those arrangements by phone.

3. NOTE TO DICK DENNIS

   In following your suggestion to locate periodicals for ICAC members to review, Gerri and I felt that we were too successful. The list of interesting publications is much longer than we had anticipated. Have any suggestions regarding best selections, procedures for review, or what to focus upon when reading such materials?

JR:ms

P.S. Have a happy holiday season. See you at Durbanville and Near Santo.

Attachment: Instructional Computing Periodicals List

■ ■ ■

INSTRUCTIONAL COMPUTING PERIODICALS LIST

The following periodicals are available at the locations indicated and would appear to be the kind that would be of interest to the committee at this time. Several other journals, newsletters, and books were found, but they seemed to be on topics which were beyond our current levels of interest and expertise. (A list of the titles, locations, and general content of these currently inappropriate resources has been filed for possible future reference.)

A. Periodicals available at East Roachmont Municipal Library

<u>Microcomputing</u>
A monthly published since 1976. Reports on timely topics and new innovations for a broad range of microcomputers and a broad range of applications; follows a "getting the most from your micro" theme. Seems to be directed to home computer applications.

<u>Computers and People</u>
Formerly called Computers and Automation. Published for over 30 years, it contains thoughtful discussions for citizens of issues surrounding information, its processing, and the industries involved. The magazine's motto: "Design, applications, and implications of information processing systems—and the pursuit of truth in input, output, and processing, for the benefit of people."

B. Periodicals available from the 14-day lending library set up by Nibble Source, the computer store in the new East Roachmont Plaza.

Creative Computing

A popular personal computing publication containing extensive reviews of hardware and software. Heavy emphasis on gaming applications; growing emphasis on school applications. Published monthly.

Personal Computing

A monthly that presents discussions of broad-ranging applications. Often prints programs to do the tasks. Good source of ideas.

Nibble Source has several more technical publications in its library (e.g., Byte, Lifelines, Microcomputing, Compute!, and journals dealing with specific microcomputing systems). These may be of help to us after we've grown a bit.

C. Periodicals available from the Oboum Senior High School Library.

(John has been working with Oboum's media specialists to build this collection of professional journals. Few issues go back beyond a year.)

Educational Technology

Discusses educational uses of many forms of technology (including computers). Regular columns on educational computing. Published monthly.

T.H.E. Journal

The "T.H.E." stands for "Technical Horizons in Education." It discusses computers as one aspect of educational technology. It contains an Inquiry Service Card by which the reader can obtain additional information regarding software, publications, and projects reported in the magazine. Six issues per year.

Educational Computer Magazine

Specifically directed to teachers using computers in the classroom. Articles about both the promise and problems of instructional computing; reports of conferences and educational projects. Book and software reviews. Published bimonthly.

Electronic Education

Dedicated to news and reviews for school computing. Discusses hardware, software, and schooling issues. Ten issues each year.

Electronic Learning

Nontechnical information about the applications of many electronic aids to instruction. Special sections regularly address educational computing issues such as funding, software, review, and inservice. Eight issues per school year.

D. Publications available from Gerri.

Journal of Data Education

Published by the Society of Data Educators. Timely articles for data processors or teachers of data processing.

Popular Computing

Aimed at a nontechnical audience, explores all aspects of personal computers and their use. Regular reviews and news on popular microcomputers and their use. A good source of ideas for applications in the home or in a small business plus regular articles on possible classroom uses. Published monthly.

Datamation

A monthly featuring broadly-ranging articles. Many surveys and reviews. Covers all types and sizes of computers. Largely business or industry directed. A good source of timely information for staying current (once we get current).

E. Periodicals available from John.

Classroom Computer Learning

Classroom-oriented periodical. Regularly reports teachers' experiences with classroom applications of computers. Articles on people and projects in the field; viewpoints on educational computing. Reviews hardware, software, and computing literature. Published six times during the school year.

The Computing Teacher

Articles by educators for educators. Although most are nontechnical items about instructional uses of computers, some present computer programs, programming problems, or programming "hints." Software and book reviews; reports on conferences and projects. Nine issues per year.

InfoWorld

A weekly newspaper covering a broad range of computing topics for a diverse audience. Articles of educational interest include items about new hardware, government actions, social and moral issues associated with computing, and the latest perceived areas of application of computers to instruction. Software reviews.

Arithmetic Teacher

Devoted to the teaching of mathematics in grades K-8, it has lately given attention to classroom uses of technology—especially calculators and computers.

Mathematics Teacher

This journal picks up where the Arithmetic Teacher leaves off and extends into the junior college level. Some instructional computing articles for the novice, but many others require programming experience.

STUDY GUIDE: CHAPTER 2

1. Activities in instructional computing can be implemented with one or both of two computing styles, *batch* and *interactive*.
   a. Describe the general advantages and disadvantages of each.
   b. Which style(s) would appear to be effective for each of the several types of instructional computing activities (tutorial, drill, practice, simulation, management, etc.)?
2. Using examples of activities, distinguish between teaching *about* computers and teaching *with* computers.
3. Within the total curriculum of a precollege subject area of interest to you, identify two or more specific activities which satisfy each of the following.
   a. The objective of the activity is to promote associative learning.
   b. The objective of the activity is to learn a step-by-step process or procedure.
   c. The objective of the activity is to provide experiences in decision making.
4. Suppose that Ocean Elementary School has decided to pilot a new computer literacy curriculum next year. The conditions are as follows:
   - Ocean Elementary will pilot the curriculum in all four of its sixth-grade classrooms.
   - Enrollments for next year are projected to be 27 students per classroom.
   - The curriculum requires eight weeks of instruction. During that period, each student must be scheduled for twelve 20-minute interactive sessions with a computer. Students cannot work in pairs for these sessions.
   - The program makes use of the Bogus Mark III microcomputer system. The school system is committed to purchasing the minimum number of Bogus systems needed to implement the pilot project.
   - All of the Bogus systems will be placed in a single room which is reserved for this purpose. The room will be open and monitored by a trained aide from 8 A.M.-noon and from 12:30 P.M.-3:30 P.M. on each school day.

   Recommend (and justify) the minimum number of Bogus systems required by the project.
5. In his letter to the ICAC consultants (12–1–82), John Russell lists six conditions which governed ICAC's selection of fourteen papers. Given those conditions;
   a. argue for or against the selections made;
   b. argue for any replacements or additions to the papers on ICAC's list.
6. Based upon the information provided by Glena Harris and Gretchen Potter, what conjectures can you make about the major sources of the implementation problems they reported?
7. Compare and contrast the planning procedures in East Roachmont (as revealed by the memoranda) with the Harris-Potter situations.
8. Carefully examine the operational procedures adopted by ICAC. What strengths or weaknesses do you see in those procedures? What additional (or substitute) procedures would you suggest?

CHAPTER THREE

QUESTIONING EPISODES: THE BUILDING BLOCKS OF INSTRUCTIONAL COMPUTING

Why a chapter on questioning? Indeed, we earlier promised that the remaining chapters would explore some specific aspect of teaching with a computer—of using the computer as a medium of instruction. All this fuss about questioning may seem tangential.

Not so! The topic at hand is central to instructional computing. Admittedly, the zeal with which we approach the whole of instructional computing springs from three axioms regarding education:

Axiom 1: The goal of education is to produce problem solvers.
Axiom 2: The key to problem solving is the skill of asking good questions.
Axiom 3: One learns to ask good questions by being asked good questions.

So there you have it. The fundamental implication of our three little axioms is that questioning is the substance of good teaching. If computers are to be admitted to the instructional process, the price of admission must be proof of their ability to pose good questions. As computer-users, teachers must expect that fundamental characteristic and must be prepared to judge how well the computer performs its role as questioner.

WHEN A QUESTION IS A QUESTION

Dear Mrs. Applegate . . . she was the second-grade pied piper of the English language at Point Pleasant Beach Elementary School. Not only did she get our *b*'s facing in the right direction and get the proper number of legs on our *m*'s, but also she taught us to distinguish among statements, exclamations, and questions by building in us an abiding faith in final punctuation. When, in later years, the mathematics teachers insisted that *8!* was not an excited eight and was not read aloud by shouting "EIGHT!," we could forgive Mrs. Applegate. (Mathematics teachers are, after all, a peculiar lot who are given to creating their own rules.)[1] On the other hand, the dear lady's faith in the **?** was clearly misplaced. Of course she expected *us* to answer her questions; she never flew the false **?** flag of the rhetorical question (like the one that opens this paper).

When we speak of questioning with regard to instructional computing, we return to Mrs. Applegate's suggestion that a question is part of a dialogue. Whenever one participant in that dialogue presents or implies a **?**, it will be assumed that it is now the turn of some other participant to respond with a **.**, an **!**, or even another **?**. Sometimes the intent of a question will be to motivate the learner, to tease him into a learning activity. Questions may also be used to help the learner to translate attitudes, interests, or beliefs into actions (decisions). At other times, questions will combine to lead the learner to the self-discovery of an idea. As clues set out by the kindly hand of Providence, they lightly guide the learner in such a way that he or she perceives that idea to be a personal creation of the moment.[2] Still another function of questioning is to determine whether or not learning has taken place. But whatever the educational context of questioning may be, a question posed for the purpose of inducing learning will be accompanied by the expectation of a response from the learner.

One of the most valuable contributions that the computer offers to education is making instruction and learning interactive. If one were to list the major failings of conventional schooling, the observation that students too often are passive participants in the learning process would be near the top of the list. (Consider the learning atmosphere of the lecture hall!) Students are experiencing what might be aptly described as "intellectual downtime."[3] As a learner, you should have no trouble recalling the experience of suddenly awakening from a reading task to the realization that your eyes were ingesting words but your mind wasn't digesting meanings. (Is it happening now?)

Appearances are deceiving. Student activity associated with school tasks is not necessarily evidence of a good learning situation. Students busily engaged in computing, writing reports, or diagramming sentences can do so in a deprived educational environment—one in which a major attribute of effective teaching may be missing. Specifically, the environment is deprived if it fails to provide the student with *feedback* (also called *knowledge of results).* To be effective, the learning situation must be more than active; it must be *inter*active. Since properly designed computer programs can simulate personal conversations between an author-teacher and each student user, the introduction of computers into teaching does not mean the abandonment of instructional dialogues.

Of course, the ability of computers to provide interactive instruction doesn't mean that this ability is always employed by the lesson designer. Computer-based instruction *can* be comprised of long sessions of information-giving. The student reads on and on while the computer serves only as an electronic page-turner. Computer-based education *can* be characterized by questioning sessions which inform a student of the correctness or incorrectness of his responses but which provide no feedback regarding the bases of those judgments. The lack of feedback to correct responses ignores the fact that the student may have given a right answer for a wrong reason (or for no reason at all). In not giving feedback to incorrect responses, it fails to provide any clue as to how the student's thinking must change in order to arrive at correct responses. Computer-based education *can* employ sets of exercises which are executed repeatedly by every student in a single order: learning is thus reduced to the task of memorizing a single sequence of acceptable responses.

Instructional computing *can* use any combination of the undesirable processes described above. The only insurance against them are the skills at interaction possessed by the human author of the materials that the computer executes and the demand of educators that the author consistently employ those skills. The authoring of sloppy, undesirable computerized lessons is far easier than the construction of interactive ones. Not all authors are endowed with a commitment to excellence. Hence, those who teach with computers must develop a firm understanding of questioning in order to demand higher standards. Knowing what to expect, the users of computer programs can put the heat on the authors of those programs. The user has a responsibility to be nasty . . . in a knowledgeable way.

The Questioning Episode

To the language specialist, a question is simply an interrogative expression. To help us recognize the question in its written form, most grammarians have seen fit to

---

[1]If one can believe it, '8!' is an abbreviation for the expression '8×7×6×5×4×3×2×1.'

[2]This use of questions is associated with a style of instruction often called "discovery learning."

[3]*Downtime* is a technical phrase you will encounter frequently as you become a computerist. *Downtime* starts when your computer unilaterally stops!

terminate such an expression with a **?**. A few, such as the Spanish, have sought to be doubly certain by adorning both ends of the expression (¿si?). But even this decorative punctuation is insufficient to the definition of questioning as it is used in teaching—especially in teaching with a computer.

For the purpose of describing and analyzing instructional computing, we need to go beyond the notion of a question (interrogative expression) in order to develop the idea of interactive teaching. The concept which will be both brick and mortar in this development is defined as follows:

> A **questioning episode** is the smallest complete unit of computer-student interaction.

Like most working definitions, this one of a questioning episode is the latest (and not necessarily the last) in a long line of trial definitions. The definition is compact, concise, and temporarily adequate. Moreover, since you weren't a participant in the struggle that produced it in its present shiny form, you won't understand it. It's probably too well polished to be understood by anyone except the authors—and you may come to view even that assertion as being optimistic. Therefore a little elaboration is in order. The procedure will be to divide the concept of a questioning episode into five component parts and to examine each. The reader is then left with the task of reweaving those five threads into the whole cloth which is a questioning episode.

A questioning episode is comprised of the following:

1. an interrogative expression (a question or prompting statement), perhaps accompanied by other statements intended to elicit dialogue;
2. a requirement of and an opportunity for the *student* to input information or to ask a question;
3. the provision for *computer interpretation* of the student input;
4. a set of computer-generated consequences, remarks, replies, or other questions which constitute specific *feedback* to the student input;
5. a procedure for determining the *duration limit* of the episode.

Each of these ingredients must be present in a learning situation if that situation is to be called a questioning episode. In order that you may recognize questioning episodes in their many colors and shades, we'll carefully examine each of their component parts in Chapter 5.

To appreciate the uses and misuses of questioning episodes in instructional computing, one needs to take a critical look at several examples of computerized courseware. We must now pause, therefore, to consider criteria and procedures for taking such a "critical look" at courseware criteria and procedures that you will refine during the pursuit of quality computerized instructional materials—the central issue of instructional computing.

Because the notion of a questioning episode is necessary to the thoughtful evaluation of computer software, a brief introduction to the concept has been placed at this point in our investigation of the instructional application of computers. The purposes of Chapter 4 are to create further awareness of the richness and complexity of computerized instructional materials and, we hope, to make clear the need to learn more about the specific characteristics of the many kinds of such materials. Since questioning episodes will have much to do with the defining of those characteristics, we'll then revisit the topic to gain a deeper understanding of their role as the building blocks of instructional computing.

Study Guide: Chapter 3

1. Go to a precollege textbook in a subject area of interest to you. Select a short-answer student exercise or study question presented by the textbook.
   a. Make a list of correct answers that a student might give.
   b. Make a list of conceptually correct but technically flawed responses that the student might give.
   c. Make a list of conceptually incorrect responses that a student might give.
   d. Identify if possible at least one response which would meet the standards of a correct answer but which could be arrived at through faulty reasoning.
2. Execute a computer activity of your choice. As you do, classify the various questioning episodes by these basic functions:
   a. giving student control of choices;
   b. promoting awareness of a concept;
   c. assessing awareness of a concept.
3. Within a computer activity of your choosing, identify a questioning episode and respond to the following items about that episode.
   a. What is the content of the interrogative expression? Is that expression accompanied by other statements?
   b. What opportunity is there for a student response? What has the student been told about *how* to respond?
   c. What provision has been made for computer interpretation of a student's response? What correct or incorrect answers are recognized by the computer? (The last question will require you to execute the questioning episode several times in order to experiment with a variety of responses.)
   d. For each correct or incorrect response identified above, what specific reaction (feedback) does the computer provide? How helpful is each such reaction to the learner?
   e. How many times can a student answer incorrectly before the computer "moves on"?

CHAPTER FOUR

Getting Hard-Nosed About Software: Evaluating Computerized Instructional Materials

Educators must make a choice. They can take a position as uninvolved spectators of computerized courseware development, or they can participate in setting and enforcing the rules governing that development. For the most part, they have thus far acted as indiscriminate consumers of instructional software.

Few educators will have the time or desire to engage in the programming of instructional software. Can they, then, engage in its evaluation? Certainly they can! One doesn't have to write textbooks in order to judge their educational value; many an established theater critic has never trod the boards; it isn't necessary to be a *cordon bleu* chef in order to recognize and reject an omelette made with rotten eggs. A teacher is not expected to be able to produce educational materials (books, films, instructional games, computerized courseware), but every teacher does have a professional obligation to judge the quality of the materials he or she uses. Any teacher who knows what can be expected from the computer as an instructional medium—the person that you soon will be—is entitled to exercise critical oversight of the computerized courseware industry and, whenever appropriate, assert, "Sorry, folks, that's just not good enough." Indeed, much of what is being hawked as instructional software just isn't good enough.

In 1980, the National Council of Teachers of Mathematics (NCTM) recognized that the quality of software (i.e., computerized courseware) rather than of hardware was to be the major concern of teachers who wished to use computers as an instructional tool. The Instructional Affairs Committee of NCTM further established the organization's position through two assertions: first, that every teacher is responsible for the evaluation of computerized courseware and, thus, for the development of computerized courseware as an educationally sound instructional resource; second, that producers of such courseware will both appreciate and rise to the expectations of informed educators. In keeping with these assertions, NCTM appointed a Task Force on the Evaluation of Computerized Instructional Materials and charged it with the development of criteria, instruments, and procedures for evaluating *all* such courseware. The task force later reaffirmed the subject-free nature of its charge by placing the following statement in the preface of its *Guidelines:*

> These guidelines are offered to *all* educators interested in the instructional applications of computers. Their development has been marked by a continuous, conscious effort to address the needs of all educators irrespective of their areas of interest, subject matter, or present level of involvement with instructional computing.[1]

Since publication, the *NCTM Guidelines* have been reproduced in part or in whole by several organizations, many of which have goals far removed from the teaching of mathematics. Now, by special permission of NCTM, an updated and slightly modified version of the *Guidelines* appears on the next several pages. Changes are few; the ideas of the task force are intact. A typeface similar to the original publication has been retained to remind the reader of NCTM's pioneering contribution.

[1]Heck, W. P., J. Johnson, and R. J. Kansky, *Guidelines for Evaluating Computerized Instructional Materials* (Reston, VA: National Council of Teachers of Mathematics, 1981), preface.

Guidelines for Evaluating Computerized Instructional Materials

prepared by
William P. Heck
Jerry Johnson
Robert J. Kansky

for the
**Instructional Affairs Committee
of the
National Council of Teachers of Mathematics**

Table of Contents

National Council of Teachers of Mathematics

ISBN: 0-87353-176-0

AN AGENDA FOR ACTION

NCTM

1980

Preface

These guidelines are offered to *all* educators interested in the instructional applications of computers. Their development has been marked by a continuous, conscious effort to address the needs of all educators irrespective of their areas of interest, subject matter, or present level of involvement with instructional computing.

The preparation of *Guidelines for Evaluating Computerized Instructional Materials* was carried out under the direction of the NCTM's Instructional Affairs Committee (IAC) as part of its effort to implement recommendation 3 of *An Agenda for Action* (see the inside front cover of this booklet). The writing and field testing were done by a special IAC subcommittee composed of Robert J. Kansky, *chairman* (University of Wyoming, Laramie, Wyoming), William P. Heck (science and mathematics supervisor, Robbinsdale Area Schools, Minneapolis, Minnesota), and Jerry Johnson (University of the Pacific, Stockton, California). The cover design was suggested by Earl Ockenga (Price Laboratory School, Cedar Falls, Iowa).

SECTION 0

A Guide to These Guidelines

What Follows 1?

The preparation of this resource presented three tasks: (1) to identify information about the location, selection, and evaluation of computerized materials that might be of interest to all educators, (2) to report that information in intellectually bite-sized pieces called *sections,* and (3) to arrange those sections in the one true order that would assure maximum understanding by each reader. With more than a little help from friends and colleagues, the authors have tried to meet the challenge of the first two tasks; the last task, however, proved too much. (Ah well, two out of three isn't bad. Given today's grade inflation, the performance probably rates a B+.) The reader should not infer that the sequence of section numbers corresponds to an optimum reading order. Section 2 may very well not be the logical successor to section 1. With one exception (section 5), the sections of this document should be of use to any educator who is concerned with the instructional application of computers. However, the best path to follow in confronting the issues of those sections depends, at least in part, on the reader's present status with regard to the instructional use of computers. The purpose of this section is to help you find the route appropriate to your interests and experiences and to suggest some useful side trips along the way.

Sign Up Here

Five "tour groups" that are defined below in terms of the instructional computing skills and goals of their members have been formed for readers. Each group has an itinerary. You are invited to join the one whose membership seems most compatible.

Tour Group A. *Members of our group have had no experiences in programming a computer. Indeed, many of us have neither the time nor the inclination to pursue such experiences. Our interests lie in becoming intelligent users of computerized instructional materials.*

Itinerary:

1. Read section 1.
2. Visit a school or computer store for an hour or so of actual interaction with a computer. Ask a lot of questions to clarify what's in section 1.
3. Read sections 2 and 3.
4. Return to the school or computer store for more hands-on experience. Try to find examples of the types of programs and documentation described in sections 2 and 3.
5. Skim section 4; ignore section 5; peruse section 6.
6. Obtain and evaluate some materials, revisiting sections 2 through 4 as needed.

Tour Group B. *All our members are experienced computer programmers. Many of us teach computer programming. We're interested in learning what characterizes instructional software. We may need to aid teachers who are trying to develop or purchase such software.*

Itinerary:

1. Skim sections 1 and 2.
2. Carefully read section 3.
3. Try classifying several available programs according to the uses described in section 3; evaluate at least one of those programs using the sample checklist.

4. Reread section 3.
5. Read sections 4 through 6.
6. Use sections 4 and 5 to guide students (and yourself) in preparing in-house documentation.
7. Rewrite a program so that it would receive a favorable review under the criteria you adopt from section 3.

Tour Group C. *Although some of our members have taught or could teach computer programming, our primary interest is in developing our own programs for instructional use in our own classrooms in subjects other than computer programming.*

Itinerary:

1. Skim section 1.
2. Read section 3. Use it to classify and evaluate some existing programs.
3. Read sections 4 and 5.
4. Develop an appropriate checklist (section 3) and documentation standards (sections 4 and 5).
5. Read sections 2 and 6.

Tour Group D. *Our members teach a variety of subjects with the help of computerized instructional materials that they have purchased or have been given. Most of us have no computer programming experience; those who have such experience do not have a strong interest in applying that experience to the initial development of computerized courseware. Our interest is in using the work of others to improve instruction in our subject-matter areas. This interest includes a wish to encourage our colleagues to make instructional uses of computers.*

Itinerary:

1. Read sections 1 through 4. (The programming members of the group may wish to skim section 5.)
2. Use section 3 to develop an appropriate checklist; use section 4 to develop local guidelines for in-house documentation.
3. Begin the evaluation and documentation of existing programs.
4. Use section 2 to seek new programs.
5. Read section 6.

Tour Group E. *Our members are interested in selling or exchanging computerized instructional materials. Each of us has programming experience, and a broad range of programming skills is represented within the group. Some of us devote considerable time and energy to producing programs that we hope will be used by many teachers; others of us are concerned primarily with improving the quality of those programs or facilitating their exchange.*

Itinerary:

1. Read sections 1 through 6.
2. Working with experienced users of computerized instructional materials, use sections 3 through 5 to develop appropriate instruments and procedures for evaluating and documenting programs.
3. Insist on use of those instruments and procedures to guide the writing or exchange of computerized materials.

Please join your tour group now. Should you choose to deviate from its proposed itinerary, the tour guide cannot accept responsibility for your safety or for any professional expenses that you may incur.

Have a pleasant journey.

SECTION 1

What, Why, and for Whom?

Let the Purchaser Beware!

The definitions, instruments, and procedures that compose the *Guidelines* are intended to be practical resources for persons involved with the selection or creation of computer programs to be used for instructional purposes. The evaluative issues that may be inferred from the instruments of the *Guidelines* (and the directions for their use) represent state-of-the-art knowledge, experience, and intuition regarding what constitutes a "good" computer program.

A cursory reading of this document may very well produce the feeling that this booklet raises more questions about evaluating instructional computer programs than any reasonable person would ever want answered. Indeed it does. Evaluative criteria in this area are both numerous and tentative. Many are expressions of group or personal values, thus being judged to be of utmost relevance by some evaluators while being viewed as totally irrelevant by others. These materials were designed to bring a wide range of evaluative considerations to the reader's attention in a format that would permit easy adaptation to meet the user's priorities. Users of these *Guidelines* should recognize, therefore, two assumptions underlying their development. First, it is highly likely that a given user will assign greater weight to some criteria than to others and will judge some criteria to be of no importance at all. Second, it is the proper and necessary task of the user to select and weigh the criteria to be employed in the local evaluation of computer programs.

The role of any set of guidelines is to *guide* the educational decision maker, supporting the careful and efficient review of an issue; these *Guidelines* are no exception. They do not attempt to employ numerical ratings to generate purchase-rejection decisions. When adapted to reflect a given user's selection of criteria, however, they will focus on the issues critical to those decisions.

Something Old, Something New

Almost every educator is eventually called on to select learning materials to be used not only in one's own classroom but also in those of many colleagues. Such selection will generally be guided by written criteria or checklists that attempt to integrate national and local professional opinions.

Most commonly, selection tasks have focused on printed instructional resources, both basic texts and supplementary materials. Selection criteria have included concerns about the scope and sequence of topics covered by the resource, instructional approaches employed, the type of student activities involved, readability, societal issues (e.g., sex or racial discrimination), appearance, durability, cost, and the relative ease with which the product can be used by both teacher and student. The order of importance of the criteria might differ from situation to situation, but the issues are familiar.

The need to evaluate computerized instructional materials may exceed that of printed materials, since computerized lessons are often executed relatively independently of teacher or user control. For example, the use of a set of textbook activities is subject to teacher control through selection, modification, augmentation, and suggested ordering. The student exercises additional control of the assignment in terms of pacing, reordering, and selective deletion. Such manipulation may be difficult (or, perhaps, impossible) in a computerized lesson.

Companies, organizations, and individuals are now engaged in the production of computer programs aimed at the educational market. The majority are intended to fulfill drill, practice, instructional-management, or limited tutorial functions and deal with isolated concepts. As the number, variety, and complexity of programs increase, we approach that desirable point at which we will be faced with choosing from among several approaches to a given teaching situation. Unfortunately, the old procedures for sampling and selection will no longer be adequate. The guidelines presented in this booklet are a response to the need for standards for evaluating the unique instructional materials made possible by computers.

Some Words about Words

The growth of instructional computing has been accompanied by the generation of considerable terminology—often the use of existing words in new and precise ways. Seven terms central to the use of these materials are defined operationally below.

Hardware consists of an individual item (or combination of items) of mechanical or electronic gadgetry required for the execution of a computer program. In addition to the computer itself, examples of common hardware items include monitors, printers, card readers, and cassette tape recorders.

Software refers to a computer program in a form that can be executed using equipment available to the evaluator. The term also includes any materials exterior to the program but referenced by it or needed to explain the instructional use of the program. (Although this inclusion represents a departure from standard usage of the term, the extended definition suits our purposes here.) These exterior materials are often called *ancillary materials* and include such things as tables, charts, laboratory equipment, lexicons, workbooks, and directions regarding appropriate uses of the program.

Software clusters are collections, usually sequenced, of interrelated programs. The procedures for evaluating such clusters give rise to sampling issues that do not apply to the evaluation of an isolated, stand-alone item of software.

Courseware is a set of computer programs with which a student has direct interaction during a learning sequence. The use of the term *courseware* is much more restrictive than *software* as used in these *Guidelines,* since software also refers to management or utility programs with which the learner has no direct interaction. For us, then, courseware is a subset of software. (Many persons restrict the use of the term *software* to computer programs that are "invisible" to the learner; the authors chose a more inclusive definition of the term.)

Documentation includes all printed materials that describe either the computer software (e.g., its purpose, cost, intended audience, effectiveness) or the equipment required for the use of that software.

Systems-error messages are statements that are generated by the computer during the execution of a program but that are not a part of the instructional computer program itself. They arise as the result of some error in the instructional program (often a result of sloppy or lazy programming) or the peculiarity of the computer system being used to execute the program. At best, such statements distress and confuse the person executing the program, since they are usually written in a kind of "computerese" that is meaningful only to a programmer. At worst, they terminate the execution of the program. Consider the plight of a teacher who, having spent several minutes typing a text passage for analysis by a computerized readability program, accidentally types "YAS" rather than "YES" to some option regarding that analysis and receives the following error message:

```
INPUT ERROR
READY
```

There will be no small amount of frustration when it is learned that the passage has been "lost" and the project must be redone.

Program listings are printed forms of computer programs. Written in the language of a particular computer, they can be entered (typed) into *that specific kind of computer* by a careful typist who has had a few hours' instruction. To be of use with a *different kind of computer,* the program possibly would need to be rewritten by a computer programmer.

Looking Ahead

The use of computerized instructional material involves five principal tasks: (1) obtaining software and its documentation, (2) evaluating the materials obtained, (3) making a decision regarding the acquisition of the software, (4) establishing a system for helping all potential users locate programs of instructional interest within the bank of programs on hand, and (5) modifying or improving the programs in the bank. These tasks must be addressed not only for purchased software but also for locally developed software and for software obtained at little or no cost from a nonprofit software exchange group.

The first four tasks can be carried out by any educator interested in making instructional use of computerized materials; they are the subject of sections 2 through 4 of these *Guidelines.* The fifth task requires an understanding of the topic addressed by a given program, general knowledge about computers, and the ability to write programs in the given computer language. Addressed in section 5, this task may require a team effort in which one team member is an experienced programmer. Section 6 goes beyond the primary goals of the *Guidelines* by providing a limited bibliography for readers interested in exploring the topics of computer literacy, the social impact of computers, the teaching of computer programming, and the use of computers in mathematical problem solving.

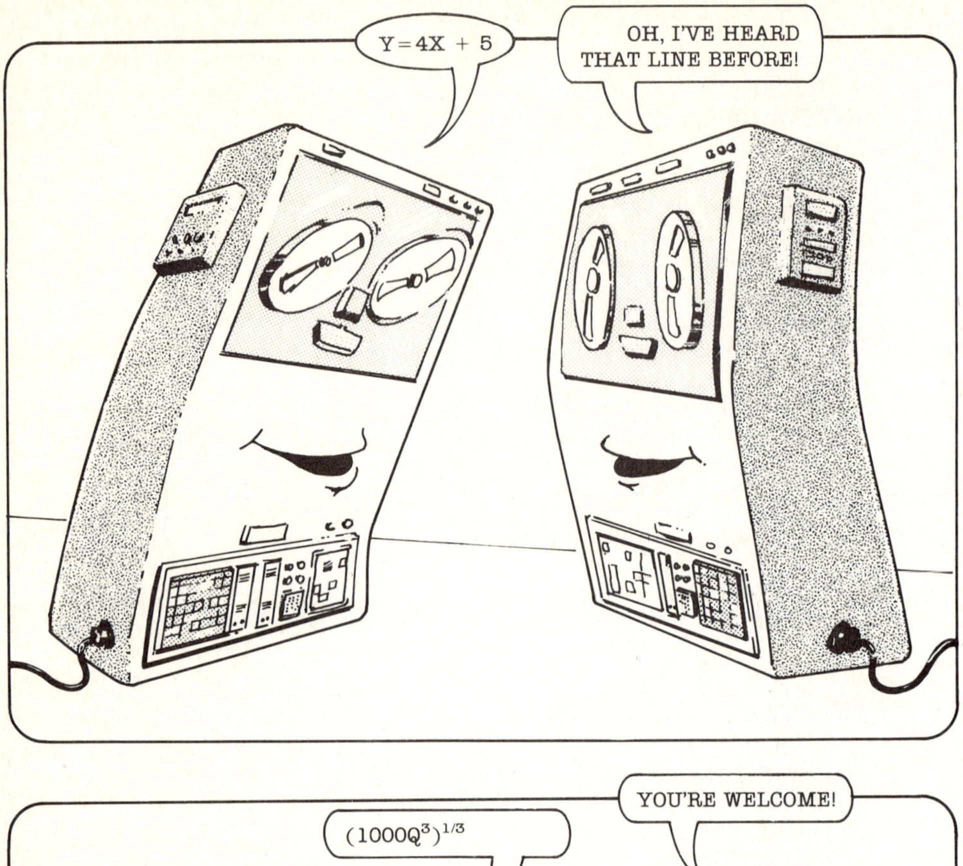
Y = 4X + 5
OH, I'VE HEARD THAT LINE BEFORE!
$(1000Q^3)^{1/3}$
YOU'RE WELCOME!

SECTION 2

Obtaining Software and Documentation

What's Out There?

There are several sources of information about commercial and noncommercial computerized instructional materials. Descriptions, sources, and reviews of commercial programs are found in a number of periodicals (see Note 1 at the end of this section). These publications often contain program listings and descriptions of programs offered for use without further charge. In addition to these periodicals directed at computer novices, there are works for those who have programming experience and/or technical knowledge of microcomputers (Note 2).

For the person wishing to survey the field of computing journals in search of appropriate resources, three publications will have special appeal (Note 3). The first of these (3a) is a where-to-find-it guide to persons, periodicals, and projects in instructional computing; included are annotated bibliographies to a variety of publications in the field. The second item (3b) is a quarterly subject index (with annotations) to the articles and software reviews of approximately 40 computing journals. The final reference (3c), comprised of reprints of the tables of contents of the most recent issues of about 70 computing journals, includes a subject index.

Publications devoted primarily to the issue of computer software can be placed in one of two categories: software directories and software reviews. Software directories (Note 4) provide basic information (name, source, topic, price) for a vast bank of software available from a wide range of producers. Some directories are indexed by subject, grade level, microcomputing system, or publisher; a few include some evaluative comments. Most directories include software for several microcomputer systems, but others are specific to Apple (4a, b, d, g, m, o, q), Commodore (4c), IBM (4h), Radio Shack (4i) or Texas Instruments (4p) systems. Software review publications (Note 5) go beyond the directories restricted to reporting factual information. Using evaluative criteria and procedures, these sources offer opinions regarding the technical and educational quality of the software referenced. While "professional" software reviews (including those which appear in the journals of educational organizations) are convenient, the convenience is not without a price. In accepting the conclusions of the reviewers, we also accept the (often unstated) criteria and procedures of the review process—not to mention the personal interests and prejudices of the reviewers. Truly, there is no such thing as a free lunch.

Software "exchanges" are organizations that provide a mechanism for the free or inexpensive exchange of computer software among a large number of users. At present the majority of such exchanges are "software jungles" that users enter at their own risk. Generally speaking, no standards of program quality are required for, or implied by, participation in the exchange. Because such exchanges are operated with little or no funding, their maintenance often depends on the freewill contributions of a handful of dedicated professionals. Local software exchanges of this type are numerous; computer users in your area probably will know of several. A partial listing may be found in the item referenced in Note 3a.

National centers for the cataloging, evaluation, exchange, or sale of software are in the formative stage (Note 6). When operational, they will offer a variety of services through a variety of means. The development of such centers is funded both publicly and privately; their maintenance will probably be through the fees and subscriptions of users.

Finally, private and governmental organizations are supporting the development of exemplary computerized materials and model plans for the use of computers in instruction. One can obtain a list of those projects funded by the National Science Foundation (NSF) or the National Institute for Education (NIE) by contacting NSF (1800 G Street, NW, Washington, DC 20550).

Into the Jungle: Two Scenarios

Given the ever growing pool of software clusters and isolated items of software, persons interested in the use of computerized instructional materials can use the sources of information just noted to identify programs of potential value. Let's assume that you've accomplished that much—that is, you find yourself in one of the following situations:

Scenario 1: You have the name and source of a given item of software or a software cluster but do not have the program in a form ready to execute on available hardware.
Scenario 2: You are in possession of one or more items of software that can be executed using available hardware.

If scenario 2 fits your situation, you may wish to go directly to section 3. If not, let's turn to the task of obtaining documented software for evaluative purposes.

Getting the Stories Behind the Names

So you've got the names of what appear to be some promising items of software. The next task is to obtain copies of that software, right? Well, maybe yes and maybe no. Are you certain that it was designed to run on the kind of hardware that you have available? Does your computer have a large enough memory to execute the program? Does the use of the program assume the availability of certain kinds of laboratory equipment, reference books, or workbooks? How much will it cost to obtain the software for review purposes? If the producer of the software will not release it for free review, is the software in use somewhere nearby? If the object of interest is a large software cluster, is it possible to obtain or even purchase selected programs from the cluster?

You may decide, depending on the answers to such questions, to drop the idea of obtaining the program (e.g., it can't be executed using the hardware available to you). Since the viewing of the software may involve paying for all or part of it, there is good reason to seek some basic descriptive information before trying to secure the software itself. The form letter on page 58 gives examples of the questions you can and should expect a software supplier to be able to answer, either directly or through promotional literature.

In listing the programs of specific interest in this letter, you will need to take special care in selecting sample programs from a software cluster. Nevertheless, you want the sample from the cluster to include programs that will reveal the extent of interdependence of programs within the cluster. Your selections, therefore, probably should include the following:

1. A program near the beginning of the cluster. This may reveal programmer/user agreements (conventions) used throughout the cluster.
2. At least two programs that form a sequence within the cluster. This sequence can suggest the degree to which review is built into the cluster. It may reveal that the programs are interdependent to such a degree that a purchase of parts of the cluster may not be educationally feasible.
3. A program near the end of the cluster. This program may give you some idea of the upper limit of the material covered by the cluster. It also may show the extent to which the style of presentation has changed or matured.

In 1981 some publishing companies were predicting that computerized instructional materials would soon account for one-third of their educational sales. That kind of market size, in turn, guarantees that brochures containing the information requested by our form letter will be available and that procedures for reviewing the materials will be developed.

The Wheat (Maybe) and the Chaff

Some items of software may be eliminated from further consideration, based on the descriptive information obtained from the vendor, because they fail to meet a critical condition of hardware compatibility, availability for review, price, and so on. Weak documentation by the vendor may make some software "iffy"; other items will show real promise. Clearly, such classification is a function both of the quality of the documentation and of the standards of the user.

Having searched the literature to obtain answers to the questions raised in the form letter, the careful reviewer would retain that information on the front page of a software documentation sheet like the one in section 4. If and when the software becomes part of a school system's instructional resources, such documentation will be invaluable to potential users other than the reviewer.

Reference Notes

1a. *Creative Computing* (P.O. Box 789-M, Morristown, NJ 07960).
b. *Classroom Computer Learning* (P.O. Box 266, Cambridge, MA 02138).
c. *Educational Computer Magazine* (P.O. Box 535, Cupertino, CA 95015).
d. *Electronic Education* (Suite 220, 1311 Executive Center Drive, Tallahassee, FL 32301).
e. *Electronic Learning* (Scholastic, Inc., 50 W. 44th St., New York, NY 10036).
f. *InfoWorld* (375 Cochituate Rd., Rte. 30, Framingham, MA 01701).
g. *Journal of Computers in Mathematics and Science Teaching* (Box 4455, Austin, TX 78765).
h. *School Microcomputer Bulletin* (Box 1326, Holmes Beach, FL 33509).
i. *The Computing Teacher* (Computing Center, Eastern Oregon State University, LaGrande, OR 97850).
2a. *BYTE—Small Systems Journal* (70 Main Street, Peterborough, NH 03458).
b. *Compute!* (515 Abbott Drive, Broomall, PA 19008).
c. *Microcomputing* (P.O. Box 997, Farmingdale, NY 11737).
d. *Micro—The 6502/6809 Journal* (P.O. Box 6502, Chelmsford, MA 01824).
3a. *Classroom Computer Learning Directory of Educational Computing Resources* (Intentional Educations, Inc., 341 Mt. Auburn Street, Watertown, MA 02172).
b. *Microcomputer Index* (Microcomputer Information Services, 2464 El Camino Real, Suite 247, Santa Clara, CA 95051).
c. *Micro . . . Publications in Review* (Vogeler Publishing Inc., P.O. Box 489, Arlington Heights, IL 60006).
4a. *The Addison-Wesley Book of Apple Computer Software* (The Book Company, 16720 Hawthorne Boulevard, Lawndale, CA 90260).
b. *The Apple Software Directory: Education* (WIDL Video, 5245 West Diversey Avenue, Chicago, IL 60639).
c. *Commodore Software Encyclopedia* (System Marketing Group, 681 Moore Road, King of Prussia, PA 19406).
d. *Educator's Handbook and Software Directory* (Vital Information, Inc., 7899 Mastin Drive, Overland Park, KS 66204).
e. *Index to Computer-Based Learning* (Instructional Media Laboratory, University of Wisconsin, P.O. Box 413, Milwaukee, WI 53201).
f. *Instructor's Computer Directory for Schools* (P.O. Box 6099, Duluth, MN 55806).
g. *Micros in Mathematics Quarterly* (Microcomputer Curriculum Project, Price Laboratory School, University of Northern Iowa, Cedar Falls, IA 50613).
h. *PC Clearinghouse Software Directory* (PC Clearinghouse, Inc., 11781 Lee-Jackson Highway, Fairfax, VA 22033).
i. *Pipeline* (P.O. Box 388, Iowa City, IA 52244).
j. *Radio Shack TRS-80 Educational Software Sourcebook* (available from any Radio Shack dealer).
k. *Reference Manual for the Instructional Use of Microcomputers* (JEM Research, Discovery Park, P.O. Box 1700, Victoria, British Columbia, V8W 2Y2, CANADA).
l. *School Microware Directory* (Dresden Associates, P.O. Box 246, Dresden, ME 04342).
m. *Skarbek Software Directory* (11990 Dorsett Road, St. Louis, MO 63043).
n. *Sources for Courses* (TALMIS, 115 North Oak Park Avenue, Oak Park, IL 60301).
o. *Swift's Software Directory: Apple II Edition* (Sterling Swift Publishing Company, 1600 Fortview Road, Austin, TX 78704).
p. *Texas Instruments Home Computer Program Library* (available from any Texas Instruments dealer).
q. *VanLoves Apple II/III Software Directory* (Vital Information, Inc., 7899 Mastin Drive, Overland Park, KS 66204).
5a. *Computer Program Reviews* (P.O. Box 331, North Springfield, VA 05150).
b. *Courseware Report Card: Elementary (K-6) Edition* (150 West Carob Street, Compton, CA 90220).
c. *Courseware Report Card: Secondary (7-12) Edition* (150 West Carob Street, Compton, CA 90220).

d. *InfoWorld Report Card on Microcomputer Software* (375 Cochituate Road, Box 837, Framingham, MA 01701).
e. *Journal of Courseware Review* (Apple Education Foundation, 20525 Mariani Avenue, Cupertino, CA 95014).
f. *MACUL Journal* (c/o Lary Smith, Wayne County ISD, P.O. Box 807, Wayne, MI 48184).
g. *School Microware Reviews* (Dresden Associates, P.O. Box 246, Dresden, ME 04342).
h. *Software Review* (Meckler Publishing, 520 Riverside Avenue, Westport, CT 06880).
i. *TALMIS Courseware Ratings* (115 North Oak Park Avenue, Oak Park, IL 60301).
6a. Microcomputer Center, San Mateo County Office of Education, 333 Main Street, Redwood City, CA 94063.
b. Microcomputer Education Laboratory, QAL/MEL, 217 Baldy Hall, SUNY at Buffalo, Amherst, NY 14260.
c. MicroSIFT, Northwest Regional Educational Laboratory, 300 SW 6th Avenue, Portland, OR 97204.
d. TABS Project, Arps Hall 202-A, 1948 North High Street, Columbus, OH 43210.
e. Technical Education Research Centers (TERC), Computer Resource Center, 8 Eliot Street, Cambridge, MA 02138.
f. CONDUIT, P.O. Box 388, Iowa City, IA 52244.

Sample Request-For-Information Form Letter

____
____
____

Dear ______________________________:

We wish to evaluate certain of your computer programs for possible purchase. This evaluation would include any related teacher- or student-support materials. The following programs are of specific interest:

______________________________ ______________________________
______________________________ ______________________________

Before requesting the programs themselves, we need information (brochures, technical reports, or your comments) to answer the following questions:

1. What are the system and memory requirements for each program's use?
2. On what media (disks, cassette tape, cartridge, etc.) is each program available?
3. In what computer language(s) is each program written?
4. For which grade levels or ability levels is each program intended?
5. What are the specific content areas or instructional objectives for each program?
6. Has each program been tested or validated in a classroom setting?
7. What kind of instructional materials are available to support a given program's use? What is the cost of such materials?
8. What is the procedure or cost for obtaining each program for a full review?
9. What is the purchase price of each program?

Please send this information to

____
____
____

Thank you for your assistance.

Sincerely,

____

SECTION 3

Getting Hard-Nosed about Software: Guidelines for Software Review

Getting the Message Out of the Medium

Once basic documentation and a program for review have been obtained, the important process of evaluation can begin. The computer program is evaluated first, followed by a review of the related documentation and ancillary materials. The evaluation serves only to provide information on which a decision can be reached; it does not use weighted scales or numerical totals to make the decision for you.

The evaluation model presented in this section is both comprehensive and detailed. It should be tailored to meet the specific needs of a given user. In doing such tailoring, however, the user should be careful to ensure that the resulting version of the model considers each of six important steps of the review process.

Step 1. Load the program on your system. Run the program briefly to become familiar with the program's "flow."

Step 2. Execute the program as a successful student would, avoiding intentional or careless errors. Extend the program when possible by interacting "creatively" as a good student would in testing the cleverness of the programmer.

Step 3. Execute the program as an unsuccessful student would. Respond incorrectly to test how the program handles student errors. If an erroneous response to a task results in the repetition of that task, make repeated incorrect responses. Be sure to repeat the *same* response and also try giving *different* incorrect responses. Finally, make other kinds of errors such as typing mistakes, incorrect form of input (e.g., "one for "1"), content errors, and errors in following the directions.

Step 4. Use the checklist for the evaluation of software on pages 63-64, adapting it as necessary to fit your own needs. Throughout, your responses should be based *only* on your observations and experiences with the program. Once completed, your responses can be compared with the vendor's claims.

Step 5. Complete the checklist for the evaluation of documentation and ancillary materials. Again, the extent of the review will depend on your needs and the impressions remaining from your review of the actual software.

Step 6. Make a decision.

The design of the sample Software Evaluation Checklist calls for items on one side of a sheet of paper and abbreviated explanations of item vocabulary or purpose on the other side of the sheet. (Detailed discussions of the terms used on this sample are presented in the next subsection of these *Guidelines.*) This one-sheet design is judged highly desirable insofar as it simplifies paper shuffling. (Of course, the items and their explanatory notes could be placed on your computer. This not only saves trees and storage space but also illustrates that you recognize another obvious advantage of computers in education.)

Although the sample checklist here purposely includes an excess of items, in practice a shorter form may do the job. Moreover, experienced evaluators would require few, if any, of the explanatory notes given on the back of the sheet.

Words to Evaluate By

The use of our checklist, or any other checklist, by more than one person requires an agreement regarding the meaning of terms used to classify or evaluate programs. We must extend the minilexicon we started in section 2. We'll do this by proceeding item by item through the sample checklist, stopping to define and discuss concepts as the need arises.

1. Instructional Range. For any given program, the appropriate grade level and ability level must be judged according to the particular instructional setting. (A program that is informational at first grade might be remedial at third). Key factors in determining grade or ability level are the concepts in the program. Other important factors are reading level, prerequisite skills, degree of student control, and intended instructional use. It is possible for a program to be flexible enough to be used across a wide range of grade levels and ability levels.

2. Instructional Grouping. The interaction between the learners and a program can be either direct or through an intermediary (the teacher). The first two groupings described below involve direct interaction; the third uses an intermediary.

Individual. Some programs are designed specifically for use by a single person. Programs of this nature may include a summary of individual performance; others may allow a specific level of difficulty—a specific set of spelling words, for example. Programs for individuals may have provisions for easier or more difficult situations, depending on the individual student's response.

Small Group. Some programs are specifically designed for use with two, three, or four students. One such example might be an arithmetic fact game involving a car race in which each student can move forward on a correct answer. Other programs for small groups might be business simulations in which each small group is a business.

Large Group. Large-group use of programs may vary in intent. A program may be used with a large group solely for the purpose of introducing the program for later use by individuals or small groups. Some programs are designed for use by a teacher in graphically demonstrating a concept. (Trigonometric functions provide one example; fraction concepts such as equivalence are another.)

3. Execution Time. The time required for the use of a program will vary considerably. The load time of the program depends on the complexity of the program and on whether it is being loaded from a cassette tape or a disk. (The disk is a much faster but more expensive storage medium.) The type of program is a factor (e.g., tutorial versus informational). The user will require additional time if responses are consistently incorrect. Another time factor is the degree of user control (i.e., how many options are available to the user). An estimate given as a range is an appropriate response for this item.

4. Program Uses. The classification of programs by the instructional uses to which they are put is difficult. Careful analysis notwithstanding, definitions seem doomed to fuzziness, and a given program may seem to fit in more than one category. Moreover, the use of a given program can often be determined by the classroom practioner; a program written with one use in mind may be used in completely different ways by each of several persons. In fact, a given person may identify more than one use for a program, leading to the necessity to indicate *primary* and *secondary* uses.

Despite the difficulties just noted, there is instructional value in attempting to identify the use or uses of a program. The following definitions are proffered as an aid to the classification of those program uses that appear on the checklist.

Demonstration. Programs that assume the intervention of an informed manager (teacher) between the program and the learner. They are designed to permit the manager to pursue the questions and suggestions of students by varying the conditions associated with some concept being developed. These programs are generally devoid of textual display relative to their purpose and operation. This lack of text, while precluding direct use of the program by the learner, permits efficient realization of the program's purpose by an informed user (teacher). External documentation is critical to demonstration programs.

Drill or practice. Programs that assume previous instruction in the concept, skill, or process to be addressed. They present a controlled sequence of exercises designed to drill the recall of certain pairings or to practice some algorithm.

Informational. Programs designed to generate data with no suggestion as to its use. They offer very little interaction with the person for whom the data is generated.

Instructional gaming. Programs calling on the user to apply one or more specific skills or concepts in a game environment. The game dimension of the environment includes the conditions of competition with oneself or others, specific (if arbitrary) rules, the need to develop a winning strategy, and the introduction of random events to force the revision of strategies.

Instructional management. Programs designed to aid the user in the flexible and efficient management of such limited instructional resources as time, equipment, workspace, instructional personnel, and consumable materials. Such programs assume, at least in part, the tasks of making instructional diagnoses, giving course assignments, evaluating student progress, keeping student records, and facilitating communication among instructors and students.

Instructional support. Programs designed to facilitate the generation of instructional products, materials, the location of instructional resources, or the selection of instructional products.

Problem solving. Programs serving either the student or the instructor; the problem to be investigated may be either within a given subject or within instruction in this subject. In practice, there are two levels of use—one that employs existing programs using known algorithms and one that requires the development of a program employing a user-defined algorithm. In fact, the development of the algorithm itself may be the object of the problem-solving activity.

Programming utility. Program building blocks (or complete lesson authoring systems) that may be used to construct instructional programs. Their availability allows instructors or programmers to make efficient use of their hardware and their programming time.

Simulation. Programs that attempt to represent key aspects of some environment within which the user will experience the necessity to make decisions and will be informed of the results of those decisions *without experiencing the real consequences of possible misjudgments.* The time required to develop and use simulations with high fidelity is justified in situations where actual experience is ruled out because of extreme expense, safety considerations, or the time required for the actual experience.

Testing operations. Programs to aid in criterion-referenced testing or tailored testing. These programs offer such services as the banking of objectives or test items, item analysis, record keeping, test generation, and test scoring.

Tutorial. Programs through which the computer assumes total responsibility for instruction. Tutorial programs are characterized by a dialogue between the student and the computer in which the direction and level of the dialogue are shaped by student input. Ideally, such programs would be high fidelity simulations of the best teaching behavior associated with a given topic and would control the variables associated with the what, why, when, and who of the instructional episode.

Whistles-and-bells. Programs designed to acquaint the user with those characteristics of a computer system that may have instructional application.

Word processing. Programs which can be used to create, store, modify, and print the text (and, perhaps, simple graphics) of letters, reports, topical papers, and standard forms. They are used to support the improvement of written materials produced by teachers and students.

5. User Orientation: Instructor's Point of View.

Flexibility. A program may permit the user or instructor to adjust it to accommodate a range of ability levels, several degrees of difficulty with respect to a given user, or the class of concepts involved. This can be accomplished through options presented by the program. For instance, a program dealing with the practice of whole number computation might offer a choice of the operation (addition, subtraction, multiplication, division) or the range of numbers involved (0-10, 0-20, 0-100). Another option might involve the difficulty of the problems presented in terms of the procedure required for a solution (i.e., borrowing versus no borrowing in the subtraction problems). Programs that do not offer such options to the student may have a provision for the execution of such adjustments by the teacher.

Intervention or assistance. Although it is a desirable goal for most programs to operate independently of the classroom teacher, there are programs for which assistance is needed and even desirable. For instance, some drill programs are "unending." Intervention to stop the program is done by the teacher and involves a judgment of what constitutes sufficient program use by a given student. (*Note:* A rating of *low* on "freedom from need to intervene or assist" would mean that considerable teacher intervention or assistance is required.)

6. User Orientation: Student's Point of View.

Quality of directions. Directions need to be concise and clear. They should be developed for the lowest level of use. Some directions can be simplified by the use of an example.

Quality of response. Responses to student input should be low-key and understandable. Responses to incorrect input should be neutral (e.g., "Incorrect. Try again." versus "Wrong, dummy! How could you get this far and know so little?").

Screen formatting. Formatting refers to the physical layout of text and graphics presented on the screen. Examples of poor formatting include a full screen of text with single spacing, too many graphics, continually flashing displays, and text scrolling off the screen. Some good examples are centering of data, a few items on the screen with the user in control of when the next items appear, and reverse-field printing of key items (i.e., light print against a dark screen versus dark print against a light screen).

Need for external information. A program may require the user to have access to information other than that printed by it. Generally speaking, the more self-contained a program is, the better. However, certain programs intentionally require the use of external items. Examples of such programs include programs dealing with dictionary skills and the use of maps.

Disruption by system error. System errors result in the involuntary termination of a program. They may be introduced by improper calculations, errors in the logic of the program, or input that is conceptually correct but does not meet the form required by the program. Programs written to prevent all system errors—syntactic errors and improper input—are the most desirable. They can be developed by using special input routines.

Simplicity of student input. A program should ensure that a user knows when and in what form input is needed. Characters with special meanings should be avoided. Input locations on the screen should be standardized throughout the program. Typing requirements should be minimal. If a special type of input is required, an example should be given.

7. Content. *Instructional focus and significance.* The program's topic should be clearly defined. The instructional objectives of the program must be viewed as important by the instructor. Also, the program should represent a valid use of the computer's capabilities. (The program should not repeat the same set of questions or present problems in exactly one sequence.)

Validity and compatibility. The concepts and terms used should be correct, clear, and precise. The rate of presentation should be consistent with the levels for which the program is intended. The content, terminology, teaching style, and educational philosophy should be consistent with those generally encountered by the student.

8. Motivation and Instructional Style. There are many options that may increase student motivation or develop a particular instructional style. Some of these options are a function of the hardware being used. Because these features are optional, a column labeled *none,* meaning the feature is not present, has been added at the left of the low-high continuum.

Student involvement. The proper degree of involvement will vary with the type of program used. A drill or practice program for one student is highly active, whereas an informational program may require little student input. Tutorial programs, being dialogues, should require student involvement.

Student control. Several concepts may be involved here. Options available to the student at the beginning of the program may include different kinds of content, levels of difficulty, or the type of response the student may wish to use. Additional examples of student control include the selection of the number of problems to be done and the provision of help (at the student's request) at any point in the program.

Game format. The use of a game format often generates favorable responses from students. Some examples are mathematics drill as a drag race or in a tic-tac-toe or concentration format. Caution must be exercised so that the game format does not overshadow the instruction. Note that a game format does not imply that the program use is instructional gaming; a drill program may use a game format. A focus on decision making strategies is required for a program to be classified as having an instructional gaming use.

Graphics, animation, color. The functional use of one or more of these features can enhance instruction; their improper or irrelevant application can interfere or cause misconceptions. The use of graphics, animation, or color must be examined carefully to ensure that they support concept development. One might begin that examination by asking what would be lost if the feature were deleted.

Voice and nonvoice audio. The use of voice input and output has considerable potential. Be aware that the quality and use of voice is dependent on the hardware. The use of nonvoice audio provides an additional means for attracting interest but may be distracting in the classroom.

Light pen. Some programs require the use of a light pen. This can be a good feature if a light pen is available, but a program employing a light pen will be useless without it.

Ancillary materials. Materials external to the program may be used. Some may be provided, but their use may not be required (e.g., pretests or posttests, worksheets, etc.). Others may be necessary but are locally available (e.g., dictionaries or local road maps). Care should be taken to note any materials developed especially for the program that must be supplied by the program's author or publisher.

As in item 4, a blank is left at the end of item 8. This is necessary because the list of special features grows daily; its length is a function both of the subject matter and the computer system involved. The listed features are in relatively common use; other examples include touch panels (the user can execute an instructional task simply by touching the screen with a finger), special keyboards for the physically handicapped, electronic devices that monitor a physical phenomenon (such as water temperature) and use it in the program's execution, and mechanical devices (robots, if you will) that interact with the program.

9. Social Characteristics.

Competition and cooperation. Some programs may be written for use by a single student, several students, or the whole class. Competition may be between two or more students or between a student and the computer; it is generally motivating. The need for cooperation among students, also desirable, might be found in a business simulation that requires several students to operate the business.

Humanizing the computer. Programs may give the computer human characteristics. Some people find this desirable, whereas others wish to emphasize that the computer is a machine. Asking for the student's name may or may not be necessary or desirable. Older students generally find it boring, distracting, or phony.

Moral issues. Items or techniques that at first create interest may be questionable from other points of view. Capital punishment as exhibited by most hangman games is one example; the violence of war games is another.

Summary of student performance. A performance summary is a feature inherent to games that result in a winner. Performance on a simulation (e.g., the use of a credit card) also calls for a summary evaluation (e.g., the credit was canceled because of the inability to meet payments regularly). Drill programs often conclude with a summary regarding the speed or accuracy of the student's performance. Depending on the manner in which these summaries are presented, they may have either a positive or a negative effect on the learner.

Notes on the Design or Redesign of the Checklist. With the exception of the few descriptive requests at the top of the form and in items 1 through 4, the use of the checklist requires only making checks, circling words, or bracketing ranges of dots on judgment scales. The design of the scales in items 5 through 9 was made with an eye to consistency; it also consistently expresses the summary prejudices of the writers. For each scale, a rating toward the left extreme (identified by such terms as *low, passive,* and *poor*) would generally be, for the writers, a negative evaluation of the software. (This technique isn't foolproof. A rating of *low* on "freedom from need for external information" would be undesirable for a drill program but might be necessary—even desirable—with a simulation.) That is, the writers felt that a program should rank *high* in flexibility, should call for *active* student involvement, should make *good* use (if any) of color, and should employ competition in a *positive* way only. This left-is-negative and right-is-positive arrangement of the scales allows one to get the general sense of an evaluation by scanning the completed checklist. When items are added or altered on the checklist, it would be a good idea to keep the design intact. Thus, should you feel that program control should be the purview of the teacher or that judgments should be within the program itself, you might reword the second part of item 8 to read as follows:

low				*high*	
*	*	*	*	*	freedom from student control

As rewritten, the word *low* would continue to be associated with an undesirable characteristic.[2]

[2]The NCTM gladly grants the reader permission to reprint an unlimited number of these forms for nonprofit purposes. It requests that the NCTM logo be retained if the forms are used without substantive alteration of their content. The user is also invited to modify the documents in any way that might improve their usefulness.

Software Evaluation Checklist

PROGRAM NAME: ____________ SOURCE: ____________ COST: ______
SUBJECT AREA: ____________ REVIEWER'S NAME: ____________ DATE: ______

1. INSTRUCTIONAL RANGE

____________ grade level(s)
____________ ability level(s)

2. INSTRUCTIONAL GROUPING FOR PROGRAM USE

_____ individual
_____ small group (size: _____)
_____ large group (size: _____)

3. EXECUTION TIME

__________ minutes (estimated) for average use

4. PROGRAM USE(S)

—demonstration	—programming utility
—drill or practice	—simulation
—informational	—testing operations
—instructional gaming	—tutorial
—instructional management	—whistles-and-bells
—instructional support	—word processing
—problem solving	—other (__________)

5. USER ORIENTATION: INSTRUCTOR'S POINT OF VIEW

low * * * * * *high*
* * * * * flexiblity
* * * * * freedom from need to intervene or assist

6. USER ORIENTATION: STUDENT'S POINT OF VIEW

low * * * * * *high*
* * * * * quality of directions (clarity)
* * * * * quality of output (content and tone)
* * * * * quality of screen formatting
* * * * * freedom from need for external information
* * * * * freedom from disruption by system errors
* * * * * simplicity of user input

7. CONTENT

low * * * * * *high*
* * * * * instructional focus
* * * * * instructional significance
* * * * * soundness or validity
* * * * * compatibility with other materials used

8. MOTIVATION AND INSTRUCTIONAL STYLE

passive * * * * * *active*
* * * * * type of student involvement

low * * * * * *high*
* * * * * degree of student control

none *poor* * * * * * * *good*
* * * * * * use of game format
* * * * * * use of still graphics
* * * * * * use of animation
* * * * * * use of color
* * * * * * use of voice input and output
* * * * * * use of nonvoice audio
* * * * * * use of light pen
* * * * * * use of ancillary materials
* * * * * * use of ____________

9. SOCIAL CHARACTERISTICS

present and negative	*not present*	*present and positive*	
_____	_____	_____	competition
_____	_____	_____	cooperation
_____	_____	_____	humanizing of computer
_____	_____	_____	moral issues or value judgments
_____	_____	_____	summary of student performance

KEY TO TERMS: SOFTWARE EVALUATION CHECKLIST

1. The grade levels and ability levels for a particular program are primarily determined by the concepts involved. Other important factors are reading level, prerequisite skills, degree of student control, and intended instructional use. It is possible for a program to be flexible enough to be used across a wide range of grade levels and ability levels.

2. Some programs are designed for use by individuals. Others have been or can be modified for participation by two or three persons at a time. Simulations or demonstrations often pose opportunities for large-group interaction. A given program may be used in more than one grouping, depending on the instructor.

3. The time required for the use of a program will vary considerably. Include loading time for cassettes. A time range is the appropriate response here.

4. Instructional programs can be categorized according to their uses. Some programs may have more than one use, thus falling into more than one of the following categories:

Demonstration: used by a teacher for leading group discussions.
Drill or practice: assumes that the concept or skill has been taught; merely reinforces.
Informational: generates data but does not direct the use of that data.
Instructional gaming: focuses on decision making within a game format; involves random events and the pursuit of a winning strategy.
Instructional management: helps manage the learning environment by assuming major responsibilities with respect to student assessment, record keeping, and learning-prescription generation.
Instructional support: generates instructional materials, helps locate instructional resources or aids in selecting instructional products.
Problem solving: an algorithm which serves the problem solver during the exploration of a complex problem.
Programming utility: helps to write other instructional programs.
Simulation: provides an electronic slice of life.
Testing operations: provide services such as item banking, test generation, test scoring, and item analysis.
Tutorial: provides for a dialogue between student and computer on a topic which is not yet understood by the student.
Whistles-and-bells: demonstrates features of the computer system—features that may be of value in instructional applications.
Word processing: permits the efficient improvement of written materials.

5. These are factors relevant to the actual use of the program from the point of view of an instructor.

Flexibility: A program may allow the user or the instructor to adjust the program to different ability levels, degrees of difficulty, or concepts.

Intervention or assistance: A rating of "low" means considerable teacher intervention or assistance is required.

6. These are factors relevant to the actual use of the program from the point of view of a student.

Directions: The directions should be complete, readable, under the user's control (e.g., should not scroll off the screen until understood), and use appropriate examples.

Output: Program responses should be readable, understandable, and complete. If in response to student input, the output should be of an acceptable tone and consistent with the input request.

Screen formatting: The formats during a program run should not be distracting or cluttered. Labels and symbols should be meaningful within the given context.

External information: A program may require the user to have access to information other than that provided within it. This may include prerequisite content knowledge or knowledge of conventions used by the program designer as well as maps, books, models, and so on.

System errors: System errors result in the involuntary termination of the program.

Input: A program should ensure that a user knows when and in what form input is needed. It should avoid using characters with special meanings, restrict input locations to particular screen areas, and require minimal typing.

7. These are matters relevant to the subject-matter content of the program.

Focus: The program topic should be clearly defined and of a scope that permits thorough treatment.

Significance: The instructional objectives of the program must be viewed as important by the instructor. Also, the program should represent a valid use of the computer's capabilities while improving the instructional process.

Soundness or validity: The concepts and terms employed should be correct, clear, and precise. Other important factors are the rate of presentation, degree of difficulty, and internal consistency.

Compatibility: The content, terminology, teaching style, and educational philosophy of the program should be consistent with those generally encountered by the student.

8. (These items are self-explanatory.)

9. Competition, cooperation, and values are concerns that may be a function of the way a program expresses them. (War gaming and the "hangman" format are sample issues.) Also, the "humanizing" of the computer may serve for motivation or to reduce anxiety, but it also may become tedious, misleading, and counterproductive.

The summary of student performance can be dichotomous (win or lose), statistical (time expended or percent of items correct), or subjective (as in the evaluation of a simulation). It may be for student, teacher, or both.

SECTION 4

Communicating with Posterity: Guidelines for Software Documentation

The Golden Rule

Only some computer-generated humanoid incorporating the joint charms of Scrooge and the Marquis de Sade would lock away program evaluations in some academic safe-deposit box. The long-term value of evaluation guidelines lies in establishing a bank of evaluations that preserves the work for easy retrieval at some future date and that earns interest through the contributions of other professionals. If, of course, you prefer the work of doing each evaluation yourself (and redoing it each time forgetfulness intervenes), this section won't appeal to you.

For the sane and humane among you, the task is clear. We need some simple way of preserving our judgments for both ourselves and our colleagues. The Sample Software Documentation Sheet that follows is meant to meet that need. Printed on a single sheet of paper, the sheet summarizes the information gathered from the vendor's documentation (see section 2 of these *Guidelines) as modified and expanded by your professional judgment based on your evaluation along the lines of section 3.*

Fact Versus Judgment

In the battle of fact and judgment, put your money on judgment. It is the task of professionals to make judgments and their fate to live with them. Facts are of value as means, not ends, of the decision-making process. However, it is our responsibility not to confuse fact with judgment. With the exception of the items regarding Program Source and System Requirements, the completion of the software documentation sheet is almost wholly a judgmental task. The items on the front of the sheet call for the evaluator's informed judgment of how the program might be used, with whom it might be used, and where it should be placed within an instructional sequence. The items on the back ask for descriptions, in terms of the evaluator's views, of the purpose and features of the program as well as for suggestions regarding its use. If the evaluator provides the additional documentation of a sample run, the selection of demonstrative segments will effect a coloring of the evaluation.

Foolish Consistency: Hobgoblin of Little Minds

It is an axiom of the instructional computing devotee that any educational process requiring repetition, speed, or prodigious feats of memory is a candidate for computerization. The use of these guidelines is such a process. Urgings of consistency demand that we consider its computerization. The letters, checklists, documentation sheets, definitions, and procedural steps all could be housed in a computer with the aid of a word-processing program. In that electronic form, they are quickly accessible to any person for use, modification, or recall of the fruits born of their use. Past evaluations can be updated or deleted as software is used, improved, or retired. Data management programs permit the efficient search for programs of potential interest and the recall of the detailed evaluation of a program so identified. Therefore, we conclude this section with the hope that you will transfer the substance of this document to your favorite computer and consign the document itself to the flames.[3]

---

[3]The NCTM gladly grants the reader permission to reprint an unlimited number of these forms for nonprofit purposes. It requests that the NCTM logo be retained if the forms are used without substantive alteration of their content. The user is also invited to modify the documents in any way that might improve their usefulness.

Sample Software Documentation Sheet

PROGRAM NAME: ____________________

SUBJECT AREA: ____________________

DATE OF THIS DOCUMENTATION

____

PROGRAM CLASS

_______ isolated program

_______ part of a ____ -program cluster

PROGRAM SOURCE

name: ____________________

address: ____________________

____

____

phone: ____________________

program cost: ____________________

INTENDED AUDIENCE(S)

_______ teachers

_______ students in grade(s) _______

_______ other ____________________

____

PROGRAM USES: (1 = primary, 2 = secondary)

—demonstration
—drill or practice
—informational
—instructional gaming
—instructional management
—instructional support
—problem solving
—programming utility
—simulation
—testing operations
—tutorial
—whistles-and-bells
—word processing
—other (__________)

SYSTEM REQUIREMENTS

computer: ____________________

language: ____________________

memory needed: __________ bytes

input mode: cassette
_____-inch diskette
cartridge
other __________
____

output mode: color monitor
B/W monitor
printer
plotter
other __________
____

CRITICAL PREREQUISITE SKILLS

____

____

NAME(S) OF PREREQUISITE PROGRAM(S)

____

____

____

NAME(S) OF FOLLOW-UP PROGRAM(S)

____

____

____

CLASSROOM VALIDATION (describe)

____

____

____

TIME FOR AVERAGE EXECUTION _______ minutes

OVER →

GENERAL DESCRIPTION OF THE PROGRAM (i.e., purpose of the program)

SPECIAL PROGRAM CHARACTERISTICS (e.g., use of graphics or sound, designed for use by groups of two or more persons at a time, level of difficulty can be modified by teacher (only) or student, exit from program is controlled by the teacher (only) or student, etc.)

DIRECTIONS FOR USE OF THE PROGRAM (e.g., directions not presented in the program itself but needed for program execution, directions regarding the use of the program within the total instructional process, notes regarding program options, etc.)

ANCILLARY MATERIALS REQUIRED (e.g., books, worksheets, charts, data lists, dice, geometric shapes, lab equipment, etc.)

ADDITIONAL DOCUMENTATION AVAILABLE (check box for each type)

☐ sample run (location ______________________________)

☐ program listing (location ______________________________)

SECTION 5

Asides to the Instructional Programmer

The comments and suggestions of this section are directed primarily to the evaluator of software who is also a programmer. For the purpose of this discussion, an *instructional programmer* is one who is capable of producing instructional software either for sale or for exchange with others. A concomitant talent or vice is the ability to alter software written by others. When evaluating software, the instructional programmer should consider both the ease with which a given computer program can be altered and the possible legal issues associated with making any alterations. It is assumed (if untested) that software can be tinkered with *if* it has been purchased and is not to be offered for resale. Nonetheless, an instructional programmer may want to consult with a good lawyer.

Numerous reasons exist as to why one may *want* to change a software program as well as to why it should be changed at all. For example, cosmetic alterations are often desirable and yet minor in terms of the programmer's intent. When more substantial changes are necessary, greater concern is raised.

The Words Have Changed, But I Recognize the Tune

Cosmetic changes are an issue when the instructional programmer likes a particular program on the whole but objects to it in part. The desired alterations may make the program palatable by changing output statements, graphics, or algorithms. For example, the instructional programmer may want to revise the language or comments made in the run of a program. The original form may have been sexist, appeared overly negative in tone, or employed poor vocabulary.

The program may need to be updated. Consider, for example, an economics simulation involving prices, sample products, and interest rates. Such data must be altered periodically if the simulation is to remain current. Finally, one may wish to alter or delete graphic or audio routines that the user may regard as childish or demeaning or that may be recognized as misleading or counterproductive. Thus, the flashing "smiley face" called up by each correct response to a drill program may soon be viewed as silly or phony. Similarly, loud noises generated in response to incorrect answers may begin to grate on the nerves.

As a group, the changes suggested above do not alter the instructional intent of the program's author. In fact, they may serve to support the author's purpose. Things may look a bit different after the program alterations, but the overall development remains intact.

Can You Still Name That Tune?

The instructional programmer may also want to make alterations that are more substantial and of greater impact than those made for cosmetic reasons. It is at this point that the toes of the program's original author begin to ache. Some obvious examples of substantive changes are the correction of known programming flaws, systems errors, poor programming, or inefficient algorithms. A less obvious example is a major alteration of the program's use (or misuse) of color that would move it from a decorative to a functional role.

At still another level, the instructional programmer may contend that the original program has a weak link in its pedagogical sequence and wish to strengthen the program by introducing a totally new subroutine. Along the same line, the wish may be to alter or rewrite a critical algorithm in an attempt to improve or extend its application.

The alterations commented on in the preceding three paragraphs can result in substantial changes in the breadth, approach, or effectiveness of the overall program. Where do the editorial privileges of the instructional programmer begin to infringe on the ownership rights of the original author? Who really is the author of the revised program?

The Many Faces of Documentation

When evaluating software with an eye to its possible modification, program documentation becomes critical. There are at least four levels of documentation; the instructional programmer must be careful that the level of the program being evaluated is sufficient to the programmer's purpose. The levels and their potential usefulness are as follows:

1. The documentation may be a brief description of the program's intent, such as that included on an advertisement or on the sample software documentation sheet of section 4. Such statements are of no real value to the instructional programmer desiring to make changes in a program.
2. The documentation may be an extended description of the details of the program's flow, possibly even in some form of flowchart. This category is again of minimal value because of its general nature.
3. The documentation may include the previous category as well as a detailed explanation of key algorithms in the program. This category is of value only if the instructional programmer can determine how each algorithm affects, or relates to, the program as a whole. For example, variables may be present in a routine that later serve as key parameters in either graphics routines or other algorithms.
4. The documentation may be very extensive and complete while also being merged within the listing of the program. It should include the definition of all key variables, descriptions of commands that control the flow of the program, and an elaboration of the steps in each subroutine or algorithm. Furthermore, the name and address of the program's original author and its creation data should also be included to facilitate any communication that may be necessary. Obviously, this category of documentation is of greatest value to the instructional programmer.

As a final concern, the instructional programmer must consider whether the program is of sufficient value to be altered. That is, the purchased form of the program may be in a specially coded form or of such complexity that the instructional programmer may conclude that it would be easier to rewrite the entire program and include the necessary modifications. This raises very real concerns regarding the authorship of the revised program because of related questions regarding whether one can copyright an idea.

Reprinted from *Mathematics and Humor*, ed. Aggie Vinik, Linda Silvey, and Barnabas Hughes. Copyright 1978 by the National Council of Teachers of Mathematics, Inc.

SECTION 6

Next Steps

What Follows 6?

We opened our discussion of instructional computing by asking "What follows 1?" and contended that the answer depended on the computing experiences and interests of the reader. Having guided you to this point by one of five routes, we hope we have stimulated an interest in further exploration of some of the issues introduced in these *Guidelines*. If so, we would be remiss in not suggesting some other places to visit when this tour is complete. The purpose of this section is to present a brief (and, hence, noncomprehensive) list of books, articles, papers, and bibliographies on four topics of possible interest. The first two sets of references assume no knowledge of computer programming; the latter two are addressed to those readers who either have such knowledge or wish to acquire it.

Computers in the Classroom

Items A through R in our first list of resources deal with instructional uses of computers, both in general and with specific reference to the teaching of mathematics. Items D and P are special-focus issues of the *Mathematics Teacher* (November, 1981) and *Arithmetic Teacher* (February, 1983) respectively; each discusses instructional applications of computers which include *but are not restricted to* mathematics education. Item K is the title of a special-focus issue of the *AEDS Journal* (Fall, 1979) that discusses many of the same issues, also apart from a specific subject matter area. Item R is a how-to-do-it guide produced by the experienced classroom teachers who comprised the Montana Task Force on Computer Education.

The remaining selections of the following list provide nontechnical information about instructional computing. These books and monographs are addressed to the person who has been seeking a simple introduction to these topics—one that isn't wrapped up in a course in computer programming.

A. *Computers and Education,* C. E. Horn and J. Poirot. (New York: Sterling Swift Publishing), 1980.
B. *Computer Applications in Instruction: A Teacher's Guide to Selection and Use,* J. Edwards, A. Willis, D. Richardson, D. Holznagel, and D. Klassen. (Hanover, NH: Time Share Corp.), 1978.
C. *Computers in Mathematics: A Sourcebook of Ideas,* D. Ahl (Ed.) (Creative Computing, P.O. Box 789-M, Morristown, NJ 07960).
D. *Focus on Computers in Mathematics Education* (National Council of Teachers of Mathematics, 1906 Association Drive, Reston, VA 22091), November 1981.
E. *Instructional Computing: An Action Guide for Educators,* J. R. Dennis and R. Kansky (Glenview, IL: Scott, Foresman and Company), 1984.
F. *Introduction to Computers in Education for Elementary and Middle School Teachers,* D. Moursund (International Council for Computers in Education, 135 Education, University of Oregon, Eugene, OR 97403), 1981.
G. *Learning With Computers,* Alfred Bork (Billerica, ME: Digital Press), 1981.
H. *Microcomputers and the 3 R's: A Guide for Teachers,* C. Doerr (Rochelle Park, NJ: Hayden Book Co.), 1980.
I. *Microcomputers in Education: An Introduction,* A. Naiman (Technical Education Research Centers, 8 Eliot Street, Cambridge, MA 02138), 1982.
J. *Microcomputers for Teachers—With Application to Science and Mathematics,* D. Zalewski (editor), Topics for Teachers Series (School Science and Mathematics Association, Inc., 126 Life Science Building, Bowling Green State University, Bowling Green, OH 43403), 1982.

K. *Microcomputers: Their Selection and Application* (Association for Educational Data Systems, 1201 Sixteenth St., NW, Washington, DC 20036), Fall 1979.
L. *Mindstorms: Children, Computers, and Powerful Ideas,* S. Papert (New York: Basic Books), 1980.
M. *Peanut Butter and Jelly Guide to Computers,* J. Willis (Forest Grove, OR: Dilithium Press), 1979.
N. *RUN: Computer Education,* D. O. Harper and J. H. Stewart (Monterey, CA: Brooks/Cole Publishing Company), 1983.
O. *Teachers Guide to Computers in the Elementary School,* D. Moursund (International Council for Computers in Education, 135 Education, University of Oregon, Eugene, OR 94703), 1982.
P. *Teaching with Microcomputers* (National Council of Teachers of Mathematics, 1906 Association Drive, Reston, VA 22091), February 1983.
Q. *The Computer in the School: Tutor, Tool, Tutee,* R. Taylor, editor (New York: Basic Books, Inc.), 1980.
R. *The Elements of Computer Education: A Complete Program* (Office of Public Instruction, State Capitol, Helena, MT 59620).

Computers Everywhere Else

The second set of resources examines the social and moral issues associated with the current and projected impact of computer technology upon society. The listing is modest and, considering the rapidly changing nature of that technology, dated. New books (and some articles) on the topic can be found by searching the bibliographies of Item B. For even more up-to-date thinking about the societal side of computing, consult the indexes of journal articles (G) under such headings as "Computer Literacy" or "Computers and Society."

A. *Are You Computer Literate?,* K. Billings and D. Moursund (Forest Grove, OR: Dilithium Press), 1979.
B. Bibliographies
   1. *Annual Bibliography of Computer-Oriented Books* (Computing Newsletter, P.O. Box 7345, Colorado Springs, CO 80933).
   2. "Computer Literacy Bibliography," S. Friel and N. Roberts *(Creative Computing,* September, 1980, pp. 92-97).
   3. *The Impact of Computers on Society and Ethics: A Bibliography,* G. Abshire (Creative Computing, P.O. Box 789-M, Morristown, NJ 07960), 1980.
   4. *The Prospect of Computers on Society and Ethics: A Bibliography,* G. Abshire (Morristown, NJ: Creative Computing Press), 1980.
C. *Computers and Their Societal Impact,* M. Holvien (New York: John Wiley and Sons), 1979.
D. *Computers and Social Controversy,* T. Logsdon (Potomac, MD: Computer Science Press), 1980.
E. *Computers and Society,* S. Rothman and C. Mosmann (Chicago: Science Research Associates), 1976.
F. *Computer Consciousness: Surviving the Automated 80's,* H. D. Covvey and N. H. McAlister (Reading, MA: Addison-Wesley), 1980.
G. Journal Indices
   1. *COMPendium* (Epicurious, P.O. Box 129, Lincolndale, New York, NY 10540).
   2. *Microcomputer Index* (Microcomputer Information Services, 2464 El Camino Real, Suite 247, Santa Clara, CA 95051).
   3. *Micro . . . Publications in Review* (Vogeler Publishing, Inc., P.O. Box 489, Arlington Heights, IL 60006).
   4. *The Index* (W. H. Wallace, Missouri Indexing, Inc., P.O. Box 301, St. Ann, MO 63074).
H. *Running Wild: The Next Industrial Revolution,* A. Osborne (Berkeley, CA: OSBORNE-McGraw-Hill), 1979.
I. *Tales of the Marvelous Machine,* R. Taylor and B. Green (Morristown, NJ: Creative Computing Press), 1980.
J. *The Compleat Computer,* D. Van Tassel (Chicago: Science Research Associates), 1976.
K. *The Computers in Our Society* and *The Computers in Our Society Workbook,* T. Logsdon and F. Logsdon (Fullerton, CA: Anaheim Publishing Company), 1979.
L. *The Micro Millennium,* C. Evans (New York: Washington Square Press), 1981.

Back to BASICs

The computing language most commonly taught in precollege classrooms at the time of this writing is BASIC, although there is developing interest in Logo for the elementary and middle schools, and for Pascal in the secondary schools particularly for students who are in college preparatory curricula. Again we have a situation in which whatever we say at this stage, will be out of date almost before the ink is dry. Each of the languages has advantages and disadvantages depending upon the purposes for which it is being used. The following discussion, however, is focused only upon BASIC for two reasons: a) it currently is the most commonly encountered language across the precollege levels; and b) stock models of current versions of school computers come equipped to communicate in BASIC (with communication in Logo or Pascal available as an add-on).

BASIC exists in many versions, each of which is evolving through constant revision. Despite these variations, there are sufficient fundamental similarities among these versions to permit one to speak of "the" BASIC language with but a slight wince. Numerous books introduce the fundamental concepts of programming in BASIC. Some are produced by the manufacturers of a particular computing system and teach the version of BASIC specific to that system. The books listed below are simply *samples* (i.e., ones familiar to the authors). Many other excellent texts—some developed for such special audiences as elementary school students—are reviewed monthly in the journals of professional associations and in computing journals.

Ten of the fourteen items in our list are books which teach the "fundamental similarities" alluded to earlier, occasionally commenting on variations of a particular BASIC concept. Items A and C present a "soft," low-level introduction to programming in BASIC. Item B elaborates upon the introductory work of Item A; the result is an extensive course in beginning programming for persons from a wide range of subject matter fields. The texts listed in Items D, E, J, and L promote the structured style of programming which is so dear to the heart of computerists (and which will capture your academic affection as soon as you've tried it). Four of the books (D, E, F, and G) give special attention to programming mathematical topics.

The remaining four items of the list deserve special mention. Items H and N could be called "companion" texts for a course in BASIC. While Item H is usually associated with the study of the language Pascal, its use might precede the study of any particular language since it develops several fundamental programming principles without making use of the concept of a variable. Item N would complement most textbooks in BASIC instruction by helping the learner to write programs in a style which is easy to read (and, hence, to debug). Once a *version* of BASIC has been mastered, Item M will prove an invaluable reference text, since it is a handy compendium of the commands and statements found in several of the versions of the BASIC language. Finally, the articles listed under Item I allow the learner to stand back from the details of a particular computing language and to consider computing languages as a generic concept.

A. *A Bit of BASIC,* T. Dwyer and M. Critchfield (Reading, MA: Addison-Wesley Publishing Company), 1980.
B. *BASIC and the Personal Computer,* T. Dwyer and M. Critchfield (Reading, MA: Addison-Wesley), 1978.
C. *BASIC: A Hands-ON Approach,* H. Peckham (New York: McGraw-Hill Book Company), 1981.
D. *BASIC: A Structured Approach,* C. Siragusa (Boston: Prindle, Weber and Schmidt), 1980.
E. *BASIC Discoveries: A Problem-Solving Approach to Beginning Computer Programming,* L. Malone and J. Johnson (Palo Alto, CA: Creative Publications), 1981.
F. *Computer Programming in BASIC,* T. P. Pavlovich and T. E. Taham (San Francisco: Holden-Day), 1971.
G. *Computer Programming in the Basic Language,* second edition, N. Golden (New York: Harcourt Brace Jovanovich), 1980.
H. *Karel the Robot,* R. Pattis (New York: John Wiley and Sons), 1981.
I. Languages in General
   1. "A Beginner's Guide to Programming Languages," S. Hughes (*On Computing,* Spring, 1980, pp. 52-59).
   2. "Programming Languages," J. Feldman (*Scientific American,* December, 1979, pp. 94-116).
   3. "What Is a Programming Language?", A. Wold (*Classroom Computer News,* April, 1983, pp. 46-49).

J. *Problem Solving and Structured Programming in BASIC*, E. Koffman and F. Friedman (Reading, MA: Addison-Wesley), 1979.
K. *Programming for Computer Literacy*, D. Moursund (New York: McGraw-Hill), 1978.
L. *Programming Primer*, R. P. Taylor (Reading, MA: Addison-Wesley), 1982.
M. *The BASIC Handbook: An Encyclopedia of the BASIC Computer Language*, D. A. Lien (San Diego: COMPUSOFT Publishing), 1978.
N. *The Little Book of BASIC Style*, J. Nevison (Reading, MA: Addison-Wesley Publishing Company), 1978.

The All-Purpose Tool

The final collection of references reveals the value of the computer as a versatile servant of the mathematical problem solver. Four apply the computer to problems in precalculus mathematics (B, D, E, and F), one presents applications in calculus (A), and one fully integrates the computer into the study of elementary statistics (C).

A. *Computer Applications for Calculus*, W. S. Dorn, G. Bitter, and D. L. Hector (Boston: Prindle, Weber and Schmidt), 1972.
B. *Computer Resource Book: Algebra*, T. Dwyer and M. Critchfield (Boston: Houghton Mifflin), 1975.
C. *Elementary Computer-assisted Statistics*, F. Scalzo and R. Hughes (New York: Petrocelli/Charter), 1976.
D. *Mathematical Problem-Solving With the Microcomputer*, L. Snover and M. Spikell (Englewood Cliffs, NJ: Prentice-Hall, Inc.), 1982.
E. *Problems for Computer Solution*, S. Rogowski (Morristown, NJ: Creative Computing Press), 1975.
F. *Problem-Solving with the Computer*, E. R. Sage (Newbury Port, MA: ENTELEK), 1969.

Study Guide: Chapter 4

Save all evaluations you prepare here. They will be used in future chapters.

1. Section 0 describes several types of people vis-à-vis their attitudes toward instructional computing. Identify the "tour group" whose membership seems most compatible with your interests, and execute the suggested itinerary.
2. Locate an instructional computing periodical or a software directory which describes courseware in a subject area of interest to you. Pick *at least three* items of interest that suggest the availability of descriptive promotional material and/or (b) a demonstration program. Send for these items. Assess what questions of selection or quality are answered (or not answered) by the material you receive.
3. Inventory the information resources relative to use of computers in your subject area or grade level which are available locally. Your search should include libraries (school and public), bookstores, computer stores, media centers, etc.
4. Use the current issue of *Microcomputer Index* (or a similar index) to locate three published reviews (evaluations) of commercial courseware of interest. Read the reviews themselves, and compare the information presented in those reviews with the information needs suggested by the evaluation procedures of Chapter 4. Prepare a short critique of each evaluation, noting the weaknesses and useful aspects of each.
5. Obtain, execute, and evaluate a computerized lesson; complete both the Checklist and Documentation Sheet of Chapter 4. Recommend adoption or nonadoption of the software evaluated, and describe any modifications or corrections you would wish to see in the lesson.

AGENDA FOR ACTION

University of Illinois
at Urbana-Champaign

Department of Secondary Education
395 Education Building
1310 South Sixth Street
Champaign
Illinois 61820

College of Education

217 333-0227

MEMORANDUM

TO: The Instructional Computing Advisory Committee

FROM: Dick Dennis

DATE: December 20, 1982

RE: ICAC Papers 3 and 4

ICAC Papers 3 and 4—like Papers 1 and 2—are best presented together. Since Paper 3 is rather short, I've been able to complete it in time for a prevacation mailing. Paper 4 is being done by Bob (for reasons that will be obvious when you see it); it will be sent in about a week. Despite their staggered arrival times, please treat them as a single package.

The purpose of Paper 3 is to introduce you to the concept of a questioning episode, a concept which we see as being common to the many instructional applications of computers which we will examine. The brief discussion of questioning episodes presented in Paper 3 is intended as a kind of advanced organizer which will aid you in understanding the evaluation issues raised in Paper 4. We'll take a much more detailed look at questioning episodes in Paper 5 after, we hope, you have had some experiences in reviewing computerized instructional materials.

We understand that several members of ICAC have had little or no interaction with a computer. Since our papers would probably make a great deal more sense alongside such experience, we urge that the committee plan a few hours of "hands-on" time in a computer store or at a school which is making use of computers. The kind of computers seen or the actual programs viewed are not important; the mere experience will produce a whole new level of expertise and critical reading power.

Paper 4 will build upon Paper 2 in describing about a dozen different kinds of programs which are useful in education. You may wish to take along those descriptions when having your hands-on experience. Perhaps the person in charge of the experience will have examples of some specific types of programs (e.g., tutorial, simulation, testing, management). If so, look at those programs, and pretend to be a student. The single critical element of the experience is that you get your hands on the computer and command the execution of some programs. (While you're at it, try to identify some questioning episodes.)

DD:glm

Enclosure: ICAC Paper 3

cc: Bob Kansky

SCIENCE AND MATHEMATICS
TEACHING CENTER

ADDRESS REPLY TO WRITER

THE UNIVERSITY OF WYOMING
UNIVERSITY STATION, BOX 3992
LARAMIE, WYOMING, 82071

MEMORANDUM

TO: Members of ICAC

FROM: Bob Kansky

DATE: 12-28-82

RE: ICAC Paper 4

The enclosed ICAC Paper comes to you with the cooperation of the National Council of Teachers of Mathematics (NCTM) and two guest authors, William P. Heck and Jerry Johnson. It is, in fact, an updated and slightly revised version of an NCTM publication which Bill, Jerry, and I prepared under the direction of the NCTM Instructional Affairs Committee. The committee's charge was that the Guidelines be written in such a way that they would be of use to all educators having an interest in the instructional applications of computers. As a result, the development of the Guidelines was marked by a conscious effort to address all educators irrespective of teaching assignment (elementary, secondary, postsecondary), area of subject matter interest, or level of involvement with instructional computing.

Dick and I are grateful to NCTM for the permission to make use of the Guidelines. To emphasize the contributions of NCTM, Bill, and Jerry, we have chosen to produce the revised document using a similar typeface and general format of the original.

BK:baa

Enclosure: ICAC Paper 4

cc: Dick Dennis

AGENDA FOR ACTION

University of Illinois
at Urbana-Champaign

Department of Secondary Education

395 Education Building
1310 South Sixth Street
Champaign
Illinois 61820

College of Education

217 333-0227

MEMORANDUM

TO: John Russell

FROM: Dick Dennis

DATE: December 30, 1982

RE: Reviewing Periodicals in Instructional Computing

Thank you for including us in the distribution list for your committee memoranda. My purpose here is to respond to your ICAC Memo #3 request for "suggestions regarding best selections, procedures for review, or what to focus upon when reading instructional computing periodicals.

You've already made the first important decision: avoid the technical stuff in favor of simpler, classroom-oriented materials. Since you appear to have access to a goodly number of the latter materials, let me suggest a procedure which we have used before with groups of educators who wish to survey the field of computing journals. The procedure has three principle features: (a) each member of the group takes responsibility for reviewing four issues of a single periodical, (b) each of the four reviews seeks to identify specific items of information about the publication, and (c) each review is shared with every other member of the group by means of a one-page summary. Here's a step-by-step outline of the procedure.

1. Using the Instructional Computing Periodicals List that you've already prepared, have each person select one periodical. Of course, the group profits most by having each person take a different periodical.
2. If the periodical is published monthly, begin with the most recent issue. If published bi-monthly, drop back to the issue preceding the most recent one.
3. Read four issues for review purposes. For each issue, prepare (and distribute to each other member of the group) a one-page review summary.
4. Each of the four reviews should be confined to a specific aspect of the periodical; taken together, they should present a total picture. A focus for each review is described below.

   *Review 1: Format Overview Describe the intended audience. Estimate the extent to which educational issues are featured. Describe main features (regular departments, letters, bulletin boards, reviews, kinds of advertisements, computer programs, inquiry cards, etc.).

   *Review 2: Content Annotation Prepare an annotated table of contents for the major articles. Summarize the software or other reviews.

   *Review 3: Selected Content Review In 75-100 words, summarize each of two articles of probable interest to the group. List the titles of any other articles of educational interest.

   *Review 4: Purchasing/Informational Summary Describe any special features not noted earlier. Estimate the quality of the articles and reviews; estimate the journal's value in helping to locate instructional computing resources. Make specific purchasing recommendations (including what institution(s) should buy it, who have access to it, and how many copies would be needed). Give precise information on cost, address of publisher, and issues per year.

DD:glm

cc: Bob Kansky

AGENDA FOR ACTION

Obourn Senior High School

200 Woodbine Avenue
East Roachmont, New York

M. Jack Stivers
Principal

(716) 568-8840

ICAC Memo #4

TO: Members of ICAC

FROM: John Russell

DATE: January 5, 1983

Refreshed by the vacation, the committee was able to move through its business and dismiss by 3:57 p.m. To bring Bob and Dick into the picture, the committee has asked me to note the following highlights of the meeting.

1. Each member has selected one publication (journal or newsletter) on which to report. Single-page summaries will be prepared and distributed. Dr. Ennis has agreed to allow ICAC to use her staff to type and duplicate the summaries. (NOTE: Allow two full days for such work.)
2. Everyone managed to get some hands-on experience with a computer during the holiday period. Donna got the most extensive demonstration from her 13-year-old niece who just acquired a microcomputer as a Christmas present!
3. Having now read ICAC Papers 3 and 4, we are aware of the superficial nature of our vacation experiences in software review.

COMMITTEE ASSIGNMENTS

1. Each member will complete the first of the four journal reviews by next meeting time.
2. Lolita, Ted, and Phil will prepare an extended annotated bibliography of journals and newsletters of possible interest. They will obtain a sample copy of each by enlisting the help of the District's media specialists. The list and samples will be submitted to the committee at the meeting of 4-1-1983. This, along with the results of our journal reviewing activity, will be used to suggest additions to the libraries.
3. Jeanne, Donna, and Phil will use the NCTM Software Evaluation Checklist and Software Documentation Sheet to review some commercial courseware which has been purchased by LaRamie Middle School. They will use this experience to suggest modifications that should be made in the NCTM documents before they are used further by ICAC or suggested for use by local teachers.

JR:ms

CHAPTER FIVE

QUESTIONING EPISODES REVISITED

The evaluation criteria and procedures that one applies to a particular item of computerized courseware are a function of the proposed instructional use of that courseware. While certain technical and mechanical standards may be applied to many types of programs, judgment of the educational potential of an instructional computer program demands that the reviewer have a clear understanding of the structure and purpose of the program being examined. Chapters 6–12 respond to that demand by placing specific types of programs (tutorial, drill, practice, simulation, etc.) under an evaluative magnifying glass.

Whatever the type of program under consideration, educational success ultimately is reduced to proper use of those basic units of computer-student interaction, *questioning episodes*. Before going on to examine the several unique patterns in which questioning episodes are put together to construct the different kinds of instructional courseware, we first must scrutinize this fundamental unit of computerized instruction.

As previously noted (Chapter 3), each questioning episode has five components:

1. an interrogative expression *(a question* or *eliciting statement)* perhaps accompanied by other statements;
2. a requirement of and an opportunity for *student input* of information or asking of another question;
3. a provision for *computer interpretation* of the student input;
4. a set of computer-generated consequences, remarks, replies, or other questions which constitute specific *feedback* to the student input;
5. a procedure for determining the *duration limit* of the episode.

Based upon your experiences in viewing computerized courseware, some of these ingredients of a questioning episode may be vaguely familiar. To sharpen your awareness (and, hence, your evaluative powers), this chapter will look closely at each ingredient. The first is of greatest importance and, hence, will command considerable attention; the remaining four will receive, by comparison, but a passing glance.

Questioning-Episode Ingredient 1: A Question or Eliciting Statement

If you accept the axiom that one learns questioning by being questioned, you might understand why one hears so few good questions in the classroom. Oh, you may hear questions which call for students to recall and regurgitate isolated facts or you may hear rhetorical questions which serve to preface teacher discourse, but the questions asked reveal—and pass on to another generation—a low level of questioning skill. You might be disappointed by this observation, but you shouldn't be surprised. After all, the teacher usually is the product of at least sixteen years of exposure to interrogative undernourishment! Like, indeed, begets like. By focusing on questioning, however, instructional computing could break that cycle.

The manner in which people, especially teachers, use language demands that we expand our notion of a question to include an *eliciting statement*. An eliciting statement is a statement intended to elicit a response from the person or persons to whom it is directed. That response might be other statements (declarative or interrogative) or some action. For instance, the eliciting statement "There's a fly in your soup" has the same purpose as the query "Do you know that there's a fly in your soup?" The eliciting statement "Name the present coach of the Dallas Cowboys" can be equated with the interrogative "Who is the present head coach of the Dallas Cowboys?" There also are eliciting statements which, as part of a discourse, have no natural interrogative counterparts. Consider the following example.

Teacher: Can someone give me three examples of a *peninsula?*
Student: May I point to them on a map?
Teacher: That's a good idea.

The teacher's use of "good idea" leaves no doubt as to the next action the student should take.

Questions and eliciting statements come in many flavors. Each implies or suggests a particular type of response. Also, each question type attempts to develop or affirm learning at a particular level such as the knowledge (fact) level, the comprehension level, the application level, the valuing level, or the organization level.[1] In good questioning, the type of response implied or suggested should match the level of learning toward which the question is directed. Thus, our examination of the first ingredient of a questioning episode must be pursued by identifying several types of questions in terms of the mode of response associated with each. Specifically, the types of questions to be explored are:

- dichotomous-choice questions,
- multiple-choice questions,
- matching questions,
- interpretive questions,
- short-answer questions,
- essay questions.

In discussing a class of questions, we'll also consider the level(s) of learning that might be developed or evaluated by members of that class.

Dichotomous-Choice Questions

Also called alternative-choice questions, these questions are appropriate for determining recognition of one of two opposing positions. The respondent must take a stand on a given issue when given some form of binary choice: true/false, yes/no, agree/disagree, up/down, positive/negative, wise/foolish. The thinkers among you may object to calling these items *questions.* In fact, many are framed as assertions. However, the insistence that the student make a response to such an assertion makes it a valid example of an interrogative expression. (Forgive us, Mrs. Applegate!) Similar situations arise in all five types of question forms to be discussed.

When used in the context of instructional computing, dichotomous-choice questions are most useful for presenting students with choices. For example, the student may be asked to choose in which of two languages he will execute a given program, whether or not more examples of an idea should be presented, whether the problems to be presented should be easy or challenging, etc. These are important and appropriate student choices—choices which can have a significant effect upon the learning situation.

As a direct aid to developing ideas, dichotomous-choice questions are something of a flop. Inasmuch as there is a 50-50 chance of selecting the correct response to an item one knows absolutely nothing about, they promote guessing and, hence, are generally unreliable for providing evidence of learning. Still, dichotomous-choice questions can have instructional value in determining whether or not a student can (a) recognize the truth or falsity of assertions, (b) distinguish between fact and opinion, or (c) discriminate between appropriate and inappropriate choices.

---

[1]Norman E. Gronlund, *Measurement and Evaluation in Teaching* (New York: Macmillan Publishing Company, 1976).

The potential effectiveness of dichotomous-choice questions, like the effectiveness of the honey bee, lies in good basic design and large numbers. With regard to good basic design (or, perhaps, to the avoidance of poor design) of dichotomous-choice questions, we suggest that you look for the following positive features.

1. *The sentence structure of the item should be a simple complete sentence; a negation should be used only if it would be very messy to state the item in a positive form; multiple negations should be shunned.* Compare the grammatical forthrightness of:

   True or false?
   One thesis of Shakespeare's *Macbeth* is that a weak man married to an ambitious woman is inclined to evil.

   with the linguistic convolutions of:

   True or false?
   It would be incorrect to assert that it is not a thesis of Shakespeare's literary masterpiece *Macbeth* that when a man of weak character is bound by matrimony to a woman consumed by ambition then the man will not be inclined to resist evil.

   The second item suggests that the questioner is employing antics with semantics in an effort to trick the learner into an incorrect response. Such persons deserve special consideration by a modern-day Dante.
2. *Generalizations do not make good dichotomous-choice items.* It is often very difficult to word the proper quantification. In such cases, the concept basic to the item becomes secondary to the learner's ability to discriminate between *some* and *a few*, between *all* and *each*, between *many* and *most*, etc. The correct response becomes debatable because of the language employed. The student becomes frustrated; the instructor will not be elected Queen of the May.
3. *When several dichotomous-choice questions are used, the length of the items should be constant.* Item length can become a cue to the correct response. Students come to recognize that, in many subjects, any lengthy item is bound to deserve a negative response. In other subjects, attempts at precision lead to long items and are a good indication that a positive response is in order.

The second consideration in making effective use of dichotomous-choice questions is large numbers. A correct response to a single dichotomous-choice question is an unreliable indicator of learning. Blatant guessing will do the trick half of the time. Moreover, possible cues provided by the item itself can increase that probability of a correct answer. In short, it's very easy to "pass" a measure of learning based on a single dichotomous-choice item.

The faith that we place in learning measures which use dichotomous-choice items can be enhanced by doing two things: (a) increasing the number of items used to test the learning of a given idea, and (b) increasing the "pass" criterion by requiring a correct answer to more than one of the items presented.

Table 5.1 (p. 82) shows how the guessing factor is reduced as the number of items involved is increased. If, for example, a lesson writer is willing to live with a criterion that will allow no more than 6 percent (0.06) of the students to pass a given test by simply guessing, the chart indicates several appropriate questioning strategies: (a) present four dichotomous-choice items and require that the student answer all four correctly, (b) present seven items and require that at least six be answered correctly, or (c) present ten items and require at least eight correct responses. (Can you identify some other such strategies?)

Multiple-Choice Questions

Multiple-choice questions are as popular as they are difficult to construct. However, with the help of training and practice, one can learn to write multiple-choice questions which can address a wide range of levels of learning. Since a full treatment of the art of preparing multiple-choice or other types of questions would be inappropriate to our purpose in this paper, we'll confine ourselves to selected tidbits and leave more scholarly discourse to the experts.[2]

To begin, a multiple-choice item consists of two parts: (a) a question or statement called the *stem* and (b) a list of alternatives which includes the correct response *(answer)* and some incorrect responses *(distractors* or *foils)*. The answer to the item may correspond to one or more of the alternatives. Variations in the basis for selecting the answer include directions to

- find *the* correct response from among the alternatives presented;
- find *all* correct responses among the alternatives presented;
- find *the best* response among the alternatives presented.

Each of these variations has its place, but the types should not be mixed within a single set of questions.

As in the case of dichotomous-choice items, there are at least two good uses for multiple-choice items

[2]See Gronlund, N. E. *Measurement and Evaluation in Teaching.* (New York: Macmillan Publishing Company, 1976) and Nelson, C. H. *Measurement and Evaluation in the Classroom.* (New York: Macmillan Publishing Company, 1970). The latter is particularly useful for science instruction.

within instructional computing. The first simply presents the student with the opportunity to make choices regarding his movement through a lesson. For instance, the student might be asked to select the learning resource (book, computer lesson, film, filmstrip, audio tape, etc.) to be used in studying a particular topic. At another time, the student might be presented with the choice of taking a test, working additional exercises, selecting an additional learning resource, or meeting with the instructor. Such choices provide richness and flexibility within a course of study. In making such a choice, the student makes a judgment and is given information but is not judged in return.

The second use of multiple-choice items is for the evaluation of learning. This can be formative evaluation (diagnosis) in which the student's responses are used to direct his further study of a given topic or in summative evaluation (testing) in which the student's responses are the basis of a judgment about whether a given topic has been learned. When used for evaluation purposes, multiple-choice items demand careful development; both the design and the number of items is important.

Computerized courseware frequently employs multiple-choice questions to control a student's progress through a lesson. As an evaluator of that courseware, you will need to judge whether the design of the multiple-choice item employed by the lesson developer is good or poor. Here are a few principles to guide you in recognizing good design.

1. *The distractors should be equally plausible.* Easily advised, this is not easily done. It's tough work to create three or more equally acceptable incorrect alternatives.
2. *The stem of the question should be a simple complete sentence and should avoid the inclusion of negations.* The stem should be short. No irrelevant material should be included. Negations should be used rarely since they foster incorrect responses due to logical confusion rather than to a lack of understanding of the topic at hand.
3. *All alternatives should match the stem grammatically.* Correct answers can be cued by grammatical mismatches between the stem and the alternatives. This often happens as a result of inadvertant changes in gender or in the number, tense, or case of a verb.
4. *There should be exactly one justifiably correct answer.* Good students can be "punished" for extra knowledge or analytic power which leads them to see a flaw in a generalization or more than one factually correct choice among the alternatives.

TABLE 5.1 PROBABILITY OF PASSING A DICHOTOMOUS-CHOICE TEST BY CHANCE ALONE

Number of Dichotomous-Choice Items Presented	*Number of Items Constituting the Pass Criterion*[a]									
	1	2	3	4	5	6	7	8	9	10
1	.50									
2	.75	.25								
3	.87	.50	.12							
4	.93	.68	.31	.06						
5	.96	.81	.50	.18	.03					
6	.98	.89	.65	.34	.11	.02				
7	.99	.93	.77	.50	.22	.06	.01			
8	.99	.96	.85	.63	.36	.14	.03	.01		
9	.99	.98	.91	.75	.50	.25	.09	.02	.00+	
10	.99	.99	.94	.82	.62	.37	.17	.05	.01	.00+

[a]This is the minimum number of items which the student must answer correctly in order to "pass" the test.

Also, items calling for opinions or judgments may be ill-suited to multiple-choice questioning.

5. *Within a question, alternatives should be about the same length.* Alternatives that stand out can both cue and mislead. Neither of these results is a proper objective when constructing alternatives.
6. *The position of the answer should vary.* In the absence of conscious effort, the question-writer often tends to place the answer at just one or two positions within the list of alternatives. Students are quick to recognize this failing and use it as a cue in locating correct responses.

A lesson designer who uses multiple-choice questions to control a student's progress through a lesson should recall that such judgments call for the safety of numbers: (a) the number of alternatives presented in a given question, (b) the number of questions presented with regard to the learning to be evaluated, and (c) the number of presented questions which must be answered correctly in order to constitute a "pass" (i.e., acceptable evidence of learning). Clever students become "test wise" with respect to multiple-choice questions. They quickly learn to check the plausibility of choices. Having reduced the field by eliminating implausible choices, they are frequently successful in guessing the answers to questions about which they have no real knowledge. Some American students who are aware of profitable guessing techniques refer to multiple-choice items as "multiple-guess" items; similarly aware students in certain parts of the world call them "monkey puzzles." Either term is a fitting tribute to poor item design.

Matching Questions

Use of the matching question is effective in learning situations which call for the establishment of associations—of pairing the elements of one set with those of another. Familiar examples of such activities include the pairing of dates and events, states and capital cities, French nouns and their English equivalents, books and authors, chemical elements and their symbols, etc.

The matching question is compact. Its tidy form promises efficient treatment of a relatively large body of content in each item. How well that promise is kept depends upon—you guessed it—careful construction of the question. Here are a few design features to look for when judging a lesson author's facility with this type of question.

1. *The content of a given matching question should be homogeneous.* The mixing of associations (say, dates/events and rulers/countries) within a single question can cause confusion.
2. *The rule for doing the matching must be stated clearly.* Some forms of this question type require that a given stimulus (member of one list) be matched with each possible response (member of the other list); there may be several responses for a given stimulus. Another form of the question asserts the existence of exactly one correct response for each stimulus.
3. *The number of stimuli should not be equal to the number of response alternatives.* This inequality ensures that the student will remain attentive throughout work on the question.
4. *The statement of the responses should be short.* This makes the item easier to read. If, for example, the item calls for matching the names of geometric figures with the definitions of those figures, the names of the figures should be used as the response list (and should be written to the right of the list of stimuli).

The manner in which a matching item is constructed will have an effect on its power to evaluate learning. Suppose, for instance, that an item presents six stimuli and ten response alternatives. Suppose further that there is exactly one correct response for each stimulus and that the student is told that no response is used more than once. One such matching item calls for six independent judgments in which the student is confronted by no fewer than five alternatives! Now that's compactness.

Interpretive Questions

Common to the social sciences, this type of question is tough to write. It is used to deal with learning at higher levels such as analysis, synthesis, and evaluation.

The interpretive question opens with a scenario which describes the question setting and which gives data or general information about that setting. Then the fun begins. The scenario is followed by one or more demands that the student recognize the relevance of some of the information, identify unwarranted generalizations, apply a principle, recognize assumptions, recognize inferences, make inferences, or interpret experimental findings. (Phew!)

With effort and practice, interpretive questions can be expressed in multiple-choice form. In that form, such questions are computerized easily and lend themselves to opportunities to individualize instruction.

One major disadvantage of interpretive questions is that they can tax the reading skills of students far more than the other types of questions we've discussed. This, of course, is not an insurmountable difficulty. By careful attention to vocabulary, sentence complexity, and clarity of expression, the writer of the question can reduce the reading problem.

Short-Answer Questions

The use of short-answer items is appropriate when the purpose is to develop or assess learning which deals with the interpretation of data or with the recall of facts, principles, or procedures. Such items often are used in association with problem-solving activities in mathematics or science.

Whereas three of the four types of questions discussed thus far (dichotomous-choice, multiple-choice, matching) require the student to *recognize* an appropriate response, short-answer items require him or her to *construct and report* a response.[3] The use of short-answer questions in a computerized environment raises special problems which, through planning and good programming, can be handled. One example of such a problem is the requirement that the computer be able to recognize equivalent forms of numerical responses (e.g., 5, five, 5.0, or even 10 ÷ 2). If the response is verbal (i.e., a written statement), errors or variations in spelling offer challenges to computer control of the situation. Again, most of these problems can be eliminated directly (by clever programming) or indirectly (by clever design). As difficult as the question form can be, the results may be well worth the efforts.

There are a number of things to look for when checking a lesson designer's proper construction of computerized short-answer items. Here are a few.

1. *An item should be designed in such a way that the answer is brief.* The more complex the response, the bigger the headache of judging the correctness of a response.
2. *An item should be designed so that the form of the answer is well defined.* By delimiting the form of the answer, the question-writer can control the number of ways in which a correct response can be given. These should be few in number and easily predicted.
3. *When responses include words, the relative importance of spelling must be decided in advance and a method of recognizing misspellings must be present.* Computers can find many spelling errors. In keeping with the teacher's purpose, a spelling error could be used to judge the response as incorrect or to judge the response to be fundamentally correct although technically incorrect. In the latter situation, the lesson designer should provide the student with feedback regarding that technical (spelling) error.
4. *A direct question is better than a fill-in-the-blanks format.* Direct questions are less likely to cue a correct answer through peculiarities in grammar or sentence structure.
5. *When numerical responses are called for, the questioner should specify the form of the response and/or the units involved.* This helps to limit the number of alternate correct responses which the computer must recognize.

[3]This characteristic of short-answer questions is shared by essay questions.

Essay Questions

Essay questions are important because they provide access to higher level learning outcomes involving the organization, integration, or relation of ideas. They offer students the ultimate in freedom to respond . . . and therein lies their disadvantage within instructional computing. Computer interpretation of free-form responses is very difficult (although possible within limited contexts). Efforts to admit essay questions to the computing environment have been limited to projects involving large educational computers or to artificial intelligence research laboratories. In view of the current state of developments in this area, we'll say little about this type of question. *Nevertheless, the essay question is important.* Teachers must know how to use it. But instructional computing systems will be of little help in doing so for some time to come.

A Matter of Confidence

In closing this discourse on the question component of a questioning episode, we should mention a questioning technique in which computers can be used to augment the information gained from a questioning episode. The technique links each question to a confidence-assertion item like this one.

How certain are you that your answer to this question is correct?

a. Quite certain.
b. Not very certain.
c. Just guessing.

By requiring that the student respond to this confidence-assertion before providing feedback or another question, the computer gathers data which permits the classification of students into four categories:

1. he who knows and knows that he knows (high comprehension and high confidence);
2. he who knows and knows not that he knows (high comprehension and low confidence);
3. he who knows not but knows not that he knows not (low comprehension and misplaced high confidence);
4. he who knows not and knows that he knows not (low comprehension and low confidence).

You probably can think of learners who fit each of these profiles. You also should recognize the importance of varying responses or consequences for such persons. Planning for instruction should take this information into account.

Questioning-Episode Ingredient 2: Student Input

The second element of a questioning episode is the opportunity and the requirement for the student to participate in the dialogue with the computer. Clearly, the form of this participation should match the form being elicited by the interrogative part of the episode, as discussed in the previous section.

Efficient learning and efficient operation of an instructional computing system demand that the lesson designer instruct the student in the mechanics of properly inputting a response. The nature of the answer and the maturity of the student are important issues to be considered. Some lessons require the use of special keyboard techniques for typing answers involving subscripts, superscripts, or language symbols such as the tilde (~). Lessons in mathematics may require the input of responses which employ complex rules of punctuation. Depending upon the user, it may be necessary to avoid questions which use such complicated forms of response. In other instances, use of such forms should be preceded by lessons whose single purpose is to teach the necessary answering skills.

Questioning-Episode Ingredient 3: Computer Interpretation of Student Input

Computer interpretation of a student's input to the interrogative part of an episode must meet four criteria regarding meaning recognition. To say that a computer "recognizes" a response means that it accepts the response and deals with it in some educationally meaningful manner. In this sense, the computer has at least four recognition tasks.

1. *It must recognize a correct input and any reasonably synonymous input.* It is a poor teacher (and, hence, a poor computer program) which will accept *Abraham Lincoln* as a correct response but which refuses consideration of *Abe Lincoln.*
2. *It must recognize responses which are literally incorrect but which are conceptually correct.* There are several ways that a student can "think correctly but express thoughts incorrectly." Typing errors *(teh* instead of *the),* conceptually noncritical spelling errors *(isoseles triangel* rather than *isosceles triangle),* or cultural differences in spelling *(colour* versus *color)* fall into this category.
3. *It must recognize an array of "common" incorrect inputs.* Insofar as such a "common" incorrect input can be attributed to a specific error in thinking, the input permits the computer to prescribe appropriate remediation.
4. *It must recognize "uncommon," probably incorrect, inputs.* Students will come up with responses that couldn't be anticipated by super-teacher. Exactly how the student arrived at that response might require extensive and creative probing. In the meantime, life—and the computer program—must go on appropriately.

The completeness and accuracy with which a questioning episode makes the above distinctions will determine, to a great measure, the overall quality of the episode. Deficiencies in attempts to deal with these distinctions during the early history of instructional computing produced considerable disenchantment among potential users.

Questioning-Episode Ingredient 4: Feedback

If an instructional computing environment is to be truly interactive, it must inform the student of more than just the correctness or incorrectness of a response. Considerable teaching can be done by messages (i.e., feedback) which accompany the confirmation or the denial of a response.

The feedback part of a questioning episode is intimately related to the interpretation of student input. One must go to great lengths, therefore, to avoid such weak or inappropriate feedback as (a) a simple *no* to an alternate form of correct input, (b) a simple *no* to an incorrect input, thus giving no hint of why the response is incorrect, (c) an *ok* to a response which appears to be correct but which has been stumbled upon despite basic misconceptions and faulty reasoning, or (d) either an *ok* or a *no* to a response indicating a request for assistance (e.g., *help* or *hint).* In fact, computerized questioning episodes should provide feedback which includes at least the following:

1. messages that confirm correct responses *and* reinforce the reasons for their correctness;

2. messages which confirm correct thinking detected in association with a technically incorrect response *and* which facilitate the construction of a technically correct response;
3. messages which deny each predictable incorrect response *and* which provide specific reasons for the incorrectness—reasons aimed at bringing about a remedy;
4. messages which label unidentifiable responses as uninterpretable *and* which suggest appropriate ways to seek a remedy to the situation;
5. messages which provide appropriate hints and help upon request.

Questioning-Episode Ingredient 5: Duration Limit

Despite all Herculean efforts at question design, careful interpretation of responses, and detailed feedback, there will exist at least one student for whom the result is inadequate. For some questioning episodes, that student will respond incorrectly time after time, all built-in corrective measures notwithstanding. In such a case, the computer *must* be equipped to decide how long such a situation should be permitted to continue and how it should be terminated.

Situations arise in which a student, for some unanticipated reason, believes an answer to be correct and, hence, continues giving it. In fact, it may be correct in some strange, unpredicted way. Nevertheless, its unanticipated nature means that the computer will continue to reject the response. Allowed to continue, this student/computer conflict can be very frustrating to the student; interest and motivation will be quickly destroyed. Therefore, every questioning episode must include a way out of such endless repetition. Such an exit can be keyed by placing a limit on the number of incorrect or unidentified responses to be permitted.

Beyond an exit procedure, careful attention needs to be given to what the computer does when one of these situations occurs. The inability to answer correctly may prevent the student from successfully going on to the next episode. It may be that he should go back through specific episodes to attempt to construct the knowledge that either is missing or was incorrectly constructed previously, or it may be that the appropriate decision is to terminate the session. The important point is that whenever a discontinuity of this type occurs in instruction, the teacher somehow should be informed of the details to the extent that they exist. This could be achieved by telling the student to consult the teacher with some form of record (paper copy, etc.) of his or her experiences. Another means of informing the teacher is through a data profile of the experience which could be put into a computer file for the teacher to consult and act upon regularly.

In Closing: A Confession

Now that you have ingested and, we hope, ruminated upon these good things about good questioning episodes, we have a little confession to make. Fortunately for us, we're not within your reach.

The fact of the matter is, dear reader, that one rarely finds computer materials which employ questioning episodes as we have described them. Whether this is because the authors of those materials are unaware of the issues we've raised or because they are unwilling to make the effort required to respond to those issues, we cannot say. The important thing is that computers and authors *are* capable of meeting the requirements of good questioning episodes. In order that there might be large scale implementation of such design standards in the future, *users must learn to recognize and to demand those standards.*

Study Guide: Chapter 5

1. Exercise 1 of the Study Guide to Chapter 3 asked you to assess a questioning episode. In light of the detailed analysis of questioning episodes presented in Chapter 5, do two things.
   a. Revise your previous assessment.
   b. Conduct an assessment of a different questioning episode.
2. Using precollege textbooks, published tests, or teacher-made tests in your field, locate at least two examples of each type of question described (dichotomous-choice, multiple-choice, matching, interpretive, short-answer, essay).
3. Using the examples obtained in the previous exercise,
   a. analyze each in terms of the attributes recommended for that type of question;
   b. select one question of each type. List all of the information needed in order to make such a question part of a well-designed computerized questioning episode.
4. Using computerized courseware in your subject area, identify three questioning episodes. For each, determine how thoroughly the possible correct and incorrect answers of students have been anticipated.
5. Imagine a topic in a subject you teach or know. Also imagine being confronted by students exhibiting the four profiles of high/low comprehension combined with high/low confidence. Discuss the variations in feedback, consequences, and instructional decisions appropriate to each profile.

AGENDA FOR ACTION

SCIENCE AND MATHEMATICS
TEACHING CENTER

ADDRESS REPLY TO WRITER

THE UNIVERSITY OF WYOMING
UNIVERSITY STATION, BOX 3992
LARAMIE, WYOMING, 82071

MEMORANDUM

TO: Members of ICAC

FROM: Dick Dennis and Bob Kansky

DATE: January 10, 1983

RE: ICAC Paper 5

The fact that this memorandum comes from both of us does not mean that we've moved together to do our work. However, we've decided upon a writing procedure which calls for both of us to proofread and edit each paper; he who is last to edit a given paper will forward it to ICAC. Our memoranda will carry both names to remind you that you can query either or both of us regarding any paper.

The enclosed "revisit" to the topic of questioning episodes is a trip upon which we place considerable value. Insofar as questioning episodes are the building blocks of computerized courseware, it follows that the quality of the episodes will determine the overall quality of that software. The goals of ICAC Paper 5 are to familiarize you with appropriate uses of specific kinds of questioning episodes and to aid you in evaluating such episodes. Our approach to the latter goal is through detailing the features that should be part of the design of a given questioning episode. By noting the presence or absence of these features in the questioning episodes of the courseware which you review, you can judge the quality of the instructional design effort put forth by the lesson author(s).

DD:BK:baa

Enclosure: ICAC Paper 5

P.S. Did you see the January 3, 1983, issue of *Time?* It was *Time*'s Man of the Year issue in recognition, as it notes on page 16, of the world's single "greatest influence for good or evil." *Time* decided that that "greatest influence" was neither a man nor a woman—hence, it modified its usual procedure in order to proclaim the microcomputer to be the Machine of the Year. Reactions of newspaper and television commentators indicated that a lot of noses were out of joint about a machine being chosen over humans for the *Time* award.

AGENDA FOR ACTION

Obourn Senior High School

200 Woodbine Avenue
East Roachmont, New York

M. Jack Stivers
Principal

(716) 568-8840

ICAC Memo #5

TO: Members of ICAC

FROM: John Russell

DATE: January 20, 1983

The committee found "Questioning Episodes Revisited" to be rather heavy going in spots but accepted the authors' assertion of the underlying importance of the concepts presented. It did make some of us think about all the test questions we've written over the years. Many of our test items wouldn't have passed muster under the standards of Chapter 5. As we critique the work of the writers of computerized questioning episodes, we hope it will cause us to look to ourselves as well.

1. The first set of journal reviews was distributed. Discussion of these format overviews revealed the diversity of the publications.
2. While the committee agreed that it cannot engage in the kind of wholesale evaluation of software that would lead to purchasing, there was concensus that regular viewing of sample software must be part of ICAC's education. We need to interact with specific examples of the issues discussed in the ICAC Papers.

COMMITTEE ASSIGNMENTS

1. The next set of journal reviews (Content Annotation) are due in four weeks (February 15).
2. Sample software will be sought to accompany the reading of each of the ICAC Papers. Using the list of proposed papers, Lolita and John will line up and borrow samples of appropriate software that can be run on John's machine. Carrinne, acting as a member of the school board, will contact the local computer vendors to explain ICAC activities and, hence, to "legitimate" the requests of Lolita and John. (Carrinne knows some of the vendors through her involvement with the East Roachmont Merchants Association.)
3. Sample software will be kept on hand for two weeks. It may be viewed at any time by making arrangements with John. Also, it may be viewed for the one-hour periods preceding and following our regular meetings (in our meeting room).
4. To help us in our critical viewing of questioning episodes, Ted will prepare a two-page summary of ICAC Paper 5. One page will note the expected "good features" of the six types of questions; the other page summarizes the main points of Questioning-Episode Ingredients 2-5.

JR:ms

CHAPTER SIX

ONE-ON-ONE: THE COMPUTER AS TUTOR

Is everyone ready to begin? Good. Please take out your *Pocket Oxford Dictionary* and look up the noun *tutor*. Ah . . . I see that a few of you have come to class unprepared. Well, those who *are* prepared can tell you that the *Oxford* defines a *tutor* as a "private teacher"—that is, as someone who is "in general charge of a person's education."[1]

Now anyone (or anything) that claims the right to be "in general charge of a person's education" needs to be queried. The person whose education is being taken "general charge of" ought to ask to see the tutor's credentials. From the *Oxford's* standard one may infer that claim to the title of *tutor* is a claim to the title of *master teacher*. Ideally, then, the tutor is a teacher whose expertise promises a maximal learning experience for any given student! Think about that as you reread the title of this chapter.

TUTORING VERSUS TALKING

For many the act of teaching is equated with monologue. The teacher selects, organizes, and delivers knowledge in word form (perhaps with the aid of some visuals). At the end of intervals defined by the teacher, students are called upon (through tests) to repeat a sample of what they have heard or read. Too often—and too late—the students discover that what they thought they heard, read, or experienced is at odds with what the teacher thought was presented. The kindly observer would point to a "breakdown in communication." In fact, any communication which has taken place

[1] J. B. Sykes, ed., *The Pocket Oxford Dictionary of Current English* (New York: Oxford University Press, 1978), p. 986.

has been almost accidental since the model of instruction has lacked *the* basic component of communication: interaction.

Of course, no teaching situation is as black as the one just painted. Even the most devoted lecturer will invite questions from students and will use those questions to initiate discussions which clarify or expand upon the material under consideration. The adoption of a model of teaching which avoids monologue in favor of dialogue is, however, a matter of degree.

In this paper, we wish to examine tutorial lessons. Guided by the *Oxford's* definition of *tutor* and influenced by the prejudice revealed in the preceding mini-diatribe on teaching monologues, we take the view that:

a tutorial lesson is a dialogue
between **two learners.**

Each participant is both teacher and learner; the lesson is a conversation in which each participant is striving to communicate. The participant having the role of tutor has the primary teaching responsibility by having been charged with the tasks of providing leadership in perfecting the dialogue and of transmitting curricular objectives. The tutor is also a learner insofar as the dialogue results in refined communication skills which affect future tutorials. Thus, when a tutorial lesson fails, we must look to both the tutor and the tutee as sources of the "breakdown in communication."

Tutorial Computer Lessons

A tutorial computer lesson (or computerized tutorial) is a simulation of a dialogue between our idealized tutor and an unidentified student. The idealized tutor is engaged in directing a very personal and highly individualized conversation regarding some concept, generalization, skill, or attitude. The student is unidentified in the sense that the tutor has no detailed information on the student's knowledge, emotional state, or physical disposition. The computerized tutor must be ready to cope with a variety of combinations of these three attributes of that unidentified student. Planning a luncheon for the entire membership of the United Nations is, by comparison, child's play.

The success of a tutorial lesson is at the mercy of two characteristics of tutors and tutees:

a. their willingness to communicate;
b. their ability to communicate.

If either participant has a mind to deliberately confound the dialogue, the other participant has no choice but to withdraw. But even when a spirit of cooperation is present, the act of communication can fall far short of the intent. It is worth noting that the likelihood of an unintentional failure in communication during a computerized tutorial is increased by current limitations in computerized media. For example, while human communication is augmented by vocal inflections, facial expressions, and gestures, the computerized tutor (or tutee) is usually restricted to print and graphics. This calls for the participants in a computerized tutorial to use its limited resources with greater precision and creativity in order to compensate for the loss of other important forms of communication. Lest this point be taken lightly, a simple example should suffice.

The story goes that the warden of Margate Prison in England was awaiting judicial response to the plea of a condemned man. As the day of execution drew near, the warden sent a telegram which concluded by asking the judicial authorities

SHALL I SPARE HIM OR HANG HIM?

The reply, arriving minutes before the scheduled time of execution, read

SPARE HIM NOT HANG HIM.

While it may be assumed that the court wished to communicate, we are confronted by a deadly example of imprecision. Depending upon what item of punctuation was lost, the warden has a choice between two significant alternatives:

SPARE HIM NOT. HANG HIM.
SPARE HIM, NOT HANG HIM.

While failures in communication during a computerized tutorial on, say, writing poetry in iambic pentameter may be less dramatic than the Margate Prison case, the computer's demand for increased attention to skillful use of the medium of communication is basic to this application of computers. American facility with the printed word is, generally speaking, less than awesome.[2] In addition, the teacher-as-artist[3] justifiably uses context, expression, gesture, students' familiarity with the teacher's style and personality, and a little bit of oh-you-know-what-I-mean to carry much of the burden of precise communication. What a teacher says in a given dialogue is often secondary to when, where, how, and to whom the statement is made. Even when sound (including speech) is used to enhance a computerized tutorial,[4] the overall communication environment must be considered deprived. Wherever the use of nonverbal communication is denied, greater precision in the use of the remaining tools of communication must fill the gap.

[2]" '81 Education Story: Good News, Bad News," in *NAEP NEWSLETTER,* (National Association of Educational Progress, Vol. XIV, No. 4, Winter, 1981–82).

[3]There'll be more said about this species in Chapter 9.

[4]This is not unheard of (if you'll pardon the pun), but it is not yet common.

Tutor, Hear Thyself!

Having pointed an accusing finger at those who attempt to teach with word and picture, we also stand in the dock with the accused. Insofar as we've failed to do a good job of communicating with you, we've done an excellent job in exemplifying the problem of the monologue. (How's that for a convenient rationalization?) In addition, pangs of guilt now goad us into using our limited literary and artistic skills as fully as possible in attempting to communicate the nature of a computerized tutorial.

Our general plan is to present a very simple and very brief example of a simulated tutorial. Its presentation will assume the willingness and intent to communicate by both tutor and tutee. Such good will notwithstanding, the example will fail to live up to expectations as a tutorial. It will, however, serve as a useful touchstone for the "intellectualizing" which follows it.

The Tutor as Computer: Simulating a Computerized Tutorial

Recall that a computerized tutorial is a simulation of a dialogue between a tutor (master teacher) and a student. To simulate a computerized tutorial, then, we must simulate that computerized dialogue. Whereas the task of *creating* a computerized tutorial is one of programming the computer to act like a master teacher, our task of *understanding* a computerized tutorial is served by trying to "program a teacher" to act like a computer!

Since our teacher is to act like a computer, we can depend upon the teacher to have a fantastic memory (in fact, total recall). On the other hand, our programmed teacher will be able to recall only those items which have been committed to memory by explicit directions in our program. Moreover, the teacher's use of those items will be restricted by the specific directions given in the program. To act as a computer, the teacher must first become a blank slate. Every bit of information and every direction for the use of such information with a student must be written on that slate by means of a detailed, carefully designed lesson plan (computer program).

A computer—and, hence, our programmed teacher—may be confronted by an unanticipated question or response from a student. Limited to what has been written on his/her/its slate, the tutor cannot react in a direct manner to unanticipated input. Realizing that such an event is likely, however, the tutor (computer or teacher) is equipped to generate the all-purpose response:

```
SORRY. I DON'T UNDERSTAND.
PLEASE RETYPE.
```

In fact, computers have a collection of such all-purpose responses built in at birth. Known as *system messages*, they provide feedback to a user or programmer who makes any one of a limited number of common, anticipated blunders. To the nonprogrammer, however, some of these messages border on the cryptographic. Imagine being the innocent user who, because of a programmer's lack of forethought, is assaulted by:

```
OUT OF RANGE
BREAK IN 3750
READY
```

In programming our teacher to act like a computer, we must make an effort to avoid such nonsense. Let's get on with it.

Background to the Lesson

Students in the fifth grade class taught by a certain Mr. C. R. Terminal have been doing a little geometry in their mathematics lessons. They're learning to classify simple figures (e.g., parallelograms, rectangles, squares, triangles, pentagons, hexagons) based upon information about side measures and angle measures. They know how to communicate with C.R.T. by typing on his keyboard. They know that his message "SORRY, I DON'T UNDERSTAND. PLEASE RETYPE." indicates that he isn't prepared to deal with a question that they've asked or a response that they've given to one of his questions. Because the students like "old C.R.T.," they try to be patient when they catch him unprepared.

Setting for the Tutorial Lesson

Estelle is Terminal's best mathematics student. Because she has mastered all of the figure classification tasks presented thus far, Terminal has decided to introduce her to the concept of an *isosceles triangle*. According to the mathematics syllabus used in C. R. Terminal's school district, an *isosceles triangle* is a triangle for which *exactly* two sides have the same measure. (There are other definitions of *isosceles triangle*, but this is the one C.R.T. is to teach.)

C. R. Terminal teaches by what he calls a "discovery method." That is, he introduces a new concept by presenting examples; students are expected to use these examples to arrive at a generalization. In the case of teaching the concept of an isosceles triangle, for instance, Terminal's overall plan is to present a student with the side measures of several triangles. For each example presented, he will tell the student whether or not the triangle is isosceles. After giving such examples, he'll describe several other triangles one at a time and have the student "guess" which of the triangles are isosceles. The student's response to each triangle will be judged correct or incorrect. As a result of these guesses, the student should be able to generalize about isosceles triangles—that is, to conclude that an isosceles triangle has exactly two sides of the same length. Just to be certain, Mr. Terminal concludes the lesson by stating this generalization.

The Lesson Plan (Teacher Program)

To prepare our teacher to act like a computer, we need a detailed lesson plan. It must show the steps of the lesson, how the teacher will decide which step to take next, and exactly what the teacher will say at each point in the lesson. The first two items are handled by the program sequence given in appendix 1 at the end of this chapter; what the teacher will say (e.g., the questions, feedback messages, summaries) during the program sequence is recorded in the program memory of appendix 2.[5] At any point in the execution of the program sequence, the teacher can reach into the program memory for the appropriate thing to say to the student. Remember: since the teacher is acting like a computer, *he can say only those things which are stored in the program memory.*

Execution of the Lesson

The planning of our simulated computerized tutorial is at an end. The program sequence (appendix 1) has been loaded. It's time for our programmed teacher, Mr. C. R. Terminal, to test the adequacy of this planning by trying to teach Estelle (his fifth-grade mathematics whiz) the concept *isosceles triangle.*

The tutorial session with Estelle is reported in cartoon form on the pages which follow. The sample cartoon frame below indicates how the cartoon distinguishes between what Estelle or Mr. Terminal *say* (i.e., *type*) to each other and what they *think*[6] but cannot communicate. Their dialogue is limited to exactly two statements by Estelle which C.R.T. can recognize **(yes** and **no)** and the few statements which C.R.T. can display (as listed in his Program Memory).

[5]A diagram (flow chart) of this sequence is shown in appendix 3. You may find the flow chart to be a nice summary of appendix 1. In fact, it was used to design the sequence in appendix 1.

[6]We take poetic license here. Although computers can't think, we'll allow our programmed teacher to reflect on what's happening. However, like a computer, he's helpless to take action on those reflections.

A CASE OF
TERMINAL INSTRUCTION

Another adventure from the simulated computerized classroom of C. R. Terminal, Programmed Teacher . . .

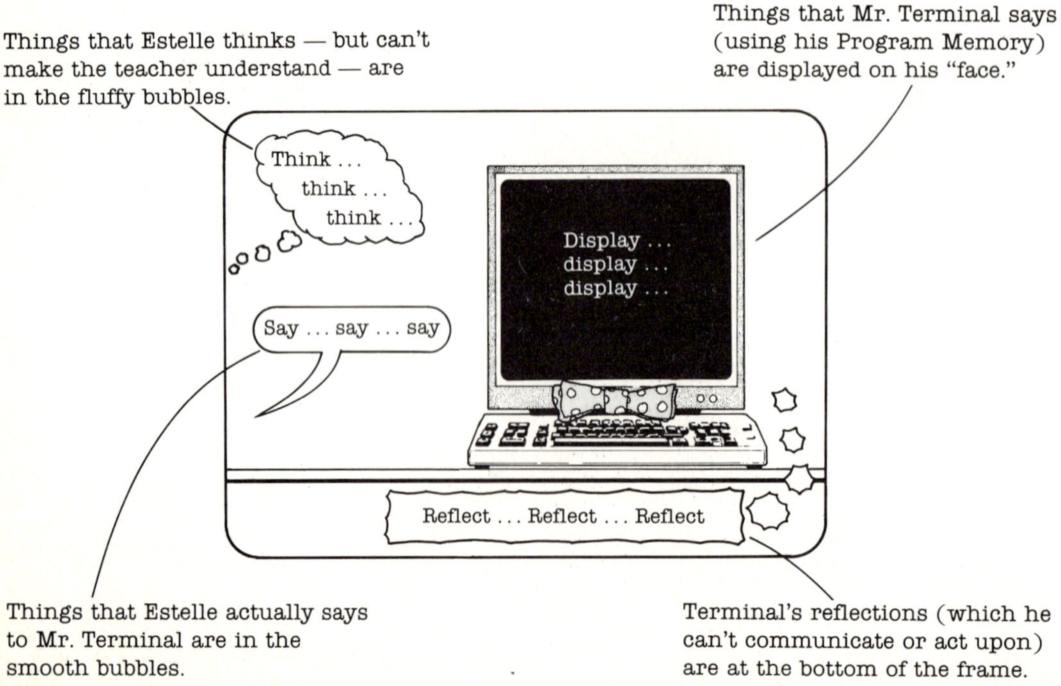

THERE ARE MANY SPECIAL CLASSES OF TRIANGLES. ONE CLASS CONTAINS TRIANGLES CALLED **ISOSCELES**. THIS LESSON WILL HELP YOU DISCOVER THE DEFINITION OF **ISOSCELES TRIANGLE**.
Looks like another of Terminal's "discovery" lessons.
Ahh . . . my favorite student! This should be easy for both of us.

HERE ARE THE SIDE MEASURES OF FOUR TRIANGLES. EACH IS AN **ISOSCELES TRIANGLE**.
4 CM, 5 CM, 4 CM
10 CM, 10 CM, 7 CM
8 CM, 9 CM, 9 CM
6.9 CM, 4.3 CM, 6.9 CM
Looks to me like an **isosceles triangle** is one that has two sides of the same length.
I'll bet she's discovered the definition already.

That third example doesn't fit. Maybe old Terminal made an error. He does seem a bit senile at times.
HERE ARE THE SIDE MEASURES OF FOUR TRIANGLES. EACH IS NOT AN **ISOSCELES TRIANGLE.**
4 CM, 5 CM, 6 CM
15 CM, 12 CM, 8 CM
9 CM, 9 CM, 9 CM
7.3 CM, 4.8 CM, 4.9 CM
That's strange. She seems puzzled. I wish that she could tell me why.

ARE THESE THE SIDE MEASURES OF AN **ISOSCELES TRIANGLE**?
(ANSWER YES OR NO.)
4 CM, 11 CM, 8 CM
Let's see. No two sides have the same length. I'd say it's not isosceles.
No

CORRECT.
ARE THESE THE SIDE MEASURES OF AN **ISOSCELES TRIANGLE**?
(ANSWER YES OR NO.)
6 CM, 6 CM, 3 CM
I was right! This time there are two sides with the same length (6 centimetres). This should be an isosceles triangle.
Yes

CORRECT.
ARE THESE THE SIDE MEASURES OF AN **ISOSCELES TRIANGLE**?
(ANSWER YES OR NO.)
7 CM, 7 CM, 7 CM
This one's like that example that didn't fit. Still it has two sides with the same length (7 centimetres) so it ought to be isosceles.
Yes
Oh, oh. She must have overlooked the third set of measures that I gave in Example 2.

Incorrect? What's going on? Terminal's just got to be making a mistake. I'll try asking for an explanation.
INCORRECT; PLEASE TRY AGAIN.
ARE THESE THE SIDE MEASURES OF AN **ISOSCELES TRIANGLE**? (ANSWER YES OR NO.) 7 CM, 7 CM, 7 CM
PLEASE EXPLAIN WHY I'M INCORRECT.
Something's wrong. I wish I could understand what she's saying.

I guess he's not prepared to explain anything to me. Maybe I can convince him I'm right.
SORRY. I DON'T UNDERSTAND. PLEASE RETYPE.
ARE THESE THE SIDE MEASURES OF AN **ISOSCELES TRIANGLE**? (ANSWER YES OR NO.) 7 CM, 7 CM, 7 CM
IT MUST BE ISOSCELES SINCE TWO OF ITS SIDES HAVE THE SAME LENGTH (7 CENTIMETRES).
More confusion. What's she trying to say?

SORRY. I DON'T UNDERSTAND.
PLEASE RETYPE.
ARE THESE THE SIDE MEASURES OF AN **ISOSCELES TRIANGLE**? (ANSWER YES OR NO.)
7 CM, 7 CM, 7 CM
The same response again. I give up. I'll respond "No" even though I'm sure it should be "Yes." Terminal's wrong on this one.
No
At last . . . she realized that an isosceles triangle can't have **three** sides with the same length.

CORRECT.
ARE THESE THE SIDE MEASURES OF AN **ISOSCELES TRIANGLE**? (ANSWER YES OR NO.)
20 CM, 13 CM, 20 CM
Correct, my foot. Oh well, might as well go on.
Umm . . . two sides have a length of 20 centimetres. This one must be isosceles.
Yes
Glad she's back on the track. I was getting worried.

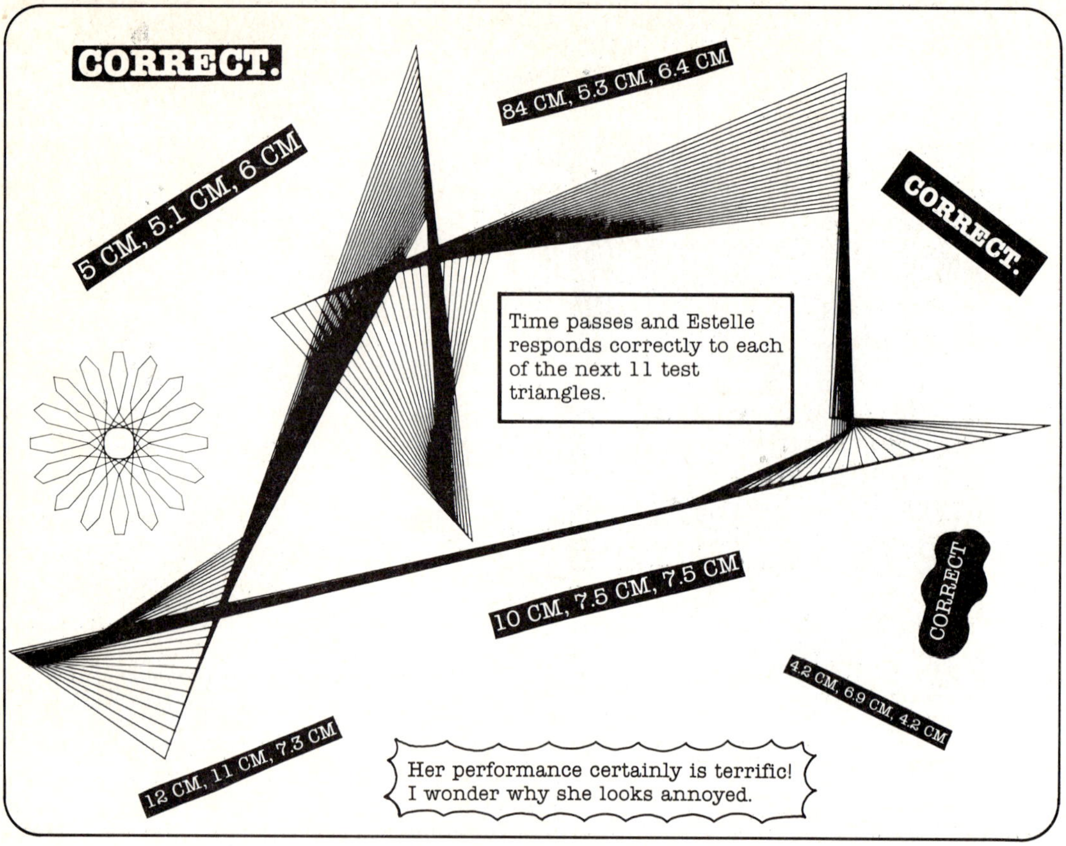
CORRECT.
5 CM, 5.1 CM, 6 CM
84 CM, 5.3 CM, 6.4 CM
CORRECT.
Time passes and Estelle responds correctly to each of the next 11 test triangles.
10 CM, 7.5 CM, 7.5 CM
CORRECT
4.2 CM, 6.9 CM, 4.2 CM
12 CM, 11 CM, 7.3 CM
Her performance certainly is terrific! I wonder why she looks annoyed.

CORRECT.
ARE THESE THE SIDE MEASURES OF AN **ISOSCELES TRIANGLE**?
(ANSWER YES OR NO.)
11 CM, 11 CM, 7.3 CM
Enough! I've got it! This is a stupid lesson ....
YES!
Wow, but she looks angry. Maybe the lesson was TOO easy for her. I should have taken that into account.

CORRECT.
ARE THESE THE SIDE MEASURES OF AN **ISOSCELES TRIANGLE**?
(ANSWER YES OR NO.)
5.6 CM, 5.6 CM, 5.6 CM
Another one of those tricky ones that Terminal doesn't understand. I know the answer should be "yes," but he'll accept only "no." Oh well, . . .
No
Great! She's got this one. I guess she now understands that an isosceles triangle must have two — but not three — sides with the same length. Still, I think my program needs some revision on that issue.

CORRECT.
THIS LESSON WAS ABOUT ISOSCELES TRIANGLES.
AN **ISOSCELES TRIANGLE** IS A TRIANGLE IN WHICH EXACTLY TWO SIDES HAVE THE SAME MEASURE.
At last it's over! What a bore. I hate math!

THE END

... but to what?

Post Mortem on "A Case of Terminal Instruction"

Although our tutorial program was a success (i.e., Estelle finally got the correct answer to each of C.R.T.'s questions), it's clear that the lesson to teach Estelle the concept of an isosceles triangle was a failure. Estelle's concept of an *isosceles triangle* includes any triangle with *at least two* sides of equal length; the concept of *isosceles* that C.R.T. was trying to communicate allowed only triangles with *exactly two* sides of equal length. Moreover, both Estelle and C.R.T. are deceived because each believes that Estelle has the correct concept of an isosceles triangle. Finally, Estelle left the lesson with a negative attitude because (a) she felt C.R.T. didn't understand the concept himself and (b) the large number of test triangles made the lesson boring. In short, the lesson was a disaster.

Blessed with the 20/20 hindsight provided by the "thoughts" of the participants in our little drama, how might we reprogram the teacher to do a better job? A number of ideas come to mind:

- Give more examples at the beginning.
- Allow the student to reexamine the examples at any time.
- Present the examples using drawings such as the following:

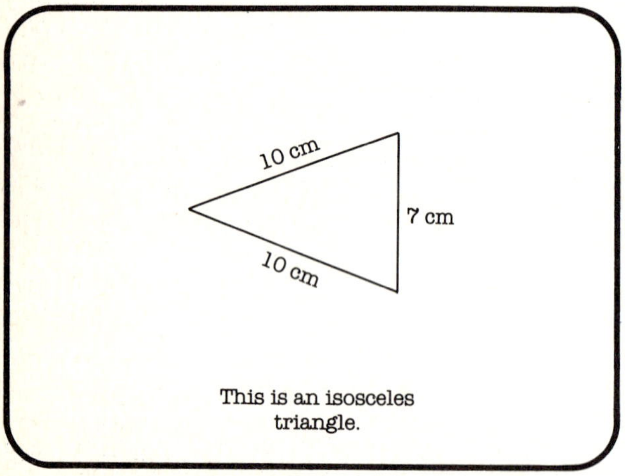

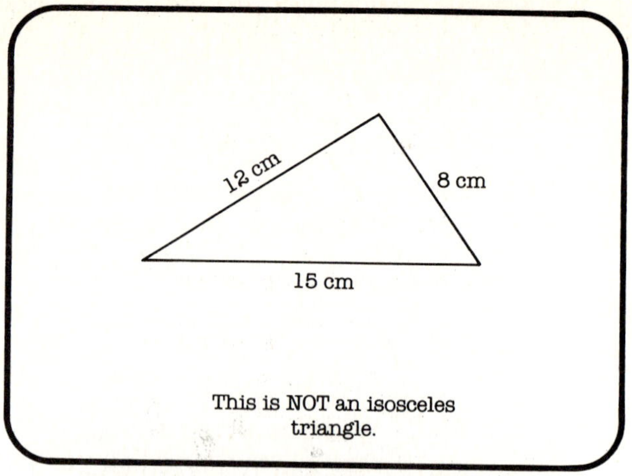

- Include a drawing in the feedback to an *incorrect* response. Thus, if a student responds that the lengths 12 CM, 8.3 CM, 8.4 CM define an isosceles triangle, the feedback (Feedback Message 1) would be:

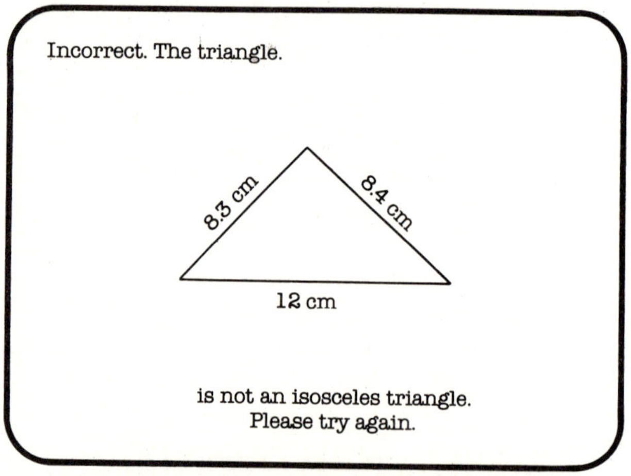

- Include a drawing of the triangle to accompany each *correct* response (in a manner similar to that used for incorrect responses).
- Provide a special feedback message for students who respond that a triangle with three equal side lengths is isosceles. Such a message might draw a picture of the triangle and say:

> This triangle has three sides of the same length. It is called an equilateral triangle. It is not an isosceles triangle.

- Include more special cases (equilateral triangles). At present, there are only two test triangles in this category. Make one out of every three to be of this type.
- Allow an "early exit" for a student who gives, say, six consecutive correct responses. Follow such a sequence with the item:

```
An isosceles triangle is a triangle which has
    1. Exactly two sides of the same length
    2. Exactly three sides of the same length
    3. At least two sides of the same length
    4. No two sides of the same length
Select one of the choices.
```

A correct response to this item would result in a jump to the lesson summary. An incorrect response would result in the presentation of more test triangles.

The suggested revisions use a form of communication (drawings) which was ignored by our original program. The revised program gives more detailed feedback, provides special attention to the problem of discriminating equilateral triangles from isosceles triangles, and provides an early exit to avoid boredom. Finally, rather than just stating the summary generalization, it asks the student to identify the condition of that generalization. In summary, the revised program is more interactive—more of a dialogue—and makes better use of the total communication capability of "old C.R.T.," our computer-like pedagogue.

A Thought About Reflections

In our cartoon simulation, we tried to get inside the "head" of a computer that is trying to act as a tutor. Our method was to imagine how a teacher would act—or be prevented from acting—if trying to conduct a tutorial lesson under some of the constraints which govern a computer.

We gave ourselves license to permit C.R.T. to see the expressions on Estelle's face and to reflect upon their meaning (as well as the possible reasoning behind her responses). As a consequence, we got some notion of both C.R.T.'s frustration and his error of interpretation. It ends with C.R.T., like any good teacher, realizing that his program (lesson plan) needs reworking and eager to get on with such reworking. *C.R.T. has learned something himself and wants to take action on that knowledge.*

It is the italicized sentence above which makes a fairy tale of our story of Estelle and C.R.T. In the real world of computerized tutorials, computers DON'T recognize errors in their own instructional procedures and DON'T give a hoot what Estelle thinks or feels. Generally speaking, computers are not equipped to *learn;*[7] hence, a computer acting as a tutor will display thoughtfulness and adaptability only insofar as the program designer has anticipated and explicitly planned for a wide range of student responses and thought patterns. Since we've defined a tutorial lesson to be a dialogue between *two learners,* the computerized tutorial has an obvious handicap. Still, useful approximations of tutorial sessions are possible on the computer if one understands the characteristics of a tutorial session and accepts the computer's limitations in dealing with them. The remainder of this chapter will explore those characteristics.

Our Role as Idealists

Any examination of computer lessons billed as *tutorial* will reveal a range of basic designs and specific features. Some authors, through their programming examples, define the tutorial style of instruction to be sequences of questioning episodes interspersed with blocks of text; the computer addresses the student by alternately giving information and asking questions about it. Examples of more elaborate refinements of computerized tutorials include provision for making adjustments in the level of difficulty of the questions asked and for defining terms or explaining phrases whenever requested by the student. Features such as these expand the tutorial to accommodate individual differences among the learners.

This discussion of computerized tutorials is admittedly idealized in terms of its overall expectations. We do not mean to present our description of a two-learner tutorial as the only truth. Rather, it is offered as a model against which one can compare and contrast a variety of sample lessons and can eventually come to a personal position regarding what does or does not constitute a computerized tutorial lesson. Idealism, then, serves a purpose: we're unlikely to get more than we

[7]Folks are working, however, to develop computerized "artificial intelligence." If a computer could be designed to exhibit artificial intelligence in the specific environment of conducting tutorials in, say, English language instruction for Spanish-speaking persons, its sessions would be indistinguishable from those of a master teacher. For a peek into the world of such dream machines, try "Artificial Intelligence—The Second Computer Age Begins" in *Business Week,* March 8, 1982, pp. 66–75.

request of those who design computerized tutorials. But let's not kid ourselves. Sanity demands that we also recognize that we're unlikely to get all that we request.

The Ultimate in Questioning Episodes

Recall that a questioning episode is composed of many elements in addition to a question or eliciting statement. Among these elements are replies to and reinforcement of correct responses, acceptance of alternate correct responses, suggestions to the student regarding the modification of conceptually correct but technically incorrect responses, feedback aimed at correcting errors in thinking which lead to certain predictable incorrect responses, and directions on how to proceed or to seek help in dealing with incorrect responses for which no specific correcting feedback has been provided or with responses which are wholly unexpected (i.e., which cannot be interpreted by the program). In a tutorial lesson, these elements must be greatly refined since the dominant characteristic of a tutorial program is its ability to give meaningful treatment to unexpected events.

There are several conditions which might cause a student to give an unexpected response.

- The question might be too difficult for the student at this particular time.
- The question might be meaningless because of unfamiliar words.
- The question might have more than one possible meaning because of "ambiguous" words.
- The question might have more than one possible interpretation because of imprecise phrasing.
- The student might be bored or tired.
- The student might be in a state of depression or excitement which diverts attention from the lesson.
- The material being taught might conflict with earlier learning.
- If the lesson involves social issues, the student might not accept the author's principles.

A master teacher senses when such conditions are affecting a lesson and takes immediate appropriate action. The designer of a computerized tutorial must try to replicate the teacher's behavior in the absence of actual contact with each of the several learners who will eventually provide cues to what condition is affecting their response.

Master Teachers Never Make Mistakes

You may have noticed an earlier assertion that the big issue in constructing computerized tutorials is "to give meaningful treatment to unexpected events." Perhaps you interpreted this to mean that the designer must try to minimize (or, ideally, to eliminate) unexpected events. After all, shouldn't the performance of a master teacher be characterized by the reduction—if not total elimination—of unexpected events? The solution seems obvious enough:

PLAN AHEAD

What we would expect of a master teacher is the ability to implement that obvious solution.

In fact, the master teacher does seem to experience few unexpected events during efforts to facilitate learning. However skillful the teacher may be in minimizing the occurrence of such events, the unexpected never really disappears—and it is the meaningful treatment of this residue which distinguishes the master teacher or the well-designed computerized tutorial.

Educators still know too little about the details of the learning act to make reliable predictions of learner behavior across all instructional settings and subject areas. Our mythical master teacher seems to mix together theory, experience, and a touch of clairvoyance in a potent brew that can be applied to the treatment of rare and subtle examples of unexpected events. To wit, the teacher learns from experience. In computerized tutorials, we attempt to simulate this artistic mastery through ever-increasing provisions for treating less predictable events and through more sophisticated procedures for using student input to identify the sources of events still classified as unpredictable.

Looking Before and After an "Inductive Leap"

Great lecturers are gifted with the talents of organizing and delivering information in an expository manner. Aided, perhaps, by animation or graphics, these talking books have perfected a style of presentation in which the learner/listener is overtly passive.

Great tutors demand that the learner be overtly active in a presentation. Socrates, for instance, is reputed to have taught by questioning his students. Each new question was a function of a student's earlier response, and the entire network of questions being guided by a predetermined strategy.

Like a dialogue with Socrates, a tutorial lesson is a network of questioning episodes which is constructed with a particular strategy in mind. In the early part of a tutorial lesson, the goal of the strategy employed may be to make the student *nonverbally aware* of a particular concept. The lesson focuses upon developing the student's ability to do something and does not call upon the student to *explain* any rules that he or she follows in order to generate correct responses. For example, an initial strategy for developing the concept of multiplication of integers would be judged successful if the student eventually demonstrated the ability to consistently give correct responses to items such as the following:

$$+3 \times -9 = ?$$
$$-6 \times -7 = ?$$
$$+5 \times +8 = ?$$
$$-4 \times +7 = ?$$
$$-2 \times 0 = ?$$

The strategy which has produced this result would not seek, however, to develop the student's ability to articulate the rules which govern his or her responses.

The success of the strategy that leads the student to the nonverbal awareness of a concept requires the teacher's careful attention to the content, ordering, and response provisions of the questioning episodes. However, the teacher does not present the student with rules for generating correct responses; neither is the student called upon to express verbally any generalizations he or she might be using to generate correct responses. Thus the strategy may take the form of a mix of examples and counterexamples of the concept. (This was the strategy employed by C.R.T. in teaching Estelle the concept of an isosceles triangle.) The examples, through their common elements, present a basis for a general concept. The counterexamples, through contrast with the examples, serve to bound and quantify the concept. Student responses to carefully designed and selected questions or exercises can then be used to reveal the emergence of the student's awareness of the concept. (Estelle's responses to the sixteen questions about triangles are a case in point.)

As a teacher-led tutorial lesson proceeds, a point is reached at which the pattern of student responses suggests that he or she grasps the concept. When this occurs, the questioning may take a different turn. (C.R.T. was unable to change direction. He just kept presenting more questions involving the sixteen triangles.) Whereas before, the questioning was aimed at creating and shaping the concept, it now may focus on asking the student to explain or justify the responses given. The change in questioning seeks to verify that the student has made a correct inductive leap from a series of examples of a concept to the generalized concept itself.

In a computerized tutorial, the program must be prepared to recognize a probable instance of an inductive leap. That is, the computer must be prepared to identify the point at which to make the transition from questioning directed at building the awareness of a concept to questioning directed at verifying the correctness of the concept which has been induced. To delay this transition can produce student frustration or boredom. (Remember Estelle!) Failure to ask the second type of question may cause the tutor to misinterpret the pattern of the student's answers to the first type of question. The student can produce correct answers to the awareness-building questions and yet have arrived at an incorrect generalization. (Again, remember Estelle.) And should the transition reveal that the student has not made the *desired* inductive leap, the computer must be equipped with some looping or recovery strategy which will refocus the lesson on correcting the student's conception.

Taking Consideration Into Consideration

The master teacher is a sensitive and considerate soul. Apart from providing the student with daily food for thought, he or she keeps in touch with the student's mental and physical states. If the student needs release from the intense demands of a tutorial lesson, the teacher can provide release. If the student feels in need of a special resource, the teacher can judge the appropriateness of providing that resource and can supply it whenever justified.

The computer is unable to see or hear the cues which teachers use to assess a student's physical or emotional condition. The student's voice tones, squirmings, and facial expressions are valuable educational input which are lost to the computer. On the other hand, the lesson designer can make sensible estimates about lesson lengths, can use natural breaks in a lesson as opportunities to let the student interrupt the lesson, can use a cluster of incorrect responses as a reason to offer the student the choice of trying another lesson or of ending the session, and can provide standard procedures which allow a student to withdraw from a lesson at any point without losing credit for portions of the lesson which have been completed.

The design of a computerized tutorial should provide for the use of references (glossaries, indices, maps, calculators, tables, etc.) deemed appropriate for a group of students. Some of these resources might be made available as integral parts of the computerized tutorial in the form of subprograms which a student can call up in a simple manner at any time during the tutorial. The availability of such resources and procedures for using them (whether they be computer programs or materials external to the program) should be a standard feature of every computerized tutorial.

When Experience Is Not a Teacher

The present state of the art of computerized tutorials makes no provision for the computer to learn from the experience of interacting with students. The computerized tutorial is forced to operate from the same decision base each time it presents a lesson to a student. It cannot make variations in execution based on past and present decisions.

Learning from experience is fundamental to good teaching, but it is an attribute which may prevent computerized tutorial simulation for some time to come. What is needed, of course, is a tutorial program which somehow "learns" each time it issues a decision and experiences (through student responses) the results of that decision. Such a tutorial program would include, at each decision point, an internal list of possible actions to be taken by the computer. Each item of the list would be associated with a measure of the instructional success resulting from past selections of that action. In fact, teachers employ a similar procedure. However, while their decisions are usually based upon intuitions arising from complex interactions with students, the computer's decisions must be guided by quantified experiences. For each possible action, this quantification might take the form of mathematical probabilities derived from previous selection of that action. Suppose, for example, that a student has responded to several questions regarding the principle of governmental checks and balances established by the Constitution. Suppose further that the student's responses reveal a lack of mastery of the topic. The computer might then select from among such actions as the following:

- Present additional questioning episodes at the current level.
- Move to a different level of instruction.
- Suggest a break in instruction and/or move temporarily to a different topic.
- Prescribe a noncomputerized instructional resource.

Each action would be attached to a mathematical probability that the student will be successful when next questioned about the principle of checks and balances.

Computer programs have been built to play games in such a way that the program retains, and subsequently uses, the results of past choices made at each decision point. While the success of such activity is of interest to those who pursue the elusive computerized tutorial, it should be noted that a game environment differs markedly from a tutorial environment. A game, by its very nature, operates in an environment which is clearly defined by a relatively small set of rules and by a scenario that establishes the context within which play will be developed. The context may be of immediate or distant relevance to everyday activities of the average citizen or to a specific area of employment. The context of some games, while well defined, may have no obvious connection with reality. In every game, however, both rules and context set absolute boundaries for participation. By contrast, the rules of a tutorial environment are often large in number, the context is often vaguely defined, and both rules and context are usually open to change.

Other chapters will contain discussions of specific principles which one can apply when constructing or evaluating a particular kind of instructional computer program (drill, practice, testing, management, simulation, etc.). The topic of computerized tutorials, however, is fraught with problems to which dedicated lesson designers have as yet found no quality solutions. One can't build sensible programming prescriptions on a foundation of "ifs," "sometimes," "maybes," and "?s."

For the moment, significant efforts in constructing computerized tutorials are being made by a small but growing group of instructional designers who have personally assimilated the intricacies of this style of teaching. Their work improves through trials and thoughtful revisions. As gross oversights are corrected, use of the programs will serve to reveal those subtle turns in the teaching act which the master teacher negotiates with unconscious ease.

Some Good News: Lesson Authoring Systems

It might seem that those of us who are interested in computerized tutorials are caught between the Scylla of complex programming based upon as yet unestablished principles and the Charybdis of awaiting the development of computerized artificial intelligence. Not so. There is a broad and promising middle ground inhabited by user-friendly programs called *lesson authoring systems,* (or sometimes, *lesson drivers).* A *lesson authoring system* is an interrelated collection of computer programs which allows the nonprogrammer to create, view, modify, and gather student data (including student comments and reactions) on computerized lessons. In short, a lesson authoring system is *a computer program which writes computer programs!*

With the aid of a lesson authoring system, a teacher who has no knowledge of programming could create a computerized tutorial lesson, drill lesson, practice lesson, or simulation. Use of a lesson authoring system requires only that the teacher who designs a given lesson have subject matter expertise in the area of instruction. The system guides the construction of the lesson by *prompts* which request the subject matter information needed. In fact, the teacher can write this information on paper forms and have the actual computer entry done efficiently by a skilled typist.

Lesson authoring systems come in two forms which we'll denote by the words *fixed* and *adaptive.* A *fixed* system is restricted to designing a particular type of lesson (say, tutorial); a different fixed system is needed for other types of lessons (drill, simulation, etc.). The format in which the lesson is displayed and the student data which is gathered by a fixed system is predetermined and cannot be altered by the teacher. A single *adaptive* lesson authoring system, on the other hand, will permit the construction of several different types of instructional programs. It offers a variety of "stock" formats or will even permit the teacher to design the lesson format. Fixed systems are already in use on large computer systems; their modification for use on smaller computer systems is under way. Adaptive systems, because of their size and complexity, are still in the experimental stage and exist on large computer systems only.

To get an idea of how a lesson authoring system works, consider Figure 6.1. Each box in that diagram represents a computerized component of the system having a specific role to play in the total lesson authoring process. The Lesson Editor is a program which is accessible only to the teacher (or clerk). Guarded by passwords, it presents the teacher with four options.

1. To create a lesson
   Under this option, the Lesson Editor asks the teacher questions which give the teacher the opportunity to select certain options of lesson design, to enter questions to be presented to the student (dichotomous-choice, multiple-choice, matching, or short-answer), to enter feedback messages, and to enter instructional text and graphics. The Lesson Editor also stores all the lesson material entered by the teacher in the Lesson Data File.
2. To view a lesson
   Once a lesson has been created, this option permits the teacher to go to the Lesson Driver and view the lesson as the student would see it.
3. To view/edit student data
   After the lesson has been used by students, the teacher uses this option to view the results of their performance and to read any comments (memoranda to the lesson author) recorded in the Student Data File. The teacher then may edit the Student Data File by erasing the data stored there.
4. To edit a lesson
   Having viewed a lesson and/or having considered the data stored in the Student Data File, the teacher may wish to make changes in (i.e., edit) that lesson. This option permits the author to make specific changes in the Lesson Data File without having to rewrite the entire lesson.

A student, again using a password, also can enter a lesson authoring system in order to execute a lesson created on it by the teacher. The student is taken directly to the Lesson Driver; additional passwords known only to the teacher bar access to the Lesson Editor. The Lesson Driver uses the teacher's input (stored in the Lesson Data File) to present a particular lesson to the student. It automatically gathers information about the student's performance on the lesson and permits the student to leave messages for the teacher whenever confusion or uncertainty warrant such action. Both performance data and comments are stored in the Student Data File for later viewing by the lesson's author.

While the lesson authoring system doesn't have the science-fiction-like appeal or broad significance of artificial intelligence, it is an *existing tool* for creating reasonably good computerized tutorials. It has the advantage of permitting any teacher to create tutorials directly (i.e., without the aid of a programmer). Because the actual entry of lesson material is carefully guided by the Lesson Editor, the skills of the teacher can be directed to lesson design while the mechanics of entry are carried out by a professional typist. But perhaps the most promising attribute of the lesson authoring system is that any improvement in the system's decision-making features results in an immediate improvement in every lesson generated by it. Thus, breakthroughs in the design of educationally sound lessons could be incorporated into individual lessons by simply changing the model lesson authoring system which generates them.

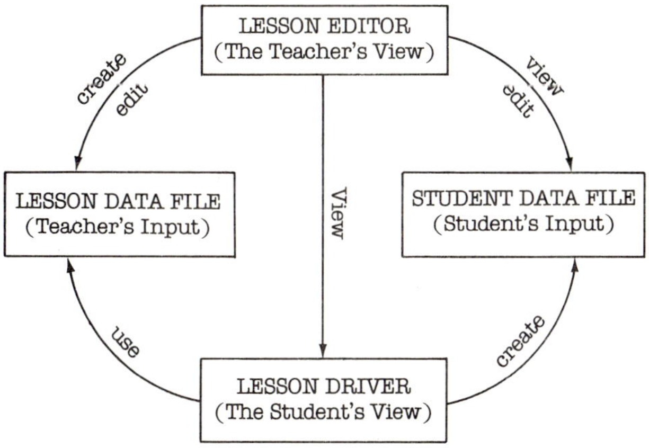

Figure 6.1
Lesson Authoring System

APPENDIX 1

PROGRAM SEQUENCE FOR A SIMULATED COMPUTERIZED TUTORIAL

1. PRESENT LESSON DESCRIPTION
   Display the Lesson Description.
2. PRESENT INSTRUCTION
   a. First describe four triangles which are isosceles triangles. (Example 1)
   b. Next describe four triangles which are NOT isosceles triangles. (Example 2)
3. PRESENT QUESTION
   a. Display the Question Stem.
   b. Display the description of one of the 16 Test Triangles. The Test Triangle Descriptions are presented one at a time with no repeats.
   c. Wait for the student to input a response.

4. JUDGE STUDENT RESPONSE
   a. If the response is not recognizable, give the System Message and await another response.
   b. If the response is incorrect, give Feedback Message 1 and await another response.
   c. If the response is correct, give Feedback Message 2. If there is another Test Triangle, go back to Step 3.
5. PRESENT LESSON SUMMARY
   When the last Test Triangle has been used, display the Lesson Summary.

APPENDIX 2

PROGRAM MEMORY FOR A SIMULATED COMPUTERIZED TUTORIAL

Lesson Description

There are many special classes of triangles. One class contains triangles called *isosceles*. This lesson will help you discover the definition of *isosceles triangle*.

Example 1

Here are the side measures of four triangles. Each is an *isosceles triangle*.

4 CM, 5 CM, 4 CM	8 CM, 9 CM, 9 CM
10 CM, 10 CM, 7 CM	6.9 CM, 4.3 CM, 6.9 CM

Example 2

Here are the side measures of four triangles. Each is *not* an *isosceles triangle*.

4 CM, 5 CM, 6CM	9 CM, 9 CM, 9 CM
15 CM, 12 CM, 8 CM	7.3 CM, 4.8 CM, 4.9 CM

Question Stem

Are these the side measures of an *isosceles triangle?* (Answer yes or no.)

Test Triangle Descriptions

4 CM, 11 CM, 8 CM	5 CM, 5.1 CM, 6 CM
6 CM, 6 CM, 3 CM	3.4 CM, 5 CM, 3.4 CM
7 CM, 7 CM, 7 CM	6.7 CM, 14 CM, 14 CM
20 CM, 13 CM, 20 CM	12 CM, 12 CM, 8.7 CM
8.4 CM, 5.3 CM, 6.4 CM	8.8 CM, 7 CM, 8.9 CM
9.3 CM, 2.4 CM, 9.3 CM	4.2 CM, 6.9 CM, 4.2 CM
10 CM, 7.5 CM, 7.5 CM	12 CM, 11 CM, 7.3 CM
12 CM, 8.3 CM, 8.4 CM	5.6 CM, 5.6 CM, 5.6 CM

System Message

Sorry. I don't understand. Please retype.

Feedback Message 1

Incorrect; please try again.

Feedback Message 2

Correct.

Lesson Summary

This lesson was about isosceles triangles.

An *isosceles triangle* is a triangle in which exactly two sides have the same measure.

APPENDIX 3

FLOW CHART FOR A SIMULATED COMPUTERIZED TUTORIAL

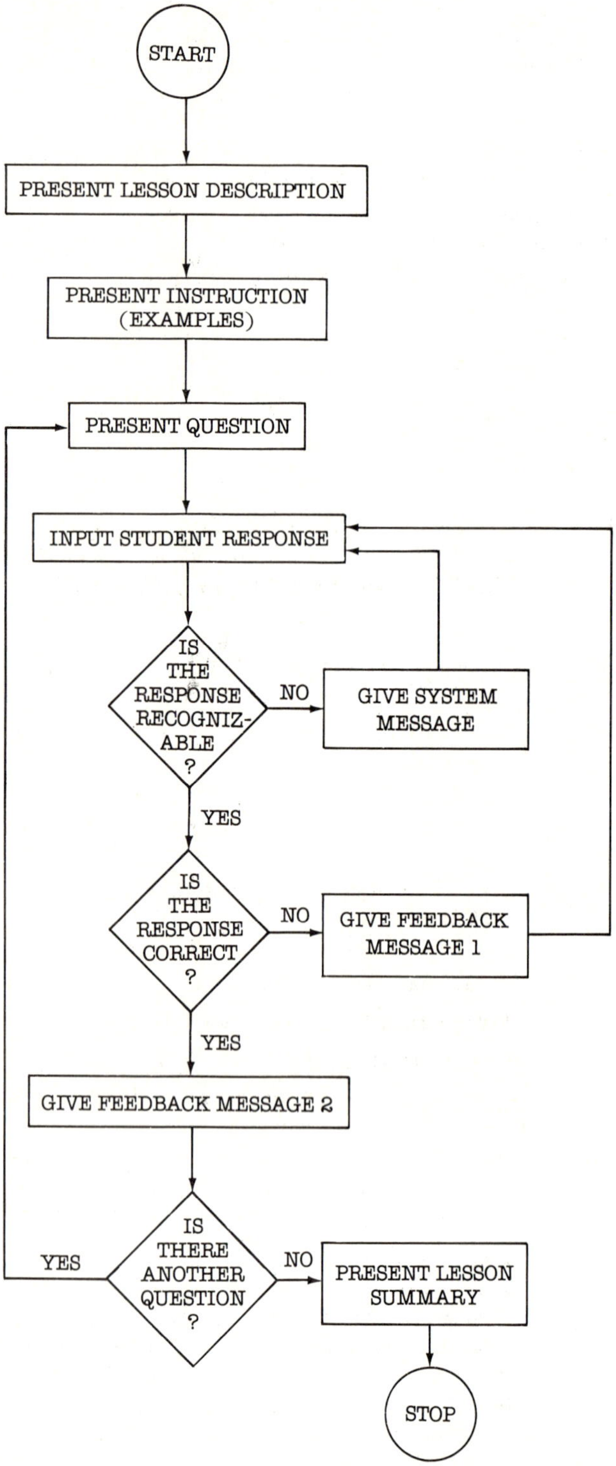

STUDY GUIDE: CHAPTER 6

1. Locate and execute a computer activity which purports to be tutorial in nature.
   a. To what extent does the lesson meet the standards for a tutorial which are outlined in Chapter 6?
   b. How, specifically, might the lesson be modified to better conform to the ideal of computerized tutorial instruction?
2. If your work on Exercise 5 of Chapter 4 involved the evaluation of a tutorial, reevaluate that same lesson and compare the two reviews.
3. Locate and execute another computer activity which purports to be tutorial in nature.
   a. Evaluate the lesson using the Checklist in Chapter 4.
   b. Summarize your evaluation using the Documentation Sheet in Chapter 4.
4. Guided by the flow chart in appendix 3 of this chapter, consider the general task of tutoring in your area of teaching interest. Develop an expanded flow chart which accounts for more extensive individual treatment of students. Include such considerations as exit procedures (voluntary or involuntary), responses to requests to rephrase a question, the use of graphics or sound (i.e., alternate forms of presentation), and HELP's available on request (both before a student inputs a response and after a student inputs an incorrect response).

AGENDA FOR ACTION

SCIENCE AND MATHEMATICS
TEACHING CENTER

ADDRESS REPLY TO WRITER

THE UNIVERSITY OF WYOMING
UNIVERSITY STATION, BOX 3992
LARAMIE, WYOMING, 82071

MEMORANDUM

TO: Members of ICAC

FROM: Dick Dennis and Bob Kansky

RE: ICAC Paper 6

DATE: January 21, 1983

The first of our four papers dealing with the applications of the computer in the role of a teacher will take a critical look at computerized tutorial lessons. We've placed it first for a very good reason. Just in case there are folks in East Roachmont who fear that the computer may replace the classroom teacher, ICAC Paper 6 should relieve them of their apprehensions!

Teaching with a computer does not mean that the computer will be used as an instructional resource to the exclusion of all other resources. (Would we be writing a book if we believed that?) As the various ICAC Papers will show, the computer will support, even change, the way we perform many components of the teaching act. The current quality of the aid or the new teaching opportunities that it offers the instructor varies with the nature of the component involved. In tutorial instruction, it faces its greatest challenge.

DD:BK:glm

Enclosure: ICAC Paper 6

AGENDA FOR ACTION

Obourn Senior High School

200 Woodbine Avenue
East Roachmont, New York

M. Jack Stivers
Principal

(716) 568-8840

ICAC Memo #6

TO: Members of ICAC

FROM: John Russell

DATE: February 2, 1983

Having read ICAC Paper 6, the committee is in unanimous agreement that (a) teachers need not rush off in search of alternate careers and (b) it would welcome an experience with even the crudest of lesson authoring systems.

1. Carrinne reports that the computer vendors initially expressed some concern with regard to loaning software to ICAC for viewing. (They fear that it might be copied.) Her being a member of the committee seems to have provided the necessary assurance of fair play, however.
2. Those who have viewed the borrowed tutorial lessons feel that there is a need for a lot of work in this area. Some lessons appeared to be computerized books (lots of text and no questions calling for student interaction); others seemed to be aimed at providing reinforcement of things that had been taught elsewhere.

COMMITTEE ASSIGNMENTS

1. There was group interest in seeing an improved "program" for C. R. Terminal's lesson, one which would make use of the improvements suggested in the "Post Mortem." Hence:
   (A) Phil and Gerri will first revise the flow chart of appendix 3 to ICAC Paper 6.
   (B) Based upon the new flow chart, Phil will prepare revised versions of both the Program Sequence (appendix 1) and the Program Memory (appendix 2).
   (C) Copies of the three new appendices will be distributed to all committee members at our next meeting.
   (D) John will execute a noncomputerized version of the revised program with his algebra I class. He'll play the part of C. R. Terminal, and individual students will replace Estelle. He'll use the whole class to review the lesson and to discuss the "problems" of communicating with a computer. He thinks it will be a useful lesson on computer literacy (for all concerned).
2. Ted and Jeanne are going to design and execute a similar computer literacy lesson in which they will try to teach the concept *peninsula*. They will prepare overhead transparencies (examples of peninsulas and test items on peninsulas) to allow "graphic displays" by C. R. Terminal. (NOTE: John will try the same technique in presenting triangles.) Jeanne will try to get one of the presentations recorded on videotape for later viewing by anyone who's interested and so that she can evaluate the lesson herself.
3. ICAC members are reminded that some tutorials are available for viewing on John's machine (for the next 12 days).

JR:ms

CHAPTER SEVEN

Play It Again, Sam: Drill or Practice on the Computer

When we think of drill or practice, one thing comes to mind—boredom. Drill or practice is to our educational experience what the American grain belt is to a cross-country drive: one has to force consciousness while in the midst of either. On the one hand, we admit the value of each; on the other, we plan life's journeys so that we have only necessary contact with either.

The purpose of this paper is to show that the computer has the capacity to make drill or practice intellectually palatable and nutritious. In doing so, we'll go beyond the common techniques of sugarcoating the drill pill by having the computer react to correct student input with monotonous displays of "smiley faces," whistles, bells, or flashing lights. True, drill or practice exercises shouldn't leave a bad taste in the mouth, but neither should they rot the mind with bells-and-whistles technology.

It's unlikely that one will be asked for the recipe to a dish that no one else has ever sampled. Requests are even less likely when a known version of the dish is widely reputed to deserve a five-yech rating. We'll start, then, by offering you a sample of the computer's wares in the area of drill or practice; then we'll tell you what went into the recipe.

Note that what follows is an example—not a model—of drill or practice. A model exercise would precisely illustrate every characteristic of good drill or practice. Since, however, drill or practice is applied to a great variety of situations, it remains somewhat amorphous. It must be adapted to applications which range from spelling drill to practice in assembling a microcomputer. There is no model which will cover every situation, so we'll settle for an (imperfect) example which reveals major features of this mode of instructional computing as applied to a rather simple drill task. Well . . . it seemed simple when we started it, anyway.

A Curricular Home for Drill or Practice

Before beginning the creation of this academic delight, let's pause a moment to ponder the general task which sends us to our computerized kitchen. Specifically, we want to consider the proper place of drill or practice within the total process of instruction. Also, there's a reason to restate the difference between drill and practice.

The use of a drill or practice activity must be a conscious decision which recognizes the proper role of such activities. The general rule is that the application of drill or practice to the learning of a given topic *assumes previous instruction in that topic.* A drill or practice activity serves to fix some association or to refine some skill. It is *not* the function of drill or practice to motivate, explain, justify, or expand upon an idea. For example, the proper goal of drill on the basic facts of multiplication is the correct and speedy recall of such associations as those between the number 24 and any one of the following expressions:

1×24	2×12	3×8	4×6
6×4	8×3	12×2	24×1

On the other hand, it is not to be expected that the best such drill episode will lend the least bit of credence to the assertion $8 \times 3 = 24$ or to present any rational case against $7 \times 9 = 72$.

The reason that the claim $7 \times 9 = 63$ will bring one rewards of praise or jellybeans, whereas $7 \times 9 = 72$ is met by exasperated looks and threats of more drill is nowhere to be found in a drill activity. However, *such justification is required before the drill activity* if the activity is to promote meaningful habituation. Stimulus-response associations or complex rules which are unsupported by some rationalization are frustrating to commit to memory and are easily forgotten. For this reason, the mathematics teacher may use buttons or pictures to convince a child that *63* is a good name for 7×9, whereas *72* is not. Moreover, having convinced the student of such great truths, the mathematics teacher must further persuade the student that the effort to commit such simple facts to memory will pay large future dividends. Clearly, carrying around enough buttons to solve 279×97 will strain both mind and pocket. Similarly, the French teacher, having provided motivation by dangling a trip to Paris before reluctant scholars, also must provide rationalization of the word associations to be memorized by presenting historical or etymological bases for those associations.

One last consideration before turning to the example promised: that is to remind you that the disjunction in "drill *or* practice" was put there with purpose aforethought. Although related to it by a common goal—to fix concepts previously learned—*drill* is not synonymous with *practice*. Thus, the word *drill* will be used to describe activities which seek to fix simple associations such as the names and symbols of the chemical elements. The object of a *practice* activity, on the other hand, will be the smooth execution of some process or procedure such as the assembling of a desk telephone. The example which follows is a drill activity.

Author! Author!: An Example of Computerized Drill

Ever hear of a fellow with the last name Darwin? Right, I mean the one who drifted around the world aboard the good ship *HMS Beagle* while collecting bits and pieces of plant and animal life. Of course, most folks remember Charles Darwin more for his pen than for his sailing adventures. In fact, the association between the surname Darwin and the book title *The Origin of Species* is so strong that most people would be surprised to learn that Charles Darwin wrote anything else. (He did.)

Darwin has another distinction. He belongs to a rather exclusive group of authors each of whom is remembered by the general public for a single book. In fact, some of these persons wrote many other things—yet the name of each is bound to a single book by steel chains. Interesting? Some people think so.

Let's imagine an English class in which the students have become fascinated (at the command of the instructor, perhaps) by the membership list of this Single-Book Authors Club. This bizarre interest finally is expressed as a determination to memorize a selected group of such authors (and the book title associated with each). Certainly, this will be a valued skill at some future social gathering of trivia buffs. To help the class realize its noble goal, we will design an appropriate computerized drill activity. Looking ahead, we find that we're faced with a nine-step task. Numbering those steps may prove useful.

Step 1: Defining the Purpose of the Activity

Done. We've already determined to fix the associations between (a) the names of authors whose public fame commonly rests on a single book and (b) the titles of the books which are those authors' claims to fame. Our motivation is the sheer joy of being able to spout academic nonsense. Such being the case, an exhaustive list of such associations is unnecessary; we'll settle for a representative handful.

Step 2: Specifying the Stimulus-Response Set

Having scanned the Single-Book Authors Club membership list, we decide on the following selections:

Single-Book Authors List

Author's Surname	Book Title
Baum	The Wonderful Wizard of Oz
Darwin	The Origin of Species
Euclid	The Elements
Hitler	Mein Kampf
Machiavelli	The Prince
Milne	Winnie the Pooh
Mitchell	Gone with the Wind
Plato	The Republic
Shelley	Frankenstein
Smith	An Inquiry into the Nature and Causes of the Wealth of Nations

Because the associations are to be made within the context of the single-book game, we settle for author *surnames* (rather than full names). We also look ahead to the dramatic impact that this surname-only decision will bring about when we later apply our knowledge. Imagine how astounded (properly) bystanders will be when a coconspirator in this little game asks, "What *was* the name of the book that that woman Shelley wrote?" and you nonchalantly reply, "*Frankenstein,* of course." Giving her entire name might provide sufficient stimulus to evoke the correct response from an outsider.

Step 3: Choosing the Type of Question

The activity involves the presentation of several questioning episodes. Construction of such episodes begins with the selection of the type of question from among those discussed in Chapter 5. The possibilities are dichotomous-choice, multiple-choice, matching, interpretive, short-answer, and essay.

Our list immediately suggests the use of a matching type of question format. On second thought, however, we note that such a style is suited to *recognizing* stimulus-response (i.e., author-title) pairs. By contrast, our anticipated use of the information will be in situations (parties) where we will have to *construct and report* one member of the pair. With that in mind, we opt for the short-answer type of question.

Step 4: Developing an Item-Presentation Style

Since associations are best learned by engaging in short drill sessions spread over time, we'll be revisiting our computer exercise several times. It would be a pity if every session looked like every other session. Certainly there is no good reason to present the questions in a single order based upon the alphabetical listing of authors. We resolve that the computer should place the list of pairs in random order at the start of each session.

Also, we don't want to be restricted to using an author's name for the stimulus. Given a book title, we want to be able to produce the surname of the author; given an author's surname, we should be able to recall the associated book title. To ensure this two-way bond, the computer should make an arbitrary decision between one of two question stems each time it presents an item. Thus, if the item is to involve Machiavelli, these two stimuli should be equally likely.

Form A: What is the title of the book for which Machiavelli is best known?

Form B: What is the surname of the author of *The Prince?*

Since Form A can be used with any author-title pair in our list by simply replacing *Machiavelli* by another author's name, the stem is a useful template for every association in the list. Form B also qualifies as a template in which *The Prince* can be replaced by any other title in our list. Computers thrive on this kind of regularity.

Step 5: Setting the Restrictions on Student Input

Students will be expected to type their responses. This form of input gives rise to two questions: (1) "Do spelling and capitalization count?" and (2) "Is it necessary to give every word of the book title?"

First we consider those cases which use Form A of the question stem. The student must type a title. If our computer is equipped with spelling-judging and capitalization-judging abilities, we'll use it to call the student's attention to any misspelled word or capitalization error. We'll insist that each such word be retyped with the correct spelling and capitalization before accepting the response as an answer. (After all, this is an activity for an *English* class!) On the other hand, if spelling and/or capitalization are the only problems with a given response, we will count the response as correct when the spelling and capitalization have been brought up to snuff. (After all, this whole exercise is just for fun!) If our computer also has the answer-judging capability to search for key words in a response and/or to cope with alternate forms of a response, we won't be fussy about full titles or underlining. Thus, *The Wizard of Oz, Origin of Species,* and *Wealth of Nations* would be acceptable responses.

When the item is presented using Form B of the stem, an author's surname is the required input. Since, after all, these are famous authors, the student should have the common decency to spell and capitalize their surnames correctly! It's decided: capitalization and correct spelling of surnames are prerequisites to acceptance.

Having set our restrictions regarding student input, we need to inform the student of the rules. One possibility would be to alter the two question templates so as to produce these examples.

```
Form A′: What is the title (approximate) of the book
         for which Milne is best known?
         (NOTE: Spelling and capitalization count!
                Underlining is optional.)
Form B′: What is the surname of the author of Winnie
         the Pooh?
         (NOTE: Spelling and capitalization count!)
```

Step 6: Providing Prompts (Cues)

There's nothing wrong with helping a student to get the correct response so long as the method of presenting prompts (cues) doesn't make the association dependent upon the prompt. Ideally, prompting should be under the control of the learner; that is, help should be available to but not forced upon the learner. One could even conceive of situations in which all such help might be withdrawn after some predetermined initial period.

In the case of our single-book authors example, let's provide a three-level student-initiated help sequence. Each presentation of a question will be accompanied by the following display near the bottom of the screen:

```
HELP available.
    PRESS 1 to learn number of words (in a book title)
            or letters (in a name).
    PRESS 2 to have each letter of the correct re-
            sponse shown as a dash.
  Any use of HELP is counted as an incorrect response.
```

If the question were:

```
What is the title (approximate) of the book for
which Mitchell is best known?
(NOTE: Spelling and capitalization count! Under-
lining is optional.)
```

pressing the key *1* would generate the cue

```
4 words
```

If this doesn't do the trick, the student could press *2* to get:

```
        ----  ----  ---  ----
HELP available.
    PRESS 3 to see some letters in the answer.
```

As a response to the student pressing *3,* the computer would randomly select, say, 20 percent of the initial number of dashes for replacement by the corresponding letters. For the question given, successive presses of *3* could generate the following displays.

```
----  W___  __e  _i_
----  W___  _he  _ind
G__e  W__h  _he  _ind
G_ne  Wi_h  _he  Wind
Gone  With  the  Wind
```

Before going on to the next question, the student will be required to type the correct response. As indicated in the earlier display, however, the student's use of the HELP option means that his response will be counted as a miss.

Step 7: Providing Feedback Messages

Specific feedback to student input is an important element of any questioning episode. When a student inputs a correct response, feedback should be provided to verify the response. In the case of incorrect student input, feedback should provide information which acts to correct errors in the student's thinking.

The feedback message for correct responses in our lesson on authors could be very simple. After all, the total task of the feedback is to affirm a correct association.[1] Just to be fancy, however, we'll have the computer *occasionally* supplement that verification with social comments intended to make the learner feel good about his or her work. Such comments, sometimes called *social evaluative feedback,* may take the form of positive remarks drawn at random from a pool of fifteen, including such gems as

That's close enough for government work.
Correctamundo!
You're good, you know.
Another good guess!
You're doing just great.
Keep up the good work.
By George, you got it!
Such a prodigious memory....
Wunnerful... wunnerful.

We'll have the computer add such a remark to the OK on an average of every fourth item. If used more often, the social evaluative remarks might be seen as ceremonial; used occasionally, they add some variety and call attention to correct responses.

Corrective feedback to incorrect responses must go beyond a mere *no* or *wrong.* In addition to enforcing spelling and capitalization as called for earlier, we'll want the computer to provide two additional bits of information.

First, the computer should state the correct response. Depending upon the form of the question, it should generate a Form A′ message like:

The correct title is:
Frankenstein

or a Form B′ message like:

The author's surname is:
Shelley

In either case, the student will be required to input the correct response before seeing the next question.

Second, we note that there are some "similar" pairs among the elements of our stimulus-response set. For instance, two pairs involve children's fantasy, three pairs involve two-word titles in which the first word is *The,* and two pairs involve ancient Greek authors. Little tricks used to aid in remembering an association may actually add confusion to the situation and create an *in-list error,* an error in which the student's response is *in the list* of target responses but properly should be associated with a different stimulus. To counter this problem, the computer will provide "discrimination feedback." If, for example, the student responds *Plato* when the correct answer is *Euclid,* the feedback message would be

No.
<u>The Elements</u> should be associated with the author
Euclid.
Plato (your response) wrote <u>The Republic.</u>

Had the student made his error on the alternate question form for the same association, the feedback message might be

No.
Euclid wrote <u>The Elements.</u>
<u>The Republic</u> (your response) was written by Plato.

Following this corrective feedback, the computer would immediately present the two items which the student had confused.

Step 8: Recycling the Questions

Clearly, some of the author-title associations will be easier to recall than will others. The ease with which one of us will remember a given association may depend upon personal history—e.g., whether your parents chose your bedtime stories from *The Wonderful Wizard of Oz* (as did mine) or from *The Prince.* It follows that we'll want the computer to desist quickly from presenting items about the associations that we know and to concentrate on presenting the items that we find hard to remember. What we need to do is to give the computer our rules for a procedure which will recycle the questions in such a way that (a) the items we find easy to recall are soon deleted from the cycle and (b) the difficult items are represented frequently in accord with some rule that the computer can follow.

[1]If the items required deductive reasoning or the correct processing of data, we might want to provide feedback messages that not only verify the result but also review a correct line of reasoning which would yield that result.

To get a grip on what would constitute a good recycling plan, it helps to step out of the wondrous world of computers and back into the primitive world of paper and pencil. Specifically, let's consider how we might conduct our little drill exercises by using flash cards. Here goes.

1. Get 10 index cards.
2. On a given card, write an author's name (e.g., Hitler) on one side and the corresponding book title *(Mein Kampf)* on the other.
3. Shuffle the deck of 10 cards.
4. Take the *top* card from the deck and hold it so that the learner can see what's written on one side. If the learner correctly states what's written on the other side of the card, reverse the card and place it on the *bottom* of the deck. Somehow remember that the learner has made one correct response to that author-title pair. Continue through the deck.
5. Each time the learner misses an association, we'll make certain that the troublesome card is presented three extra times in a scheduled manner. The schedule we'll use will follow a 2–3–4 sequence. That is, we'll put the missed card just behind the next card in the deck, making it the second item to be presented. If the learner gets the association right that time, we'll place it in the third position back. If its next appearance brings a correct response, we'll put it into the fourth position back. If the learner gets that presentation correct, we'll move the item to the bottom of the deck. Of course, any error made during the 2–3–4 sequence will cause us to start still another 2–3–4 sequence with that card.

The memory task for the person presenting our flash cards is awesome! A few errors on the part of the learner, and the presenter finds himself faced with executing multiple (and overlapping) 2–3–4 sequences. Poor mortals that we are, perhaps we should abandon the whole idea of recycling.

Ah, but recall that it is a computer that will have to do all this reshuffling of items! Since two of the fundamental charms of a computer are its ability to recall accurately all manner of trivia and its willingness to pursue a mindless task with unflagging zeal, the recycling task we've described is made to order for computer execution. We will, therefore, insist that our author-title drill program have this recycling plan built into it. Having so decided, we transport ourselves out of the world of flash cards and back into the world of flashing lights.

Step 9: Terminating the Lesson

You may have detected a tiny flaw in our flash-card recycling plan—it never ends. That simply will not do. In fact, we want the lesson to systematically delete from our electronic flash-card deck those items that we have shown (through a sequence of correct responses) that we remember. Such a procedure will, in time, leave us with no cards in the deck—i.e., it will terminate the lesson. Also, it would be a good idea to plan for voluntary termination of the lesson in case the learner must leave before reaching a no-card situation. In short, we want the lesson to have procedures for both involuntary termination and voluntary termination.

- *Involuntary termination.* Each response to an item results in one of two things: (1) the author-title pair goes to the "bottom of the deck" following a correct response or (2) the author-title pair goes into a 2–3–4 recycling sequence following an incorrect response. To produce involuntary termination of the lesson, we must specify how many correct responses (i.e., trips to the bottom of the deck) will be equated with learning the pair. Specifically, let's set a learning criterion of three correct responses. Thus, the pair will be deleted from our deck after the third time that it is answered correctly outside a 2–3–4 corrective cycle.
- *Voluntary termination.* Should boredom set in or should other commitments demand our attention or call us elsewhere, we need a polite way to dismiss the computer from its task as drill master. Let's agree that typing the response *bye-bye* to any question will signal our desire to terminate the program voluntarily. Upon receiving that signal response, the computer will terminate the lesson and respond "See you later."

PS-RSQ-TSI-PSS-IRPFMQRTP

And so we come to the end of our example of computerized drill. Although many of the decisions made during the discussion of the proposed computer program are peculiar to the general nature of the example (drill rather than practice) and details of the example itself (memorizing author-title pairs), the steps of the program design are common to all drill or practice programs. In building or evaluating any such lesson, then, we expect the resulting program to show evidence that each of the following design issues was considered.

1. Purpose
2. Stimulus-Response Set
3. Question-Type Selection
4. Item-Presentation Style
5. Student-Input Restrictions

6. Prompts
7. Feedback Messages
8. Question Recycling
9. Termination Procedures

The nine design issues are important enough to be given explicit attention whenever preparing or reviewing drill or practice lessons. You can keep them in mind by using the handy acronym

PS-RSQ-TSI-PSS-IRPFMQRTP

If you find the acronym unpleasant, you could design a computerized drill program to help you associate the number of each issue with the key words describing that issue. If that doesn't appeal to you, you might copy the list on a card and keep it nearby whenever you are working with drill or practice programs. Whatever your method for recalling the acronym, recall it you must. Drill or practice lessons may often lack panache, but each is obligated to have PS-RSQ-TSI-PSS-IRPFMQRTP.

A Broader View of PS-RSQ-TSI-PSS-IRPFMQRTP

Each of the nine steps in the development of the author-title drill called for decisions by the lesson designer. In some cases, the decision reflected the personal interests or purposes of the authors. Many, however, were guided by research-based principles.[2] We'll conclude this chapter by revealing those guiding principles and by noting how they might be applied in ways which were not appropriate to the example of drill (author-title) that we examined so minutely.

The titles of the following subsections should look familiar. No, we didn't run out of ideas for headings. Rather, the choice is designed to help you locate that part of the author-title example which illustrates the use of the principles to be presented.

Defining the Purpose of the Activity

Drill or practice activities serve to *reinforce* learning. Their use assumes that the associations to be memorized or the procedure to be perfected have taken on value within some broad educational context. Specifically, use of *drill* follows the establishment of a purpose for fixing some selected stimulus-response associations. *Practice* lessons, while they may include exercises which help to refine or extend the application of a procedure, *follow* instruction directed at demonstrating and rationalizing the procedure and/or attaching some significance to its use. On the other hand, it is not necessary for *every* procedure to be rationalized in terms of the theory which supports it. The personal significance attached to being able to execute the procedure followed in baking a great souffle can make the practice activity meaningful to the learner. Discussion of the chemistry which supports the successful procedure becomes unnecessary and, perhaps, counterproductive.

Specifying the Stimulus-Response Set

Drill lessons are used to assist in memorization, quick recall, or distinguishing among stimulus-response pairs. The set of such pairs may be both complete and mercifully short, as in the case of name-birthdate pairs of all American presidents. If the set of pairs is very long (as it would be if the name of each member of Congress were paired with the amount of his or her 1982 pretax income), it is likely that a subset of the pairings would suffice for whatever political purpose is to be served. The task of associating each English monarch with the name of each spouse introduces an additional complication because the stimulus-response set must contain all of the pairings appropriate to a given monarch. (Henry VIII, for instance, would require six pairings!)

Practice lessons, insofar as they consist of exercises in executing a procedure or in applying a combination of concepts to solve a problem, do not permit the listing of all stimulus-response pairs. The designer's task, then, is to identify exercises which include (a) experiences with common variations of the procedure being practiced or (b) representative examples of problems that might be solved with the aid of a given set of concepts. If a practice lesson in subtracting whole numbers doesn't include examples in which there are adjacent zeros in the minuend (e.g., 3004–219), practice in the use of a subtraction procedure may fall short of its purpose. Also, practice exercises in agricultural decision-making which inadvertently call for the application of only five of eight principles studied do not comprise an adequate stimulus-response set.

Choosing the Type of Question

The form of the question used in presenting a stimulus is, in part, a function of the general type of learning that was the object of the lesson which preceded the reinforcement (drill or practice) lesson. At least three types of learning—generalization, discrimination, and transfer—may be identified;[3] each has implications for question design.

[2]James T. Stewart, Drill and Practice on a Computer, Illinois Series on Educational Application of Computers, Paper 7e, (Urbana, IL: Department of Secondary Education of the University of Illinois, 1979), mimeographed.

[3]Lawrence M. Stolurow, "Theory of Feedback and Retention," *Journal of Educational Psychology* 67, no. 6 (December, 1975).

- *Generalization.* The learner is presented with sequences of associations in which the same response is to be made to different stimuli. For example, in teaching the generalization called *round,* the student would be presented with stimuli such as a pie plate, a Frisbee, a ring, a circle, and a ball; the student would be expected to respond to each with the word *round.*
- *Discrimination.* Here the learner is presented with sequences of associations in which different responses are to be made to different stimuli. Thus, discrimination between *round* and *not round* would call upon the learner to apply one of the two responses to stimuli which include triangles, squares, circles, cubes, spheres, and pyramids.
- *Transfer.* In this case, the learner is expected to respond by employing previously learned principles or procedures when presented with a stimulus which differs from that used at the time the principle or procedure was taught. A typical situation would be one in which the learner is asked to combine several separately taught skills to solve a problem.

The questions of a drill or practice lesson must be constructed to conform to the type of learning desired.

When instructional computing was just getting started, lessons required that students *construct* answers to the tasks presented. Lesson designers felt that the constructed response was necessary to show that learning had occurred, a feeling that was supported by research. However, later studies have suggested that response *recognition* in a selected-answer format such as multiple-choice also gives good results. The choice of effective format (constructed or selected answer) now appears to be linked to lesson content. That's worth examining.

Three factors appear to influence the effect of the response mode chosen for a lesson. First, the *completeness* of the item (stimulus) can make the two types of responses equally effective. This is the case when the item has enough prompts (cues) to give equal assurance of a correct response under either selection or construction. Second, the *difficulty* of the content is a significant influence, with the constructed response being more effective where highly technical material is involved. If the items involve nontechnical material, constructed responses and selected responses are equally appropriate. Finally, the student's overall familiarity with the material of the lesson interacts with the response type. The constructed response is more effective with material that is new (unfamiliar) to the student; the two modes are equally effective with familiar material.

Apart from the three factors just discussed, the selected response has two major advantages over the constructed response. Selecting responses saves time, and it can be used with those computers having limited answer-judging capabilities. In general, the total time that a student invests in a constructed-response task will be at least twice that invested in a corresponding selected-response task. This difference in total times is more than can be attributed to the extra typing effort required to input a constructed response; it suggests that the student spends more time in the actual processing of the material.

So what have we learned thus far from the investigations of those who research questioning? For one thing, we know it is important that the mode require the student to attend to the meaning of the response. If the student can answer a question without processing the information in the task, then the question style is ineffective. This seems obvious enough, and yet computerized lessons exist in which the answers follow a pattern that makes it possible for the learner to consistently make correct responses without processing the material of the stimuli. Also, it is generally the case that constructed response items and selected response items are equally effective with nontechnical or familiar material. New or technical material calls for constructed responses. Finally, the selected answer format is less time-consuming during execution. The resulting shorter lessons reduce student fatigue and allow more students to use a given computer facility.

In our Chapter 5 discussion of six types of questions, there are notes regarding the general types of learning situations in which each type is applicable. Since more than one type of question might be acceptable for a given drill or practice lesson, the final choice often involves such considerations as (1) the type of response which is most appropriate in situations in which the acquired skill will be applied, (2) input or answer-judging limitations of the computer to be used, (3) the specificity of the feedback to be provided, (4) the kind of decision making called for by the items, and (5) the range of responses that can be associated with a given stimulus.

Step 3 of our author-title exercise provided an example of the first of the five considerations listed above. In that example, we were led to the decision to employ short-answer questions rather than dichotomous-choice questions. The second consideration would force us to seek an alternative to short-answer questions if the computer's answer-judging capability did not permit the recognition of multiple forms of the correct answer or would reject a correct answer because of noncritical typing or spelling errors. The third consideration, specificity of feedback, is at issue when the items have predictable incorrect responses which correspond to identifiable errors in thinking. In such a case, the multiple-choice format provides a convenient way of shaping student thinking by providing analytical, factual, or prompting feedback messages which are specific to a given response.

The consideration of the kind of decision making called for can be justified by examining three different practice tasks. In the first task, students' opinions are pitted against author's opinions by using dichotomous-choice items. A second task calls for decision making in which the data provided may lead to any of several decisions; this calls for a multiple-choice format. In a third instance, decision making which calls upon the learner to use known principles to practice ordering steps in a process might best be handled by matching questions.

The fifth and final condition important in selecting the question type is the range of possible responses. If the lesson is to provide drill or practice on a topic for which the set of incorrect and/or acceptable responses is not well-defined, the short-answer form may be useful in identifying such responses. If the lesson calls for practice of discrimination skills (calling for the best response), multiple-choice items are indicated. If the task is to identify all possible responses that may be associated with a given stimulus, either multiple-choice or matching items may be appropriate.

The choice of the best type of item requires a good deal of thought about the student, the purpose of the lesson, the subject matter, and the capabilities of the computer system available. Although guidelines and examples have been given to raise pertinent issues and suggest alternatives, the number of variables involved places art above science in the selection process. In the end, the choice is limited by two simple rules. As you evaluate computerized lessons, you must judge whether these rules have been obeyed by the lesson author.

1. *Use only one type of item in a given drill or practice lesson.*[4] If the material to be reinforced is such that more than one type of item is required, create a separate lesson for each type of item (or break the single lesson into clearly defined sublessons).
2. *Take your time.*[5] The type of item selected is most important. Careful analysis and a little experimenting with students before lesson development will avoid the investment of resources in an unacceptable format.

[4]RULE: *To every rule there is an exception.* An exception to this rule is discussed under "A Matter of Confidence" in Chapter 5.

[5]This is a rule which is an exception to the rule in footnote 4. The take-your-time rule allows no exception.

Developing An Item-Presentation Style

The selection of the type of item, a task which may have at first appeared to be simple and objective, turned out to be a rather complex art. The matter of developing item-presentation style, on the other hand, is more a matter of science than of art. Development should follow two guidelines.

1. *The lesson should vary the entry point and the item sequence within the lesson.* Drill or practice is best done in several short sessions. If each such session begins with the same item and/or follows a single sequence of items, the task becomes stale; learning is replaced by the memorization of a sequence of responses. When a lesson consists of the presentation of all members of a single set of items, the order of presentation should be as varied as the topic permits. Better yet, the items making up a given session should be selected at random from a large pool of equivalent items. Where the capability of the computer permits, the student's exit point from a given session should be recorded and should be used to avoid needless repetition when the student begins a new session.
2. *The lesson should interchange stimuli and responses.* In Step 4 of our author-title example, a two-way bond within each author-title pair is supported by the random selection of one of two item stems. The one stem names an author and asks for a book title; the second stem reverses the task. This was particularly simple in our sample lesson since there was a one-to-one correspondence between authors and titles.

The interchanging of stimuli and responses in a drill lesson on simple division problems poses a much more complex task than the author-title exercise. The lesson starts out simply enough by presenting expressions such as

$$6 \div 3 \qquad 0 \div 2 \qquad 20 \div 4$$

and asking the student to record the single number which is the quotient indicated. Since previous instruction would have included the discussion of expressions which do *not* name whole number quotients, expressions like

$$6 \div 0 \qquad 0 \div 0 \qquad 20 \div 0$$

would be presented. The student would be expected to indicate that no numerical solution exists for these problems.

So far, the stimulus presented has involved a *pair* of numbers; the response expected has been the *single* number (if any) which is the quotient of that pair. Interchange of stimulus and response suggests that now the stimulus presented should be a *single* number (one of the quotients); a student's response should be a *pair* of numbers which have that given number as a quotient. That is, students would be asked to input a pair of numbers for problems like

$\square \div \triangle = 2 \qquad \square \div \triangle = 0 \qquad \square \div \triangle = 5$

Since any one of the last three problems has several solutions, the computer would need to recognize each. But wait, then . . . . Is this really an adequate way of reversing the original stimulus and response? When the stimulus was

$$6 \div 3,$$

there was only one response—2. But when the stimulus is

$$\square \div \triangle = 2$$

there are many responses, only one of which uses the numbers 6 and 3. If a student always responds to

$$\square \div \triangle = 2$$

by inputting 6 and 3, the process of reversal isn't complete.

The interchanging of stimuli and responses in a drill or practice program is a nontrivial problem in any situation in which there is a many-to-one correspondence between those stimuli and responses. The division problems above comprise one drill situation which has this inherent difficulty. Foreign language vocabulary drill is another example since a given word or phrase in a foreign language may have many possible translations. Any given translation is but a single example of the possible meanings.

Like drill lessons (involving associations), practice lessons (involving procedures) give rise to problems when stimuli and responses are interchanged. Practice in solving so-called worded problems in science usually involves situations in which the student is provided (in written, oral, or cartoon form) with certain information relevant to the solution of a given task. There may be several ways to use the information to solve the task. Reversal of this practice lesson might present a task *and* a method of solution; the student would be called upon to specify the *information needed* to use the given method in solving the given task.

Drill or practice lessons, properly constructed, answer the call to interchange stimuli and responses in a manner which will ensure a two-way bond. How well that call is answered depends upon the subject-matter skills and creativity of the lesson designer, the versatility of the computing machinery used, and the skills of the programmer who translates the lesson designer's ideas into computerized form. It follows that a courseware evaluation procedure that will identify how well the call has been answered would involve both persons who have expertise in teaching the subject matter involved (to the lesson's indicated student population) and persons with technical/programming knowledge of the computer system used.

Setting the Restrictions on Student Input

Restrictions on student input have two sources: the equipment and the lesson designer. For selected-response questions (i.e., dichotomous-choice, matching, multiple-choice), rules for responding are easily described to the user and the judging of responses is no serious challenge to any computer. Still, even an item with the simple and familiar multiple-choice format of the following example requires clear instructions regarding how the student is to respond.

```
How many days are there in a fortnight?
  (a) 4
  (b) 7
  (c) 10
  (d) 14
```

Surely, you say to yourself, the student will respond by typing one of the four letters corresponding to the choices. Maybe so, maybe no. *Should* the student input some other response, the computer should be prepared to react in a manner which will prevent an involuntary termination of the lesson because the computer isn't prepared to deal with alternate responses. What alternate responses? Here are a few.

- Response: *(d)*
  Will the response be rejected because the student has included parentheses?
- Response: *four* or *4*
  This response could be incorrect (i.e., the student is indicating the number in choice *a*) or it could be *correctly* indicating that the answer is the fourth choice listed.
- Response: *fourteen* or *14*
  It is highly likely that the student knows the correct answer but has ignored input directions.
- Response: *forteen*
  Here a spelling error compounds the technical error of ignoring the input directions.
- Response: *s*
  Since the *s* and *d* keys are adjacent on the keyboard, this could be a typing error.

Constructed-response answers such as were used in the author-title sample raised (in Step 5) questions about spelling, capitalization, punctuation, the "completeness" required in a response, and the acceptability of alternate responses. Insistence upon a single representation of the correct answer has the appeal of apparent simplicity in program design, but such rigidity is rarely justified by lesson objectives. Moreover, the program still must be prepared to *accept* responses which differ from the single acceptable answer and to provide appropriate feedback messages that inform the student as to why the response has been rejected. Placing multiple restrictions on the form of an answer also necessitates detailed instructions to the learner regarding what constitutes proper input. Unless such detailed and (probably) complex directions are justified by lesson objectives, they can be a source of frustration and may retard learning.

Relaxation of the rules governing the form of a constructed response is made at a price. If multiple forms of a correct response are to be accepted, the designer must anticipate each of those forms, and the computer must be able to recognize each. If the computer has a spelling-judging facility that makes it possible to recognize otherwise correct responses, it also should be prepared to inform the student of that technical error in the accepted response. (Sound pedagogy further suggests that the student input the technically correct—i.e., correctly spelled—answer before continuing.)

It is possible, furthermore, for the computer to search for *key words* within a constructed response; it then accepts the response as correct if the key words are present and ignores all other parts of the response. For example, suppose that the key word list for the question:

What American city has the largest land area?

consists of "Jacksonville" and "jacksonville." Acceptance based on the presence of a key word would admit each of the following.

It's Jacksonville.
Jacksonville, Florida.
I think it is Jacksonville.
jacksonville, of course

Unfortunately, it would also accept

Jacksonville, Illinois
Either Jacksonville, Los Angeles, or New York

Some responses may require special input techniques or the use of nonstandard notation. For instance, many computer keyboards will not permit the entry of an expression like 5^3 in the form shown here. Instead, alternate forms such as *5**3* or *5↑3* must be adopted. Keyboards which do allow 5^3 must be manipulated in a special way to attain the expression. In all cases, the student must be given instruction in the use of such notation; this instruction should be the subject of a lesson separate from the one in which the technique is applied.

Computers are capable of presenting items which involve graphics. For example, the computer might present the map of the continental United States and ask the learner to indicate the general location of each state named by the lesson. Since the usual way to describe such locations is with coordinates, the map might look like this:

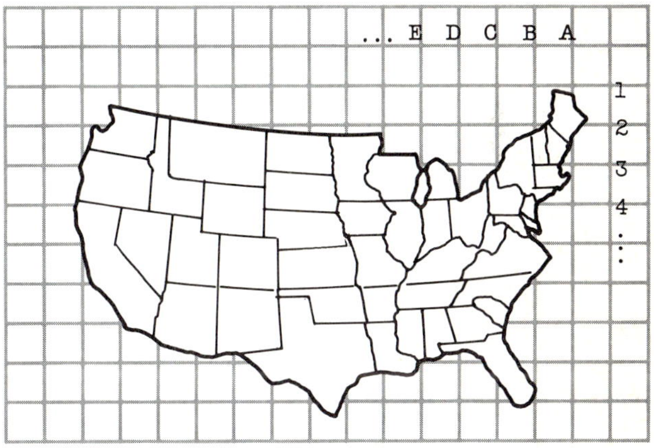

Asked to tell the location of New Jersey, the student (and computer) must know which of the following forms of response will be accepted:

B,4	4,B
B4	4B
(B,4)	(4,B)
B 4	4 B

If this is too complicated, each state could be indicated on the map by a number. This would make it relatively easy to design a lesson which would both (a) indicate a location and ask for the state's name as well as (b) name a state and ask for the number that indicates its location. There even are computers which permit the learner to indicate a location on a screen by touching that place with a finger or a sensing stylus. This touch-sensing feature also could be used to have students locate the specific named parts on an anatomical drawing.

Providing Prompts

Your own experiences to the contrary, most teachers *do* want students to give correct, meaningful responses. In preparing questions, several techniques can be used to help the student get a correct response (without reducing the exercise to rote learning). These techniques use helpers called *prompts* or *cues*. Providing prompts in the early part of a drill or practice session helps build the learner's confidence and allows the learner to better organize his previous learning within the context of the reinforcement lesson. The following list describes some useful prompting techniques you should look for when examining computerized courseware.

1. *Underlining words or numbers which are important to generating the solution.*
2. *Constructing the size of the answer space to reflect the size of the desired answer.*
3. *Constructing the answer space for a written answer by using dashes to represent the letters of the desired response.*
4. *Placing some letters in the answer space.* This may be done randomly as illustrated in Step 6 of the author-title example. However, it could involve the placing of specific letters such as the first and last letters of each word, or entire prefixes or suffixes.
5. *Providing graphic illustrations which suggest the desired answer.* Care must be taken that the illustrations are pertinent to the task. Any diagram, chart, or picture which is not necessary to the solution of the task will be distracting (no matter how "cute").
6. *Giving bounds for a numerical response.* Cues would include such remarks as *It's negative, It's greater than 10,* and *It's between 1.5 and 3.5.*
7. *Prompting should occur only in the early exercises of a lesson.* It should be withdrawn as soon as possible. A student's success rate can be used to key the removal or reintroduction of prompts.

Providing Feedback Messages

Adequate feedback goes beyond simply informing the student that a response is right or wrong. It should, in fact, meet five conditions.

1. *Feedback should confirm a correct response by telling why it has been judged correct.* The student may have made a lucky guess or may have arrived at the answer through faulty reasoning. Feedback to correct responses serves to connect those responses to correct reasoning.
2. *Feedback should point out errors that have been "forgiven" in accepting a conceptually correct but technically incorrect response.* There may be good reasons for accepting a response which differs from the "best" one because of an error in typing, spelling, punctuation, capitalization, or completeness.[6] Feedback should note such an error and present the desired response. The student should then be required to input the desired (corrected) response before new material is presented.
3. *Feedback should tell why a response has been judged incorrect.* This condition might be met by stating the correct response and telling why that response is correct. However, this is not always satisfactory, since the student still may have reason to believe that the rejected response is correct as well. Insofar as specific incorrect responses can be anticipated and related to specific errors in reasoning, feedback should point to the error in judgment which has given rise to the rejected response.
4. *Feedback to "in-list" errors should focus on discriminating between the associations that have been confused.* Step 7 of our author-title example suggested that the presence of two Greek titles *(The Elements* and *The Republic)* in the list of responses could cause confusion when the stimulus *Plato* is presented. A student's in-list error of associating Plato with *The Elements* should generate feedback which gives discriminatory practice in associating Plato with *The Republic* and in associating Euclid with *The Elements.*
5. *Feedback of a social evaluative nature may follow the response verification (correct or incorrect) feedback of Items 1–4.* Inclusion of such remarks involves judgments regarding the student. Positive social evaluative feedback such as *Good work* or *Ah, more proof of your superior intellect!* may be useful at the beginning of a practice session. As students gain confidence through several correct responses, however, the remarks tend to be ignored. Negative comments such as *You're slipping* or *How could you come so far and still make such silly mistakes?* can be effective in shocking confident students into devoting more time and attention to the task being reviewed. In fact, there is evidence that students receiving negative social feedback following incorrect answers on an achievement test tend to do better than students receiving only positive social feedback or no social feedback at all. On the other hand, less confident students may be discouraged by negative feedback. The

[6]The completeness issue deserves special attention. If *Jacksonville, Florida* is the desired response but *Jacksonville* is also accepted, the student's response needs shaping. Feedback might say *There are many states having a city called Jacksonville. The correct response here is Jacksonville, Florida.*

decision to use social evaluative feedback should, then, take the target population into account. When used, evaluative comments should vary in their wording and should be displayed on an intermittent schedule.

Recycling the Questions

The 2-3-4 recycling schedule illustrated in Step 8 of the author-title example says it all. If you were overwhelmed by its detail at the time (or underwhelmed by its apparent significance), give it a second look now.

Of course *recycling* is a term that has acquired social and economic connotations related to crises involving energy and natural resources. We *recycle* wrecked cars to get new cars, *recycle* used aluminum cans to get new aluminum cans, and *recycle* old newspapers to get fresh newsprint. Recycling is done with a mind to transforming garbage into useful products. The recycling of questions, on the other hand, is aimed at the improvement of the learning process; it in no way transforms the basic material—the questions themselves. The recycling of academic garbage yields the same academic garbage. The most elaborate question-recycling routine is only a means of delivering (and redelivering) questioning episodes in a manner that retires those items the learner has mastered and focuses attention upon the items the learner has not mastered. The quality of learning is a function of the questions and the feedback messages. There is still no market for sow's ears in the silk purse industry.

Terminating the Lesson

For those of you who have read of James Bond, the word *terminating* may suggest unintended finality. Perhaps we should speak of *interrupting* a lesson. Since a person may have several sessions with a given drill or practice lesson, learning may involve several interruptions. Lesson exits must be carefully planned and clearly marked.

Like this paper, a computerized drill or practice lesson should allow the learner to leave voluntarily. Unlike this paper, it might limit the points of exit to what the designer sees as "natural" breaking points in the flow of the lesson.

Ideally, the computer should make an electronic ✓ next to a learner's exit point. Upon returning to the lesson, the learner should have the option of picking up where the last session terminated or of beginning the lesson anew. This practice is a matter of basic academic courtesy; why should a computer be less courteous than a book?

The lesson designer should set forth built-in criteria for lesson interruption. For instance, Step 9 of our author-title example points out that the question recycling plan includes a criterion for retiring a given associative pair from the list and, in time, brings the session to a close. If the learner is not convinced that the internal criterion allowed sufficient practice, the lesson can be rerun. In setting a criterion which will result in the involuntary (from the student's point of view) termination of a session, the designer is not claiming that the student who meets that criterion *has learned the material.* Rather, the designer is asserting that meeting the criterion is evidence that the student *is learning the material.*

Lesson design also should allow for the interruption of a session in which a student's incorrect responses indicate that further attempts at drill or practice are inappropriate. If the purpose of the lesson is to practice a procedure (e.g., diagramming certain kinds of sentences) presented elsewhere, a sequence of incorrect responses may indicate inadequate introduction to the procedure. Left unchecked, the student may attain rote—and, hence, false—mastery of the finite set of examples presented by the lesson. To guard against this, the lesson could be designed to terminate a session based upon some "criterion of failure." Lesson termination would be accompanied by a feedback message explaining why the session was interrupted and directing the student to take some specific remedial action. Some computer systems permit the further use of that criterion to "lock out" the student from further interaction with the lesson until the remedial action has been verified.

This lesson is hereby terminated. Would that its termination were based upon evidence that learning has taken place. Ah well, voluntary reentry at any point is permitted and invited.

Study Guide: Chapter 7

1. In general terms, distinguish between drill lessons and practice lessons.
2. Suppose that the students in a course entitled Contemporary U.S. Political History decide that their work would be aided if they would commit to memory the names and terms (dates) of the U.S. presidents from 1933 to the present. The stimulus-response set of interest to them is:

President	*Dates in Office*
Franklin Roosevelt	1933–1945
Harry Truman	1945–1953
Dwight Eisenhower	1953–1961
John Kennedy	1961–1963
Lyndon Johnson	1963–1969

Richard Nixon	1969–1974
Gerald Ford	1974–1976
Jimmy Carter	1976–1980
Ronald Reagan	1980–

Note: There were *two* presidents in office during each of the *transition years,* 1933, 1945, 1953, 1961, 1963, 1969, 1974, 1976, 1980. (In 1933, by the way, they were Herbert Hoover & Franklin Roosevelt.) CONSIDER THIS FACT IN DESIGNING STEMS.

a. Give two item stems which are appropriate for this activity. (The combination of these two stems should support a two-way bond between the names and dates.)
b. For each of the two stems just given, describe and justify the conditions required for the inputting of a response which will be judged as correct. Also indicate how the program will respond to input which does NOT meet the conditions of a correct response.
c. Suppose that there is to be a HELP menu associated with each stem. A student not knowing the response to an item would type *HELP* and would be presented with a menu of possible prompts to aid him or her in responding to the item. Describe appropriate choices for the prompts available for each item.

3. For any three of the following subject areas, give a brief description of a *drill* activity which might be appropriate for computerization. The description should identify several pairings within the appropriate stimulus-response set and should give the two item stems that would link them.

arithmetic	foreign language
algebra I	geography
art	geometry
auto mechanics	history
biological science	music
driver training	physical education
English	physical science

4. Give a brief description of a *practice* activity (appropriate for computerization) for each of the three fields chosen in Exercise 3.
5. Locate and execute a computer activity which purports to be a drill lesson.
   a. To what extent does it meet the standards for a drill lesson as outlined in Chapter 7?
   b. Specify modifications which would bring it into better conformity with the proposed ideal of computerized drill.
6. If your work in Exercise 5 of Chapter 4 involved the evaluation of a drill lesson, reevaluate that lesson and compare the reviews.
7. Locate and execute another purported drill activity.
   a. Evaluate the lesson using the Checklist of Chapter 4.
   b. Summarize your evaluation using the Documentation Sheet of Chapter 4.

AGENDA FOR ACTION

SCIENCE AND MATHEMATICS
TEACHING CENTER

ADDRESS REPLY TO WRITER

THE UNIVERSITY OF WYOMING
UNIVERSITY STATION, BOX 3992
LARAMIE, WYOMING, 82071

MEMORANDUM

TO: Members of ICAC

FROM: Dick Dennis and Bob Kansky

RE: ICAC Paper 7

DATE: February 7, 1983

The ICAC paper which accompanies this memorandum examines one of the more common ways in which the computer takes responsibility for a specific aspect of teaching. In this case the computer, in its role as teacher, manages a reinforcement (drill or practice) activity.

Computerized drill or practice can make exercising more efficient and individualized than is possible in the textbook-homework environment. This greater effectiveness follows from special attributes added to the learning situation by the computer, attributes such as

* sophisticated procedures for using individual student response patterns to control the repetition of items,
* informative feedback messages which are tailored to fit student responses,
* lesson management techniques based upon principles of efficient mastery achievement, and
* time-use optimization methods.

All in all, the preparation of an effective drill or practice program is not a trivial affair to carry out. Neither is it easy to explain. After a good deal of paper-crumpling, we finally decided to approach the topic by constructing what we think is a well-designed drill lesson. Having done so, we try to stand back from the example and review it in terms of the principles used to design it.

To get the most out of this paper, use it as the basis for examining (evaluating?) some computerized drill or practice lessons. Any store that sells computers and computer software will have such programs available for viewing. We think that you'll find it interesting to view "what is" against a background of "what could be."

DD:BK:glm

Enclosure: ICAC Paper 7

AGENDA FOR ACTION

Obourn Senior High School

200 Woodbine Avenue
East Roachmont, New York

M. Jack Stivers
Principal

(716) 568-8840

ICAC Memo #7

TO: Members of ICAC

FROM: John Russell

DATE: February 17, 1983

Having read and discussed ICAC Paper 7, it's pretty clear that the "drillanpractice" programs which we've examined fall short of the proposed standard although it appears that there is an abundance of programs aimed at reinforcement. In retrospect, it seems that the computing machinery was up to providing many of the features proposed as characterizing an effective lesson. However, the program quality suggested that the programmers were unaware of good questioning techniques or of effective design of drill or practice lessons. Their failure to make full use of the capabilities of the computers on which the programs were demonstrated suggests that (a) the programmers were unaware of those capabilities, (b) the programs were designed for other (or earlier) computer systems having lesser capabilities, (c) the program designers had more enthusiasm than expertise, or (d) a good bit of software is produced in a slap-dash manner. These general observations (feelings?) about the state of software development give rise to the assignments which follow.

COMMITTEE ASSIGNMENTS

1. John and Gerri will use John's personal microcomputer to program an approximation of the author-title drill lesson of ICAC Paper 7. The program will be demonstrated at a future committee meeting.

2. Jeanne reported that students in the computer programming classes at Sinclair Senior High School (Bellville) are involved in a thing they call a Faculty-Support Programming Project. In brief, the students write instructional computer programs to meet the needs of faculty members. The programming teacher told Jeanne that there are more students than projects; she's always seeking more ideas from faculty. Sooo . . . Jeanne will ask if the students will program some projects of our design. If so, she will let us know in order that we might submit our own 'drillanpractice' projects along the lines of the example in ICAC Paper 7.

   (NOTE: Jeanne was successful. Anyone interested in the Sinclair Senior High School service should prepare a lesson design like that in the example and submit it through Jeanne. Nice going, Jeanne!)

CHAPTER EIGHT

An Examination of Computer-Assisted Testing Operations

Evaluation is fundamental to effective teaching. *Diagnostic* evaluation reveals what a student can already do; it tells the teacher where to begin instruction. *Formative* evaluation keeps track of a student's progress within a unit of instruction; by showing the success or failure of a given instructional procedure, it guides the teacher in selecting "next activities" for the student. *Summative* evaluation verifies student mastery or nonmastery of an instructional objective; it is the basis of the teacher's major decisions in designing a student's curriculum. At selected points, summative evaluation may be condensed into a "grade."

Many people, including all teachers, must design and execute evaluation activities. When these activities call for the use of written examinations, teachers must invest considerable time in the preparation and scoring of those examinations. Evaluation work can quickly become burdensome for, say, the elementary school teacher who is responsible for instruction in language arts, reading, mathematics, science, and social studies. At the secondary school or college levels, testing activities are complicated by a teacher's need to evaluate a broad range of cognitive skills in several courses related to a single discipline (as in the case of a secondary school teacher of U.S. History Since 1868, Current World Political Theory, and Social Aspects of Scientific Development). As a teacher becomes aware of the need for more diagnostic and formative evaluation activities, good intentions are overwhelmed by the magnitude of the test construction and scoring tasks. Certainly, there is little or no time to devote to the study of the test materials themselves—to identify their strengths and to correct their weaknesses. Teachers simply do not have the time to write and grade the number of tests needed—much less to worry about the quality of the test items. Or do they?

Testing Operations

Before we argue an answer to the question above, let's take a quick look at the major operations involved in testing. Each is as necessary as it is obvious. The trick is to perform those operations with such ease and speed that frequent evaluation can be a reality. Guess what that suggests.

First, we need lots and lots of test items. These must be related to specific objectives in our courses and must be filed in such a way that we can quickly locate the items which are associated with a given objective. It will be necessary to make frequent additions to, deletions from, or modifications of the items in this "pool." In fact, we'll want to add or delete whole objectives (and, hence, to add or delete clusters of items dealing with those objectives). Moreover, we need a procedure for wading through our item pool in search of a combination of items that can be used to build one or more parallel tests—tests of the same general form and degree of difficulty—for a given set of objectives.

Once items have been selected, they must be arranged into logical groups (perhaps by item type) with appropriate sets of directions. To permit efficient scoring, it's often wise to design a response sheet which will control the order, length, and format of student answers. This entire test package then must be placed in the form in which it will be presented to students (accompanied by such drawings, pictures, objects, measuring instruments, laboratory stations, or recordings as are required) and reproduced in the quantity necessary. If typing is involved, the test should be read by more than one person to ensure freedom from errors introduced by typists or artists.

After students have taken it, the test will be scored and interpreted. Scoring should make it possible to assign different numbers of points to different questions and, perhaps, should allow for the awarding of "partial credit." The scores must be interpreted in terms of the specific objectives tested. Student performance data also should be recorded in such a way that it can be used to evaluate the quality of the test items used.

Finally, we want to guarantee the security of our item pool and of each test that we build from it. Believe it or not, there are students who would sneak a peek if given the opportunity. This, of course, would invalidate our tests; a lot of hard work would come to naught.

Item Pools: Benefits and Warnings

The construction or purchase of computer-accessed pools of questions should sound attractive to schools for many reasons.

- Teachers may be encouraged to test more frequently.
- Testing can be increased with a minimum of increase in teacher effort.
- Computer feedback on tests (and individual items) may encourage teachers to revise tests more frequently.
- Tests may be designed to fit the needs of individual students or small groups of students.
- The availability of large numbers of questions could make it possible for students to use many items in practice exercises and self-testing activities without a loss of testing integrity.

Even the computer's current inability to score essay items does not preclude the storing of such items (with sample answers and scoring schemes) in an item pool.

Before using computerized item pools, however, you should keep some limiting factors in mind. These are *solvable* issues, but they can prevent the implementation of item pooling if ignored.

1. Creating item pools can require significant effort. More rapid start-up can justify the cost or effort of acquiring existing pools.
2. Existing pools may contain errors or items which need updating or modification. Permission and provision for local editing must be assured.
3. Capabilities of printing equipment are crucial to successful use of the pool. Questions may require superscripts, subscripts, underlining, special alphabets, special symbols, or graphs. If so, careful attention must be paid to the selection of printing equipment. The fancier the printing required, the higher the price of the equipment.
4. On-line testing requires much terminal time. If every student is to be presented with the same test, on-line testing may be an inefficient use of equipment.
5. The grading of tests taken off-line requires a device to read student answers. Without this device, the benefits of machine scoring and test analysis are lost. Such machines exist, at relatively reasonable cost, even for microcomputers.

Computer-Assisted Testing Operations

Can teachers survive the ordeal of testing? Can *anyone* cope repeatedly with the tasks posed by testing operations? Can you? Let's see.

Imagine yourself as a teacher (your choice of subject) about to prepare a test (your choice of purpose: diagnostic, formative, summative) for a particular group of students (your choice of group size). Because we like you, we're going to perform a fine bit of magic for your benefit. We're going to transport you (not far) through time to a wondrous school which is equipped with a well-designed instructional computing system, one that has a special facility to aid teachers in testing operations. Sit back and see yourself as you might behave in such a school. Ready? The magic word is

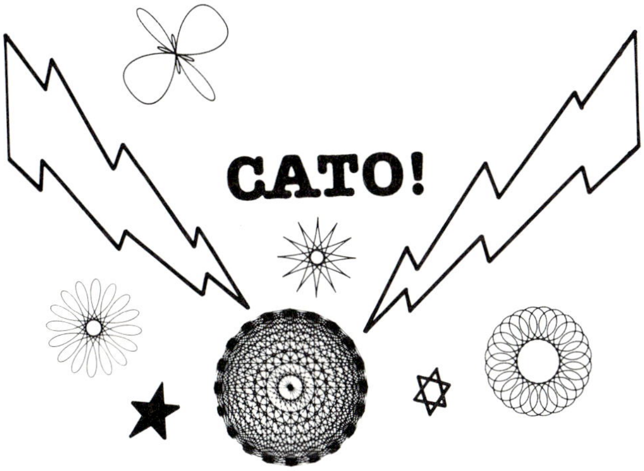

WELCOME TO
CATO

This computer is equipped with a special program which assists teachers in carrying out testing operations.

Note that the keyboard has a **HELP** - key. Pressing the **HELP**-key will allow you to see special displays of information.

Please press the **HELP** - key now.

CATO SECURITY CONTROL

Please identify yourself by typing the following information.

A. Your name. ≫
B. Your subject group name.
C. The group password.

Press **HELP** to continue.

Although security was the last issue discussed with relation to testing operations, it's the first item of business in a computerized testing system. As the display indicates, entry into the school's testing system would require proper identification. The entry of your name and subject group alerts the computer to your claim that you are one of the persons allowed to use the item pool of that group to prepare tests; the computer checks its memory to see if your claim is true. If it isn't, you can go no further. This subject-by-subject control isn't caused by the fear that some unscrupulous mathematics-type may seek to finance a new car by selling questions from the physics test-item pool. Rather, it ensures that any breach of security will be confined to just a portion of the total system.

But since a lot of people know your name and what subject you teach, the procedure offers little real access control to this point. It's the third item—the group password—which unlocks the test files. This secret code word is known only to members of the subject group. For even greater security, each member of the group can be assigned an additional personal password which is not known by any other member of the group but which is required for entry into the testing system.

For this demonstration, we have enrolled you in the CATO system under the subject matter group called *multisubject* (because its item pool has a variety of materials in it). The password for the group is *snoop-about*. Please enter your last name, the subject group name, and the password. Then press the **HELP**-key so that you can continue.

CATO MAIN CHOICES DISPLAY

Type the number of the testing operation that you wish to perform now.

1. Build a test.
2. Administer a test.
3. See test statistics.
4. Perform item-pool updates.

≫

Very good! The system has let you pass through its security control and has taken you to a display which lists the four main choices available. Let's explore the choices in the order given. Please type a *1* now.

1. Build a test

1. TEST-BUILDING OPERATIONS

Type the letter of the test-building operation that you wish to perform now.

a. Specify objectives to be tested.
b. Specify item characteristics.
c. Select test items.

>

Press **HELP** to see a list of course objectives.

As the display indicates, you can now engage in the details of test construction. The logical place to begin would be with the specification of the exact course objectives to be tested. Note that the system will take you to a complete list of these objectives if you press the **HELP** key. When the list is displayed, you will be able to choose each objective you want simply by indicating the objectives's number within the list. When you indicate that you've finished your selecting, the system will return you to this display so that you can specify the characteristics of the test items to be drawn from the item pool. In the case of a large computer system, this item pool would be stored in a library file which would be automatically requested by the CATO system. If a microcomputer were being used, you might need to insert the diskettes which contain the item pool.

The items of the test item pool are grouped by such characteristics as objective, level of difficulty, level of cognition from Bloom's *taxonomy,*[1] and type of item (e.g., multiple-choice). The computer would now engage you in a dialogue in which you would be asked to indicate the number of test items you wish to select for a given objective and the mix of characteristics (cognition and difficulty levels, item type, etc.) that the selected items must meet. With only a few queries, the computer would have determined all of the necessary characteristics of your test and would return you to the display which lists test-building operations. Nothing magic here—the computer has been programmed to do all of these nice things.

[1]Benjamin S. Bloom, J. Thomas Hastings, and George F. Madaus, *Handbook on Formative and Summative Evaluation of Student Learning,* (New York: McGraw-Hill, 1971).

By now taking option *c* (select test items) of the testing-building operations, you command the computer to search its test item pool for the number and kinds of items that you've specified. This might take a few minutes, the time required being a function of both the power of your computer and the manner in which the question pool is organized. When suitable items have been located, the computer can display them to you one at a time. If you accept a given item, it is added to the collection of items which will make up your test. If you reject an item, the computer would jump back into the item pool to find a different question which fits the specifications of the one rejected. This accept-reject procedure would continue until your item selection is complete. The final collection of items selected (i.e., the test) would then be given a name (say, 'PHYSQUIZ-1A') to permit easy reference later. The computer would then return you to the CATO Main Choices Display where you would type a *2* to set the conditions of test administration.

2. Administer a test

TEST-ADMINISTRATION OPERATIONS

Please type the letter of the test-administration operation you wish to perform now.

a. Specify administration mode.
b. Specify scoring procedure.

>

The first of the two administration options would allow you to choose the mode, on-line or off-line, in which the test will be presented to students. If you choose on-line administration (which has students input their responses through a computer keyboard), the system would present you with the following queries:

- What is the name of your test?
- What group(s) of students will take this test?
- On what day will testing begin (end)?
- Will students need to enter a security password in order to gain access to the test? If so, what is the password?

- What testing directions are to be given to the student?
- Should the order of presentation of the test items be exactly the same for all students?
- What are the time limits (if any) for a student's completion of the test?
- Will a student be permitted to review and change test responses?

If the test is to be administered on-line, you will also need to instruct the computer on how to score student responses (option *b*). This information would be provided through your responses to computer queries about such things as the number of points to be assigned to each question (for both full or partial credit) and the total number of points required for mastery of a given objective.

Off-line testing requires that the test be printed. Computer queries about the generation of a printed form of the test would deal with the following issues:

- In what order should the questions be presented?
- What directions are to be inserted?
- Are answer spaces (blanks) or work spaces to be provided?
- Will there be a need for alternate forms of the test?[2]

Having satisfied the computer's need for test-administration information, you would again be returned to the CATO Main Choices Display. Typing a *3* would then bring you to a list of options regarding test statistics.

3. See test statistics

TEST STATISTICS OPERATIONS

Type the letter of the test statistics operation that you wish to perform now.

a. View item statistics.
b. View whole-test statistics.
c. View student performance statistics.
≫

[2]An alternate form is one in which the same questions are presented in a different order or in which the response sets to multiple-choice or matching questions are reordered. Such features reduce the need for careful monitoring when the test is given.

Whether scoring is done by the computer, the teacher, or a combination of the two, the computer test service would be prepared to offer detailed reports regarding individual test items, the entire test, or the performances of students (as individuals or in groups). If some scoring is done off-line, the system would permit the results of that scoring to be entered into the data banks which would be used in generating these reports. Of the three options presented, two (*b* and *c)* assume that the test which you have just constructed has also been administered and that student scores have been recorded in the computer's data banks. Option *a,* on the other hand, could be used to view the results of past users of any test item.

A decision to view test item statistics would allow you to investigate the pattern of student responses to any given item. The computer would alert you to such information as the statistical difficulty of the item by classifying the item *easy, medium,* or *hard* according to the percentage of students getting the item correct. It would tell you how well the item discriminates between those students whose overall test performance was rather good (say 80 percent or better) and those whose overall test performance was generally poor (say 25 percent or below). If generally good students are choosing an incorrect response to a matching or multiple-choice item, it would note this fact so that the item could be checked for such problems as misleading phrases or, perhaps, two correct responses. All such information is aimed at helping you to improve the test items themselves.

A look into whole-test statistics (option *b)* would provide more than the mean, range, and standard deviation of student scores. It would give graphical summaries of performance on both individual objectives and the complete test. It would use a table to compare the statistical difficulty (easy, medium, hard) of an item with the level-of-difficulty classification under which that item is currently stored in the item pool. It would suggest the overall difficulty of the test by summarizing the total number of test items which fell into each of the three difficulty classes.

Student performance statistics (option *c)* would let you review the entire "test paper" of any individual student or to view a summary of a group's performance. The summary would include a list of the class members (alphabetical or by ranking of test scores) with such things as raw scores, percentages, and number of objectives mastered. For any specific test item or objective, it would list all persons who answered the item incorrectly or failed to master the objective. Such reports would allow you to focus group discussions of test results and to prescribe remedial activity for small groups of students having common problems.

Let's return to CATO's Main Choices Display one more time. Our purpose is to see what's available by typing *4* to engage in the creation of test items.

4. Perform item-pool updates

```
ITEM-POOL UPDATE OPERATIONS
     Type the letter of the item-pool update operation
that you wish to perform now.
     a. Delete an item or objective.
     b. Modify an item or objective.
     c. Create a new item or objective.
     >
```

The need to update any pool of test items may arise in any of three ways: (1) the changing of course objectives calls for the deletion of existing items/objectives or the addition of new items/objectives; (2) the review of test-item statistics suggests the need to modify or delete an item; and (3) the accept-reject procedure used during test-building operations reveals that the pool has an insufficient number of items which fit a given mix of characteristics. The three options available under Item-Pool Update Operations will allow you to meet all of these contingencies.

The deletion option (option *a)* can handle any specific item or objective (with all associated items) which is judged to be unworthy. It will pluck offending items or objectives from their hiding places in the computer's data banks and cast them forth into Everlasting Darkness.

Option *b* is less dramatic. It will call forth a given objective or item and permit you to change its wording. Thus misspellings can be corrected, ambiguities can be eliminated, and the choices to selected response items can be improved. In addition, this option will allow you to alter an item's classification by changing, for instance, its difficulty classification from *medium* to *easy*. In fact, you could detach an item from one objective and add it to another.

Finally, the last option (option *c)* guides the entry of whole new objectives and items. The entry of a new test item would be accompanied by queries which have you specify the characteristics (objective, level of difficulty, etc.) of the item.

```
                 THE END
of the beginning of CATO's services. Watch for soon-to-
be-added features such as
     * adaptive testing and
     * test-item templating.
```

Now that we have completed the updating of CATO's item pool, our tour of a sample computer-assisted testing facility comes to an end. Before we look to CATO's soon-to-be-added features, it should be noted that systems like CATO already exist. And while a computer-assisted testing facility can have a life of its own, it also may be just one component of a computerized instructional management system—but that's a topic for Chapter 9.

Adaptive Testing

A likely feature of future computerized testing systems having an on-line testing mode will be the generation of individual tests which adapt in difficulty to the achievement level of the student. Such tailoring would modify the test as the student is taking it; the student's performance on the items already presented would be used to determine the next item to be presented. As a result, any two students taking a particular test might be presented with different questions and/or a different number of questions. If a student's test performance shows a profile of success, next questions would be selected from more advanced objectives or more sophisticated levels of the item-classification scheme. Such a student might need but a few questions to satisfy the evaluative purpose (diagnostic, formative, summative) of the test. On the other hand, students experiencing difficulty would be better served by being presented questions which would aid in achieving a diagnosis. The overall purpose of such tailored (or adaptive) testing is to optimize the evaluative power of the testing situation. It's a purpose that is the goal of a good deal of research.

Test-Item Templating

The success of a computerized test service is obviously dependent upon an adequate supply of testing's raw material—test items. One needs great pools of items which will produce the mix of characteristics arising in a variety of testing situations. Early efforts in computer-based testing have burdened instructors with gathering or creating the items to be entered into the pools. As computerized test systems become popular, however, there will be ample reasons for computer courseware firms to market question pools for many courses.

Another possible source of questions is the computer itself. Eerie? Well maybe, but it is true that computers can "create" questions. Actually, computer generation of test items is not mysterious. The computer simply follows a recipe provided by the teacher. The recipe, usually called an *item template,* is a pattern from which many questions of a given form can be produced. However, such computer generation of questions requires the topic being tested to have an explicit set of rules by which each question's answer can be determined. Such sets of rules are found in structured disciplines such as mathematics, the sciences, and grammar (any language); they are present to a lesser degree in the social sciences and humanities.

Item templates are sentences with "holes" in them. The computer's job is to fill each hole in the template with a word, numeral, or drawing in such a way that the result is an "un-holed" statement which makes sense and which has the form of a certain type of item.

Birth of an Item Template

Actually, item templates aren't born—they're made. (We just like the catchy section heading.) That is, one doesn't start with an item template and go immediately to the generation of items. Rather, one starts with a sample item, uses that sample to construct a template, and then uses the resulting template to generate items like the sample (and including the sample).

Suppose you were teaching about subtraction of the whole numbers from zero to twenty. An example of the simple worded problems which you might give to students is

> Greta had 12 snakes. She gave 4 snakes to her friend Leander. How many snakes did Greta have left?

Since you want your students to do several problems like this one, you decide to develop an item template to do the job. You can make a template that will use *numbers* other than 12 and 4 by replacing those special numbers by holes (sometimes called *variables).* Using **X** and **Y** to show the location of these holes, you get the item template shown below.

Item Template 1

Greta had **X** snakes. She gave **Y** snakes to her friend Leander. How many snakes did Greta have left?

This simple template can be used to generate lots of subtraction items about Greta and her snakes. All you have to do now is to instruct the computer regarding exactly what kinds of numbers it is allowed to put in place of the **X** and the **Y**. If you don't do this, the computer could generate some really stupid items by making replacements like these.

Replacement for the **X**	Replacement for the **Y**
6	13
87,641,385	-7
2 4/9	π

To prevent such absurd replacements of **X** and **Y**, it's necessary to send the computer a note (part of the computer program) about how to do the job correctly. In the case of **X** and **Y**, the note would say something like this.

Programming Memo 1

Dear Computer:

With regard to Item Template 1, use the following rules when replacing the **X** and **Y**.

1. Replace the **X** by a randomly chosen whole number which is greater than 2 but less than 21.
2. Replace the **Y** by a randomly chosen whole number which is less than or equal to the one you chose for the **X**.

Thanks a bunch.

Commandingly yours,
Master Teacher

If you use Problem Template 1 and Programming Memo 1 to generate several items, you'll find that each makes sense. You'll also find that you're getting sick of hearing about Greta and Leander! But you can correct that by making the template more general—by putting four more holes in the item to get a new template.

Item Template 2

N1 had **X** snakes. **A1** gave **Y** snakes to **A2** friend **N2.** How many snakes did **N1** have left?

Two of the holes (**N1** and **N2**) should be replaced by names of snake fanciers, and the other two (**A1** and

A2) should be replaced by pronouns which match the sex of **N1.** We'd better write another memo to keep the computer informed.

Programming Memo 2

Dear Computer:

When using Item Template 2, use the following rules.

1. Replace **X** and **Y** using the rules in Programming Memo 1.
2. Replace **N1** with a name chosen at random from one of the following lists.

List A	List B
Greta	Neil
Mona	Dan
Lisa	Louie
Claudia	Andreas
Carrol	Phil

3. (a) If you choose **N1** from List A, replace **A1** by 'She' and replace **A2** by 'her.'
   (b) If you choose **N1** from List B, replace **A2** by 'He' and replace **A2** by 'his.'
4. Replace **N2** with a name chosen at random from among the following.

Chris	Leander
Betty Ann	Sharon
Duane	Sybil
Melfried	Igor
Alan	Max
Yusef	Tillie

Make just one mistake in any of this and I'll pull your plug.

Watchfully yours,
Master Teacher

Using Item Template 2 and Programming Memo 2, the variety of items would include such examples as

Carrol had 17 snakes. She gave 9 snakes to her friend Sharon. How many snakes did Carrol have left?

or

Louie had 5 snakes. He gave 5 snakes to his friend Tillie. How many snakes did Louie have left?

Things have been made a bit more interesting by Item Template 2, but why the fixation on snakes? Also, would Louie and Tillie still be friends if such a gift were unsolicited? Let's have a third go at the template by using holes for *snakes* and *friend.*

Item Template 3

N1 had **X C. A1** gave **Y C** to **A2 R N2.** How many **C** did **N1** have left?

To explain the holes in the latest template, we need to rush the following memo to the computer.

Programming Memo 3

Dear Computer:

Pay attention! I know that you're not very bright, but you can follow rules. The rules for using Item Template 3 are as follows.

1. Replace **X, Y, N1, N2, A1,** and **A2** using the rules in Programming Memo 2.
2. Replace **C** by randomly selecting the name of one of the following critters.

snakes	aardvarks
gerbils	koalas
tarantulas	piranhas
goldfish	elephants
bats	rabbits

3. Replace the **R** by a random choice of one of the following relationships.

friend	cousin
neighbor	late friend
classmate	favorite enemy

Okay, now churn out those items.

Expectantly yours,
Master Teacher

Guided by Programming Memo 3, Item Template 3 can generate over two million different items! Among them are such innocuous selections as

Dan had 10 goldfish. He gave 5 goldfish to his cousin Sybil. How many goldfish did Dan have left?

as well as such satisfying surprises as

Claudia had 18 tarantulas. She gave 16 tarantulas to her late friend Igor. How many tarantulas did Claudia have left?

In summary, then, the item templates from which the computer generates questions for tests or classroom exercises will have two kinds of elements.

1. There are *constant elements* which remain the same for each item generated by the template. (In our example, the constant elements of Template 3 were *had, gave, to, How many, did, have left,* and the three punctuation marks.)
2. There are *variable elements* for which the computer generates replacements from a defined set of information (given in our Programming Memos) each time a new item is generated.

The extent to which the items generated by a template look different is dependent upon the number of variable elements in the template and the teacher's cleverness in chosing the replacements for each variable element. Thus, one could improve upon Template 3 by introducing additional variable elements.

- Introduce the variable element **V1** to replace the constant element *had.* Then let the computer choose a replacement for **V1** from the list

bought	had	found
inherited	stole	won

- Introduce the paired variable elements **V2** and **V3** to replace the constant elements *gave* and *to*. The replacement list for the new variable elements could be like this.

V2	V3
threw	at
traded[3]	for[3]
gave	to
mailed	to
had	delivered to
had	hidden in the bed of
sold	to

- Introduce **V4** in place of *How many*, and allow **V4** to be replaced by either of the following:

How many
What number of

- Introduce **V5** for *did* and select the replacement for **V5** from among the following:

should
would
did

- Introduce **V6** for *have left*. Then select the replacement for **V6** from these choices.

keep
have left
hold back
have then

An item template incorporating all of the variable elements we've discussed would leave only the three punctuation marks as constant elements. The final template would look like this:

Item Template 4

N1 V1 X C. A1 V2 Y C V3 A2 R N2.
V4 C V5 N1 V6?

and would have the power to generate over two billion different items! We need have little fear that anyone will memorize all of these items before the next test.

Looking at the form of Item Template 4, it should be clear why we said that templates are made and not born. We certainly didn't have Template 4 already in mind when we began. It just "happened" as we continued to work with our original item about Greta, Leander, and the snakes. Remember them?

Study Guide: Chapter 8

1. While reading a professional journal in your field, you encounter an advertisement from National Test Banks of Meeteetse which claims to have computerized test item banks in each of the following areas:

arithmetic: grades 3–6	science: grades 5–6
Algebra I	American history: grades 5–6
Algebra II	American history: secondary
spelling: grades K–2	world history: grades 5–6
spelling: grades 3–4	world history: secondary
spelling: grades 5–6	biology: secondary

Each bank is keyed by learning objectives so that tests can be generated by clusters of objectives. Each bank costs $300. What would you want to know about any one of these banks before placing a purchase order?

2. National Test Banks of Meeteetse (NTBM) also advertises a $280 program (prepared for use with the microcomputer system available to you) which will perform "test scoring and analysis functions." It requires the purchase of a card reader and a printer. Money has been set aside by your school for the purchase of hardware and software to support such computer-assisted testing operations.
   a. What specific instructional services would you expect from such a program?
   b. What further definition of "test scoring and analysis functions" would you need before purchasing? (Express your needs in terms of specific questions to be addressed to NTBM.)
3. Suppose that you wished to develop an item template based upon the following item.

Stepans' General Merchandise, Inc. advertises 4 styles of refrigerators.

Each of these styles of refrigerators comes in any one of 3 colors.

How many different refrigerators must Stepans' keep in stock?

The first two stages of template development introduce variables as shown in the following:

STAGE 1

Stepans' General Merchandise, Inc. advertises 4 styles of **I$**.

Each of these styles of **I$** comes in any one of 3 colors.

How many different **I$** must Stepans' keep in stock?

STAGE 2

Stepans' General Merchandise, Inc. advertises 4 styles of **I$**.

Each of these styles of **I$** comes in any one of 3 **V$**.

How many different **I$** must Stepans' keep in stock?

It is decided that each template variable that deals with words or phrases (e.g., **I$** and **V$**) should have at least five

[3] These particular replacements present some interesting prospects.

possible replacements. In using the template, the computer program will select a replacement for **I$** *at random* from those available; it will then select a replacement for **V$.** For each replacement for **I$,** *there should be more than one appropriate corresponding selection from* **V$.**

a. Simply list the possible replacements for **I$.**
b. List the possible replacements for **V$.**
c. Write the "programming memo" for Stage 2. (In doing so, assume that a programming memo has been written for Stage 1.)

4. Stage 3 of the development of the item template in Exercise 3 involves the replacement of Stepans' General Merchandise, Inc. List a replacement set of five members and write the associated programming memo.
5. Take the item template of Exercise 3 to Stage 4 by selecting a next constant to replace. List a replacement set and write a programming memo for Stage 4.
6. In ICAC Memo #8 which follows, the Committee Assignments section suggests six item-template subjects. Suppose that each templating program also had to generate the correct answer(s) to each item. For each of the six templates, discuss the programming problems introduced by this answer-generating task.

AGENDA FOR ACTION

University of Illinois
at Urbana-Champaign

Department of Secondary Education

395 Education Building
1310 South Sixth Street
Champaign
Illinois 61820

College of Education

217 333-0227

MEMORANDUM

TO: Members of ICAC

FROM: Dick Dennis and Bob Kansky

RE: ICAC Paper 8

DATE: February 21, 1983

Members of ICAC who have begun reading journals and newsletters on instructional computing may wonder why we're devoting an entire paper to computer-assisted testing operations. Many folks would treat testing as just one aspect of instructional management (a subject that we'll address in ICAC Paper 9). Indeed, we'll return to the issue of testing in ICAC Paper 9, but we've isolated it as a major application of the computer as teacher for two reasons. First, computerized-testing facilities can be established independently of broader instructional management programs. That is, computerized testing need not be linked to a comprehensive management package in order to be useful. Second, testing operations are such an important part of teaching that they deserve separate consideration. To present an adequate discussion of testing as a part of ICAC Paper 9 would interrupt the flow of its overall discussion of management.

We wish to thank you all for the copies of ICAC memos, lists of errors and suggestions regarding earlier papers, journal summaries, and committee assignments that you've sent to us. They will be of great help as we begin to revise the papers. We were tempted, in fact, to ask you for permission to use the revised flow chart, program sequence, and program memory that Phil and Gerri prepared (ICAC Memo #6) on the saga of C. R. Terminal and the isosceles triangle. But then we realized that had it not been for the obvious need to do something better than we did, you wouldn't have dug into the revision. Even more important, we might never have received that photo of John wearing a cardboard terminal over his head when teaching the improved lesson!

By the way, Ted and Jeanne's tutorial on the concept of a peninsula was excellent. For one thing, it brings out the common features of instructional design which support the introduction of a new concept in any subject. It is such commonality which lends credence to our assertion that tutorial lesson authoring systems useful in any subject are close at hand.

DD:BK:glm

Enclosure: ICAC Paper 8

AGENDA FOR ACTION

Obourn Senior High School

200 Woodbine Avenue
East Roachmont, New York

M. Jack Stivers
Principal

(716) 568-8840

ICAC Memo #8

TO: Members of ICAC

FROM: John Russell

DATE: March 2, 1983

First, some general observations which the committee felt would be of interest to our goads and mentors, Dick and Bob.

(A) The computer programming classes at Sinclair Senior High School enjoyed programming the 'drillanpractice' projects that we sent them after reading ICAC Paper 7. They've asked for more projects!

(B) Lolita noted that the generation of the items in the author-title drill program was done by crude item templates. It would seem that item templates would be central to many drill or practice programs.

(C) Phil pointed out that his work in rewriting the tutorial on triangles (ICAC Paper 6) would have been simplified by the use of an item template. Hence, templates could be useful in tutorials which build a concept by presenting examples. (NOTE: There could even be templates for generating the examples and counterexamples—Examples 1 and 2—of the tutorial on isosceles triangles. This would allow the program to respond to student requests for more such items.)

(D) Ted mentioned that he and other social studies teachers have card files filled with multiple-choice test items that they've developed over the years. He predicts widespread cooperation in pooling such items if a CATO-type program could be obtained. Gerri, Donna, Phil, John, and Lolita felt that there could be similar poolings in their areas. In each case, of course, someone would need to be given time (and authority) to do a lot of editing since writing styles would differ and grammatical/spelling errors are a sure thing.

COMMITTEE ASSIGNMENTS

The committee decided to accept the offer of the students at Sinclair Senior High School by putting them to work at designing and programming item templates. The plan is as follows.

1. John and Gerri (our only programmers) will enter Templates 1-4 (from ICAC Paper 8) on John's microcomputer. He and Gerri will arrange to spend two days with the students at Sinclair in demonstrating and teaching the concept of an item template.
2. Sinclair's students will be given sample items from which to develop templates. Their designs will be checked by subject experts before being programmed. The sample items and subject experts are as follows.

(A) Expert: Lolita

Item: Give the present simple tense of the sentence: He ran.

Note: The template could take on a multiple-choice form. It should cover six tenses (simple present, past, and future; present, past, and future perfect) and several verbs.

(B) Expert: Carrinne

Item: If a 100-gram tin of sardines is priced at 56 cents, a store will sell 1220 tins each month and make a profit of 11 cents per tin. Experience shows that for each 1-cent increase in price the store will sell 65 fewer tins per month. What price should be charged for the sardines in order to make the greatest monthly profit?

Note: Carrinne can provide prices on several other items, both canned and fresh.

(C) Expert: Jeanne

Item: Mix 1 part of primary red pigment (oil paint) with 1 part primary blue (oil paint). What is the color of the resulting mixture?

(D) Expert: Ted

Item: A family has been spending 23 percent of its total income on food. If the price of food itself increases 1.7 percent, what percent of the family's total income will then be spent on food?

Note: Ted has information on budget distributions for a variety of population groups. Also, he thinks the program should be optimistic by allowing for a decrease in prices.

(E) Expert: John

Item: The dinner bill (2 persons) at the Platinum Penguin Pavilion comes to $47.50 with a sales tax of 4 percent yet to be added. Louise leaves a total of $55.00 in bills, the "change" being a tip for the waiter. What percent of the dinner bill did the waiter receive as a tip?

(F) Expert: Donna

Item: For the following key signature name the key.

Note: The item would provide questions in either key signatures/keys or chords/chord symbols. It should include exercises involving both treble and base clef.

JR:ms

CHAPTER NINE

Individualization and Instructional Management with a Computer

The person who asks you "Is effective teaching a science or an art?" is probably seeking an argument rather than an answer. While a logically adroit listener might respond "Yes" and confound the questioner's little game, most of us would take the bait. We'd assume that the query is the stem of a dichotomous-choice item and that we must come down on one side (art or science) and argue against the other. Having done so, we're trapped.

The questioner's trick has been to pose an issue in such a way that we accept a dichotomous-choice format as being both intended and appropriate. In fact, the classification of so complex a phenomenon as *effective teaching* demands at least the freedom of choice found in the multiple-choice item:

Effective teaching is ______________.
1. wholly an art
2. wholly a science
3. both an art and a science

Of course, the primary reason for raising the question might be to have the responder recognize the existence and relevance of the third alternative. Indeed . . .

Education has a history of attending to dichotomies. Battles are joined under educational banners which suggest irreconcilable poles; efforts, funding, and opinion somehow move from one pole to the other without passing over the ground between! Thus, we have experienced "sight" versus "phonics" in reading and spelling, and "the basics" (yawn . . .) versus "the new math" (ugh!). The terms used to label the positions acquire strong emotional values such that anyone who is not an uncompromising advocate of one position is assumed to be wholly committed to the opposing point of view. So it is that educational dichotomies—specifically, *false* dichotomies—are born and nurtured. We'll consider a few garden-variety examples in which the characters involved are composites of real persons.

False Dichotomy 1: Art Versus Science

Studies have shown that a person's decision to enter the teaching profession is rooted in his or her interaction with a particularly effective teacher. The reason is common, but the examples of that effective teacher are diverse. One teacher recalls the college history instructor who gave each lecture dressed in the costume of the era under discussion and who ended each lecture in mid-sentence, refusing to "give more" than he was "paid to deliver." Another recalls a secondary school instructor who slipped into an old phone booth prominently displayed in one corner of the room, reappearing in a red and blue Superman suit in order to help students "overcome some difficult mathematics problem."

Art or science? Certainly the costuming and performances of the two teachers showed a certain flair for the dramatic, a flair that some might prefer to label *clowning*. On the other hand, it is reported that the teachers were effective in securing good class attendance and good test performances by their students. Was the style exhibited by the teachers simply an expression of personality or was there very deliberate method in apparent madness? Did the history teacher plan his costumes as another form of visual enhancement of his lectures (like textbook photographs or slides)? Did he halt in mid-sentence to support an instructional view of history as a great story to be told? (Tune in tomorrow for the next thrilling episode of . . .) Did the history teacher also know that lack of closure which characterized his "continuing story" style of presentation causes listeners to seek their own closure, thus extending lesson involvement? Was the use of costume by the mathematics teacher part of a plan to cause students to focus on selected mathematical concepts and to identify with their "conquest"? Could the students fail to recognize that each performance was an expression of planning, personal enthusiasm for the subject, expertise in the subject, and a desire to have others understand and become involved in the subject? Art or science?

False Dichotomy 2: Discipline Versus Instruction

While discipline (social order) and instruction have been recorded as inhabiting the same classroom, there are teachers who believe that these are just happy accidents resulting from unique circumstances. There is a belief that one of the two conditions (discipline, instruction) must dominate. Thus we hear "My students may not learn all that they should, but I have discipline!" thrown up against "I know my classroom is pandemonium, but my students are learning things!" The teacher in the first example probably defines good discipline to be absolute-silence-with-eyes-forward-and-hands-on-desk. Like the man who took literally his mentor's advice to "keep your ear to the ground, your shoulder to the wheel, and your nose to the grindstone," students may find it quite difficult to work in so unnatural a position. The second example sets classroom disorder as the price of learning, perhaps assuming that any sort of social restraint will warp student psyches and hinder intellectual growth.

The definitions of and research findings regarding discipline and effective teaching weave a tangled web. Yet a somewhat dated review of the research on discipline suggests that discipline/instruction is a both/and rather than an either/or situation.[1] It indicates that good discipline is found in those situations in which

- the teacher clearly understands the subject being taught
- the teacher exhibits a desire that the students come to understand what is being taught.

The conditions for good discipline could just as well be the basic principles of effective instruction.

False Dichotomy 3: Individualization Versus Management

The title to this paper mentions both *individualization* and *management*. For many educators, these terms have emotional connotations. For the teacher who prefers to be classified as a humanist, *individualization* is a "good" word. It suggests interest in each student and a flexibility in presentation aimed at meeting the needs of

---

[1]William J. Gnagey, *Maintaining Discipline in Classroom Instruction* (New York: Macmillan Publishing Co., 1975).

each student. To our humanist (our teacher-artist) the term *management* is associated with rigid, impersonal, or mechanistic instruction; it's "bad." On the other hand, the person who holds that planning and organization are the sum and substance of effective teaching sees these terms in quite a different light. To this teacher-scientist, *individualization* may be equated with a model of instruction which places each student on one end of a log and a teacher on the other. Individualization is unacceptable (i.e., "bad") because (a) such one-to-one instruction is impossible in practice and (b) such instruction is an ill-defined function of the talents and personality of the teacher. The teacher-scientist favors *management* insofar as it organizes and standardizes the delivery of the curriculum.

Being the clever person that you are, you have no doubt observed that individualization-or-management, as applied to teaching, does not present a simple dichotomy. Just like the art-or-science and discipline-or-instruction choices, the terms *can* be associated with extreme, emotion-laden positions. In classroom practice, however, the associated instructional processes or styles can and should enjoy peaceful coexistence. Rational discussion demands that we recognize individualization-or-management as a false dichotomy and that we explore the advantages of an individualization-*and*-management position. (In general, we'll find the pursuit of *both/and* to be much more profitable than the resolution of *either/or.)*

Management and Individualization: Means and End

Instructional management is a means to an end. The end which it serves is the utilization of the learning environment in a manner that best serves the individual needs, talents, and interests of both students and teachers. In computer-managed instruction, the computer facilitates the management process by executing a wide variety of necessary but complex and tedious tasks. In its role as electronic paper shuffler, it provides a form of clerical assistance formerly unavailable because of the magnitude of the tasks presented and the speed of response required. As a ready source of both summaries and details regarding teaching resources and student progress, it supports the teacher's decision-making role as the designer of instruction. The computer is, then, *a means to* instructional management—a means to a means to an end.

The basic motivation for the development of computer management of instruction is evident. After all, one of the major roles of the classroom teacher is that of manager. What isn't quite so evident is the fact that there are two levels to the teacher's management activities, levels which make quite different demands upon the teacher's professional skills.

Supervisory management activity involves clerical functions such as recording, assigning, evaluating, arranging, and reporting. The activities called forth by these functions are familiar to every classroom teacher. They are routine and almost mechanical, but their execution consumes significant blocks of time. Insofar as they do not call upon the teacher's specialized professional talents (e.g., expertise in a subject, knowledge of how children learn, creativity in lesson design), they come to be resented by teachers who feel that they are squandering time on the mindless (even if necessary) repetition of tasks tangential to teaching while instructional challenges go unanswered. It's not surprising to find that activities at the supervisory management level are among the first duties that teachers assign away when blessed with the services of an aide or a student teacher. Boring! The computer, a creature given to the relentless pursuit of mindless tasks, is a prime candidate for application at the supervisory level of classroom instructional activity.

The second level of instructional management involves, shall we say, more art than science. It involves the *executive* functions of planning, organizing, commanding, coordinating, and controlling instruction. While the sophisticated decision-making at this level draws upon complex teaching skills, the computer can aid the teacher by providing data useful in making those decisions. The computer's role in instructional management is to help the teacher move away from supervisory-level functions toward greater involvement in executive-level functions. The computer system required must be able both to assume most of the supervisory functions and to support the teacher's increased involvement with the executive functions.

The New Kid on the Block

Computer managed instruction (CMI) is "the new kid on the block" of instructional applications of computers. As reported in Chapter 1, early emphasis on teaching *about* computers gave way to teaching *with* computers in the drill, practice, and tutorial modes. Lessons in these modes could be relatively short and could be developed in isolation as presentations of specific items of subject matter. The use of computers for instructional management, on the other hand, requires a detailed analysis of the entire teaching act (independent of a specific subject) and the development of an integrated system of programs that comprise a single instructional management facility. Moreover, the demand for such a facility presupposes teachers' acceptance of the goal of individualizing the educational experience.

Recent in arriving, CMI has rapidly gained acceptance as *a,* if not *the,* most important application of computers to instruction. While the growing availability of computer equipment in schools has promoted all forms of instructional computing, there are specific conditions which may explain the sudden gains being made by CMI.

First, the acceptance of individualization as an educational goal has led educators to realize the magnitude of the task of monitoring and facilitating this style of education. Simply put, the educator's task under the individualization model is to deliver each daily lesson (example: spelling the possessive form of a plural noun ending in *s* or *z*) of each major topic (example: spelling the possessive form of a noun) at each level (example: grade or level 6) within each strand (example: grammar) of each curriculum (example: English) to each student in one or more forms appropriate to the student's level of achievement, interests, and learning style. Viewed from the personal perspective of a given secondary school teacher of English, the task needs to be translated into specific activities for 150 students whose achievement is spread over six school years. Oh yes, and don't forget (a) to keep detailed records (both individual and class) for reporting to parents, administrators, and assorted government agencies, (b) to keep track of the location and condition of teaching resources in use, (c) to regularly retire outdated teaching materials, and (d) to identify new learning resources and to revise lessons to make use of those resources. Having done this, of course, the teacher will have lots more time to spend with individual students. Students will find the teacher very easy to locate since she now is at the school some 8760 (i.e., 24 x 365) hours of the year.

Declining school resources also have increased educational interest in CMI. Existing resources must be put to optimum use. The request for new resources must be accompanied by an assessment of need which justifies the purchase of those resources. The public, demanding accountability in education, holds the schools responsible for verifying that they are attaining the goals set for them. Each request for resources must be related to those goals; subsequent evaluation must show that the new resources have been effective in attaining those goals.

CMI: The Dimensions of the Task

So much for the preamble to CMI. We hope you're convinced that education needs managing and that the computer should be harnessed to aid teachers in performing overwhelming management tasks. It remains for us to identify the activities which comprise the task of instructional management and to describe the characteristics of a computer system that is a match for that task. The purpose of this section is to define the task faced by CMI; the next major section of the chapter will examine the components of the computing facility required.

Understanding the phrase *instructional management* is comparable to understanding the phrase *French language.* Either topic is so complex as to demand the development of understanding by stages. First, we can *talk about the topic* in broad terms which describe its purpose and major characteristics. Next, we *seek mastery* of specific components of the topic. Finally, we *apply our knowledge* by weaving together the individual skills that we've acquired into a smooth performance. It is at this final stage that we realize that any major idea is more than the sum of its parts.

In the next eight subsections we will attempt to reach the first level of understanding of instructional management. Our purpose will be to *talk about the topic* by breaking it into the tasks of diagnosing progress, prescribing study, monitoring study, evaluating learning, collecting data, reporting evaluation results, managing resources, and supporting interpersonal communications. While the analysis is made with good intentions, the reader should keep in mind that this kind of academic dissection reveals only the gross anatomy of the subject. It does not purport to explore any task in depth, it does not seek to develop the reader's skill in dealing with any component task, it ignores the fact that each task takes place in union with each other task (thus making their separation a convenience of discussion only), and it tends to obscure the fact that understanding of instructional management as a whole requires more than an understanding of the tasks which have been identified as comprising it.

Diagnosing Progress

There's a story about a very timid fellow who was making his first airplane flight. Seeing the copilot strolling down the aisle, the passenger nervously inquired as to how the flight was progressing. "Well," said the copilot, "I've got some good news and some bad news. The good news is that we're two hours ahead of schedule—the bad news is that we haven't the foggiest notion of where we are." The story has often been used to illustrate the overall condition of schooling.

To determine educational progress, we need signposts to tell us where we began, which way to go, and when we've arrived. In educationese, these signposts are called *behavioral objectives*. Their construction and use are the subjects of an impressive volume of literature;[2] they are also among the specific skills of instructional management that we won't stop to develop here. Sufficient to say that when we speak of "diagnosing a student's progress" we mean "diagnosing a student's progress toward specific objectives."

Progress toward a major objective may take place in several steps (subobjectives) over a period of years. Consider, for example, this objective from a course in music appreciation.

> Played 15-second opening passages of duets selected at random from two operas by each of ten composers (Mozart, Wagner, Rossini, Donizetti, Verdi, Bizet, Strauss, Puccini, Busoni, Britten), the student will identify orally both the name of the opera in which the duet appears and the name of the composer. The student will identify both items correctly for at least 16 of the 20 passages played.

Diagnosis of a student's progress is concerned with the pattern of successes and/or failures he or she has recorded at each step along the way. In particular, it seeks to identify any pattern in the failures and to determine the reason(s) for the failures so that remedies can be applied. Based upon the results of this diagnosis, the student's progress will be routed in one of several directions: toward a remedial assignment in a prerequisite concept, toward a remedial assignment on the same concept but involving a different mode of instruction, toward a remedial assignment on the same topic and involving the same mode of instruction but using fresh examples, toward a new assignment relative to the same concept, or toward an assignment on a new concept. Each routing calls for a correct interpretation of the student's learning profile which is crucial to the use of the student's learning time and the available learning resources.

Prescribing Study

Prescription is the natural companion of diagnosis. Each prescription assigns the student to a specific learning activity, the appropriateness of which is a function of both the quality of the diagnosis and the range of learning resources available.[3] Sometimes the pattern of student errors is so familiar and so specific that a well-established treatment immediately suggests itself as the only reasonable prescription. At other times; a wide range of possible activities might be prescribed. In the latter case, the learning resource could be a textbook assignment, a group activity, individual practice, consultation with a teacher, laboratory work, or the use of new media such as films, slides, audio tapes, television, or a computer-based activity.

Although a computer-based management system need not be designed to include the direct delivery of computerized instruction, its prescriptive function can integrate the use of computerized lessons involving drill, practice, simulation, problem solving, etc. That is, computer-based *management* can live a life apart from computer-based *instruction*. However, its prescriptive facility should direct the student to an available computerized lesson in the same manner that it would direct that student to a book, film, or laboratory exercise. Appropriate computerized lessons merely constitute one category of learning resources in management's bag of remedies. And whereas a computer can be useful in managing an instructional environment which has no computerized lessons among its resources, computerized lessons—like the science kits in the closet—aren't really "available" until they are linked to the prescriptive facility of instructional management.

Monitoring Study

Orwell's *1984* aside, it's sometimes comforting to know that Big Brother is watching. In fact, one of the important tasks of an instructional management system is to provide a study-monitoring system which not only watches the student but also whispers suggestions aimed at making the study session of greatest value to him or her.

In many classrooms, individual study is really independent exercising. The student, assigned a variety of in-class or homework exercises, often is expected to carry out his labors in monkish solitude. To consult with others is to cheat. Consequently, a student may work through a long list of exercises without the benefit of feedback on the correctness of that work. The student may, as a result, refine and reinforce an erroneous procedure! Surely, the value of such a procedure is in doubt.

---

[2]We offer two of the more helpful volumes:
R. F. Mager, *Preparing Objectives for Instruction* (Belmont, CA: Fearon, 1962); N. E. Gronlund, *Stating Behavioral Objectives for Classroom Instruction* (New York: Macmillan Publishing Co., 1970).

[3]To be *available* is more than to be physically accessible. Many a teacher has been found to have physical access to a closet filled with kits of excellent elementary science activities; however, these resources were unavailable to students because the teacher did not know how and where to use them in instruction.

An instructional management system facilitates learning by providing the student with self-study monitoring. This feature is designed to give the student immediate knowledge of the correctness of a response and to give specific suggestions for dealing with errors. In effect, this "Big Brother" service includes the characteristics of a well-designed questioning or practicing facility. When management is computer-assisted, the service can be implemented interactively by having students go to terminals to participate in a questioning session or it can be implemented in a batch mode by using a computer to read and evaluate responses previously recorded on special forms. In interactive CMI, the student might get feedback on each question as it is answered. In batch CMI, the student completes the entire set of questions before receiving feedback.

To facilitate study, the answer-judging elements (feedback messages and performance summaries) must be evaluative, but they should not be judgmental or penalizing. The object is to improve self-study and not to assign a grade. There should be no stigma attached to answering questions incorrectly. Rather, the monitoring system seeks to use incorrect responses to support learning by attaching those incorrect responses to specific and carefully designed feedback messages.

The system also should provide periodic performance summaries. While these don't fit into the grading process, they provide the student with knowledge of how the performance *would* be rated *if* a grade were assigned. This kind of formative evaluation helps the student judge how well learning is progressing. It's nice to know that you're making progress; it's also valuable to know that you're not.

Evaluating Learning

In monitoring study, questions and feedback are used to guide the student along a path of study leading to a specific objective. There comes a time, however, when the student may wish to prove mastery of that objective in order to move on toward something new. Now the management system must verify that learning has taken place (i.e., that the objective has been met). Evaluation at this level will make use of sets of questions or tasks which require the desired behavior described in an objective. The data gathered may be used to assign a grade or to prescribe the next learning activity; it always becomes part of the student's performance history—the pattern of success and nonsuccess which is the basis of diagnosis.

Let there be no doubt, we're talking about *testing*. Terms like *evaluating* and *assessing* may better describe our purpose, but the student view focuses upon method rather than purpose. The teacher's motives may be most noble. The manner in which the student will benefit from evaluation may have been presented with sensitivity and crystal clarity. Still, for the student, it all boils down to a test and a judgment—"You have learned" or "You haven't learned yet." Remember your last test? Feel a little tense? If so, you may understand that some students fail to appreciate the overall good of evaluation;[4] a few even go so far as to feel that the objective of test taking is to "beat the system."[5] Teachers, in response, require that an evaluation facility have some degree of security so that the results of evaluation will be valid evidence of learning. One must beat the system of those who are out to beat the system.

The security of an evaluation system can be achieved through question pooling. Each objective is represented in its pool by several questions (tasks) which are similar in item form, level of difficulty, and physical appearance. In the case of a computer-based evaluation facility, the interactive form of test presentation presents fewer security problems since there are no printed copies of the items to be carried away. Security in batch mode calls for the printing of alternate forms of a test, with each copy accounted for and destroyed after use. In either case, evaluation must take place under supervised conditions with local conditions dictating individual or group testing.

Collecting Data

Data is the fuel of any instructional management system. The system needs data about the past and current performances of students, data about available resources, data that relates student performances to prescriptions, data which links student performances to past study resources used, and data about the quality of the data. Teachers' decisions—whether announced directly by the teachers or announced indirectly by a computer acting on behalf of the teachers—are rooted in that data. Because of the size and complexity of the data base, the teacher-manager, operating at the executive level, must be able to quickly manipulate it in a variety of ways in order to make decisions regarding an individual student, a group of students, a particular learning activity, a group of learning activities, or (and, perhaps, most important of all) the effectiveness of the decision-making process in the system.

---

[4]Shame! Can it be? How extraordinary!

[5]How shortsighted! Whatever is the world coming to? Certainly *we* never felt that way . . .

Reporting Evaluation Results

Data must be summarized and reported to a variety of participants in the education game: students, parents, teachers, school administrators, agencies supporting particular instructional programs, government agencies, and the general public. Everybody wants to know; everybody wants to know something a bit different. What any individual or group is entitled to know is, of course, a function of legal right and academic usefulness. Thus a management system must be both open enough to generate the reports needed and secure enough to guarantee a proper (and legal) balance between information access and individual privacy.

Data must be summarized and reported in a variety of ways to a given participant in the education game. Suppose, for example, that a group of students has completed a diagnostic test dealing with four objectives of a unit on theories of the formation of continents. A given student is entitled to know what the objectives were, what the criterion for passing (demonstrating mastery of) each objective was, and how he or she performed relative to each objective. The student may or may not be entitled to know the answers to questions missed or how the class performed as a group. The student definitely is not entitled to information regarding the performance of another individual. For the same test, the teacher may need access to all of the information mentioned as well as to summaries of class performance on each test item and each objective. In the interest of improving the diagnostic process itself, the teacher also may need item and test statistics which include data from several classes of students.

As a further example, suppose that a student is routed to a study prescription which lists a choice of six possible learning resources. The student is entitled to a brief description of each resource, some estimation of the time required to study each resource, and the location of each resource. In addition, the teacher should be able to obtain a report of the frequency with which any given resource has been chosen and the effectiveness of that resource with each of several groups of students. Such information regarding a resource is needed if the teacher is to refine the process of assigning students to appropriate learning experiences.

Managing Resources

Teacher-managers need to distinguish between a situation and a problem. Whereas situations ask only to be described, problems demand solutions. Some examples are in order.

Situation A: Bob invites Dick to go trout fishing. Dick accepts. There is no problem since Bob has two fishing poles.

Situation B: Bob invites Dick to go trout fishing. Dick accepts. Their wives decide to accept, too. Now there is the singular problem of what Dick and Bob will do with their day while the ladies take to the stream. Four into two won't go!

The problem associated with Situation B demands a solution. One solution is for Dick and Bob to quietly abscond with the poles. However, the probable consequences of this solution must give Dick and Bob pause. An acceptable solution might be to develop a plan to share the limited resource (i.e., the fishing poles) on a time schedule while providing some alternate and desirable activity (reading, cards, frying the latest catch) for whatever pair is awaiting access to the resource. Problem solved.

The management of limited resources (driver-training cars, laboratory stations, sporting equipment, computer terminals) is an everyday teaching task. The teacher must make the arrangements by which students and learning materials get together in the right places at the right times. If the resource is a book or worksheet, the supply usually exceeds the need. On the other hand, the following situation is common.

Situation C: Ms. Echinodermata's biology class is studying single-celled life forms. She wishes to set up laboratory stations on such forms; the following resources are available:

- 5 microscopes
- 3 slides of *amoeba proteus*
- 4 slides of *paramecium caudatum*
- 2 slides of *gymnodinium breve*[6]

Each of her 28 students is given a copy of a worksheet which presents two exercises.

1. Use a microscope to view each of the three life forms. For each one, you must answer correctly at least eight of the ten questions on this sheet which deal with it.
2. Draw and label a sketch of one of the three forms (your choice). NOTE: The sketch must measure at least 15 cm along at least one of its dimensions.

Because the resources are limited relative to the class size, Ms. Echinodermata's situation poses a problem in resource management. Although five laboratory stations can be set up, the supply of slides dictates that the stations will be different. In order that each student may work with each life form, the teacher must establish time blocks (say, 30 minutes for viewing and 15 minutes

[6]Single-celled gym shorts?

for sketching) and design sign-up procedures for each pair of students to visit a combination of stations.

The teacher-time spent on supervision tasks like Ms. Echinodermata's mounts quickly. It reduces the time available for tasks demanding the teacher's professional skills; thus, valuable student learning activities may be denied because of the time and energy that must be invested in clerical duties associated with those activities.

As described earlier, a CMI system includes a study prescription facility that takes the major responsibility for matching students with appropriate assignments. The system stores data about those prescriptions and reports the assignment to the teacher as requested. Were the computer's contribution limited to arranging learning activities to end with those services, the clerical-supervisory burden of the teacher would be reduced but little. The system not only should know what assignments to make to students but also should aid the execution of those assignments by scheduling student use of limited resources. In particular, the system must take into account the resources needed for each activity, the quantity of each resource relative to number of students that may use it simultaneously, the number of spaces available for making use of the required resources, and the amount of time that each student must spend with a given resource. With such information, the system can cope with the prickly Echinodermata-type scheduling problem. It concentrates use of a resource by as many students as possible in order to minimize set-up time required and to give all students access to the resource as quickly as possible. Given information about alternate assignments that are appropriate when a given resource is being fully used, it also can maintain meaningful study activity among students waiting to use the resource.

Perhaps *the* resource most in need of scheduling is the teacher. Individualized education should not be equated with independent study. Individualization includes group activities and seeks to promote individual student-teacher interaction. In the case of a self-contained elementary school classroom, the teacher's scheduling of sessions with groups and individuals is aided by extended daily contact; computer supervision of such sessions may constitute management overkill. However, environments such as secondary schools, community colleges, professional schools, and colleges usually reduce the time for formal meetings between teacher and class to three to five hours per week. These situations—situations in which the majority of study takes place outside the classroom—are characterized by limited and irregular student-teacher contact and, often, by a large student-teacher ratio. The scheduling of education's central learning resource, the teacher, is a must under these conditions.

Supporting Interpersonal Communication

Education is an elaborate exercise in communication. At one end of the line is a student; at the other is some source of information about a concept, generalization, or skill. Education has the job of linking students and sources in such a way that the information is transferred from source to student with minimal interference. At the classroom level, the teacher functions both as the switching system and as a source of information. In particular, the teacher functions as a focal point for communication among all persons involved in the education of students in that classroom.

Teachers seeking to individualize instruction have been quick to recognize the importance and difficulty of operating a network of interpersonal communications. As students become dispersed throughout the extended learning environment which typifies individualization, the problems of interpersonal communication are magnified. The teacher needs to make specific announcements to small work groups, to respond to queries from individuals or groups, to get information from individuals or groups, and to relay private information to individuals. Individual students need to communicate with the teacher, members of a study group, or other individual students without having to depend upon personal contact. When the management of an individualized program falls to a teacher-manager, maintenance of the interpersonal communications network can become impossible. This breakdown probably is a reason that teachers using these alternate instructional plans report that they feel "out of touch" with their students.

Computer management of an individualized environment can put students and teachers back in touch through the use of computerized bulletin boards and computerized mailboxes. A bulletin board provides a public forum for a given group; any member of the group (including the teacher) can post a notice. Whenever a member of the group signs on to the computer, he or she is immediately shown a display of any new announcements. Old notices can be recalled as needed. Computerized mailboxes, on the other hand, are used for private correspondence; only the "owner" of the mailbox can read or erase the messages it contains. These mailboxes support the efficient exchange of confidential information between any two persons using the system.

CMI: Features of an Adequate System

Having faced up to the task of managing instruction in an individualized environment, we're now ready to call upon some "assistant" to relieve us of much of the clerical burden at the supervisory level and to support our work at the executive level. Barring some sudden and radical alteration in our human ability to store, sort, recall, and replace the countless items of data necessary to the operation of an individualized system, we need help! For those of us who aren't able (or willing) to juggle the mental bin of dusty facts required, computers are more than an alternative—they're *the* alternative. There is no other resource which offers the combination of memory, speed, devotion to detail, and unquestioning obedience that is necessary to do the job.

As we get ready to make up our shopping list of things we expect to find in a computer based MANAGEMENT system, there's one word that needs to be emphasized. (Guess which word.) Since a CMI system is charged only with the MANAGEMENT of instruction, it follows that responsibility lies elsewhere to provide whatever it is that CMI is to manage. A CMI system cannot operate without a large amount of specific information to process and to present to its users. The majority of this information must be created *before* the CMI system can begin to function. Other information (e.g., student performance records) is gathered as the system chugs along.

The kind of information needed to get a CMI system operating is that which describes the content, organization, and learning resources of a curriculum. Thus, the curriculum must be spelled out in detail in terms of specific objectives. There must be an instructional plan which includes the bases for guiding students through the maze of objectives along individually defined paths. The system must be supplied with the sets of questions to be used in diagnosing progress, monitoring study, and evaluating learning. The CMI prescription facility will need a detailed description of each study assignment and of each learning resource to be employed. These objectives, questions, prescriptions, and resources form a curriculum; their location (or creation), and organization must be carried out by a skilled teacher. At this level of professional judgment, the computer is worthless. The computer within the environment of instructional management is a doer, not a thinker. However, once the information about a curriculum is in a form that a computer can handle, it will execute the aforementioned eight tasks of management for time unending.

The computer is a wellspring of supervisory services within the arid land of management minutia (or "administrivia"). To make the services flow, however, you first have to prime the pump. Part of that priming is the development of a curriculum (an executive-level management task); the other part was glossed over by the condition "once the information . . . a computer can handle." To accomplish the latter task, one needs a simple means of teaching the curriculum (objectives, etc.) to the computer. In fact, any CMI system worth considering must include a facility—called a *curriculum authoring* facility or *authoring language*—for doing just that. Designed for use by folks who are not computerniks, the facility uses simple questions which guide the user in entering the details of the curriculum. With a little training in the language of instructional management,[7] a clerk could be given the task of entering the information which constitutes a particular curriculum.

Let's now assume that some talented teacher (or group of talented teachers) has put together the bits and pieces of a curriculum in ———, where ——— may be art, botany, driver education, geography, music, welding, or whatever turns your crank. That is, let's assume that the objectives, questions, decision points (for curriculum routing by student or teacher), learning resources, and evaluation criteria of our curriculum are known. We can then use the ideas generated by our discussion of the eight tasks faced by an instructional management system to define Super-CMI.[8] As explained in the subsections to follow, Super-CMI will be comprised of a curriculum authoring facility, an individualized study/monitoring facility, a records/reporting facility, a resource management facility, and a communication facility.

Curriculum Authoring

A curriculum authoring facility is a computer program which provides a simple way in which teachers can answer the Super-CMI question "What is the curriculum that you want me to manage?" The facility aids the teacher in answering that question by responding to more specific questions about curricular objectives, prescriptions, questions of various sorts used for a variety of reasons, etc. It allows the teacher to "author" the curriculum by providing a nontechnical way of entering the following kinds of information about the curriculum.

1. *Text*. This includes all of the written material associated with the Items 2–4 which follow. For example, text is involved in course descriptions, the statement of objectives and questions, feedback messages, instructions, and lesson assignments.
2. *Questioning episodes*. In addition to the text associated with an episode, the user must be able to specify all acceptable forms of the correct answer, all familiar incorrect responses to which specific

---

[7]That is, such terms as *objective*, *resource*, *criterion*, etc.

[8]Super-CMI is the unregistered trademark of a CMI system of literary invention that will answer every demand we have ascribed to a "well-designed" instructional management system. No single computer system offers Super-CMI but *it does exist* as a combination of the management features of computer systems now on the market.

feedback messages will be attached, and information on the number of points to be assigned for any given response or combination of responses. Also, graphic or other visual material which may accompany the episodes will need a facility to simplify its creation.

3. *Student-controlled decision points.* The system must be informed of the types of decisions a student may make in selecting a learning resource, determining the sequence in which assignments will be done, tests taken or already completed materials (tests or lessons) reviewed.
4. *System-controlled decision points.* The CMI system must be given the criteria by which the teacher-creator will route students through the curriculum. Such decision points may (a) alter a student's path within a single unit of instruction or (b) cause the student to leave one unit and enter another.

Super-CMI not only must help the teacher create a computerized curriculum but also must ensure the easy *re*-creation of the curriculum. One of the attractions of Super-CMI is its ability to keep a curriculum current and "clean" by providing a "no-sweat" procedure for deleting out-of-date material (e.g., terminology, methods, learning resources, specific lessons, or whole units of instruction), inserting new material, and correcting errors in the text, answers, or decision-making structure of the curriculum. Specifically, the system must offer at least three *re*-creation features:

- *insertion* of new letters, words, or lines of information at any point;
- *deletion* of any part of existing material without disturbing the adjoining material;
- *alteration* of specific letters, words, or lines of information in the text.

And since we know you are an alert reader, we hasten to point out that alteration really is distinct from the combination of deletion and insertion! In Super-CMI, the editing capability of the system lets the user introduce change with a minimum of effort by limiting the change to the specific offending letter, symbol, or phrase. It also will execute a recurring textual alteration with but a single stroke: for instance, it can update a text on African geography by locating each of 138 appearances of the name *Rhodesia* and replacing it by the name *Zimbabwe.*

Individualized Study-Monitoring

The individualized study/monitoring facility of Super-CMI is the teacher-defined medium of contact between each student and the curriculum. It provides the student with appropriate assignments and employs monitoring services to ensure that the student's self-study of those assignments leads to the desired learning.

The student's view of the study/monitoring facility is dependent, at least in part, on the mode of delivery: batch or interactive. In batch mode, a terminal directs the student to printed self-study booklets containing diagnostic tests, information and questions related to a topic to be studied, or to a test to verify that a given lesson has been learned. The student records answers to questions on a computer-readable form (card or sheet) and submits the form to a computer-operated form reader. Having checked the students' responses, the computer uses a printer to give the student such feedback as (a) an analysis of the responses, (b) a remedial assignment to aid the student in areas where the profile of responses indicates a weak performance, or (c) an assignment to a new activity. When operated in batch mode, CMI requires a form reader and a printer to provide detailed analysis of the responses and to prescribe the activities suggested by those responses. Clearly, batch-mode CMI needs aides, test monitors, a large space for storing study and test booklets, and a location where students may collect the computer's printed feedback to performances on question sets.

Life is simpler for the student who encounters Super-CMI in an interactive mode. All questioning is done on-line; analyses and assignments are generated immediately. While this eliminates the need for storing and working with printed question sets, it requires many more terminals to serve a given audience. (That need for more terminals is, of course, a need for more money and work space.) Even given those extra terminals, a student using CMI in the interactive mode must be able to interrupt his computer session at points both within and between lessons and to resume his work at an appropriate place at the next session.

Whatever its mode of delivering a study/monitoring service, Super-CMI must provide for two levels of achievement with respect to a curricular objective: the *attaining* level and the *maintaining* level. At the first level, the system manages the student's study of a topic until his performance satisfies some criterion specified by the teacher. Student study activity which precedes the satisfying of that criterion is aimed at attaining achievement. When the criterion is met, the system's feedback from the teacher says "You've got it!" But "getting something" is just part of the learning game; a trickier part of learning is hanging on to whatever you "got." So, having reached the you've-got-it point, the student moves into the maintaining level of achievement. At this second level, Super-CMI faces the task of keeping knowledge alive. To this end, a newly attained objective is added to a set of objectives needing periodic review.

The length of the period associated with periodic review at the maintaining level depends on many considerations, including:

- the difficulty experienced by the student during the attaining stage,
- the relative importance of the objective within the total curriculum,[9]
- the pattern of success recorded within the maintaining stage (with low success resulting in a shortening of the period between reviews).

Objectives deemed most likely to require extensive maintenance are represented by questions (tasks) in the Super-CMI review pool. The computer then initiates review sessions by presenting the student with a random selection of items dealing with the objectives which are under maintenance. A less sophisticated procedure (for smaller and not-quite-so-super computer systems) would have the computer advise the student of those objectives needing review and have the student assume responsibility for conducting that review by selecting activities from a suggested menu of appropriate things to do.

Super-CMI will permit any student to review any objective at any time. There are, after all, motivated students who march to the beat of their personal academic drummers. For important objectives, it also must provide a system-controlled schedule of achievement maintenance which responds to (a) a student's profile of past performances relative to those objectives and (b) the need to review objectives which are prerequisite to the successful study of a new topic. There is, after all, the rare student who will turn a deaf ear to all academic drummers.

Students do not excel at designing their own achievement maintenance schemes. Studies have shown that students will not initiate adequate review and will use review time ineffectively. When an individualized environment puts the students in total control, their work will be characterized by long periods of no activity, short periods of frantic effort (the well known "procrastination phenomenon"), and inefficient use of the facilities available. It will come as no surprise to the experienced teacher (and/or the reflective reader) that these characteristics are most pronounced among the least successful students. Until we find the secret of fostering self-motivation in all students with regard to each valid objective of education, Super-CMI can provide appropriate and insistent prodding as needed.

Records/Reporting

The records component of our Super-CMI records/reporting facility is the means by which the system continuously updates information relative to anybody or anything in touch with the system. The reporting component summarizes that information in a variety of ways and presents it in a form which is useful to anyone with a justified "right to know." To serve, it must let the teacher quickly accomplish the following tasks:

1. enroll a student in any course at any time;
2. specify the data to be kept relative to students;
3. specify the course requirements (units, sequencing, completion criteria) for students;
4. enter initial data regarding any student;
5. alter a student record;
6. keep student records secure from unauthorized eyes;
7. protect student records from unauthorized alteration;
8. define the form of needed reports;
9. generate reports as needed.

Students also may wish to review their records from time to time. Such interest in investigation is particularly strong (frequent) during students' early contact with CMI, a period during which the student is understandably suspicious of an "automatic" record keeping system. In fact, concern for the contents and uses of computerized files of information is worth encouraging in an increasingly electronic world. Individuals should be concerned about what is in those files, who may inspect the files, and who may alter them.[10]

Others in the instructional setting—administrators, government groups, funding agencies, educational researchers—may have a justified need for specialized summaries of data. In general, such justifications deal with measuring the educational progress of the system and planning future activity. In these cases, Super-CMI should be able to make such reports available to the authorized persons in interpretable form (preferably with suggested decisions noted wherever the data implies them). The impact of such data-based decision making could be quite dramatic. The hiring of staff and the purchase of learning resources could be based upon documented evidence of educational need rather than upon vague notions, public emotion, tradition, clever salesmanship, or whims of the local educational power structure. Conversely, the same system could be used subsequently to record evidence of educational change which might be ascribed to the hiring and purchasing decisions made. (We'll soon have reason to recall this "validation" feature.)

---

[9]Okay, so one objective of a certain tenth-grade English course is to recite (from memory) at least one poem of 10–25 lines by each of six nineteenth-century American poets. If attained, should it be maintained through grade twelve? Until marriage? Until death us do part?

[10]A certain amount of malaise is a good thing, provided that it is based on an understanding of potential misuses of the computer and an investigation of the public's role in preventing those misuses. To develop such an "informed malaise," try sampling relevant chapters from the books listed under "Computers Everywhere Else" in Section 6 of Chapter 4.

Resource Management

Our Super-CMI resource management facility has two general functions.

1. It ensures maximum efficiency in the use of space, equipment, staff, and other instructional resources.
2. It minimizes the loss of instructional time caused by the unavailability of needed instructional resources.

The *obvious* overall task of resource management is to squeeze every drop of use out of every instructional resource. But, aided and abetted by the records/reporting facility, it answers to a secret agenda as well.

The managers of education are a curious lot. Given that the football team at Oulde Intelligensia State College has just lost the last thirty-three games, the trustees will conclude that the only solution is to build a new stadium, increase the number of coaches, raise salaries in the Athletic Department, and offer more scholarships. Should the students at Mishmash High School show a 0.8 percent drop in scores on some standardized test, an irate citizenry will direct the local board of education to freeze teacher salaries, cut the number of teachers, refuse the purchase of frills (e.g., computers, microscopes, films, new textbooks), build a new stadium, increase the number of coaches, etc.

Okay . . . so we exaggerate a tiny bit. Still, school budgets are being tightened, and the budget category containing equipment and supplies is the first to feel the pinch. In the absence of data verifying that learning resources are being used with maximum efficiency, that real shortages do exist, that the areas of shortage can be linked to weaknesses in the educational program, and that the effect of eliminating the shortages can be measured in terms of learning progress, school teachers and administrators have no foundation for a convincing argument. In this atmosphere of educational accountability, the public may argue from opinion (and the fact of the 0.8 percent drop in scores); educators must present facts. The secret agenda served by Super-CMI is to provide such facts by verifying efficient use (the resource management facility) and educational outcomes (the records/reporting facility).

Even with the best of political maneuvering on the part of educators, many learning resources never will be supplied for entire classes on a one-to-one basis. Some items are very expensive and/or have a limited academic life because of the development of more advanced resources. In other cases (e.g., microcomputers) it may be undesirable to limit students' experiences to a single version of the resource. As a result of the shortage or diversity in a given resource, detailed plans must be made for the use of the resource—plans which include alternate activities for students awaiting access to the resource. The resource management facility of Super-CMI addresses these problems.

The primary service performed by a resource management facility is the optimal scheduling of learning resources. From the teacher's point of view, the service must permit flexible scheduling: some activities require twenty minutes, while others take two hours; some can accommodate only one person at a time, whereas others can be pursued by pairs or groups of students. Super-CMI must permit the teacher to define such conditions of flexible use easily and should maintain scheduling (and rescheduling) under those conditions for extended periods of time. The following list illustrates, for a drivers' education class, the variety of appointments that might need scheduling in a fully individualized environment. The suggested times are illustrative only.

- Supplemental text resources (single-person appointments in time-unit multiples of 30 minutes)
- Audio-tutorial facility (up to six persons per time unit in multiples of 15 minutes)
- Film projector and viewing room (up to room capacity of eight persons in time-unit multiples of 15 to class size of forty in time-unit multiples of 15 minutes)
- Outdoor measurement activities (five two-person teams in time-unit multiples of 30 minutes)
- Computer terminals for viewing of programs (six single-person stations; one 10–15 minute lesson per any given person on a given day)
- Practice in automobile operation (three persons maximum at any time for a period of 60 minutes)
- Student-initiated conference (single persons in time-unit multiples of 10 minutes)
- Teacher-initiated or group-initiated conference (up to class size of forty in time-unit multiples of 15 minutes)

In order that the teacher may take advantage of special events (visitors, television programs, mobile laboratories) or recover from unexpected disasters (illness, equipment breakdowns, school closings due to bad weather), the system should permit the teacher to block out time periods and/or reschedule planned activities. Thus, the system must provide information about the current appointment schedule so that the persons affected can be directed to take appropriate action.

The principal users of a resource management facility are students and teachers. Any one of these users should be able to schedule any one of the several types of appointments. The user should be able to view his own schedule and to change or delete personal appointments. Whatever the resource—space, equipment, or human—Super-CMI must keep it in continuous use and must keep all participants active on productive tasks.

One final thought regarding computer management of instructional resources: since the computer is itself an expensive instructional resource, it is subject to public scrutiny as part of the general demand for accountability. Good enough. Note that the efficiency produced by adding resource management to the system's list of intended uses can increase its educational attractiveness. You might want to add that item to the secret agenda.

Communication

As individualization aids students in the development of greater independence and lets them expand the physical settings and the time frames in which they do their work, communication troubles arise. Super-CMI can alleviate the problem of maintaining communication among participants in an individualized system by means of a computerized mailbox. This permits any person in the system to deposit a message in the electronic mailbox of any other person (or group of persons) in the system. Each person receives such messages the very next time he uses a terminal.

A CMI mailbox system should provide certain minimal services. Specifically, it should permit any user to

- enter and edit a message,
- send a message to one person,
- send a message to several persons,
- read any personal message sent to him by another individual,
- read any message sent to any group to which he belongs,
- delete any messages received.

Deluxe models of a mailbox system also might allow the user to

- forward a message to another person,
- print a message on paper,
- establish a date after which a message will be automatically deleted.

A somewhat different message feature available on really super Super-CMI systems is a "page-and-talk" facility. Such a Super-CMI system allows any two users to have a private conversation using terminals which may be physically separated by a considerable distance. (The super-duper models will permit several persons to engage in what is called "computer conferencing.") To use the page-and-talk feature, a user (say, Mark Twain) first consults a current list of persons using the system. The user can then page any one of those persons, and a message such as "Mark Twain wants to talk to you" will appear on the screen of the person paged. If the person paged chooses to respond, the two can engage in an interactive conversation (typed) through their terminals. During the conversation, each person's screen displays the last message from each of the two parties. When the conversation is complete, the system returns each user to the computer activity that was in progress prior to the page-and-talk session. The system also allows any user to refuse all calls from the page-and-talk feature. This ability to play "nobody's home" is important if, say, the user is involved in taking a timed test.

CMI: The Teacher's Role

Certainly you have been able to infer much about the teacher's role in CMI as you've read the preceding sections. By way of summary, however, we'll close this paper by depositing five messages in your uncomputerized mailbox facility.

Message 1: Planning is Everything

Before any CMI system can go into operation, it must be "taught" a curriculum. It must know the content of the curriculum, the bases for instructional decision making in routing students through the curriculum, and the action to be taken as a result of any given decision. Teachers have the job of planning and preparing all of the information which defines the curriculum. The scope of that executive-level management task is suggested by the following *nonexhaustive* list of questions for which teachers must have detailed answers.

1. What are the specific instructional objectives?
2. What are the prerequisites for each objective?
3. For each objective, how will mastery of that objective be viewed?
4. How will routing through the curriculum be determined (e.g., one fixed sequence, branching by student option, branching in accord with individual performance)?
5. At what points in the curriculum are remedial resources likely to be needed?
6. For each such point, what remedial resources are available?
7. What action will be taken when no more remedial resources are available?
8. What information about student performance is to be gathered?
9. How is the information to be processed and reported? (For whom and for what reasons is this done?)
10. What instructional pacing procedures will be used (and under what conditions)?
11. What types of tests are to be used and how often are they to be used?

12. What are the criteria for beginning or ending a testing session?
13. What learning resources will be used?
14. What resource scheduling will be needed?
15. What are the conditions which determine the maximal use of a resource?
16. If grades are used, how and when will they be assigned?

Message 2: Mighty Oaks from Little Acorns Grow

Think big but start small. To avoid overwhelming yourself, start CMI efforts at a low level defined by carefully selected services. Studiously avoid overadvertising your first efforts.

Although it is not very likely at present, you may fall into a teaching situation in which a total Super-CMI system already exists for every subject and every class. Our "small-thinking" suggestions are still apropos if you're a stranger to such educational utopia. The fact that the system is fast and shiny doesn't mean that you should expect to be able to operate all of its bells and whistles on the first day. As with learning to juggle glass balls, one is likely to be discouraged by the results of starting with ten.

Message 3: Bees Do It

If bees and ants have enough sense to divide up the labors of life, surely educators can learn to recognize the need to have certain jobs done by other folks. With regard to CMI, teachers have the full responsibility of making the detailed curricular preparations required by a CMI system as given in Message 1. Teachers should *NOT* try to create the CMI system software! Preparation of such software should be left to an outside source; the teacher's interaction with that software production is to specify what it is that the resulting system should be able to do. If some of this software has already been developed for a given computer system, teachers must carefully examine what it can do and decide if it is adequate. When modification ("tailoring") of such software is required, that too should be left to the software specialists. Any such modification should be preceded by a careful examination of copyright law and should be clearly defined in a written contract with the software specialists doing the work.

Message 4: The Lesson of the Four-Wheel Drive Donkeys

The story (probably apocryphal) is told about a rich nation (Nation R) that was trying to help increase the agricultural productivity of a poor nation (Nation P) that was wholly dependent upon hand tools. Nation R noted Nation P's need to move agricultural products quickly over long distances. Since Nation P found this difficult to do with its simple donkey carts, Nation R supplied large numbers of four-wheel drive trucks. During an inspection tour a year later, representatives of Nation R were horrified to find the trucks abandoned and rusting in fields and ditches. When asked for an explanation, the farmers of Nation P explained apologetically that their donkeys simply weren't strong enough to pull the trucks.

The inappropriate use of sophisticated resources isn't confined to Nation P. Students' first few weeks of exposure to CMI can produce comparable confusion. For example, many CMI assignments will direct students to make off-line use of a textbook and then to return for a questioning session over what has been learned. In practice, however, one finds students sitting at terminals with those textbooks in their laps, flipping pages in search of the answer to each question asked. The procedure is inefficient, wastes computer resources, and misses the whole point of the interaction between the computer and other learning resources. Students need to overcome the fear of answering a question incorrectly when it is part of an activity which is not graded. In fact, the student must realize that there is merit in incorrect answers since the feedback message of the questioning episode provides corrective information and, perhaps, tells the student of the possible consequences of the incorrect response. Students, for all that they seem favorably disposed toward computers, need to learn to use them properly.

Message 5: Chatter Matters

Watch for opportunities to get small groups together for a chat. Although theoretically students *could* scatter themselves throughout an individualized curriculum so that no two were working on the same topic, this would rarely happen in practice. People are social creatures; they tend to cluster themselves so that there will be an opportunity to share problems and ideas. The teacher should capitalize on this natural academic clustering by organizing sessions in which group members can talk about their work and what they're learning. Oral interchange among peers is an important activity in any learning situation. At even the highest levels of research, participants depend upon such interchanges to identify "holes" in their thinking and to suggest new directions to take in search of solutions. Learning individually should not be misinterpreted to mean learning in isolation.

STUDY GUIDE: CHAPTER 9

1. An instructional management system must serve at least eight functions *whether or not* it is computerized:

A.	diagnosing progress	E.	collecting data
B.	prescribing study	F.	reporting evaluation results
C.	monitoring study	G.	managing resources
D.	evaluating learning	H.	supporting interpersonal communication

   a. Write a capsule description (25–50 words) of each.
   b. *Distinguish between* Elements A and D.
2. The eight functions of instructional management are purportedly served by five "facilities" of a well-designed CMI system.
   - curriculum authoring
   - individual study monitoring
   - records/reporting
   - resource management
   - communication

   For each of the five facilities, describe in 50–75 words which of the eight functions it serves (and how it does so).
3. CMI calls for the shared governance of instruction. The teacher, students, and computer each participate in that governance.
   a. What benefits does a well-designed CMI system offer to a teacher?
   b. Compare and contrast the roles of teacher and computer within a well-designed CMI system.
   c. Compare the traditional role of a student with the role of a student participating in a well-designed CMI environment.

AGENDA FOR ACTION

SCIENCE AND MATHEMATICS
TEACHING CENTER

ADDRESS REPLY TO WRITER

THE UNIVERSITY OF WYOMING
UNIVERSITY STATION, BOX 3992
LARAMIE, WYOMING, 82071

MEMORANDUM

TO: Members of ICAC

FROM: Bob Kansky and Dick Dennis

DATE: March 10, 1983

RE: ICAC Paper 9

This is the fourth and final paper which explores those instructional applications of the computer in which the computer performs "as teacher." Specifically, the paper looks at the ways in which the computer can support the managerial role of the teacher.

We've found the task of describing computer-based instructional management to be something like trying to disarm a porcupine. There's really no good place to begin; attacked from any quarter, the subject reacts as a whole and immediately suggests that we turn elsewhere.

Our solution to the problem of describing computer-based instructional management was to separate the discussion of the instructional management task from the description of the computer facility that is required to give the teacher control over that task. Recognizing that some readers may be predisposed toward or against the idea of "managing" instruction and that others will have given the topic no thought at all, we've chosen to digress on occasion to speak of art versus science, of fishing trips, and of four-wheel drive donkeys. We ask that you forgive us our digressions, realizing that each leads to a point regarding computer-based instructional management.

BK:DD:baa

AGENDA FOR ACTION

Obourn Senior High School

200 Woodbine Avenue
East Roachmont, New York

M. Jack Stivers
Principal

(716) 568-8840

ICAC Memo #9

TO: Members of ICAC

FROM: John Russell

DATE: March 18, 1983

Gerri and I have agreed to forgive all of you for your snide remarks and unsuppressed howls of laughter during the demonstration of the "Author! Author!" drill program that we promised in ICAC Memo #7. We've corrected many of the spelling errors (although I think our Gone With The Wine was a more intriguing title). We also accepted the criticism of our historian-come-lately, Ted Kanaley, who argued that both Hitler and Schicklgruber are technically correct responses to Mein Kampf. We drew the line at Phil's request to list Judy Garland as the source of The Wonderful Wizard of Oz.

COMMITTEE ASSIGNMENTS

1. Gerri and John will create "variations" on their drill program using the question stems and associative-pairings submitted by other folks on the committee. (In the case of Donna's drill program on music, we plan to delete the program termination condition and to call the resulting exercise "Song Without End.")
2. Jeanne will take a copy of "Author! Author!" (as revised) to the computer programming class at Sinclair Senior High. Our purpose is to find out
   (a) What improvements the students suggest, and
   (b) What improvements the students can program!
3. To get student reaction to some of the variations on the drill program, John has asked Glena Harris to use it with students at Near Santo (LaRamie Middle School).
4. Since CMI sounds like it is what we need to keep afloat in teaching's sea of forms and reports, Phil will use the microcomputer brochures he's been collecting to seek information regarding CMI programs for those systems. Some of the microcomputers do claim that they can be "linked" to form a classroom system with some CMI features.
5. Carrinne will arrange for Computers Count, Inc. to give us a demonstration of a "text processor." This should help us to better understand the deletion-insertion-alteration features of a curriculum authoring facility. (To accommodate the schedules of most of us, she'll ask for two demonstrations—one at each of the times and dates agreed upon.)

JR:ms

CHAPTER TEN

ELECTRONIC SLICES OF REALITY: THE INSTRUCTIONAL ROLE OF COMPUTERIZED SIMULATIONS

The story is told of a high-school senior who found a magic lamp. The genie of this particular lamp claimed an ability to see into the future and offered to answer any two questions the student might pose about it. After some thought, the student asked, "Genie, is there life after high school?" The genie, quite taken aback by the question, replied, "Before I answer, Master, might I know why you ask that?" "Well," said the student, "if there is, my teachers seem to be unaware of the fact."

Unfortunately, both the lamp and the text of the genie's answer have been lost. However, it is known that the student's second question was posed four years later: "Genie, is there life after college?"

ACCORDING TO A GENIE WE KNOW . . .

Over the centuries, the school curriculum has evolved into the current set of diverse and curious activities. Today's well-schooled individual can find the square root of 2746.931 correct to hundredths, recite fifty lines of poetry by each of five selected authors, interpret the works of literary giants, sketch the lineage of English monarchs (with all appropriate side trips into France and Spain), name the parts of a cell as indicated on a drawing of same, outwit almost any multiple-choice test, and locate a set of encyclopedias in the school library. It is reported that schooling has gone so far as to produce a few students who have composed a two-paragraph letter, read a newspaper, learned to operate a hand-held calculator, asked a question, and visited a library voluntarily.

According to a genie we know, the school curriculum will continue to evolve. Unless our genie's mind has become fogged by his own smoke, the curriculum of the future will engage students in—get this, now—*decision making*. That's right, folks, students will be called upon to make decisions, will rationalize the decisions made, will learn the consequences of those decisions, and will go on to make new decisions which take into account the consequences reported. Moreover, those decisions will be concerned with such diverse activities as using a credit card, managing a business, guiding the workings of government, purchasing insurance, preparing for a career, diagnosing automotive engine problems, raising livestock or crops, performing complex experiments, resolving social/moral issues, borrowing money, administering justice, and answering the questions of a prospective employer. If there is life after high school, this is the stuff of which it will be made. Skills such as knowing how to find the square root of 2746.931 correct to hundredths may be necessary conditions for making some of life's decisions, but they are not sufficient.

Learning to ride a bicycle requires that one ride a bicycle. One does by doing. It is reasonable to propose that students will learn to make decisions by making decisions. But if the decision-making experiences are to involve realistic issues, the consequences of a poor decision can be a bit more painful than falling off a bicycle. Consider, for example, the potential disasters inherent in asking an inexperienced person to make decisions in the following situations.

1. You have been selected for jury duty. The first case involves armed robbery. The accused, a school teacher who has three children, faces a possible jail term of fifteen years.
2. You've been given a credit card that has a $1500 limit. Its use is up to you.
3. You need to select and train for an area of employment that will promise reasonable income for many years. Depending upon your choice, you may have to undergo as much as seven years of education before you'll be qualified to begin work (and, hence, to realize *income*).
4. You've decided to buy a house. Although you have saved some money, the purchase will require that you borrow much more than you've saved.

Now realize that most persons actually confronted by such situations *are* inexperienced decision makers relative to those decisions!

Consideration of any one of the four sample situations reveals that its resolution involves a complex network of decisions, many of which will be called for as the results of earlier decisions are revealed. Some decisions will affect movement toward a successful resolution of the situation, other decisions will amount to delaying actions which allow the decision maker to await the results of other decisions, and still other decisions will be directed at gathering information. Some decisions will have catastrophic results. The task of education is to provide an opportunity for students to make all of these kinds of decisions within an environment which (a) presents realistic situations in which to practice decision making, (b) quickly informs the learner of the results—both immediate and potential—of each decision, and (c) protects the learner and society from suffering the actual consequences of catastrophic decisions. "And just how does education carry out that task?" you may ask. Good question.

Wherever has that genie gone to now?

Education's Magic Carpet

Even early applications of computers included attempts to replicate the behavior of a wide variety of physical and social phenomena. These replications, referred to as *simulations* or *simulation games*, were the magic carpets of education. They transported the student to believable make-believe worlds to practice decision making previously denied. Specifically, simulation activities allowed the student to seek understanding of phenomena which formerly were inaccessible because of the costs, dangers, or time constraints associated with actual experiences involving those phenomena. It is this "magic carpet" characteristic of simulations which has led to their use in school settings.

Many areas of instruction have used simulations to facilitate learning. Medical schools employ them to provide instruction both in the diagnosis of disease and in the prescription of drugs. Such activities have been reported to be helpful during initial instruction, during individual student practice, and during the evaluation of student performance. Business schools employ simulations as part of problem-solving training and other management activities. Both the civilian and the military aircraft industries are noted for their extensive application of simulations in the training of flight personnel. There is even an instance in which two authors decided to use a noncomputerized simulation to help educators understand the instructional application of computers.

WHAT *IS* A SIMULATION?: AN ATTEMPT AT A DEFINITION

Can you imagine the images called forth the first time a child hears a mathematics teacher use expressions like "finding a square root," "reducing a fraction," "constructing a right angle," or "balancing an equation"?[1] Communication problems arise because the listener already has attached meanings to words which the teacher wishes to use in a more precise, technical manner. Our use of the word *simulation* poses this kind of problem.

There are several ways to assist you in understanding our use of the word *simulation*. Our first attempt will be to state a definition of the word in terms of other (we hope) meaningful expressions which will dissolve the language barrier. How about this?

Definition

A simulation is a replication of the behavior of some phenomenon in one's universe.

Well, it is. Still, there is a good chance that our definition isn't altogether useful for the person who hasn't experienced several simulations. Like all definitions, this one is the end product of a long line of attempts to produce a statement which will encompass the many instructional examples—some computerized and others not—that we would like to refer to as simulations.

A necessary starting point in seeking to understand the general concept of a simulation is to experience a simulation. The wide array of available examples include airplane flight simulators, replications of stock company transactions, computerized replications of laboratory experiences, replications of several business competition environments, replications of travel through or survival within foreign countries or imagined worlds, and replications of decision-making activities within teaching, to mention but a few. Some of these simulations are computerized, others take the form of board games, and still others are packaged as elaborate workshops in which experts and learners act out assigned roles.

To acquire the understanding that we need here, your experience with simulations need not be in your field of special expertise; neither is it necessary for the simulations to be computerized. Such being the case, perhaps we can be of help.

[1]Can one also "fatten" a fraction? Are there angles which are "wrong" or "left"? Is an "unbalanced" equation sufficiently dangerous that it should be institutionalized?

WHAT *IS* A SIMULATION?: ANSWERING BY EXAMPLE

At this point, we really should pause while you go off to experience several simulations. Instead, we choose to present a simple example of our own so that (a) we'll have a common experience which we can use for discussion and analysis and (b) you'll have a guided view of one simulation which can aid you in appreciating and evaluating other simulations. Also, we want to present an example that will communicate our particular view of the nature of a simulation.

Seeing Things Our Way

Although the majority of the discussion of our little simulation will be in a looking-back mode, you might find it enjoyable to try to detect elements of our simulation construction plan as you go through the simulation for the first time. To that end, we'll give you a few clues regarding what to look for; later we'll see how good a detective you have been. Here are the "clues."

- Learning involvement is enhanced by describing an environment and a task with which the learner can associate.
- The learner must make decisions to gather specific data, to take actions which may alter the environment, to seek the advice of authorities, or to express or reflect personal feelings.
- Decisions result in specific consequences, some of which are immediate and others which temporarily are hidden or delayed.
- A pairing of a decision and a consequence brings about change regarding completion of the task. The pair may be necessary to a successful solution, may be unnecessary but useful, may have no effect on progress, may delay progress, or may ensure failure.
- There can be several different paths to a successful conclusion or to a failure.

Rules For Playing "Lights Out"

The next several pages show screen displays from a computerized simulation called "Lights Out." Because there is no machinery to drive this simulation (i.e., to take you from one display to another in keeping with your decisions), the displays have been labeled so that you can be the machine that drives it. The rules for operating "Lights Out" are as follows.

1. Read Display 1. Go to Display 2 as directed by the phrase at the bottom of Display 1.
2. Read Display 2. Go to Display 3 as directed.
3. Read Display 3. Make a decision and branch to the display indicated by the phrase in parentheses following your particular choice. (No fair peeking at other displays!)
4. Keep reading and branching until you conclude the simulation.

To get the most out of "Lights Out," run through it several times and try different sequences of decisions.

Ready? Go. (Don't forget to use the clues mentioned earlier to try to detect method within this bit of madness.)

"LIGHTS OUT A DARK AND CHILLING TALE"

LIGHTS OUT . . . A DARK AND CHILLING TALE

Knowing of your interest in skiing, a friend offers you the weekend use of her "cabin"—a new, all-electric mobile home located in a small village high in the Rocky Mountains. You accept!

Having obtained her key, you leave for the village on Friday afternoon.

It's snowing.

—Press the SPACE BAR to continue—

(Go to Display 2)

Display 1

Slowed by the snowfall, you reach the cabin at midnight. The snow has now stopped, but it is *very* cold. You turn on lights throughout the cabin, set the heater on HIGH, unpack, and take a hot bath.

Being hungry, you start the coffee and put some cheese sandwiches in the broiler.

As you reach for the latest copy of *Skiing Today,* the lights go out.

—Press the SPACE BAR to continue—

(Go to Display 3)

Display 2

What will you do? (Press the letter corresponding to your choice.)

(a) Check to see if any of the cabin's lights is working. **(Go to Display 4A.)**
(b) Search for a flashlight. **(Go to Display 4B.)**
(c) Check to see if lights are on in neighboring mobile homes. **(Go to Display 11C.)**
(d) Pile on some blankets and go to bed. Leave the electrical problem for morning. **(Go to Display 4C.)**

Display 3

None of the lights will come on. Also, you notice that neither the broiler nor coffee pot are working.

—Press the SPACE BAR to continue—

(Go to Display 3)

Display 4A

You find a flashlight, but the batteries seem weak.

What do you want to do now? (Press the letter corresponding to your choice.)

(a) Search for more flashlight batteries. **(Go to Display 5A.)**
(b) Telephone for help. **(Go to Display 10C.)**
(c) Seek help from a neighbor. **(Go to Display 8C.)**
(d) Repack and go home. **(Go to Display 8C.)**

Display 4B

Good Morning!

It's very cold (-18°c) in the cabin this morning.

What will you do now? (Press the letter corresponding to your choice.)

(a) Telephone for help. **(Go to Display 7A.)**
(b) Seek help from a neighbor. **(Go to Display 6B.)**
(c) Search for the cabin's electrical panel. **(Go to Display 9B.)**
(d) Repack and go home. **(Go to Display 5B.)**

Display 4C

You search for several minutes but are unable to find more batteries.

What's your next move? (Press the letter corresponding to your choice.)

(a) Telephone for help. **(Go to Display 10C.)**
(b) Seek help from a neighbor. **(Go to Display 8C.)**
(c) Search for the cabin's electrical panel. **(Go to Display 6C.)**
(d) Go to bed. Leave the electrical problem for morning. **(Go to Display 4C.)**

Display 5A

The temperature is so low that your car won't start. You realize that you'll have to leave it in the sun for several hours to get it warm enough to start.

—Press the SPACE BAR to continue—

(Go to Display 4C.)

Display 5B

Only two neighbors are showing lights.

The first home is occupied by an elderly insomniac. He's sympathetic but is unable to help.

A kind but somewhat nervous lady lives in the second mobile home. She loans you a good flashlight and suggests that you check the breaker-switch electrical panel often located inside the cabinet above the refrigerator.

What will you do? (Press a letter.)

(a) Search for the breaker-switch panel. **(Go to Display 6A.)**
(b) Telephone for help. **(Go to Display 10C.)**
(c) Go to bed. Leave the electrical problem for morning. **(Go to Display 4C.)**

Display 5C

You locate the breaker-switch box in the cabinet indicated. The switch marked MAIN seems to be out of position. You move the switch up and down until the lights come on.

After turning off some lights to avoid another overload, you enjoy your late-late snack and look forward to a pleasant weekend.

END OF DARK AND CHILLING TALE

Display 6A

A neighbor quickly solves the problem. He resets a switch in the breaker-switch electrical panel concealed inside the cabinet above the refrigerator. He suggests that you shut off some lights and appliances to avoid an overload.

You shut off everything except the heater, grab your skis, and take off for a restaurant breakfast and a glorious day on the slopes!

—Press the SPACE BAR to continue—

(Go to Display 11A.)

Display 6B

You begin a careful search. Before you can locate the electrical panel, your flashlight gives out.

What will you do now? (Press a letter.)

(a) Seek help from a neighbor. **(Go to Display 5C.)**
(b) Telephone for help. **(Go to Display 10C.)**
(c) Search for more batteries. **(Go to Display 5A.)**
(d) Go to bed. Leave the electrical problem for morning. **(Go to Display 4C.)**

Display 6C

There is no one else waiting to use the public pay phone, and you have enough coins to make several calls.

Whom do you wish to call? (Press a letter.)

(a) The friend who loaned you the cabin. **(Go to Display 8A.)**
(b) The town's only electrician. **(Go to Display 8B.)**
(c) The local police. **(Go to Display 11B.)**

Display 7A

The electrician, very annoyed at having been awakened, says he doesn't make night calls.

He suggests that you check the switches on the cabin's electrical panel and then slams down the receiver.

What do you do now? (Press a letter.)

(a) Search for the panel mentioned. **(Go to Display 6A.)**
(b) Seek help from a neighbor. **(Go to Display 5C.)**
(c) Make another telephone call. **(Go to Display 10C.)**
(d) Go to bed. Leave the electrical problem for morning. **(Go to Display 4C.)**

Display 7B

The police dispatcher explains that no general electrical failure has been reported in your area and that your problem is not a police matter. She suggests, however, that you locate the cabin's electrical panel and try resetting any switches that seem to be out of line.

What will you do? (Press a letter.)

(a) Search for the panel mentioned. **(Go to Display 6A.)**
(b) Seek help from a neighbor. **(Go to Display 5C.)**
(c) Make another telephone call. **(Go to Display 10C.)**
(d) Go to bed. Leave the problem for morning. **(Go to Display 4C.)**

Display 7C

She doesn't answer her telephone. What will you do now? (Press a letter.)

(a) Telephone someone else. **(Go to Display 7A.)**
(b) Go back to the cabin. **(Go to Display 4C.)**

Display 8A

The electrician says he can't get to you until late morning or early afternoon. The time is uncertain, but you must be there when he arrives. There is an initial charge of $35, and his hourly rate is double because it's Saturday.

What do you want to do? (Press a letter.)

(a) Wait for the electrician. **(Go to Display 9A.)**
(b) Tell the electrician to forget it and call someone else. **(Go to Display 7A.)**
(c) Go back to the cabin. **(Go to Display 4C.)**

Display 8B

On Saturday, you call your friend and report the problem.

She calls the owner of the mobile home park (who has a key to her mobile home). He quickly solves the problem by resetting a breaker switch and reports that the heater is working again.

—Press the SPACE BAR to continue—

(Go to Display 10B.)

Display 8C

The electrician arrives at 4:30 P.M. and soon locates the cabin's electrical panel inside a storage cabinet over the refrigerator. He resets some switches; the lights come on.

The charge is $50.

Since it is too late to do any skiing today, you decide to go out to dinner.

—Press the SPACE BAR to continue—

(Go to Display 10A.)

Display 9A

Despite a long search, you are unable to locate the cabin's electrical panel.

—Press the SPACE BAR to continue—

(Go to Display 4C.)

Display 9B

She tells you to reset any breaker switch which is "thrown" up in the box concealed inside the storage cabinet above the refrigerator. Also, she warns you to shut off some lights and appliances to avoid another overload.

You follow her directions, and the lights come on again.

Problem solved . . . vacation begins!

END OF DARK AND CHILLING TALE

Display 9C

You return from dinner to find the carpet soaked with water!

You telephone the village's only plumber who explains that the pipes must have frozen and burst during the night while the heat was off. When heat was restored, the ice melted and the water ran out of the broken pipes.

He can't help you until Monday afternoon.

Big mess . . . big expense!

END OF TALE . . . BEGINNING OF BILLS

Display 10A

Your friend arrives at her cabin a week later to find a soggy carpet and warped paneling.

A plumber explains that the waterpipes froze and burst during the night the electric heater was turned off. When heat was restored, the water in the broken pipes melted and ran out of the broken pipes.

Big mess . . . big expense!

END OF THE TALE . . . AND, POSSIBLY, OF A FRIENDSHIP

Display 10B

There is no one else waiting to use the public pay phone at this late hour. You have enough coins to make several calls.

Whom do you wish to call? (Press a letter).

(a) The friend who owns the cabin. **(Go to Display 9C.)**
(b) The town's only electrician. **(Go to Display 7B.)**
(c) The local police. **(Go to Display 7C.)**

Display 10C

You return from your day of skiing to discover a major disaster—the water pipes have burst and the cabin's carpet is soaked!

A plumber explains that the pipes froze and burst during the night while the heat was off. As the cabin reheated during the day, the water in the broken pipes melted and ran out of the broken pipes.

END OF TALE . . . END OF VACATION . . . START OF PAYMENTS

Display 11A

The police dispatcher is very busy. He tells you that your problem is not a police matter. He suggests that you call an electrician.

What will you do now? (Press a letter.)

(a) Telephone someone else. **(Go to Display 7A.)**
(b) Go back to the cabin. **(Go to Display 4C.)**

Display 11B

Lights are on in two nearby mobile homes, but all others are dark. The street lights are on.

—Press the SPACE BAR to continue—

(Go to Display 3.)

Display 11C

What Is a Simulation?: Elements of Construction

Even after experience with so simple an example as "Lights Out," our earlier definition of *simulation* should make a bit more sense. The simulation serves as a surrogate, a substitute for an experience with an electrical problem under a specific set of conditions. It replicated the situation (phenomenon) as closely as the medium (a limited number of written pages), the author's cleverness, the anticipated interests of the intended audience, and the purpose of the simulation (an example for analysis) permitted. Further understanding of the nature of a simulation can now be obtained by examining "Lights Out" under the magnifying power of an analysis of the basic elements used to construct it. In the process, you can rate your own astuteness at using the clues we gave you regarding our construction plan.

Simulation Element 1: The Scenario

A simulation can be constructed for any phenomenon which presents a problem to be solved, a goal to be reached, or an environment to be understood. While a simulation's representation of that phenomenon is generally as realistic as possible, realism is a characteristic which is limited both by *necessity* and by *choice*. The restraints related to necessity are basic to the reasons for introducing simulations in the first place: the real situations involve costs, dangers, complexities, or time constraints which the simulation seeks to avoid. With regard to the restraints introduced by choice, it is the purpose of a simulation to ignore selected aspects or details of the real situation in order to focus the learner's attention on a central "field" in much the same way that a television camera can be used to focus one's vision on a central subject by removing or blurring details surrounding the viewing field. However, enough complicating detail must be included to retain the veracity of the simulation. If the facts and ideas necessary to solve the problem are not partially concealed by scenario irrelevancies, the fun (challenge) and realism of the exercise is lost. Consider the loss of fidelity which would result were the author of a detective mystery to have all relevant clues (and only relevant clues) printed in red ink.

One important element of a simulation, then, is the *opening scene (scenario)*. The scenario presents the setting for the simulation. It may include some selected irrelevancies to achieve a modicum of realism or to capture the interest of the learner. It seeks to make the learner assume the role of an involved participant in the simulation rather than view the simulation from the standpoint of an observer. The scenario also details the learner's role in the simulation, states (or implies) a task or goal, and reveals any limitations imposed upon time, assistance, or related resources.

Displays 1 and 2 of "Lights Out" constitute the scenario. It presents such relevant items of setting as the location, time of day, weather conditions, and activities which lead to overburdening the "all-electric" environment. Irrelevant details (cheese, coffee, and the name of the magazine) help the learner to settle into the situation. The problem is introduced; the participant's task may be inferred. For this simple simulation, no specific restraints are introduced with respect to time or available resources. Were this a simulation of landing a spacecraft on the moon, such things as time and fuel supply restrictions *would* be included in the scenario.

Simulation Element 2: Decision Pairs

The scenario can be thought of as the simulation's costume and make-up. Its function is to make the simulation attractive and interesting. The intellectual holding power of the simulation, however, is a function of a network of *decision pairs* which support the scenario.

A *decision pair* is comprised of a *choice* and a *consequence*. In Display 4B one might elect the choice of searching for more flashlight batteries (Choice 4B, *a*). This choice is matched with the consequence (Display 5A) that time is lost without any more batteries being located. This particular decision pair can be denoted by

$$4B,a \rightarrow 5A$$

The decision pair denoted by 10C,b → 7B is one in which the choice of a late night call to a sleepy electrician has as its consequence the possibly useful (if angrily delivered) suggestion to search for the cabin's electrical panel.

There are at least four classes of decision pairs that can play a part in a simulation. The number and mix of these decision pairs will determine the character and complexity of the simulation.[2]

1. *Management Decision Pairs.* These pairs involve actions that can be taken in the environment described. They have the potential of altering that environment. For example, the decision pair 3,d → 4C involved an action which changed the environment by allowing the cabin's temperature to drop to −18°C.

---

[2]Categories and descriptions used here are adapted from those first presented in *Construction and Use of Written Simulations* by C. McGuire, L. Solomon, and P. G. Bashook (The Psychological Corporation, 1977). Changes from this earlier work reflect consideration of a new medium of simulation delivery, namely, an interactive computer.

2. *Consultation Decision Pairs.* Such pairs make use of consultants (outside authorities) to aid in things like the collection of data, the interpretation of data, or the making of management decisions. A consultation decision pair like 7C,b → 5C calls upon neighbors for help, a move which eventually produces a good flashlight and the probable location of a breaker-switch panel that may be the key to the problem.
3. *Valuing Decision Pairs.* A choice could call for (or reflect) an expression of personal attitude or opinion about the problem or setting of the simulation. This kind of choice would be derived from an assessment of various possible value positions toward the situation. While there are no valuing decision pairs in the "Lights Out" simulation, an extension of the story could introduce them. An additional choice in Display 4C could have allowed you to go skiing, leaving the cabin to warm in the sun. Returning in the evening, you discover the broken pipes yourself. The simulation could then present alternatives about whether or not to admit responsibility for the mess.
4. *Data Gathering Decision Pairs.* A choice may call for access to accumulated information (charts, tables, reports, etc.), some of which is necessary to completion of the task. Such a data gathering pair could be added to "Lights Out" by listing choices on Display 9B after claiming that you have found a drawer containing various schematic diagrams of the cabin including the electrical diagram. If you then made the choice to see the electrical diagram, the consequence would be a display of the diagram. (This data gathering decision pair might be followed by consultation decision pairs which permit you to get help in interpreting the diagram.)

If you took a few moments to think about the decision pairs of "Lights Out," you could easily identify pairs which were (in retrospect) "good" in that they moved you toward a successful completion of the task. Other decision pairs had consequences which led you down the road to disaster. In between these were pairs whose consequences were helpful, harmless, or stalling in nature. In fact, each decision pair can be placed in one of five classes according to its effect in moving the participant toward completion of the task of the simulation.

1. *Necessary.* A necessary decision pair is one required for successful completion of the task. Having reached Display 3 the decision pair 3,b → 11C is a necessary management decision pair. From Display 10C the decision pair 10C,a → 9C is a necessary consulting decision pair.
2. *Expediting.* The results of these decision pairs are not necessary to task completion but will facilitate that event. The decision pair 3,a → 4A is expediting in nature because it reveals that the problem is a general electrical failure; the pair 3;c → 11C is expediting in that it suggests that the problem is confined to the one cabin. A search for additional flashlight batteries could be an expediting management decision if it resulted in the discovery of the electrical diagram for the cabin.
3. *Neutral.* Some decision pairs are of a do-nothing nature in that they neither aid nor hinder the participant's pursuit of the task. Suppose that Display 3 contained the choice "Wait 30 minutes to see if the lights come on again." The consequence would be that no progress will have been made 30 minutes later. Although some time will have been wasted, the original situation would remain unaltered. Such is the nature of a neutral decision pair.
4. *Impedimental.* A decision pair can result in the complication of the original task. That is, new impediments are placed between the participant and the completion of the task, impediments which hinder but do not prevent completion. For instance, a young couple's wish to save money could lead to the decision to rennovate an old house themselves. As a consequence, they find that they must study books on plumbing, wiring, carpentry, glazing, masonry, and interior decorating. The decision results not only in an expenditure of much time but also introduces several necessary learning tasks. Thus, the decision pair can be classified as impedimental.
5. *Aborting.* An aborting decision pair leads to eventual failure to complete the task. The decision pairs 3,d → 4C/4B,d → 8C/5A,d → 4C/ and 5C,c → 4C of "Lights Out" are aborting decisions. Each is a first step on the road to burst pipes; no future decision pair will prevent disaster.

The two schemes for classifying decision pairs attend to the two dimensions of a decision: its character and its quality. The combination and relative concentration of decision pairs of the four different characters described will be determined by the general nature of the overall simulation, a topic that will be discussed in a later section presenting a taxonomy of simulations. The quality of a particular decision (in terms of the five classes just presented) places the choice involved along a continuum from very good (necessary) to very bad (aborting). Between these extremes, expediting decision pairs reveal or suggest related necessary choices by providing clues to required actions. Necessary and expediting decision pairs represent good decisions;

impedimental and aborting decision pairs represent poor decisions or decisions based upon misconceptions or inadequate information.

It should be noted that the two components of a decision pair (choice and consequence) are inseparable when one discusses the nature or quality of a decision. For instance, in the simulation of a welding procedure, one would expect the choice:

Turn on the welder.

to be part of a necessary management decision pair. However, if this choice is selected before proper equipment is assembled and environmental preparations have been made, the action could result in mild to very serious damage of the welding machine or its operator. In these cases, the choice becomes a component of an impedimental or aborting decision pair.

Simulation Element 3: Solution Paths

While the preceding discussion of decision pairs has been very erudite, we'll have to admit it lacks drama. An individual decision pair just isn't very exciting in itself. The problem is that we've thus far examined decision pairs as distinct, relatively independent items. To grasp their value, we need to step back and see them in sequences—as subsets of all the pairs available—which lead us to a successful conclusion of the task or to a disaster. These sequences are called *paths;* those paths which terminate in a successful resolution of the task are called *solution paths* for the simulation.

There are many possible paths through the decision pairs of "Lights Out." Six of those paths are shown in Table 10.1. Paths I and IV end in the same disaster; the person following Path IV simply takes a bit longer to get there. Paths II, III, V, and VI are all solution paths. Paths II and V share a common successful conclusion as a result of a telephone call to the cabin's owner, while Paths III and VI share a different successful conclusion as a consequence of consulting a neighbor.

Among the several solution pairs of a simulation, a few paths represent superior decision making by the participant. These paths, such as Paths II and III, reach a successful conclusion of the task without including any neutral or impedimental decision pairs. They represent an efficient achievement of the task. Such "better paths" are called *optimal solution paths.* Obviously, there must be at least one optimal solution path through any simulation; in "Lights Out," there are two.

The notion of *optimization* used here is more than a matter of efficiency in concluding a simulation. For instance, Path I leads to disaster more quickly (efficiently) than Path IV. However, we choose not to recognize efficiency when it is related to failure. Our notion of optimization is, then, reserved for solution paths—paths which lead to success.

TABLE 10.1. SAMPLE PATHS THROUGH THE DECISION PAIRS OF "LIGHTS OUT"

Path I			*Path II*			*Path III*		
choice		*consequence*	*choice*		*consequence*	*choice*		*consequence*
3,d	→	4C	3,b	→	4B	3,b	→	4B
4C,b	→	6B	4B,b	→	10C	4B,c	→	5C
6B.	→	11A	10C,a	→	9C	5C,a	→	6A

Path IV			*Path V*			*Path VI*		
choice		*consequence*	*choice*		*consequence*	*choice*		*consequence*
3,d	→	4C	3,a	→	4A	3,b	→	4B
4C,c	→	9B	4A	→	3	4B,a	→	5A
9B	→	4C	3,c	→	11C	5A,c	→	6C
4C,a	→	7A	11C	→	3	6C,c	→	5A
7A,a	→	8A	3,b	→	4B	5A,b	→	5C
8A,b	→	4C	4B,a	→	5A	5C,a	→	6A
4C,b	→	6B	5A,c	→	6C			
6B	→	11A	6C,b	→	10C			
			10C,a	→	9C			

Simulation Element 4: Strategy Initiation Sections

A simulation will have one or more points at which strategies are formulated. It is in these *strategy initiation sections* that the participant selects from among the categories of data gathering, managing action, consultation, and valuing. The participant will return to a strategy initiation section each time all of the consequences of a strategy previously initiated have been realized. In other words, "So much for that strategy, back to square one!" The related strategy initiation section is "square one."

Although "Lights Out" is a rather puny simulation, it does have a strategy initiation section in Display 4C. The choices presented in Display 4C start strategies which may be terminated by a "back to square one" at any of ten other displays.

The strategy initiation section of "Lights Out" has a multiple-choice format. However, since computers can be prepared to recognize and respond to several phrases which might be input by the participant, a constructed response format also is possible. Figures 10.1 and 10.2 present a scenario and strategy initiation section for a simulation involving the preparation of an unusual culinary delight. Note the difference in the level of task presented by Figure 10.1 (where one simply has to *select* a reasonable move) and that posed by Figure 10.2 (where one must *construct* a reasonable next move). Of course, the programming problem presented by Figure 10.2 is more complex than for Figure 10.1. The multiple-choice format of Figure 10.1 allows the programmer to limit carefully the number of strategic choices possible. The "open" nature presented by Figure 10.2 suggests that a broad range of possibilities will be accepted. For this reason, the use of constructed responses is usually restricted to situations where the range of probable choices is rather narrow because the task is specific or the participant has had previous training. Initial learning simulations would employ the multiple-choice format to acquaint the participant with an array of reasonable choices. Later, practice simulations—simulations aimed at developing mastery—would use the constructed response format to force the participant to recall and use that array of reasonable choices.

```
Your International Foods Cooking Club (IFCC)
decided to make an African meal this month. Because
you missed the menu-planning meeting, you were
assigned the task of preparing "waterblommetjiebre-
die" for 14 persons.

What do you want to do now?

(a) Consult a dictionary.
(b) Look for some cookbooks.
(c) Go shopping.
(d) Call the IFCC chairperson.
(e) Begin preparation of the dish.
(f) Leave town.
(g) Substitute a dish you know how to make.
```

Figure 10.1
Strategy Initiation Section: Multiple-Choice Format

```
Your International Foods Cooking Club (IFCC)
decided to make an African meal this month. Because
you missed the menu-planning meeting, you were
assigned the task of preparing "waterblommetjiebre-
die" for 14 persons.

What do you want to do now? (Type your decision
below.)

>
```

Figure 10.2
Strategy Initiation Section: Constructed-Response Format

Simulation Element 5: Transition Messages

The last major element of a simulation deals with the mechanics of the simulation rather than with its content or logic. This element is a collection of statements whose purpose it is to keep the participant informed regarding any mechanical features affecting the progress of the simulation. Examples of such *transitional messages* in "Lights Out" include:

Press the letter corresponding to your choice.
Press a letter.
Press the SPACE BAR to continue.

In fact, the three transition messages listed above are the only ones that would be necessary were "Lights Out" to be computerized. However, since computerization has been simulated, additional transitional messages are needed to do the job that the computer would do for the participant. Typical of those extra transition messages is "Go to Display 4C."

In a computerized simulation, transition messages

also can be used to tell the student what types of assistance are available,[3] to explain how to use special features of the keyboard[4] or other input devices,[5] to indicate a choice, to provide access to particular data needed in the simulation,[6] or to temporarily terminate interaction with the simulation.[7]

WHAT IS A SIMULATION?: A MATTER OF INTENT

Is a boot always a boot? If you use it to hold a door open on a windy day, is it still a boot? If you first fill it with cement and then use it to hold a door open, is it still a boot? If it is placed on display in a museum, is it still a boot? If someone were to wear it with a tutu, would it become a slipper?

You now know a great deal about the word *simulation*. You've seen a definition, experienced an example, and examined the elements of its construction. Still another method of understanding an educational simulation is to categorize examples in terms of the learning goals or objectives which each appears to have. Thus, the simulation is seen to be partially a matter of *intent:* the *intent* to replicate a performance, the *intent* to extract information about the operation of an environment, or the *intent* to have an encounter with a new environment.

Replicable Performance Simulations

The goal of a *replicable performance simulation* is to execute a series of behaviors in an optimal sequence. Examples of this type of simulation include

- medical diagnoses, involving people or pets;
- technical trouble shooting such as that involved in the diagnosis of problems in an engine, printing press, computer, or television set;
- laboratory procedures such as the preparation of a hydrogen generator, the construction of special glassware, the use of radioactive materials, or the care of bacteria cultures;
- mechanical performances such as driving a car, flying a plane, or operating the controls of a giant crane;
- emergency situations such as those arising in a nuclear power plant.

Such simulations may be characterized as task oriented, with both the task and the best methods for its solution being definable.

The phenomenon dealt with by a replicable performance simulation has two components: a procedural logic and a procedural execution. The purpose of the simulation is to have the learner gain proficiency with the procedural logic. That is, the purpose is to learn "what to do next." However, simulations also present opportunities to deliberately explore the consequences of decisions which are not within optimal solution paths. (They may, in fact, lead to what would be disasters in the real situation.) These procedural executions permit maimed or dead patients, irreparably damaged machinery, blown up laboratory apparatus, crashed planes, and nuclear core melt downs. The participant learns of the consequences of alternate choices without having to suffer the actual results. In simulations having a high degree of fidelity, the participant may be so immersed in the situation that the consequences of these surrogate performances can have a strong impact upon learning.

High fidelity is called for in a replicable performance simulation since it is intended that the learner will later execute these simulated performances in real situations. Behaviors or ideas mastered during the simulation must have guaranteed association with behaviors or ideas called for in the real setting. Should the real situation call for the efficient manipulation of a control board comprised of dials, switches, and levers, there is little fidelity in a simulation which uses a typewriter-like keyboard to represent that control panel. Situational fidelity seeks to guarantee that application of the procedures learned in the simulation will be as effective in a real situation as in the simulated situation. For this reason, a replicable performance simulation demands that the procedures of the real situation must be well defined, that the consequences of specific decisions or actions can be well defined, and that there is a precisely defined connection between each action and its consequences.

Information Extraction Simulations

Just in case we haven't yet broken a common mindset, we'll warn again:

Don't confuse problems and exercises!

---

[3]Example: "Press the HELP-key to see a list of cookbooks available at the local library."

[4]Example: "Type NOTE to learn how to use the keyboard to draw musical notes."

[5]Example: "Type PEN for information on how to use the light pen to draw figures."

[6]Example: "Type DATA to see a list of the chemical elements and their atomic weights."

[7]Example: "Press the STOP-key if you wish to leave this lesson temporarily."

An exercise is a clearly stated task which requires the student to apply selected principles, procedures, or skills. The exercise arises in a context which clearly indicates the principles, procedures, or skills needed for its solution. By contrast, a problem usually arises in a situation far removed from the context of its solution. The problem may be but vaguely defined; the discovery of its underlying dimensions may present a major task in itself. The problem solver must clarify the problem situation, propose methods of investigation which may provide useful information, test those proposals, analyze results, redefine the problem, and make new proposals for its investigation—the cycle of activities hopefully leading to the solution of a then clearly-defined problem.

The goal of an *information extraction simulation* is the securing of relevant information about the facts and principles which govern the operation of some phenomena. The setting of the simulation does not provide a clear statement of a performance task or goal. This style of simulation is used to experiment with such processes as

- genetic reproduction in fruit flies or molds;
- population growth as affected by birth rates, death rates, disease, critical resources, and specific social programs;
- economic growth as affected by natural resources, manpower, conservation programs, and marketing considerations;
- predator-prey relationships among the inhabitants of a particular physical environment (e.g., a large lake in Wisconsin);
- ecological system performance as affected by food webs, climate, and environmental change.

In each example just given, the phenomenon involved is a process which operates under a set of principles well understood by experts in the field but which may be unknown to the participant. Interactions among the variables involved (e.g., crossing a male fruit fly of one eye color with a female fruit fly of another eye color) have been reduced by experts to probabilistic laws.[8] The role of the problem-solving simulation is to transmit information about the phenomenon. Such transmission may take the form of statements of fact about the state of the phenomenon under any user-specified set of conditions. At more sophisticated levels, transmission may take the form of awareness of (a) principles of cause and effect which govern the phenomenon or (b) principles which achieve stable states of the phenomenon.

The participant in an information extraction simulation may at first have very vague goals in mind or may be executing specific experiments on the surrogate environment. In either case, the participant introduces changes in certain variables of the phenomenon (e.g., the reduction in number of certain elements of an aquatic food web) and seeks data on the changes in state which result (e.g., the change in population sizes of other elements of the food web). If the simulation is successful, this defining of experiments and observation of consequences will be transformed into the ability to define experiments and *to predict consequences prior to further execution of the simulation*. Between the early stages of random manipulation/observation and the final state of definition/prediction, there is an intermediate stage in which the participant defines an experiment and explains the results observed.

Encounter Simulations

Some simulations provide experiences with phenomena which are neither completely definable nor completely predictable. The purpose of such a simulation is to allow the learner to achieve a goal or to function effectively in a setting in which no clearly defined principles or optimal procedures exist. The problem lies in the fact that the phenomena of interest have loose cause-effect relationships. Any underlying "laws" are, at best, probabilistic; the behavior of the phenomenon is influenced by considerations which are neither scientific nor logical. As a result, these simulations allow the student to encounter a phenomenon which defies complete mastery.

Encounter simulations most commonly provide surrogate experiences with a variety of social phenomena. Sample simulations of this kind include

- competing in business development,
- responding to discipline episodes arising in a school classroom,
- resolving local, national, or international political conflicts,
- locating missing persons in an unfamiliar environment,
- interacting socially with a radically different culture.

The looseness of an encounter simulation reflects the fact that the phenomena which underlie such simulations are not well understood. They often involve moral, cultural, or religious issues. The variables influencing these phenomena are not all identified; known interactions among the variables may be influenced by unpredictable events or conditions. Encounter simulations are simulations at their fuzziest.

[8] Probabilistic laws take the general form "If you do this-and-that to so-and-so under thus-and-such a set of conditions, then the specific result la-ti-da is guaranteed about X percent of the time." Social and natural scientists like to talk that way.

The role of the encounter simulation is to provide opportunities for the learner to become familiar with major features of the phenomenon and with the nature of the chance influences that affect it. There are few solid cause-effect relationships to be discovered. The hope is that the learner will derive understandings (even if incomplete) of the varying relationships between precipitating events or actions and an array of possible changes in the environment.

The Price We Pay

As you may have begun to suspect, good simulations are beastly difficult to design and program. Time is money, so simulations can be costly to construct or purchase. "Lights Out" certainly doesn't qualify as a good simulation, but it again serves as a good example of what the simulation builder faces.

Once the general idea of the "Lights Out" simulation had been sketched, a display-by-display program was laid out using index cards. The scenario was presented in Displays 1 and 2; the first set of choices appeared in Display 3. From Display 3, each choice was pursued along a variety of paths leading (a) to a solution, (b) to a disaster, or (c) back to Display 3. The array of index cards (displays) began to grow. Next, additional choices were introduced on many of the displays which had been created in response to Display 3. Each of these new choices had to be pursued to its logical conclusions. Some choices had to be deleted to keep the simulation to a reasonable size. The simulation then was subjected to several "run-throughs" to check the connections of decision pairs, verify the logic of the simulation, and edit the displays wherever experience demanded change. Consideration also was given to the format of each display including the possible use of graphics. Score so far:

27 possible displays
815 minutes of time invested

Thus the pilot version of a 27-display simulation represented an investment of over 30 minutes per display!

That's just the beginning. To be at all confident that there are no major flaws in the logic of the simulation, it was next programmed into a computer, run through several more times, and edited as needed. Even without investing the effort to program the graphics required by the final product, the score card then read:

27 trial computerized displays
2790 minutes of time invested

That's a total cost of about 103 minutes per display for an initial computerized version of a simulation that can be executed by some student in at most a few minutes. Since the designers and programmers of computerized lessons charge about $10–$15 per hour, "Lights Out" carries a price tag of *at least* $465.00. Try to imagine the cost of a high fidelity replicable performance simulation of medical diagnosis that engages the student for an average of 30 minutes!

Computerized Simulations: Cheap at Twice the Price?

Before deciding to construct or purchase a computerized simulation, the educator needs to answer the following questions.

1. Is the learning objective to be addressed by the simulation deemed to be important?
2. Is there *any* reasonable alternative method of teaching that objective?
3. Does the simulation promise a significant improvement in instruction of that objective?
4. Can the simulation be used properly given existing time and equipment constraints?

If you answer *no* to Question 2 and *yes* to the other three, you are probably justified in considering a simulation. Under such circumstances, the simulation becomes the only reasonable way to attack the presentation of a significant objective. Insofar as a simulation holds a monopoly on instruction for that objective, the simulation is probably worth the purchase price as expressed in time or money.

Is the Objective Important?

The importance of an objective is a function of many things including the age of the learner and the local priorities set for education. The examination of a few objectives is in order.

The following objective[9] was part of the published curriculum guide of a large school district. Even given the affluence of the district's residents, the meaningful use of a credit card is not a grade 1 activity. A grade 1 student can't even read the oh-so-important fine print, much less understand it.

Objective A

Each child in grade 1 shall have a real or simulated experience with the use of a credit card.

[9]Like the other objectives to be discussed in this section, it is really the statement of a goal rather than a measurable objective. Let's not quibble. We'll here focus on the statement's general intent rather than its form.

Were the objective involving the credit card to be placed a bit later in the curriculum (as Objective B), it acquires relevance. The students involved may soon be holders of credit cards. As part of its efforts to deal with possible life after high school, the school very well may call upon its social studies and/or mathematics teachers to prepare students to enter the jungle of consumer credit.

Objective B

Each student in grade 12 shall have a real or simulated experience with the use of a credit card.

Some science teachers use the word *science* as a verb in order to emphasize their belief that science is a participant—not a spectator—sport. To learn science, one must *science* (i.e., do science). When expressed in the design of local curricula, this belief in a student's need to science takes the form of objectives requiring laboratory activities. Some objectives (such as Objective C) call for the replication of classical experiments in order to give concrete affirmation of textbook theory, to illustrate experimental design, and to introduce students to the procedures (and problems) associated with laboratory science. The overall science program requires that students science in every course (chemistry, physics, biology . . .) and that they science as often as possible in any given course. Seen in this light, Objective C is part of a fundamental curricular goal.

Objective C

Each student will design, execute, and present an analysis of the results of an experiment in classical genetics.

Is Simulation the Only Reasonable Procedure?

Having decided that Objective B is significant, we now consider instructional alternatives. How can the school provide each grade 12 student with an effective credit card experience—an experience that will cover such variables as initial service charges, interest rates, minimum payments, changes in the credit line, penalties, liability for lost cards, and the need to budget? One possibility is to get the parents to loan their credit cards to their children for six months. Following a classroom discussion of the variables just noted, the students would be turned loose in the local shops. While to our knowledge no such an instructional activity with credit cards has yet been attempted, three results seem certain if it should be done. First, the activity will teach the *parents* a great deal about their credit cards. Second, the activity will provide an acid test of the parents' commitment to Objective B. Third, the cost of a computerized simulation will appear more reasonable.

Many schools may have the budget, physical facility, and faculty to meet Objective C in a real laboratory setting. Providing every student with the opportunity to experiment with live media presents, however, a number of problems. Let's begin by considering some of the practical difficulties associated with the use of fruit flies.

An adequate supply of genotypically pure parental fruit fly stock requires the constant attention of a skilled instructor. The preparation of fresh food calls for special equipment. Disposal of old food, cleaning of glassware, preparation of new food, and transferring of stock to new containers is an ongoing activity which cannot be suspended during school holidays. Experiments involving more than one generation of flies will take several weeks of care and observation (again, uninterrupted by extended absences on the part of the experimenter). Students must be taught how to handle the flies (for population count purposes) without killing them and without inhaling large quantities of the substance used to anesthetize them. Then there is the sanitation problem posed by old food and escapee flies. Still, if the teacher is *really* determined. . . .

Approaching Objective C through other media simply raises other problems. Guinea pigs, mice, or gerbils don't require the preparation of specialized food; neither do they pose the handling or anesthetization problems of fruit flies. However, most of the other problems have their counterparts. In addition, these larger animals require more living space. There is also the tactical/moral problem of what to do with all the offspring.

Amateur geneticists seeking refuge in experimenting with the plant kingdom will find little solace. Plants such as the sweet pea need space and a controlled climate; meaningful experiments would require months of careful attention. Speedier experiments involving the irradiation of molds revive many of the headaches of fruit fly work and introduce problems associated with the accurate and safe administration of radiation.

Documentation of the trials and tribulations of the biology teacher who wishes students to science need go no further. While the creative teacher may present students with some opportunities to science within biology, only the doggedly determined semifanatic would attempt the laboratory activities suggested above. On the other hand, genetic experiments with each medium mentioned have been thoroughly documented. Reaction of a medium (fruit flies, etc.) under the manipulation of each of several experimental variables has been reduced to mathematical laws. Thus, computerized simulations of those experiments offer a reasonable alternative if the primary purposes of Objective C are to have students engage in the problem solving aspects of experimentation or learn optimal procedures for handling the medium in a surrogate laboratory setting.

Will Instruction Be Improved?

The improvement of instruction by use of computerized simulations is a function of at least four variables: (a) the effectiveness of current instruction, (b) the extent to which the simulation utilizes the special characteristics of the computer, (c) the limitations of the computer system which delivers the simulation, and (d) the manner in which the teacher utilizes the simulation. For the purpose of discussion, let's assume that we have a significant learning objective. Our task will be to try to answer the query regarding "improved" instruction in the situation in which there is no reasonable alternative to simulation and in the case where alternative instruction is now used.

If there is no reasonable alternative to a simulated experience, our question would appear to have an obvious answer of *yes*. After all, something should be better than nothing. Well, it should be—but that doesn't guarantee that it will be.

In introducing the use of a simulation to close a gap in the curriculum, we must make a choice between purchasing an existing simulation and constructing a new simulation. Either task takes time. The teacher must approach the selection/construction task with clear notions of what basic learnings must be addressed by the simulation, what nonnegotiable demands should be made about the manner in which those basic learnings are presented, what kind of instruction will be done to prepare the students to use the simulation, and how the learnings imparted by the simulation may be reinforced and evaluated. Possible simulations—both computerized and noncomputerized—must be located and *thoroughly experienced* by the teacher. Are there conceptual errors? Is the presentation at a level that the students can understand? How much preparation must be done before students can be exposed to effective use of the simulation? Does the simulation allow for adequate manipulation of significant variables? Is the simulation interesting? Is it sufficiently realistic to give one a feeling of involvement?

As an example, consider a computerized simulation of genetic experiments using fruit flies. While textbooks may present a detailed discussion of the mechanism of genetically dominant and recessive traits, the teacher may wish to have students execute experiments which will reveal specific examples of the mechanism in action. A good simulation would allow the student to experiment with several variables (e.g., eye color, barred eye versus normal eye, dwarfed wing versus normal wing, the sex of the parent having a given characteristic) either individually or in combinations. Selection of parents would be done either on the basis of the outward appearance of the parents or on the basis of guaranteed genetic make-up.[10] Suppose the student decides to use outward appearance as the selection criterion and to determine the genetic makeup of a pair of flies by means of an experiment. Specifically, the experiment will cross a red-eyed fly with a sepia-eyed fly. The simulation should permit daily observations of the results. It should permit the student to isolate the offspring of this cross at any time (including the maggot stage) in order to provide the stock needed to extend the experiment to additional generations as may be required. While the simulation simply may tabulate (red-eyed versus sepia-eyed) the appearance of a generation of offspring, an improved simulation would permit the student to actually see selected flies and to observe their eye color. If this were done, the simulation might be expanded to provide surrogate experiences in the laboratory procedures used in taking such counts. An elaborate simulation would use the variable of time to introduce the issues of stock pollution and food preparation. The total experience could be further enhanced by a slide presentation (or motion picture film) which would help the student to identify with the role of an experimenter.

The question "Will instruction be improved?" is even more difficult to answer in a situation where some reasonable alternative to simulation is currently in use. If the current alternative has been evaluated and is satisfactorily meeting all expectations, there is little incentive to invest time or funds in introducing a simulation. To be a viable candidate for replacing an existing experience of known value, a simulation must promise (a) to serve learning objectives which are beyond the current alternative or (b) to provide economies in the use of time or funds. The question of improvement then is reduced to evaluating two things:

- Is the simulation *as effective* as the existing experience in meeting the primary objectives of that experience?
- Does the simulation do an adequate job in meeting the expectations set for additional learning objectives or economies?

---

[10]The case of guaranteed make-up is the equivalent of purchasing "thoroughbred" stock—stock issued from a long line of carefully bred generations. The criterion of outward appearance allows no such assumption of "pure" breeding; what you see is not necessarily what you get.

The stress laid upon *as effective* in the first question is a reminder that we are happy with what the current alternative is doing in this area. The improvement we are seeking is in terms of realizing the extra learnings or improved administration promised by the simulation.

There is no guarantee that a given simulation will live up to your expectations. The results that others may have had with a given simulation are subject to so many variables of use that reports of the simulation's success are, at best, suggestive. If the simulation you seek is not yet available, the risk is even higher. In the end, one must decide whether or not the promised returns are worth the risk. If so, you take the plunge with the realization that it probably will take more than one use of the simulation to determine its effectiveness.

Are Existing Time and Equipment Adequate?

All simulations introduce a time requirement; computerized simulations carry equipment-related requirements. If a new simulation requires an increase in the time devoted to a topic or demands the purchase of additional computing equipment, the preceding discussion of instructional improvement is complicated still further. The educational and financial risks have been increased. The decision to take such risks is again reduced to an examination of the significance of the educational objective(s) to be served and the availability and effectiveness of instructional alternatives.

To Simulate or Not to Simulate?

The answer really isn't all that difficult to come by. If the learnings sought are valued highly and existing educational experiences don't live up to educators' expectations, a simulation may be cheap at twice its price. If the learning objective is of low priority or the design of the simulation to be introduced is of limited relevance because of local constraints on funds, time, equipment, or programming talent, it may be too costly at half the price.

Study Guide: Chapter 10

1. A simulation is comprised of at least five types of information (or elements):
   - the scenario,
   - decision network(s),
   - solution path(s),
   - strategy initiation section(s),
   - transition messages.

   Describe the content and purpose of each of these in less than 50 words each.
2. Select any instructional simulation available to you. Identify in it
   a. the data gathering choices and consequences,
   b. the management choices and consequences,
   c. the consultation choices and consequences,
   d. the valuing choices and consequences.

   Find a solution path for the simulation and outline (or make a flowchart of) the steps in it. Also, find a path which does *not* lead to a solution (the goal is impossible to achieve) and outline (or make a flowchart of) the contents of it.
3. The simulation "Lights Out" in this chapter contains no valuing decision pairs. At no time do we have the choice to ignore or avoid dealing with the problem while having full knowledge of a possible disaster.
   a. Add to the example by creating a display (decision point) *of at least five alternatives* which constitutes a strategy initiation section for valuing decisions.
   b. Beginning with one of the alternatives (options) in your valuing strategy initiation section, describe (with a sequence of decision pairs) a successful resolution to the valuing issue.
   c. Repeat *b* above, but this time describe an unsuccessful resolution of the valuing issue.
4. The list below describes several possible simulations. Based upon discussions with other people, classify each simulation as replicable performance, information extraction, or encounter.
   a. flying a jet plane
   b. investing in the stock market
   c. securing job tenure in an elementary school
   d. controlling human population growth in Japan
   e. defining pollution controls for a lake near a large city
   f. assembling a telephone
   g. conducting fractional distillation experiments in chemistry
   h. handling radioactive materials
   i. vacationing in New Delhi
   j. negotiating the Korean cease-fire
   k. counseling drug addicts
   l. presiding at an arms control debate of the UN General Assembly
   m. counting bacteria
   n. setting up a relief program for flood victims
   o. repairing the engine on a jeep
   p. managing a fast-foods restaurant
   q. acting as a personnel manager for a business firm
   r. securing a loan to purchase a house
   s. defining predator control methods in a sheep-ranching area
   t. managing a presidential election campaign
   u. using a credit card
   v. delivering a baby
   w. welding superstructures for ships and bridges
   x. maintaining classroom discipline in a junior high school
5. Chapter 10 discusses three kinds of simulations:
   - replicable performance
   - information extraction
   - encounter

Describe an example of *each* of these kinds of simulations which would be applicable to the teaching of a
  a. doctor or nurse,
  b. physical or biological scientist,
  c. teacher,
  d. farmer or rancher,
  e. school administrator,
  f. a parent,
  g. automotive mechanic or electrician,
  h. police officer.
6. In one's college education it is necessary to make personal decisions about courses to take. There are both effective and ineffective ways to make such decisions. Assume that you are building a simulation of the course selection process.
  a. Write an opening scenario.
  b. Identify the choice-consequence elements (pairs) of an optimal solution path.
  c. List a variety of other data-gathering, managing, consulting, or valuing elements as they come to mind. Try to include elements of a variety of qualities (from necessary to aborting) for each type.
7. Locate and execute a computer activity which purports to be a simulation.
  a. Identify which of the three types of simulations it purports to be.
  b. To what extent does it meet the standards for a simulation as outlined in Chapter 10?
  c. Specify modifications that would bring it into better conformity with the proposed "ideal" for a computerized simulation.
8. If your work in Exercise 5 of Chapter 4 involved the evaluation of a simulation, re-evaluate that simulation and compare the reviews.
9. Locate and execute another purported simulation.
  a. Identify the type of simulation involved.
  b. Evaluate the lesson using the Checklist of Chapter 4.
  c. Summarize your evaluation using the Documentation Sheet of Chapter 4.

AGENDA FOR ACTION

University of Illinois
at Urbana-Champaign

Department of Secondary Education
395 Education Building
1310 South Sixth Street
Champaign
Illinois 61820

College of Education
217 333-0227

MEMORANDUM

TO: Members of ICAC

FROM: Dick Dennis and Bob Kansky

RE: ICAC Paper 10

DATE: March 21, 1983

With the discussion of simulations in ICAC Paper 10, we begin our examination of the role of the computer as a partner in instruction. The topics of this paper and the paper which follows it (instructional games) share an emphasis on decision-making activities in which the computer and the user share the responsibility for controlling the learning environment.

While we're on the topic of shared decision making, we'd like to express our interest in learning more about your experiences in sharing program-construction activities with the students in the computer programming class at Sinclair Senior High School. Have you been pleased with the results? What, if any, problems have you encountered?

We're firm believers in the division of labor with respect to instructional computing! The development of courseware can be divided into tasks for lesson designers (e.g., teachers) and lesson programmers (e.g., students). For large projects involving several items of related courseware, there also may be need for a "project manager" whose task it is to enforce programming standards, ensure continuity in development among the items of courseware, and maintain production schedules. (The teacher in charge of the student programmers might fill the position of project manager.)

We must admit that such team approaches to courseware production are not without their pitfalls. Experience has shown that the product envisioned by the designer is often far removed from that delivered by the programmer. One reason for this is the differing reasons for interest in such a project: the designer is interested in a program which teaches, whereas the programmer is interested in exercising his programming skills. Left unattended, the two interests can produce programs which are illustrative of clever programming tricks but which show minimal concern for communication with the learner. In other cases, a disappointing product may be the result of the designer's lack of appreciation for the limitations of the computer system involved or for the programming skills of the students.

One solution is to require detailed written lesson design specifications from each lesson designer. These can be in the form of display-by-display illustrations (as we'll show in Paper 10), descriptions of the general intent and expected flexibility of the lesson, or both. These must then be discussed with the student programmers (and/or their instructor) to make certain that the designer's expectations are clear and—in terms of the equipment and programming skill at hand—reasonable. Sometimes the design will need adjusting to meet the criterion of reasonableness; at other times, the programmers may be able to suggest options that will make the lesson more flexible!

So again we ask: how are things working out with the projects at Sinclair Senior High? We're eager to add to our bank of practical experiences (with the depositors being teachers like yourselves).

DD:BK:glm

■ ■ ■

AGENDA FOR ACTION

Obourn Senior High School

200 Woodbine Avenue
East Roachmont, New York

M. Jack Stivers
Principal

(716) 568-8840

ICAC Memo #10

TO: Members of ICAC

FROM: John Russell

DATE: April 1, 1983

These several weeks of work by ICAC are beginning to show some returns both in terms of our own growth and in the further commitment and interest of the school board. With regard to the latter item, we are most appreciative of Carrinne's effort to keep the Board informed of our activities.

1. Lolita, Ted, and Phil have submitted their annotated bibliography of journals and newsletters on instructional computing. The list also contains several books and is subdivided by level of interest: Elementary School, Secondary School, General. Only a few of the items are now available at the high school; none were found at the junior

high and elementary schools. (This was checked by the media people at the schools.) Carrinne has volunteered to take this information to the school board; she feels she can get a district-wide recommendation that the libraries acquire some of the suggested materials.

2. Gerri and Jeanne reported viewing three computerized management packages. None had all of the features described in Paper 9, but at least one looked promising in terms of school applications.

3. There was much discussion of the designer/programmer issue raised by Dick and Bob in their memorandum of March 21. Indeed, we have already experienced the "conflict of interest" between teacher and student in the production of courseware. (Note to Dick and Bob: This conflict was what led us—see ICAC Memo #9—to send an "interpreter" to explain item templates to the Sinclair High programmers. Two templates have been returned already; the improvement in usefulness is proof that the effort was worthwhile.) The committee has agreed to experiment with a somewhat more formal designer/programmer relationship in an effort to produce some exemplary courseware to use in possible demonstrations to the school board or to teacher groups. It is clear that we need to greatly improve the initial product as it is difficult to interest the students in doing extensive program revisions. In a sense, it is also unfair to ask for those revisions—we should have done a better job of describing what we wanted in the first place.

4. Carrinne called this morning to report that the school board is willing to entertain a proposal to purchase computing hardware and software for next year! (NOTE: Contrary to today's date and to this writer's unwarranted reputation, this is NOT an April Fool's joke.) Carrinne took our part by responding that we would prepare such a proposal but that we needed to do further study first.

COMMITTEE ASSIGNMENTS

1. Gerri wants to use a modified version of "Lights Out" as part of a unit on human values that she will soon begin in a grade 9 social studies class. She'll follow the index-card procedure in preparing screen displays for several paths that will make use of valuing decision pairs.

2. John and Donna will oversee the preparation of a short Courseware Standards Guide for use by both teachers (lesson designers) and students (programmers). The Guide will seek to remedy major problems that have been observed in both the students' work and commercial programs. The plan is to add more pages to the Guide as we continue to work with the students. Some items to be covered are:

   A) All text must be double-spaced, and each paragraph is to be indented.
   B) A standard format will be used for presenting multiple-choice items (such as Display 4C).
   C) A standard title page (with designer and programmer credits) will be placed at the beginning of each lesson.

   Several other standards were discussed but not recorded. Each committee member is to submit suggested standards (with a clear example of each) in writing at our next meeting. Just remember all the faults you've seen!

3. Jeanne will contact the programming class at Sinclair to explain our planned Guide and to get suggestions from the students. (She'll also attempt to enlist the teacher as our project manager.) A draft of the Guide will later be discussed with the students in order to identify the need for revisions or additions before it is "published."

JR:ms

CHAPTER ELEVEN

In Search of Strategies: Computerized Instructional Games

As kids, we lost many a golden opportunity by committing the tactical/semantic error of asking, "May I go play?" Had we known better, we would have tried, "Mother, may I go learn?" or "Dad, may I go work?" Looking back, we (along with educational philosophers and researchers) can see that play was an important part of the "work" of our youth. How we labored to learn the complex rules of the games we played! How we studied (and often were forced to interpret) the directions for assembling some toy. Then there were those experiences in model building which forced us to invent several special "tools" or techniques in order to complete a step in the construction which must have been designed for an octopus. One might also recall the sudden social growth that occurred at the dinner table of that valued friend when the table setting turned out enough knives to equip a band of pirates.

For many of us, a significant portion of our learning has come not from studying textbooks or listening to school teachers but, rather, from engaging in a variety of activities called *play*. The contexts of those activities varied (e.g., sports, board games, parties, plays, construction tasks), but they all qualified as play because we wanted to do them. The cultural association of the word *play* with pleasure seeking is so strong that even those of us who take great pleasure in our occupations would never dare excuse ourselves from that late-night dinner by explaining that we've "got to be going in order to be in shape for play tomorrow."

In play, one collects a wide variety of experiences in situations which can be highly motivating. Although play is closely associated with the learnings of childhood, the attributes of play also can be found in adult learning and work activities. For instance, the player of a game often discovers a master strategy, only to later find it ineffective in an unanticipated situation or because of a logical flaw. Adult problem solvers are confronted by similar situations in which the logic behind a proposed solution is revealed to be faulty. In either case, further progress requires a return to the cycling of such basic gaming processes as observation, testing guesses, and jumping to (tentative) conclusions.

There is evidence of an increasing use of games as teaching devices. Supply catalogs and professional publications increasingly display a wide variety of instructional game material for sale. (This suggests that someone must be buying.) Teachers' journals and the programs of professional meetings give considerable attention to games as a medium of instruction. Textbooks include game-type activities intended for instruction in core content as well as for diversion or enrichment. While the presence of such activities is not new to instruction, the increased visibility of games as accepted—even recommended—tools of instruction is significant.

Settling Down to Some Serious Play

Since this chapter is supposed to be an academic endeavor, we've just got to get serious about play! At any rate, we need to establish a respectable link between play and learning if our use of games is to be viewed as educational rather than wholly hedonistic. In short, we need to know what we are doing or can do by using instructional games.

Play has many attributes which educators associate with good educational episodes. First, one can never be passive when engaged in play. A restatement of this first principle might be "Spectators don't qualify as players." In play, as in a well-designed educational activity, each participant easily identifies with the context, assumes a role, and takes a degree of personal responsibility for consequences. Play is individualized; what we get from it depends upon the previous learnings we bring to it. Play encourages the formation and testing of strategies, the examination of guiding principles (rules), and the exploration of the effects of modifying the guiding principles. Play often leaves some success to chance or sudden flashes of insight—features common to life in general and to the world of research in particular.

What is learned from play—or, at least, how efficiently something is learned from play—can be influenced by structuring the play activity. Young children, given a large box of brightly colored rods of different lengths, will manipulate them (i.e., play with them) for long periods of time on several occasions. Left to such unfettered educational activity, children form many ideas having mathematical import. One could conjecture that, left alone long enough, the child might discover all of the mathematics of elementary school. Maybe so, but it would be hard to find teachers or parents who would place a child's education at the mercy of such a conjecture. Instead, teachers prefer to use structured activities with the rods (activities that are *games* from the student's point of view) to pursue specific mathematical concepts. Play need not be unrestrained; learning need not be drudgery.

What's in a Game?

A game is one way of structuring the learning environment. In trying to understand games as potential learning devices, it may help to examine that structuring in terms of common attributes of games. Simply put, a game is a decision-making activity which usually includes the following features:

1. One or more players (i.e., decision makers)
2. Rules of play which govern the behavior of the players
3. One or more goals that the players are trying to reach
4. Rules of scoring which define goals to be reached
5. Conditions introduced by chance
6. A spirit of competition[1]
7. A strategy—i.e. pattern of action-choices to be taken by a player (or team)
8. A feedback system for revealing the state of the game at any moment
9. A winning player or team

A game may have a single player. For instance, there are many card games in which a single player is pitted against a task presented by a wholly "uninvolved" deck of cards. When more than one person is involved in a game, the players may participate as individuals or as teams. Finally, a computer may be counted as a player provided that it has been programmed to simulate the decisions of a human.[2] If the computer simply makes the game possible (e.g., it generates tasks for the players, records the decisions of players, or describes

[1]This has several forms. In some cases, each player is in competition with each other player. As a variation, the members of a team may cooperate with each other in order to compete with another team. In some games, all players cooperate to solve some task; hence, the competition is with the task rather than with other players.

[2]There are situations where *all* of the players are computers. Human involvement is in the writing of the programs which govern the play of the competing computers.

the state of the game following the action of a player) but does not make independent decisions which affect the competition, it is not a player. A player must actively participate in the decision making which eventually produces a winner.

Each decision by a player is governed by the rules of play. Usually, there will be several possible choices for a given decision. On occasion, the player's strategy (or the game's elements of chance) may produce a situation in which only a single action is permitted by the rules. From decision to decision, the choices available under the rules will vary as a result of chance, the player's strategy, or the goal being sought.

A goal of a game is a set of conditions which, when achieved, mark a conclusion of play; that is, a goal is a set of conditions under which (a) one player (or team) has won part or all of the game, (b) further play will never result in a winning state for any player, or (c) no further play is possible. These conditions are, of course, a consequence of the rules of the game—rules which may include a time limit for play, a score to be achieved, a position to be reached, or a task to be completed. If the game involves the participation of more than one player or team, the fact that only one player (or team) may attain a winning state creates the game's element of competition. In some games, the "opponent" which introduces competitive stress is a task. In such games a player, or a group of players acting in cooperation, is pitted against the task rather than against other players.

The rules of the game also give value to specific game-related resources such as cards, game pieces (as in chess or in word-spelling games), wealth, order of play, information, or special options which offer flexibility of play to one player or which restrict the play of an opponent. A player's capacity to act within the rules of the game is determined by these resources insofar as they define or restrict the pattern of actions which comprise the player's strategy.

The game's feedback system provides data regarding changes in the state of the game which result from actions taken. This data helps the player to decide what resources to commit to a particular strategy. In some games, the decisions to be made are logically independent; outcomes are based upon chance and, hence, information about the results of one decision does nothing to provide the basis for the next decision. However, most games supply feedback which can be used to improve the conditions of play (i.e., to implement winning strategies). While some feedback is available to all players, other information may be hidden from some players. In the latter case, success in gaming requires the further management of information flow through bargaining, negotiating, bluffing, or cooperating.

The Games People Play

Instructional games are essentially decision-making activities designed to take place within a context which "tickles the fancy" of the player. The decisions may have a marked similarity to those made in the everyday activities of the players or may have no apparent relationship to such activities. The degree of reality associated with the game's decisions, the skills called for in making those decisions, and the motivation for engaging in the game affect the choice of games that people will play. It is helpful, therefore, to take a look at three different types of instructional games.

The Games of Life (Simulation Games)

Simulation games are characterized by a scenario which presents the context within which play is to be developed. The context may be of immediate or distant relevance to the everyday activities or work prospects of the player; the decisions to be made in playing such games carry a guarantee of practical value when transferred to situations outside the game. The context of some simulation games, however, may be quite removed from practical reality; the decision making to be done may be of generic value but carries no guarantee of applicability.

Context-relevant simulation games are used in such learning settings as farming, ranching, small business management, military training, and nuclear plant emergency procedure training. The play involves behaviors obviously congruent to the behaviors desired in the setting being simulated. Although the game may present the players with a large number of decision-making opportunities (with several choices at each opportunity), the given rules and goals of play rigorously define the game. That is, the player cannot introduce new rules, modify existing rules, or propose new goals. Exploration beyond the bounds imposed by the given rules and goals is neither permitted nor suggested. Pursuit of interesting alternatives which would involve alteration of game variables is not possible.

Simulation games need not have the rigid form just described. Considerable freedom is typical of the simulation games used in fields such as political science, sociology, social psychology, and counseling. A distinguishing feature of these games is that the positions taken, the goals set, or the rules governing play may be challenged, altered, or created as part of the play activity. This flexibility means that successful play calls for imagination and innovation on the part of the players. Moreover, the players' freedom to manipulate the basic constraints of the game enables them to experience aspects of problems not described in the scenario.

Although the problems involved in these games are of the same type as problems encountered in their real-life counterparts, no two problems are identical. The problems are not static; they require solution behaviors which are similar to, but not congruent to, the real-life solution behaviors. Given the creativity of the human mind on the one side and the program dependency of the computer on the other, it is clear that this type of simulation game is not easy to computerize.

Every simulation game involves the players in the replicating of a performance, the solving of a problem, or the experiencing of some new environment. In short, each simulation game is a simulation (as discussed in Chapter 10). On the other hand, not every simulation is a simulation game. In particular, encounter simulations lack such game features as stated rules, specific goals, and a spirit of competition. The principal object of an encounter simulation is to explore a vaguely defined environment rather than to conquer a task or attain a winning state.

Academic Games

Teachers are both clever and practical folk. It's not surprising, therefore, that they have long employed games as a means of motivating the study of some less attractive topics. They have used the excitement created by gaming to drive out the pain of repetitious activities and to force students to ingest some otherwise unpalatable academic ideas. In this manner, teachers seek both to have students refine specific skills and to provide them with a variety of opportunities to formulate and test problem-solving strategies. In most academic games, the primary objective is to provide development, drill, application, or practice of a concept or skill which has been embedded in the game. In some cases, it is the search for winning strategies which is the only instructional purpose of the game; any academic skills (e.g., mathematics, English, science) employed in that search are incidental.

Examples abound of academic games in which the teaching of subject matter is paramount. The word game called "hangman" can be used to provide spelling drill in any language (and permits complete control of the words to be used). Crossword board games provide practice in the use of a dictionary (any language) and encourage vocabulary development apart from the constraint of a particular word list. The card game "concentration" has hundreds of variations used for associative drill activities. A few simple examples which should suggest many more concentration games would include:

- Geography: matching map outlines with names of countries or states
- Biology: matching the names (or pictures) of organs with their primary functions
- Cooking: matching specific foods with vitamins
- Woodworking: matching woods with characteristics of workability
- History: matching political figures with positions on a given issue

Mathematics has been a rich source of academic games which have been (a) translated for use in other subject areas and (b) adapted for use on a computer. For instance, one game makes use of five dice and a five-by-five array of numbers. A sample set of dice ("exploded" to reveal their faces) and a sample array are shown below. The computerized version creates the array by randomly selecting 25 of the numbers from 0 to 50 and placing them at random within the display; no number is used more than once. It then "throws" the five dice to get a display like:

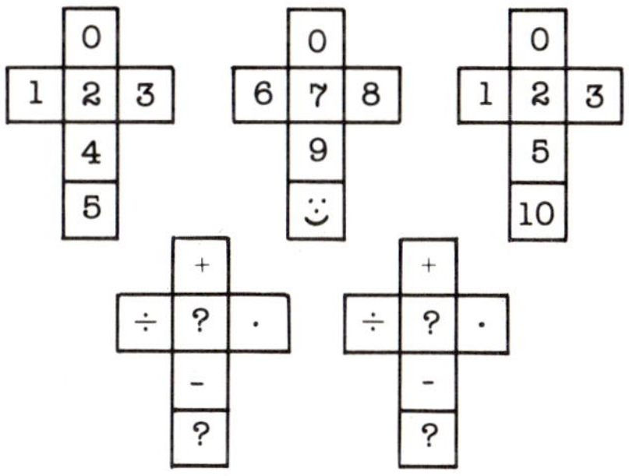

DICE

10	16	35	6	32
13	45	3	9	19
43	15	14	27	17
20	31	40	39	48
30	42	2	7	1

ARRAY

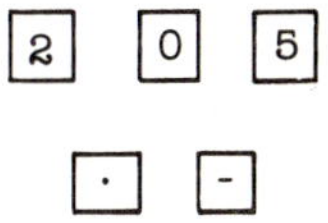

A player (one of which can be the computer) is to combine the three numbers using the two operations to obtain one of the numbers in the array. The throwing of the smiling face permits the player to select any whole number from 0 to 10 to replace it; the throwing of a **?** permits the player to use any one of the four operations in its place. All five dice must be used or the player loses a turn. Some possibilities are

$(2 \cdot 5) - 0 \qquad 5 - (2 \cdot 0) \qquad 2 - (5 \cdot 0) \qquad (5 - 2) \cdot 0$

Only two of the four expressions result in numbers included in the array. The element of the array which the player chooses to claim (in this case, 10 or 2) is further dependent upon rules for scoring which assign extra points for selecting a number in a square sharing a side with one or more previously selected squares. There also is a penalty for claiming a number which cannot be obtained with the dice faces thrown. A player has the option of claiming no number (if this might deny some advantage to the opponent) or of rethrowing from one to five of the dice to get a "better" set *but* at the cost of penalty points for the number of dice to be cast a second time. Winning the game requires a combination of arithmetic skill, strategy, and dumb luck. As in all academic games, strategy and the correct use of a curricular skill are the important components of success. The elements of chance (the selection and placement of numbers in the array, the numbers/operations obtained on any throw of the dice) introduce the need to alter a strategy.

Academic games tend to reflect "school reality" rather than reality outside the school. Game rules which place special requirements on method, answer form, precision, syntax, answer length, and speed of performance are not typically real-life conditions, but they are very handy devices for promoting school objectives of the game. Also, the search for numerical solutions apart from a problem context (and, hence, the lack of a requirement that the numbers be interpreted in that context) further reveals the contrived nature of academic games. Still, such games are popular with educators (since they can be related to specific curricular skills) and are enjoyed by students as a variation within the overall restrictions of school-based instruction. Moreover, special restrictions characteristic of its school reality make the academic game a prime candidate for computerization.

Games to Set the Mind Free

A third and final class of games contains those in which neither the problems solved nor the behaviors employed are congruent to real-life situations. Good players clearly exhibit behaviors different from beginners, but how (if at all) those behaviors relate to the solution of real-life problems is unclear. In such open games, problem solving is context free and of a general nature.

Chess is a good example of this class of game. It is an exercise in decision making within a set of rigid rules which govern the movement of the pieces, rules which claim no real-life counterparts. The essence of the game is problem solving, and much learning takes place along the road to becoming a good player. Still, the problems presented by chess are synthetic—unique consequences of a set of arbitrary rules.

Politics has been referred to as "an exercise in chess." An adroit politician will often be credited with being "a shrewd poker player" or "a good chess player." Many people hold that chess playing has positive influences on both political and mathematical behaviors (popular wisdom has it that chess fosters skills in geometry). Whether these claims are true, or just how chess improves one's performance in political or geometric spheres, hasn't been demonstrated. In fact, we really don't know what learnings are required to make a good chess player! The only safe claim that one can make about chess is that playing chess will improve one's ability to play chess. The claim that chess (or any general, context-free game like it) is an *instructional game* must be restricted to learning the activity itself: chess teaches chess, poker teaches poker, bridge teaches bridge, backgammon teaches backgammon, whist teaches whist. (One might even get away with such claims as "whist teaches bridge" because of the similarities in the games.) However, unsupported arguments that such games teach general problem-solving skills which will magically be transferred to the solution of real-life problems will cut no ice with the local school administrators (unless they are avid fans of chess or whatever).

The context-free (purely recreational?) type of game does permit creative exploration of the set of problems presented. However, this very freedom of exploration has the effect of reducing the teacher's definition and control of the behaviors learned or practiced. By contrast, academic games and context-relevant simulation games are easily related to specific learning objectives of the school curriculum. While academic games may reflect "school reality" rather than life situations, they permit the practice of accepted academic learnings such as solving equations or increasing vocabulary in a foreign language. Context-relevant simulation games are attractive to schools because they engage students in the use of flexible problem-solving strategies within a "real world" environment. Context-free games like chess, attractive as they may be, are not relevant to the school curriculum or applicable to the real world. To put it another way, it can be argued that simulation games and academic games constitute a *means* of instruction; a context-free game, on the other hand, appears to be its own *object* of instruction.

Games in the Classroom(?)

A teacher once remarked, "Game-playing will never be accepted in my school district—the idea is in conflict with too many school principles." The statement not only presents a nice play on words but also reminds us of an important source of justifiable challenges to game-playing in the classroom. In order for a teacher to assert that such-and-such a game is an *instructional* game, the teacher must be able to identify the motivational or learning outcomes associated with its use.

As any teacher knows, the school day is a kind of academic battleground in a war against time. Several possible activities compete for each portion of the day, and the teacher's task is to select those activities which best serve the goals of instruction. If an educational activity offers only vague promises, its life is in jeopardy.

Despite the current growing popularity of instructional games, the outcomes of gaming are not easily defined. Although there is general agreement that games do teach, it is often difficult to pinpoint the precise nature of what is learned and just how it is taught by the game. Games are in the position of being an instructional technology which "works" (i.e., game playing produces changes in behavior), but which has been introduced into the classroom without theoretical support. It's a situation which invites challenge.

Instructional games are not without claims to educational respectability, claims that are worthy of examination so long as one maintains an open mind. As you read the claims which follow, it would be healthy to interject occasionally the cautionary thought, "However, the evidence is far from complete."

1. *Games are self-judging.* Although chance plays a role in a game's outcome, a player's success also is clearly related to his/her own actions. Success is not the subjective judgment of a nonparticipant. The notion here is that the player must take responsibility for any outcome, but the claim is flawed if the nature of the game allows the player to attribute failure to chance or to the actions of team members. Still, games do offer feedback which is clear, objective, and immediate; these conditions often are not characteristic of teacher-led learning activities.
2. *The teacher's role is favorably moved away from that of judge and toward that of partner.* Insofar as the teacher must pass judgment on students' performances, the teacher is seen as an authority figure. Student reactions to authority figures (e.g., hostility, servility, alienation) can interfere with learning. By using games, the teacher *momentarily* avoids the role of judge and assumes the role of a partner in learning. Of course, the role of partner in learning is confined to the gaming episodes. The teacher still must give grades and maintain discipline. The effect of the claim is, then, that games release the teacher from selected judgmental activities and even provide the opportunity for the teacher to participate and *lose* (without trying).
3. *Games provide immediate goals for which the content of classroom instruction is relevant.* Students—covertly and overtly—are known to wonder "What is knowing about *XXXX* really any good for, anyway?" Some have the temerity to challenge the study of *Hamlet,* the Battle of Vicksburg, the anatomical wonders of earthworms, and the proof of the Pythagorean theorem! Games enable the teacher to devise situations in which students will have immediate need for such bits and bites of school substance. It has been observed repeatedly that the very student who will resist completing a written assignment calling for the completion of twenty simple arithmetic problems will enthusiastically attack ten times that many problems when they occur in the context of a game (such as the academic game of five dice described earlier). But does the student really see the classroom content (e.g., the arithmetic) of the game as relevant? Or does the student *accept* the irrelevancies as the price for playing the game (i.e., engaging in competition)? The game has motivated the study of certain material, but has it really justified that study to the student? The fact that the student may gain greater facility with some curricular concept as a result of the game should not be confused with the student's attaching revelance to the study of that concept.
4. *Games provide students with the opportunity to engage in roles which they see as important in their future lives.* This claim certainly would apply to simulation games. Well, maybe. Many games will assign students to roles that they will never play in real life (e.g., leader of a country or president of a large corporation) and which they may have no interest in pursuing. Other games may assign them roles that they view as unimportant or unnecessary. While games force students to make decisions and to face the consequences of those decisions, it must be recognized that games tend to reward those players who think like the designer of the game and, often, to punish players who develop innovative strategies. Thus, games may be useful in developing behaviors which are similar to some existing or approved model, but may not be useful for exploring alternatives to that model. It follows that a simulation game in a social science, a game in which success is equated with conforming to an underlying "approved" social model, could come under attack as educational brainwashing.
5. *Games promote positive student attitudes toward education.* Games will motivate students to study materials which they otherwise view as uninteresting. In fact, students will request to play some games long after the teacher's educational objectives have been met. On the other hand, some students are threatened by the competitive nature of games and regard game playing as unsatisfying. Teachers who require such students to participate in game playing may generate hostility and alienation. It's wise to keep in mind that not everyone likes to play games and that anyone may dislike a particular game.
6. *Games provide instructional variety.* Games can be constructed in such a way that success requires the

use of specific skills, concepts, facts, or insights. The learning objectives of such games can be clearly identified; the success of the game in teaching those objectives can be verified. All other things being equal (time expended, level of learning attained, expense) the game is a promising alternative by which some students may study a given topic. There is some evidence that games reduce differences in the learning rates of high, average, and low ability students, and that they result in comparable levels of learning by all students. However, if the game resource is limited so that gaming groups become large, the potential value of the game is reduced. Specifically, players will learn the game rules less efficiently, will interact less, and will lose interest in the activity.

Is there a place for games in the classroom? The answer clearly must be a resounding Yes!—and No! Instructional games have great promise and are gaining in popularity. Their effectiveness, however, is at the mercy of such variables as student acceptance, clarity of purpose, excellence of design, and method of classroom use. Games do motivate some students to acquire traditional learning objectives, and they offer opportunities to approach nontraditional objectives.

With the possible exception of some academic games and some content-relevant simulation games, it is not an easy matter to argue the case for instructional games. Their justification requires thoughtful advanced planning by the teacher. While games are motivating and exciting and may comprise the memorable events of the school day, students seldom remember the instructional objective of the game. Indeed, students may not be aware—nor really need to be aware—of the purpose for including certain academic games. The teacher may even wish to conceal that purpose if, say, it is to "force" students to develop facility with some process they usually seek to avoid. On occasion, the teacher's only reason for including a game is as a diversion or release. Teachers use such departures to clear away cranial cobwebs in preparation for lessons that demand active involvement by the students.

A public relations problem can then arise when students, unaware of or forgetful of a teacher's purpose, report to parents, "We didn't do any work in our XXXX class today—we just played games!" Hence, from both a learning and a public relations perspective, the teacher who uses games must be forearmed against the academic challenges of parents, administrators, and other teachers. Games must be components of an overall instructional plan which includes organizing activities preceding the games and summarizing/relating activities following the game.

Parents will (and should) continue to question the credentials of any game which claims to be *instructional.* They must also understand that a game need not be instructional in itself to have value; the way in which it is employed by the teacher may imbue it with instructional worth. Finally, the teacher who is convinced of the value of instructional games must not despair of defending their use to parents who, in grand inconsistency, justify their own purchases of electronic TV games (ping-pong, chess, hockey, space games) with "But they're so educational, of course." Of course.

Computerized Instructional Games

Computerized games are a dime a dozen. At that, some are overpriced; others are electronic masterpieces of human ingenuity. The point is that there is a large supply of such games. Many were not designed with classrooms in mind but, happily, can be used there. Of late, large numbers of games are being generated specifically for education.

The Criterion for Computerized *Instructional* Games

In the remainder of this chapter, we'll address the everyday concerns of teachers who wish to select and use computerized educational games. While the qualification *computerized* should require no elaboration, the qualification *educational* should be understood to imply one condition:

The activity encourages the player to develop strategies.

Educational gaming is a search for strategies. This search may or may not involve the student in (a) the use of school-related academic skills or (b) contexts which have real-life counterparts. By equating educational gaming with the search for strategies, we avoid prejudging the possible educational value of context-free games.

The strategy criterion also permits a useful distinction. There *are* games which provide students with drill or practice experience. To be specific, academic games or context-relevant simulation games often do this. On the other hand, there are many drill or practice activities that do not qualify as games because they do not call upon the student to develop problem-solving strategies. Gamelike feedback such as smiling faces, colorful graphics, sounds, electronically dispensed candies, or other rewards are not sufficient to classify an activity as a game. Such activities may develop a skill or its application quite apart from the development of problem solving strategies. For instance, consider a computerized activity which makes use of the following five dice. With

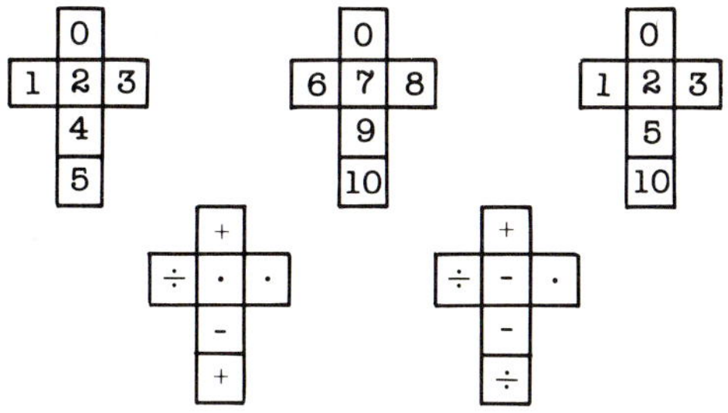

minor differences, these dice look like the ones used in the academic game on page 177. In this activity, the student's task is to generate whole numbers by forming and evaluating an arithmetic expression which makes use of all five dice. If a computerized throw of the dice produces:

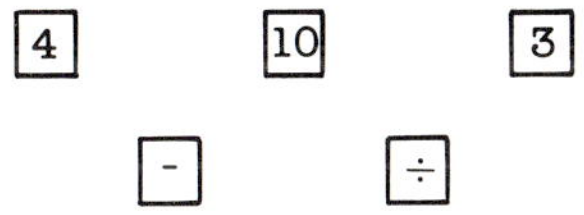

the student might type the expression 10 ÷ (4 − 3) and its value: 10.

The computer would judge the student's play to be correct and would award a score of one point.[3] Play then passes to the next player; the first player to score a total of 50 points is the winner. However, this identification of a winner in the activity is not enough to give it game status. Student involvement in this activity is limited to practicing the generation and simplification of simple arithmetic expressions. Winning the activity does not call for the development of a winning strategy. By contrast, the rules of the academic game on page 177 encourage the development of strategic planning.

Management of Computerized Instructional Gaming

Management of the use of computerized instructional games must deal with two issues: (a) the physical demands of the type of instructional computing implied and (b) the twofold issue of the purposes/sources of the games employed. The first of these issues is a practical consideration arising from the fact that the use of instructional games almost dictates the interactive use of computer terminals by individual students or pairs of students.[4] Since some games are open-ended (i.e., they have a logical termination but can be repeated) and since it is often necessary for students to play a game several times to develop the desired strategies or to otherwise meet the teacher's instructional objectives, a limited resource (the terminals) will be tied up by a few students for extended periods of time. If few terminals are available and many students are to be provided with the gaming experience, the activity must be spread over several days. The teacher must be prepared to deal with related problems of scheduling the terminals for maximal use and of providing productive activities for each student who has had or is awaiting a place at the computer.

The second management issue is a twofold one. First, it recognizes that the broad purpose of introducing a computerized instructional game may be (a) to use the game as a means of developing some specific item of subject matter or (b) to involve the student in the task of designing and programming the game itself. The former use of instructional games is intended to provide all students with relatively equivalent experiences with the subject matter. The latter use provides each student with a unique learning experience which may be difficult to classify within the bounds of traditional school objectives. These two uses are linked to the sources of the computerized games, a topic that we'll examine in the remaining sections of this chapter.

Ready-To-Use Computerized Games

Hundreds of computerized games have been prepared for several computer systems. Many are available at reasonable prices from the shelves of shops that sell computing equipment. Others are available by mail from courseware companies who advertise their products in computing magazines and courseware catalogues. Vendors of a particular brand computing equipment will usually be able to list several sources from which one may obtain game programs for their machines. There are also groups of educators who are willing to provide copies of the games that they've written; the charge is usually minimal, sometimes involving only the cost of preparing the programs for shipping.

Programs from any one of the sources suggested above are in a load-and-go format. That is, you receive

[3]The computer could even be programmed to award a point to a student who types *impossible* when confronted with a throw of the dice such as the following. (No combination of these five dice will produce an expression having a whole number value.)

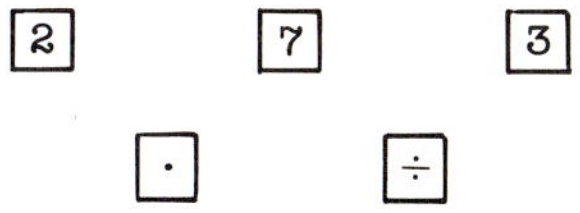

[4]One can conceive of simulation games which could be executed in batch mode. However, delayed feedback may take the "zing" out of the game and reduce needed involvement.

the programmed games on an electronic medium (disk, magnetic tape, punched cards, punched tape). You simply load those programs into a particular kind of computer (by pushing the appropriate buttons) and immediately start using them. Anyway, things are *supposed* to work that way.

In practice, the selection and use of ready-to-use computerized games raises two questions (in addition to those of price and the reliability of the supplier).

1. Can the game be used on the computer system available?
2. Will the game do an effective job of teaching some relevant learning objective?

The first concern reminds us that any program is prepared for execution by a particular computing system; some are available in several versions, each corresponding to a different computing system. Thus, the program is ready-to-use by *your* computing system if and only if there is a version that has been designed for the name brand (and model) of your computer, uses the same version of programming language as your system,[5] and does not require peripheral devices (printers, disc drives, sound systems, color monitors, etc.) which are not available on your system.

The second concern, that of instructional value, is by far the more complex issue. The educational claims made by the producer often will differ considerably from the expectations of the teacher obtaining the program. The "deception" need not be intentional. The teacher wishing to use the program may have misunderstood the statment of its purpose, may have overestimated the programming skill of the producer, or may disagree with the pedagogical approach of an otherwise well-designed program. Resolution of the concern demands that the teacher make a careful evaluation of the computerized game from an instructional viewpoint. The procedures for evaluating computerized instructional materials merit a paper unto themselves. We will be content here with posting a warning.

Ready-To-Computerize Games

One step away from the load-and-go format of a game is the printed program listing. This is a line-by-line listing of the computer code (for a particular computer) which constitutes the game. Entire books of such programs have been published, and computing magazines often contain such programs as a regular feature. Groups of computer-using teachers use club newsletters to display such listings or to announce their availability (at the price of copying the computer printout of the listing). A listing is usually accompanied by an explanation of the game's purpose and/or procedures. Since listings are offered for use, it follows that the programs may be modified to better serve the intent of each teacher using them.

Use of printed program listings presents some new problems. The most obvious problem is the need for people to remove the program from the printed page and to place it in your particular computer. The task requires both time and a modest understanding of the programming language used. If the program was written in the version of BASIC employed by the Model-T Flivver Microcomputer, it may call for nontrivial modification before it will run on your Stumblebum Micromarvel. Aided by an understanding of the differences in the versions of BASIC used by the two systems,[6] a student or teacher usually can make the programming changes that are needed or desired.

Almost Ready-To-Computerize Games

A procedure by which students may participate in the creation of a computerized game makes use of a game which already exists in some noncomputerized setting. The game itself need not be one which later can be employed to teach some item of subject matter to other students. The educational aspect of this kind of gaming may be confined without apology to the learnings of the student (or group of students) involved in its creation. The task of the student creator(s) is to adapt the game to the computer—both to design such a computerized version and to program it. This is not a simple task (few worthwhile endeavors are), so the teacher should be aware of some of the problems involved.

To begin with, the teacher must address the problem of programming the game. If the student needs instruction in a programming language, the teacher must see to the matter of instruction. (After all, one component of this use of instructional games is to have the student do the programming.) In fact, simple games provide excellent instructional projects when teaching computer programming. They permit easy "problem definition," insofar as students are familiar with the game's materials, rules of play, and strategies. They also

---

[5]Languages such as BASIC have several versions which are "updated" from time to time. Programs written with one version may not execute on a machine which makes use of another version *even though the machines themselves are identical.*

[6]A useful aid to such BASIC translations is *The BASIC Handbook: An Encyclopedia of the BASIC Computer Language* by David A. Lien (San Diego: COMPUSOFT Publishing, 1978, second edition, 1981).

contain examples of the structures found in programming tasks (inputting data, evaluating expressions, executing branching (*if-then-else* structures), generating random numbers, repeating procedures through *loops,* and formatting data for output). Many games use graphics as well.

The game to be computerized should be one that is easy to represent on a computer terminal. Board games cause special problems. Not only do the boards require special programming skills to present the graphics, but it also may be impossible to display the entire board on the screen. Other kinds of games are more easily adapted to computer display. Dice are simple to represent, and the use of cards can be simplified by agreeing to use symbols such as

4♥ K♣ A♦

rather than drawing entire cards.

Another important feature of game design is the matter of how the computer participates in the play of the game. It may simply make the play of two persons possible, or it may itself take the role of a player. The initial design of a computerized game should be confined to the first (and easier) of these options: it merely records the moves made by human players. The design demands of the second option are much greater since the student must analyze the entire strategy behind the game and develop a computer algorithm which will permit the computer to play against a human opponent.[7] Even a game as seemingly simple as tic-tac-toe has a rather complex decision algorithm to control the play of the computer. Asking students to develop an algorithm which permits the computer to participate as a player may be asking too much at first.

Computerized Originals

At its least structured level of application, instructional gaming calls upon the students to create and to computerize an entirely new game. This task requires the kind of creativity used in producing an original painting; computerizing an existing game is, by comparison, a paint-by-numbers exercise. It follows that the creation of a game is not something which can be done easily or well by all people. Nevertheless, inventing a new game can be a valuable instructional experience since it usually involves many problem solving episodes. Its value as an instructional tool is further enhanced if its play or design makes use of curricular content of current interest. In fact, students may find it more interesting (fun) to play a game designed by "one of their own" than to use a slick, professionally designed game.

[7] An extension of the second option makes use of several computer algorithms, each representing a particular level of sophistication in the playing ability of the computer. The game then offers the human player the opportunity to choose the level of ability. Good instructional games have this feature.

Study Guide: Chapter 11

1. Select several (2 or 3) popular games used in teaching your subject. Study the game and articulate what you think to be the learning outcomes of playing the game. Be sure to consider both thinking and problem solving as well as skill outcomes.
2. You decide to use one of the games studied in Activity 1 (above) in your classroom. A parent becomes upset and complains to the principal that there is too much fun and not enough learning. Neither the parent nor the principal has thought about the game from the perspective of teaching your subject. You are requested to prepare a written defense of your decision to use the game as a learning activity. Do so.
3. Distinguish among the three major classes of games by filling in the cells of the following chart.

Type	Defining Characteristics	Place or Role in the Classroom
Simulation Game		
Academic Game		
Context-free Game		

4. A game called "Prime Dice" uses the chart and five dice described in the "Academic Games" section of this chapter. Items a to d below explain how those materials are used to play "Prime Dice." Remember! A prime number is a whole number that has exactly two *different* factors (divisors), namely, the number itself and 1.
   a. Construct the dice by putting masking tape on the faces of cubes and marking the faces with a pen as indicated in the chapter.
   b. Use the array given in the chapter as a game board.
   c. Follow these rules of play (two players):
      i. Roll all 5 dice.
      ii. Using the values of all 5 dice create a numerical expression such as

      [2] [·] [5] [-] [0]

      which names one of the unclaimed spaces on the game board.

iii. Players use an *X* or an *O* to claim spaces on the board.
iv. The smiling face can be used as any whole number 0 through 10; the player must declare the number intended.
v. A [?] can be any of the operations, +, −, ·, or ÷; the player must declare the operation intended.
vi. A player who makes an error in evaluating the arithmetic expression formed *or* is unable to create an expression that names the value of an unclaimed space on the board loses the turn.

d. Use these scoring rules:
i. One point for each prime factor possessed by a number claimed—e.g., claiming 12 yields *two* points for prime factors 2 and 3 (4 and 6 are *not* primes).
ii. *Loss* of two points for an error in arithmetic when evaluating an expression.
iii. Four points for claiming a space whose value *is* a prime number.
iv. No points for being unable to claim a space.
v. The first person to gather a total of 15 points is the winner.

Activity 1: Play the game several times under the above rules. What are the learning outcomes of the game? Can you identify any playing strategies that will facilitate or guarantee a win?

Activity 2: Consider the rules of play. What changes might be made in them or the scoring procedures to make the learning situation better? Describe these changes.

Activity 3: Consider computerizing this game. Describe any desirable changes in the board, the rules, or the scoring needed to do this. Sketch the computer screens needed, assuming the screen layout of a computer accessible to you.

5. Invent a board game for language arts instruction. Use eight dice and put the letters of the alphabet on the faces. Eight dice make 6 × 8 = 48 faces, so you will need to decide on repeated letters.
   a. Invent the playing and scoring rules and test these in actual play. Describe the desired learning outcomes. Pay attention to maximizing them.
   b. Describe (including screen sketches) a computerization of the game.
6. Locate and execute a computer activity which purports to be an instructional game.
   a. What type of game (of the three types described in Chapter 11) is it?
   b. To what extent does it meet the standards for an instructional game as outlined in Chapter 11?
   c. Specify modifications that bring it into better conformity with the proposed "ideal" for a computerized instructional game.
7. If your work in Exercise 5 of Chapter 4 involved the evaluation of an instructional game, reevaluate that game and compare the reviews.
8. Locate and execute another purported instructional game.
   a. Identify the type of game.
   b. Evaluate the game using the Checklist in Chapter 4.
   c. Summarize your evaluation using the Documentation Sheet in Chapter 4.

AGENDA FOR ACTION

SCIENCE AND MATHEMATICS
TEACHING CENTER

ADDRESS REPLY TO WRITER

THE UNIVERSITY OF WYOMING
UNIVERSITY STATION, BOX 3992
LARAMIE, WYOMING, 82071

MEMORANDUM

TO: Members of ICAC

FROM: Dick Dennis and Bob Kansky

RE: ICAC Paper 11

DATE: April 4, 1983

In ICAC Paper 10, computerized simulations cast the computer in the role of a partner in instructional decision making. This educational partnership also is the primary characteristic of the application to be examined next, the application known as instructional gaming.

To youth, the word game has a very positive connotation; the same word often sends teachers and school administrators into paroxysms of educational indigestion. Permit us, then, to preface ICAC Paper 11 with one point, subtly made:

ICAC Paper 11 April 4, 1983

In fact, the educational focus of computerized instructional games will be the search for problem-solving strategies. The game aspect of the activity will provide the means of instruction (both motivation and experience in decision making) toward an end of strategy development.

P.S. ICAC Memo #10 just arrived, bringing the good news that your school board has expressed interest in purchasing some computing equipment. Apparently Mrs. Calabresi has been able to bring the exemplary work of your committee to the attention of the board.

We heartily agree with your decision to delay preparation of the proposal; some of the remaining ICAC papers should provide you with useful information on planning and purchasing.

Professional meetings in your various subject fields also can be a rich source of information regarding hardware and software. We would urge you to attend any such meetings that you can before writing your proposal. Many large professional groups offer presentations on instructional computing which cover grades K-12 and which are NOT confined to the subject matter of the host organization.

DD:BK:baa

■ ■ ■

Obourn Senior High School

200 Woodbine Avenue
East Roachmont, New York

M. Jack Stivers
Principal

(716) 568-8840

ICAC Memo #11

TO: Members of ICAC

FROM: John Russell

DATE: April 13, 1983

What ever happened to all that time we thought we had when ICAC was formed 'way back in November of 1982? With so much yet to do, June seems very, very close.

1. Superintendent Ennis has suggested that the committee have its computer purchase proposal ready for the board meeting of June 17, 1983. It should be in her hands no later than June 10. The proposal is to cover hardware, software, and inservice teacher training.
2. Suggestions for the Courseware Standards Guide (including those obtained from the Sinclair students by Jeanne) have been turned over to John and Donna. (Note: An interesting format guideline has resulted from the work on "Lights Out." It was decided to reserve an area of each display for graphics; this will permit the later addition of graphics as time and experience permit. The space was limited to 1/6 of the screen area to keep the graphics from overwhelming the content of the display.)

3. Mr. Woody Absher, computer programming instructor at Sinclair Senior High School, has agreed to serve as our project manager. He'll enforce use of the Guide and will keep notes regarding needed changes.
4. Lolita and John leave tomorrow to attend the annual meeting of the National Council of Teachers of Mathematics. The program for the meeting gives major attention to instructional computing.

COMMITTEE ASSIGNMENTS

1. Carrinne will meet with Superintendent Ennis to propose that some members of ICAC be released to attend major professional meetings. It will be argued that this is a worthwhile investment in view of the committee's original charge "to develop a plan for implementing the instructional uses of computers in the East Roachmont schools" as stated in the Superintendent's letter of October 26, 1982.
2. Lolita and Phil will write to several organizations to gather information regarding professional meetings to be held between now and the middle of May. The letter will include a request for the program of any such meeting (or of any meeting already held this year). The list of presentations and commercial displays found in these programs can be used to measure professional interest in the instructional application of computers.
3. John and Donna will complete the preparation of the Courseware Standards Guide before our next meeting.
4. Looking ahead to the writing of our proposal to the Board, we will prepare a software matrix. Ted, Gerri and Jeanne will examine all available software catalogs and create numerical lists of "interesting" items of software. A different list will be maintained for each subject area and each list will undergo continuous augmentation. All ICAC members will copy announcements of any promising software found in the magazines they're reading and will send them to Jeanne.

   The number of each recommended item of software will be placed in the cells of a matrix (John's fancy word for chart) which will serve to classify the item in two ways:

   - The kind of application (tutorial, drill, simulation, etc.) represented by the item.
   - The brand(s) of computing equipment on which the item is available.

   A matrix will look something like this:

	Type of Computer System			
Type of Application	Brand X	Brand Y	Brand Q	Etc.
Tutorial Drill Practice Testing Operations Instructional Management Simulation Instructional Game Problem Solving Aide-de-Camp				

   A different matrix will be prepared for each subject matter area. This should give a practical view of the courseware coverage available in each area and should aid in purchasing activities.

JR:ms

CHAPTER TWELVE

THE COMPUTER AS AIDE-DE-CAMP

In Chapter 2, we tried to organize our study of the instructional application of computers by asserting that the computer is, educationally speaking, three-faced. Its faces are those of *teacher, educational partner,* and *aide-de-camp.* The expressions of its teacher-like face are those of tutor, drill master, examiner, and instructional manager. It reveals the visage of a partner in education as it shares the decision-making tasks of simulations and instructional games. Finally, the computer may assume the placid countenance of a competent aide, an electronic servant devoted to the careful execution of educational tasks characterized by mind-shrinking tedium. The important thing to recognize now about these three fundamental educational personalities is that they comprise overlapping bands along the continuum of control of the teaching act.

MAINLY A QUESTION OF CONTROL

When assuming the role of teacher, the computer uses its own decision-making scheme (i.e., program) to *provide principal direction and control of the teaching act.* As tutor, for example, it may engage the student in a dialogue about some new topic. It may reinforce such introductory instruction by an appropriate level of drill aimed at fixing simple associations or by practice designed to produce facility with some step-by-step procedure. To verify learning, the computer can generate, score, and analyze several kinds of criterion-referenced tests. Finally, the computer-as-teacher can manage each student's educational progress by using test results to prescribe objective-specific learning resources which have been selected for the purpose of (a) developing skills prerequisite to a new topic in the curriculum, (b) reteaching a just-covered topic in a different way, or (c) providing experiences which go beyond the basic curriculum. While the activities of this role as teacher are devoted to meeting the unique needs of each student, it is the computer which both identifies the student's learning difficulties and provides appropriate instructional intervention. Except when overruled by a flesh-and-blood teacher, the computer is in charge of the teaching act.

If it is to perform as a partner in learning, the computer must *share educational decision making with the student*. In fact, a major objective of this sharing is to teach decision making. During a simulation activity, for instance, student decisions effect alterations in the learning environment. As the simulation progresses, the student is informed of the results of earlier decisions and can seek to alter basic decision-making strategies in order to cope with the altered environment. The computer also can capitalize upon the motivation inherent in instructional games to engage students in the search for problem-solving strategies. The student's control of the progress of a simulation or instructional game will vary in *degree* according to the nature of the particular simulation or game, but significant decision making always must be partly the responsibility of the student whenever the computer is performing as a partner.

This chapter describes a potpourri of instructional computer uses which fall under the rubric *aide-de-camp*. As a group, the applications to be discussed present a wide range of educational activities. On the other hand, they share certain characteristics which bind them together and which distinguish them (as a group) from the teacher and partner applications.

1. *Minimal control of instruction.* The uniqueness of aide-de-camp applications is mainly a matter of control. In this type of application, the computer offers an educational service but has no overt control over its application. The application of the service offered is largely dependent upon the user. In short, the user gets from the service what the user sees in that service. User control is maximal; computer control is minimal.
2. *Lack of clear definition.* The applications of Chapters 6–11 are characterized by considerable clarity of definition. This was demonstrated, in part, by the listing of nine design issues associated with constructing drill or practice lessons (Chapter 7) and the listing of the five elements of a simulation (Chapter 11). While the definitions of those applications certainly will undergo modification and refinement, the applications do already have a recognizable shape. Each is relatively distinct from any of the others. By contrast, the applications classified as aide-de-camp do not occupy a specific niche in the educational scheme of things. Some (e.g., word processing) were first developed in other fields; their places in education still are tentative and limited owing to their recent entry into the classroom. Others appear to have so many possible uses that they defy classification.
3. *Unknown life expectancy.* Like the dinosaurs and many brands of American cars, several of the aide-de-camp applications are destined for extinction. Some will fail to live up to their promises, some will fade into obscurity because their services are no longer valued, and some will be absorbed by more general applications. Conversely, new aide-de-camp applications surely will appear as computers continue to develop and as educators become more experienced and creative in instructional computing.

The Current Roll

At the time of this writing, *our* roll of aide-de-camp applications contains seven terms.

1. Classroom Demonstration
2. Problem Solving
3. Programming Utility
4. Instructional Support
5. Word Processing
6. Information Generation
7. Whistles-and-Bells

The purpose of this chapter is to exemplify and roughly define each of these applications. Neither the order of presentation nor the relative length of the discussions should be interpreted as indicating the educational significance of the applications. The order is simply one that had a certain logical appeal to the writers; the length of a given discussion often reflects the authors' assumptions regarding readers' familiarity with the application being considered.

Aide Application 1: Classroom Demonstration

Those who train, hire, and evaluate teachers are in constant pursuit of *The List:* that collection of observable teaching skills which will identify the competent teacher. There seem to be as many different lists as there are teacher trainers, administrators, parents, students, and teachers themselves. And while the entries on *The List* appear destined for long debate, we find little hazard in suggesting that one characteristic which will make the final form will be:

skilled example-giver

In fact, we would guess that this characteristic will be high up on *The List*.

The motivation for and introduction of a topic is often effected by presenting and discussing relevant examples. The mathematics teacher uses examples to introduce the concept of an isosceles triangle. The history teacher invokes examples to establish the influence of individuals on the course of international affairs. Language teachers depend upon examples to develop the understanding of structure; the appreciation of literary style proceeds by example. Coaches (drama, voice, athletic) use examples both to introduce and to refine performance techniques. It would be difficult to imagine a teaching endeavor that did not have *for example* at its center. Consider, for example, this book.

A teacher's skill as an example-giver is bounded by two conditions: (a) personal knowledge and creativity and (b) practical constraints inherent in the examples. The computer can be of direct assistance in extending the latter boundary—and, indirectly, in perhaps extending the former. Specifically, the computer can be used to quickly generate examples of phenomena which are controlled by a complex set of well-defined rules. Without the aid of a computer, the teacher's ability to produce relevant examples of these phenomena is confounded by such practical considerations as the time required to produce the examples.

Computer programs designed to assist the example-giver are designed for use in classroom demonstrations and are called *demonstration* programs. The physical arrangement is one in which the displays of a single computer terminal (operated by the teacher) are made available to an entire class. This can be accomplished in one of several ways.

- A *video projector* can be used to project the terminal's image onto a large screen (much like an overhead projector is used to display transparencies).
- The display can be replicated on several large TV sets (or video monitors) which are connected to the teacher's terminal through a *"daisy chain,"* in which the terminal is connected to a monitor; that monitor is chained (connected) to a second monitor, etc.
- The several terminals of a computer laboratory can be made "slaves" of the teacher's terminal by means of special software which establishes a master-servant relationship within a network. Whatever is generated on the teacher's terminal is also displayed on every other terminal. All control is vested in the teacher's terminal; the students' terminals function only as monitors.
- The terminal can be attached to a printer; a machine for making overhead transparencies is at hand. In this situation, the teacher generates the example on the terminal screen, prints the result, makes a transparency, and uses an overhead projector to share the example with the class.

Since any one of these techniques involves special physical arrangements, the usual procedure is to establish a computerized classroom which can be scheduled for demonstration use by many teachers.

Note that three of the four forms of the computerized classroom require but a single terminal. These are efficient and economical configurations for many kinds of demonstrations. In schools where the number of terminals is not sufficient to support one-on-one experiences in simulations or problem solving for all students, the computerized classroom can be used to provide groups of students with modified versions of such experiences. For example:

- *Athletics: designing offensive/defensive strategies*
  For a variety of team sports such as football, a collection of offensive and defensive strategies can be displayed in animated form. Theoretical opposition to these strategies also can be illustrated. Weaknesses can be detected and strategies can be modified.
- *Environmental studies: countering pollution*
  The teacher can illustrate the long-term effects of a given type and volume of pollutant upon the animal and plant life of each of several aquatic environments (large lake, small lake, swift-moving stream, slow-moving river, etc.). Students can "experiment" with antipollution schemes which vary in kind and degree.
- *Mathematics: graphing "what-if"*
  The ability to quickly sketch the graphs of functions is an important mathematical skill which is developed by constructing point-by-point graphs of examples. Since point-by-point plotting is a beast with an insatiable appetite for time and graph paper, teachers usually resort to trying to force generalizations based upon a few sample graphs. Many a variable is left unexplored; any examination of the interactions among variables is an unaffordable luxury. On the other hand, the computerized exploration of graphs like

$$y = 3x$$

opens the world of "what-if." The computer can swiftly display flawlessly plotted responses to

What if the *3* were replaced by *4*? By *5*? By *10*? By *2*? By *1*? By *0*?
What if the *3* were replaced by a negative number like *−1*, *−2*, *−3*, or *−15*?
What if *3* were replaced by a positive fraction?
What if *3* were replaced by a negative fraction?
What if the *x* and *y* were interchanged to get $x = 3y$?

- *Agriculture: playing chicken*

  The game of "what-if" isn't confined to the mathematics classroom. The successful wheat farmer has to know more than how to plow a straight furrow. The student of poultry farming must understand that the difference between making a profit and getting plucked clean involves the intelligent control of several production variables.

  What is the most economical feed mix schedule to use in the production of frying chickens having a market mass of one kilogram?
  At what rate must breeding stock be replaced?
  What is the break-even point in the egg-laying productivity of a hen?
  What would be the financial consequence of a 3-cent per dozen drop in the market price of large eggs?
  How long would it take to recover normal production (eggs or chickens) if it was necessary to meet a financial crisis by marketing 30 percent of the breeding stock?

At this point you might conclude that computerized demonstration (example-giving) programs are just computerized simulations that are presented to a group using one of the computerized demonstration classrooms described earlier. Indeed, computerized simulations could be used in this way to produce the examples needed to develop a concept or to give an example of how to use a computerized simulation to explore a topic.[1] That is, programs designed as simulations can be pressed into service as demonstration programs. However, programs which are *designed* to be used in classroom demonstrations have a special characteristic which increases their effectiveness: economy of presentation.

True demonstration programs are devoid of screen displays which explain their purpose or operation. They present the user with a menu of options and then get directly to the business of executing those options. The user is expected to understand the meaning and limitations of the options presented and is expected to be ready to supply the information necessary to the execution of the program. Explanatory text relative to *input* is at a minimum; emphasis is upon the generation of high quality *output*.

The *planned avoidance of text* which characterizes a demonstration program permits efficient realization of the program's purpose. However, it also precludes the use of the program by an inexperienced person. Demonstration programs require the intervention of an informed manager (i.e., teacher) between the program and the learner. It is assumed that this manager possesses expertise in the subject explored by the program. The manager is informed of the purpose, capabilities, and operation of the program by means of external (written) documentation. With the aid of that documentation and a little bit of practice, the manager is ready to manipulate the program in order to efficiently explore the questions and suggestions raised by students during a demonstration lesson. Thus, demonstration programs permit the teacher to engage students in directing an exploratory experience while freeing them from the burdensome details which would discourage (or, perhaps, rule out) that exploration.

[1]The latter activity is important in its own right. Students often do not know how to make proper use of a computerized simulation. A demonstration experience can be used to prepare students for effective individual interaction with that simulation.

Aide Application 2: Problem Solving

Problem-solving activities pervade the instructional application of computing. In fact, each of the applications presented in Chapters 6–11 has involved a discussion of how computers may be used to solve an instructional problem of the teacher or a learning problem of the student. These papers substantiate the assertion that problem solving is both the purpose and substance of education.

The applications of the computer as teacher or as instructional partner each had a problem-solving component. Similarly, each of the aide-de-camp applications in this chapter serves to teach problem solving or to support the problem-solving work of teachers or students. It is simply impossible to isolate problem solving from the other applications of computers—i.e., to present problem solving as an application separate from all others. On the other hand, it is possible to identify computer programs which have problem solving as their *raison d'etre.* It is this special type of program—rather than the whole of computerized problem-solving activity—which is the object of interest here and which we will refer to as a *problem-solving* program.

A problem-solving program is a computer program which has been designed to aid the user in exploring and solving some complex problem. The key words are *aid* and *complex.* It is the user rather than the computer who solves the problem; if the problem is simple, the computer has no part to play since a cheap calculator or some paper and pencils would suffice. It is NOT the purpose of a problem-solving program to crank out the solution to some textbook-like question about some rigidly defined situation. Rather, a problem-solving program helps the problem solver to examine the dimensions of complex and, perhaps, poorly defined problem situations. It provides, upon request, the heavy computational support needed as the problem solver follows a cycle which includes (a) making conjectures about investigations that may generate useful information, (b) testing those conjectures, (c) analyzing the results of some experiment, (d) making new conjectures, and so forth. The program is a means, not an end. It serves rather than directs.

Algorithms to Guide the Search for Solutions

The sum and substance of a problem-solving program is an *algorithm*[2]—a step-by-step procedure which is guaranteed to produce consistently excellent/correct results. Here the key phrase is *consistently excellent/correct* as illustrated by the following examples.

- It is impossible to name $\sqrt{2}$ using decimal notation. However, there is a procedure which you can use to find the decimal name of a number which is as close to $\sqrt{2}$ as you wish. If being within 0.00000005 of the extact value of $\sqrt{2}$ is close enough, the procedure consistently yields a value of 1.4142135. Because of the consistent correctness of its approximation power, this procedure is an algorithm.
- Industrial chemists and physicists have described a procedure which, executed as specified, will consistently generate steel to meet preset specifications of malleability and tensile strength. The fortunes of the steel magnates depend upon the excellence of this algorithm.
- Alchemists sought a rule for changing base metals such as lead to gold. Had they succeeded, the Golden Rule might have been overshadowed by the Golden Algorithm.
- A certain Carol Cioffi knows a procedure for producing superb cinnamon rolls. Since it does not always present excellent results in other hands (and occasionally fails Carol), it, alas, does not qualify as an algorithm.[3]
- We are all supposed to know a procedure for reducing:

$$\begin{array}{r} 7306 \\ \times\ 537 \\ \hline \end{array}$$

to 3,923,322. For some folks, the procedure involves sixty seconds of put-down-the-?-and-carry-the-?. For those of us who do not delight in such mathematically based masochism, the procedure involves ten seconds of finger exercise on a pocket calculator —twenty seconds if one double checks. Either procedure qualifies as an algorithm, since the correct application of either will give 3,923,322 as a result.

The results generated by an algorithm, no matter how consistently excellent or correct, are not necessarily the solution to a problem. Remember, problems are complex and often poorly defined situations. Commonplace, step-by-step procedures such as those which compute products, approximate square roots, test the tensile strength of a metal, assess the probability that a certain event is a random occurrence, identify all known criminals who have certain specified traits, or approximate the number of animals of any given kind living in a certain habitat simply provide information. These are generally *known* algorithms that can be used to generate data; the data, in turn, will guide their users as they seek solutions to new problems. On the other hand, the search for unknown algorithms (such as a procedure for halting the growth of any cancerous cell) may itself be a problem; the problem solver seeking to develop that new algorithm will depend upon facts and ideas generated by relevant known algorithms from the fields of, say, biology, chemistry, and mathematics.

An algorithm's change in status from being a *problem* (an unknown procedure) in its own right to being an *aide* (tool for seeking solutions to other problems) is a function of the user. For instance, the ancient Romans had no simple "symbol-pushing" procedure for adding or multiplying two large numbers. Their algorithms involved pushing physical objects on a device we call an *abacus*. The discovery of the speedier put-down-this-and-carry-that algorithms which you learned in elementary school had to await the development of Hindu-Arabic numeration; when discovered, these algorithms (now tools) were introduced into the curriculum of Europe's universities as what was then the "new math."

Algorithm Users Versus Algorithm Developers

The problem solver may be either a *user* or a *developer* of a computerized problem-solving program—that is, of a computerized algorithm. The job ot a *user* is to find the program (or combination of programs) which will aid in translating data and conjectures into information and reasonable conclusions. For instance, every five years the National Assessment of Educational Progress (NAEP) gathers data regarding the reading skills of four age categories of Americans.[4] Computerized statistical programs help the NAEP staff to draw conclusions from that data. Thus NAEP is a *user* of problem-solving programs.

Any person who is able to write computer programs may move from the level of *user* to the level of

[2]Those with less agile tongues may prefer the synonym *algorism*.

[3]An algorithm is, in fact, partially a matter of standards. If the standard for "superb cinnamon rolls" were expanded to include cinnamon-flavored dog kibbles, my products would make the grade and Carol might have an algorithm.

[4]In fact, NAEP has investigated several subject areas. For information about its work, contact the National Assessment of Educational Progress, c/o Educational Testing Service, Princeton, NJ 08540. Ask for its list of publications.

developer of problem-solving programs. As a *developer,* the problem solver searches for and computerizes the algorithm itself. Universities still search for algorithms that will use data such as school grades, standardized test results, interviews, letters of recommendation, work experience, and extra-curricular activities to make reliable predictions about the probable academic success of persons applying for admission to a given course of study. Employers in industry seek algorithms that will predict the on-the-job success of university graduates. Some of us are in pursuit of an algorithm for Carol's cinnamon rolls.

The student who is engaged in developing a problem-solving program is operating at a higher educational level than the person who simply uses such a program. For one thing, the developer must be able to express a problem-solving procedure as a computer program—a task that calls for more than mere programming skill. The developer must identify, often by trial and error, the variables which are critical to the problem's solution. These variables must be measured in a way that is acceptable for computer manipulation, and an algorithm must be developed which correctly expresses the interactions among the variables. Finally, the developer must know how to interpret the results of the computer's efforts in order to know whether or not the algorithm is generating "consistently correct/excellent" information. In short, the developer of a problem-solving program must know a great deal about the problem situation. The user, by contrast, simply supplies prespecified data and interprets the computer output along prescribed guidelines.

A Few Words About Programming Of all the instructional applications of computers we have mentioned and will mention, only the application that engages the student as a *developer* of computerized problem-solving programs calls for instruction in a programming language. It is not an objective of this book to deal with the content or procedure of teaching programming. However, having identified the need for programming skills in this one application, we are obliged to record a cautionary few words on the subject.

Teaching computer programming is not a trivial task. The task is one, in fact, of teaching the use of languages by which one may communicate with computers in order to solve problems. The language to be taught is, in part, a function of the problems to be solved. The manner in which the language is taught affects the efficiency and clarity of the communication between human and machine in this problem-solving endeavor. Like the use of any language, proper use of a computer language draws upon both content and style.

Teacher certification laws make the common assertion that the right to teach any subject at any level requires extended personal involvement with the subject. That involvement must go beyond the content to be taught so that the teacher can grasp the purpose of the subject within the whole of education. What is taught at any level and (of greater importance) *how* that content is presented demand that the teacher have an unobstructed view of the long-range goals of that instruction.

Even in the absence of certification laws, a teacher of science would hesitate to teach English, a teacher of mathematics would argue against assignment to an American history class, and few foreign language teachers would feel comfortable teaching physical education. Despite the fact that each of these teachers probably had extensive contact with the subject matter of the "other field" during precollege and college education, he or she would likely refuse the proposed assignments on the grounds of inadequate preparation. Strange, then, that many educators view the teaching of computer programming as an exception to the rule of adequate preparation—perhaps because *adequate preparation* has yet to be given careful definition.

Prior to 1970, few educators gave any thought to the study or teaching of computer programming. Most of the teachers now in the schools have never taken a course in computer programming; many hope to avoid ever having to do so. As of this writing, it is a rare state department of public instruction which recognizes the teaching of computer topics as a certification area. Recall, however, that studies show that the major use of computers in today's precollege classrooms is teaching of programming languages. Therein lies a potential problem of no small import.

The vendors of computing machinery often advertise that learning to program is simple. In fact, learning to write *simple* programs is simple. Learning to write good programs to solve significant problems is a different matter. Furthermore, good program design, like good surgical procedure, is rarely a result of self-instruction. Oh, there are always the gifted few who can perfect learning in isolation, but most of us need to share the vision of scholars and the experiences of other students.

Initially, the teaching of computer programming was viewed as akin to the teaching of mathematics. This was a natural consequence of the fact that most of the early problems addressed by the computer were numerical. But although computers teethed on "number crunching," they have long since come of age and are able to handle a wide range of information processing tasks. As computers have matured in their ability to deal with these general information processing problems, people have changed their view of the nature of computer programming. More and more, today's teaching of computer programming is being likened to the teaching of a language. Motivated by the need to solve some problem which defies paper-and-pencil procedures, we choose a particular computing language as the means of communicating a possible solution procedure (algorithm) to a computer. The choice of language is related to the nature of the problem; just knowing which language will best communicate the proposed solution is an important part of problem solving.[5] Regardless of the language chosen, its use requires the learning of a vocabulary, a grammar, a syntax, rules of punctuation, a procedure for assembling all of the previously listed elements into communicative packages equivalent to sentences and paragraphs, and techniques for arranging these component packages into a complete program which is easily understood both by the computer and by other humans. Sounds very much like teaching the Mother Tongue, doesn't it? Indeed. It follows that some very good candidates for the job of teaching computer programming are good teachers of the Mother Tongue—be it the tongue of Shakespeare, Molière, Goethe, Dante, Aristotle, or Khayyám.

In addition to becoming fluent in the elements of a programming language (as outlined above), the emerging teacher of programming also must become knowledgeable about a sizable collection of concepts involved in the organization, storage, and retrieval of information. These concepts carry across all programming languages. First, there are the various ways to contain information in a computer. Such structures include lists, arrays, queues (special lists in which the *first* information entered is the first information retrieved), stacks (another special list in which the *last* information entered is the first retrieved), linked lists (in which each piece of information is "tied" to a successor or to a predecessor), and various types of trees (linked lists in which each entry is tied to more than one successor). Furthermore, the competent programming teacher will be familiar with several techniques for sorting information into order (alphabetical or otherwise) and several methods of efficiently searching out information after it has been stored in any one of the above structures.

If the preceding description of computer programming sounds a bit overwhelming, it is not meant to be so. Our purpose in presenting the description is to make it clear that the credentials of a good programming teacher are not to be derived from a one-day workshop or even from several one-day workshops. A little knowledge of programming can be a good thing if your purpose is to engage in limited rudimentary programming for your own purposes. A little knowledge of programming is dangerous if it is to be the basis of instruction of others. Schools planning to offer computer programming activities should make provision for the teachers involved to attain at least the level of education described in the preceding paragraph.

Examination of the current precollege curriculum in the teaching of computer programming reveals one final problem which deserves mention. Current curricula appear to strive for the presentation of several programming languages at the probable expense of a thorough understanding of and facility with any one of them. However, the competent student of computer programming is not simply a collector of languages. Rather, schools must decide to give students a high quality and extended experience in one language. That "extended experience" would be realized, by the way, through the application of the language to the solution of a variety of problems.

First We Need a Problem The important thing to note about the use of computerized problem-solving activities in the classroom is that instruction begins with a problem and not with a computer program. The program comes to the rescue when the need to do repetitious calculating bars a problem solver's way to the solution of a significant problem. The student approaches the program with problem-oriented questions that have been developed in other activities. This pedagogical aspect of problem solving is the focal point of our concluding example.

The problem-solving scene of our example is a coeducational secondary school class called "Planning for Living," which is taught by the Department of Home Economics. A discussion of financing the purchase of a house has already addressed the broad social, legal, and financial aspects of borrowing money for such a purchase; students are now concerned with the financial details associated with a given loan. They have identified the following as variables which affect those details:

a. amount borrowed,
b. interest rate (and changes in same),
c. duration (in years) of the loan,
d. monthly payment.

Guided by the teacher, they have raised questions (problems) such as the following.

- What will be the monthly payment on a loan of $20,000 made for 30 years at 12.8 percent?

[5]Some common problem solving languages used in the schools are BASIC, Pascal, and Logo. Business-oriented problems often employ the language COBOL. To a lesser extent, FORTRAN and assembly language also have found their way into precollege applications.

- What will be the total interest paid on that loan?
- If I can budget a maximum of $450 per month for the loan payment, what is the largest 30-year loan that I can afford under an interest rate of 12.8 percent?
- Suppose that the local bank wants 12.9 percent for a 25-year loan of $18,000. Another bank in town offers an interest rate of 12.6 percent for the same loan if I'll move both my savings and checking accounts to that bank within 7 days. If I do this, I'll lose $358 in interest on my savings account. Is the move financially advantageous?
- After securing a 20-year loan on $12,000 at 11.7 percent, I discover that I can make monthly payments of $10 more than I had estimated. If I were to do this, how much sooner would the loan be paid off and how much (total) interest payment would I save?

Of course, one could always rely upon the services of local bankers to answer such questions, but that isn't necessary. A whole new world of financial understanding can be explored with a simple computer algorithm (problem-solving program) which can use

- proposed amount to be borrowed,
- interest rates,
- proposed duration of loan,
- proposed monthly payment

to compute

- the sufficiency of the proposed monthly payment,
- the actual duration of the loan under the payment proposed,
- the total interest paid during the actual duration of the loan.

Such a program will answer all of the questions raised (and many more). The user or developer can be elevated to the world of higher finance. This rather edifying experience, previously open to few students because of the heavy "number crunching" required, is accessible to any user of the problem-solving program described!

Aide Application 3: Programming Utility

A *programming utility* is a computer program which directly aids a programmer by offering one of two services: program enhancement or program creation. In either case, a programming utility is a program of many uses.

Programming utilities designed to provide enhancement services are of interest to the instructional programmer who is writing a program in the language used by the utility. The utility is a block of code which can be immediately attached to the larger instructional program in order to perform some common and useful instructional service.[6] In a sense, these utilities are modular units that can be used to build instructional programs since they perform actions common to many such programs. Moreover, many utilities are complicated enough that a programmer would be foolish to write them afresh each time they are needed. Familiar examples of utilities (which are often used as stand-alone programs as well) include those which alphabetize lists, judge the spelling accuracy of a student's response, or compare a student's input to a question with each of several acceptable responses. Somewhat more esoteric utilities perform such functions as creating/clearing/deleting data files or storing values of variables during chaining operations between programs.[7]

There also are utilities which are designed to perform program creation services for the teacher who is *not* (and, perhaps, has no wish to be) a computer programmer. Also known as lesson authoring systems or lesson drivers, these utilities were described in some detail at the end of Chapter 6 with regard to tutorial lessons. They constitute a new breed of computer program which will permit nonprogrammers from several subject areas to create original computerized lessons of many types (tutorial, drill, practice, simulation).

There is a simple lesson authoring system which will create a drill lesson in associating the elements of any two lists of verbal items (e.g., books with their authors, chemical elements with their symbols, metric units with the attributes they measure, French words with corresponding English words). The user—either student or teacher—of this program has only to supply the two lists; directions which guide the user in inputting those lists are provided by the computer. While this drill lesson driver is restricted to lists of verbal items, a more general driver would permit the elements of a list to be pictures or sounds.

Existing tutorial lesson authoring systems represent points along a continuum of program generality. One driver is restricted to generating tutorial lessons in the single subject field of foreign languages. Although it can be used for several languages, it uses a fixed format for all choices. This single-subject/single-format tutorial

---

[6]This attachment business is not quite as simple as it seems. The variables employed in the utility must not conflict with those used in the larger program. Some programming languages are structured in such a way that the variables of the utility are independent of the larger program. In other cases, the programs can be altered in such a way as to avoid conflict.

[7]Such utilities may be written in machine language. When loaded into the computer, they act as new commands within the higher-level language used in the instructional program.

system can be contrasted with one which serves a wide range of subject areas and makes automatic adjustments in format according to the choice of subject. Still, the format for a given subject is fixed. Finally, work is being done on tutorial lesson systems which will generate lessons in many fields and will allow the instructor to tailor the format within a given field.

Lesson authoring systems also offer promise of relief from the time-consuming task of programming simulations. The system will guide the teacher in inputting the elements of the simulation; it will then help fashion the complicated branching structure used by the student in executing the simulation.

Aide Application 4: Instructional Support

The direct beneficiary of *instructional support* computer programs is, of course, the instructor. Students benefit indirectly insofar as these programs help the teacher to expand and refine materials used in the classroom and to improve communication with students and their parents. Aided by a modest text editor, a teacher can use the computer's vast memory capacity to store, retrieve, and modify a wide variety of instructional products. Using an inexpensive graphics printer, the teacher can generate clean and up-to-date copies of such useful items as

- outlines of laboratory activities,
- class newsletters,
- worksheets and other teacher-made lesson materials,
- transparency masters,
- periodic progress reports for parents,
- individualized study assignments.

Effective use of a wide variety of teacher resources (books, articles, films, slides, audio tapes, video tapes, computer programs, laboratory activities, visiting speakers, field trips) can make use of a computerized inventory system that allows the teacher or student to readily locate those resources. Such an inventory permits the easy filing of new resources and the quick deletion of outdated or ineffective ones. The same inventory program can use a different set of files to store the addresses of firms that sell or repair the equipment or supplies used. Still another set of files would keep track of consumable resources (handouts, chemicals, paints, etc.); regularly updated, they would advise the teacher of the need to reorder. Mailing label programs will generate typed labels for sending materials to parents or request the latest brochures from educational supply houses.

In education, the term *scheduling* usually brings to mind the problem of matching students with courses. At the classroom level, scheduling becomes a pairing of students with some limited resource (such as the teacher). Also, equipment must be scheduled for regular examination, preventive maintenance, and replacement. Computer programs can handle all such tasks.

In addition to generic instructional support programs (text editors, inventories, schedules), there are programs which generate variations of a specific product. For instance, there are programs which generate word mazes or word scrambles for any list of words; a given list can be used to produce a different version of the maze/scramble for each student. Geography teachers would be served by a program which could generate maps of countries, states, oceans, cities, sample terrains, or peculiar geographic regions. The printed masters of such maps could be used to make transparencies or to define classroom exercises. In elementary arithmetic, a teacher can use a single program to create tailored versions of thirty different worksheets on the basic computational algorithms (i.e., multidigit problems in addition, subtraction, multiplication, or division).

Aide Application 5: Word Processing

A *word-processing* program is devoted to the efficient and inexpensive preparation of typed material. It's an item that should be on the Christmas list of every computer-using teacher. Any teacher who prepares classroom materials will benefit from the use of a word-processor program to create, store, modify, and print those materials.

The features which characterize a word-processing program are of two kinds: editing and work-assist. The editing features are those which allow the user to manipulate the content and general format of a document. Work-assist features aid in reviewing or printing the document.

Put yourself in the role of a teacher. You have just typed a fourteen-page paper on, say, the uses of word processors in the business world. Upon reading the draft, you are filled with assorted misgivings. For instance, the section on Automatic Addressing really should have come before the section on Form-Letter Generation. Oh, oh! Somehow *processor* got spelled *processer* throughout the paper, and it appears on every page! There's a four-word phrase missing in the middle of a paragraph on page 3, and you forgot to footnote the quote in the second paragraph on page 5. (Inserting either the phrase or the footnote means retyping at least four pages; moreover, all the footnotes beyond page 5 must be renumbered.) You also realize that you will need to insert a definition of *boiler plate* into the middle of page 8 in order for the reader to understand word-processor applications to constructing legal contracts. Subheadings would certainly help the development on pages 6, 11, and 12. The block style format and 12-pitch typing make the document rather difficult to read; the ragged right-hand margins are less than attractive. Things will really look crummy if you use pencil to insert even the most critical corrections; still, the paper is needed in class tomorrow. What will you do?

If you've been working on a word processor, you can make *all* of the desired changes in a few minutes and then produce a crisp new typed copy at a minimum typing speed of 180 words per minute (or under two minutes per double-spaced page).

Now put yourself in the role of a student *and reread the two preceding paragraphs.* Imagine what a word processor would do to the quality of your term papers!

In fact, teachers can use word processors to improve the writing skills of students. The trick is to have the student enter a first draft of the paper into a computer with the help of a word-processing program.[8] The student generates a typed copy for the teacher. Some word processors now include automatic spelling checks tailored to specific misspelling habits. The teacher, no longer burdened with the need to decipher student handwriting, quickly enters comments on the draft. The student returns to the word processor to make the teacher's suggested improvements; a typed copy of the improved draft is returned with the original (marked) draft. This comment/revise process continues until the student has produced a document that meets the teacher's expectations.

The procedure is one which focuses on the improvement of the student's writing and the use of current technology rather than upon laborious retyping or rescripting. The student operates in the real world of writing where drafts of a document are a matter of course and "final copy" isn't really final at all—it's just the most recent draft.

Remember Super-CMI, the instructional management program of Chapter 9? Well, prepare yourself for Super-Pen,[9] a word-processing program *par excellence.* The appendix to this chapter describes Super-Pen in terms of its several features. Read and drool.

[8]Right . . . this means that students must learn to type, but error-free typing will not be a premium. Editing supported by technology to the rescue! In our computer-oriented world, nominal typing skill may soon join reading as a basic skill (until spoken computer input is available, anyway).

[9]Super-Pen is the unregistered trademark of a word processing system which has the basic features teachers will come to know and love. While Super-Pen is our invention, there are existing word processing programs which have our Super-Pen features (and many more).

Aide Application 6: Information Generation

It appears that there is no item of information so obscure that no one is interested in it. In fact, the item's obscurity may be the very thing that makes it interesting. Moreover, several persons may be interested in the same item of information for widely differing reasons. To illustrate these assertions we submit the following.

Item

The identity of the consonant used most frequently in the noncommercial items of the first section of the March 2, 1983, Wall Street Journal.

First, you have got to admit that the item is obscure. On the other hand, it would be of interest to a cryptographer who wishes to use the *Journal* to develop an alphabetical code or to a mathematics teacher who is developing some probability problems for students. Its extreme obscurity might even cause it to attract the attentions of the host of a "trivia bowl" quiz.

An *information generation* computer program does just that: it generates information. These programs produce specific (and peculiar?) things such as lists of prime numbers, entire calendars for any year since 1 A.D., synonyms for hundreds of words, chemical formulas, definitions of terms associated with a given topic, symbols used in a given field, the Greek alphabet, the current time to the nearest 0.01 of a minute, the dates of the full moons in any given year, or the time of today's high tide in the Bay of Fundy. Want a list of all of the square numbers[10] between 2635 and 8937? Ask an information generation program. Need to know of the English king who came to the throne upon the death of King William IV? An information generation program would tell you that it was *Queen* Victoria.

Looking at the output of an information generation program is like looking at a lump of iron pyrite: one person sees gold, another sees a paperweight, and still another sees iron pyrite. The value of an information generation program is largely a function of the user. Such a program might be used by a problem solver to produce data relevant to the problem under investigation, might be attached to some other program and used as part of a drill or tutorial lesson, or might be exercised for reasons of entertainment. The usefulness of the program is a function of the user; the face value of the program remains one of data generation.

[10]Numbers such as 0, 1, 4, 9, 16, 25, and 49.

Aide Application 7: Whistles and Bells

Whistles-and-bells programs allow a computer system to show off. These bits of electronic exhibitionism are a computer's version of "Look what I can do! Look what I can do!" From a computer-using teacher's point of view, they can be seen as a display of those (perhaps unique) characteristics of a computer system which can be employed in developing instructional applications. Whistles-and-bells programs run the gamut from carefully documented displays of system features to mindless productions of color or sound in an effort to "wow" the consumer.

Whistles-and-bells programs are of instructional importance because they can raise the teacher's expectations about lesson design. Through such programs educators can learn about and reflect upon the possible instructional value of a number of tantalizing items.

- *Graphics.* What degree of screen resolution is possible?[11] Can animation be produced? How fast is a full-page graphic plotted?
- *Color.* How many colors are available? Is that number a function of the degree of resolution employed? What happens when a graphic in one color is plotted over a graphic of another color?
- *Keyset versatility.* Are both upper and lower case letters available? Can simple graphics characters be typed? Can the keyboard be "programmed" with a set of author-created characters (i.e., special symbols, small pictures of objects, the Greek alphabet)? Can typing be done using several type faces? Can the size of the type be changed? What special function keys are on the keyset (and what do they do)?
- *Sound.* What is the range and quality of nonvoice audio? Can chords be produced? Does the computer's speech sound more like Richard Burton or like Hal (in *2001: A Space Odyssey*)? What is the range of spoken words; can you input new words? Can the computer be addressed by speaking? Is voice recognition possible? If the input is sung, can it be analyzed in terms of pitch and volume so that it can be compared with a written score?
- *User security.* Is there a built-in password system?
- *Screen formatting.* Can displays be made on a split screen (where one portion of the screen changes while other portions remain static)? Can portions of the screen be "protected" against student write-over? Does the screen accommodate reversed displays (both light characters on a dark screen and dark characters on a light screen) or blinking displays?
- *Language versatility.* Does the computer's version of a particular language (such as BASIC) have any special features? What is involved in switching from one language to another—and how many "others" are there?

Some of the wonders displayed by a whistles-and-bells program are features of the system's hardware and others are features of the system's software. These features vary from system to system and from month to month. The whistles-and-bells program provides an invaluable service by keeping the user (and sales staff) abreast of the latest advances. While both the user and sales staff should be thankful for such programs, it falls to the educator to be thoughtfully critical of the instructional value of each new hoot and tinkle.

About Face

So we come to the end of an examination of instructional applications of computers which we started in Chapter 2. From our present vantage point, we must take a final glance backwards to get a summary view of the acquaintances we've made. We've seen that the computer presents three faces to education: those of teacher, instructional partner, and aide-de-camp. As teacher, the computer assumes primary responsibility for control of the educational decision making that guides tutorials, drill, practice, testing, and instructional management. This control is altered markedly to introduce shared decision making within the educational partnerships of simulations and instructional games. As aide-de-camp, the computer relinquishes all control of decision making to the user of an array of programs designed to perform a wide variety of educational services.

Three faces today, but what of tomorrow? As new educational applications are developed, the computer—having already done Janus one better—may turn still another cheek.

Appendix

A Glossary of Attributes of the Super-Pen Word Processor

The purpose of the next few pages is to acquaint you with the word processing attributes of Super-Pen. In creating Super-Pen, we selected attributes that should be of interest to most teachers. (Some word processors have many more features

[11]The screen resolution—"smoothness" with which a picture can be drawn—depends upon the size of the smallest element of the video screen that can be turned on/off under program control. Crude graphics (called "block" graphics) are displayed on a screen using as little as a 40 X 40 grid (with 1600 elements). Increasingly finer graphics ("dot" graphics) can be presented on screens having grids of 128 X 128 (16,384 elements), 512 X 128 (65,536 elements), and 512 X 512 (262,144 elements), with the basic dimensions of the visual area remaining about the same.

than we have listed here.) The attributes are listed in alphabetical order and are printed in italics wherever they appear within any description. This has been done to aid the reader in cross-referencing the terms.

Super-Pen has been designed with the educator in mind. The educator should interpret the attributes of Super-Pen in terms of possible application to the generation of written materials in his or her field of interest.

Administrative Functions will permit the user to establish calendars, time schedules, and files that issue reminders of important actions to be taken at particular times.

Arithmetic Capability is the ability to incorporate arithmetic tasks within word-processing routines. Useful in calculating answers to test questions or preparing departmental budgets.

Automatic Carrier Return automatically returns the carrier to the left margin when the last word that will fit on a line has been typed. The typist may type without pausing to press the carrier return key at the end of each line.

Automatic Centering uses a keystroke to instruct the system to center the next (or previous) text segment. Text can be centered between margins or around a designated point. The system also can center between tabular settings to allow the centering of column headings within a table.

Automatic Decimal Tabulation automatically aligns columns of decimal figures on the decimal point when tables or columns of data are set up.

Automatic File Selection uses characters in data field (i.e., coded "flags") to automatically select certain data from a file. (Example: Using a postal ZIP code, the system could select all addresses with the 82070 code to receive one letter and all those with the 82071 code to receive a different letter. Mailings also could be sorted by sex, subject matter, class level, etc.)

Automatic File Sorting arranges files in alphabetical or numerical order. This is useful in manipulating address lists since changes in the list need not be made in alphabetical order.

Automatic Footnote Linking links each footnote to the page with the referenced text segment. If the segment is moved to another page, the footnote automatically accompanies it. This automatically handles the spacing of text and footnotes. A useful feature for both students and teachers involved in the writing/revising of documented papers.

Automatic Headers/Footers places identifying information (title of paper, author's name, etc.) at the head or foot of each page of a multipage document. The text of the header/footer need be specified only once.

Automatic Line Spacing allows the line spacing (single, double, triple) of any block of text to be changed after the text (such as *Boiler Plate)* with newly entered text.

Automatic Margin Adjustment permits the alteration of the margins of any block of text after the text has been entered. The text is automatically retyped in the new line length to fit the new margins.

Automatic Page Numbering generates page numbers within a document and automatically renumbers the pages if the text of the document is rearranged.

Automatic Pagination automatically divides the text of the document into pages having a specified number of lines. Can be linked to *Automatic Page Numbering* and *Automatic Margin Adjustment.*

Automatic Repagination automatically redivides the text into pages following (a) insertion or deletion of blocks of text within the original document or (b) a decision to change the specified number of lines per page or the margin settings.

Automatic Underscoring allows underscoring to be created by indicating only the beginning and ending of the text to be underscored (rather than back-spacing and typing the underscore).

Automatic "Widow" or "Orphan" Prevention automatically prevents a title, heading, or first line of a paragraph from being the last typed line of a page (a widow) or the last line of a paragraph from being presented as the first line of a new page (an orphan). This is particularly useful when *Automatic Pagination* or *Automatic Repagination* is employed.

Automatic Word Wraparound causes a word that is too long to fit on the line being typed to be automatically placed on the next line.

Block Text Copying allows a block of text to be copied and sent to a storage location so that editing work can be done without altering the original block of text.

Block Text Movement permits the movement of a block of text from one location in a document to another.

Boiler Plate permits the use of stored blocks of text to create new documents. Such blocks might be things like directions commonly used in quizzes or standard explanations which accompany periodic progress reports.

Character Sizing allows the elements of the Character Set (alphabet, numerals, and special symbols used in a document) to be displayed in each of several different sizes. Smaller sizes might be useful in footnotes; larger sizes could be employed with young children or persons who are visually impaired.

Column Delete allows the deletion of a vertical column of text (such as found in a table).

Column Move allows the movement of a vertical column of text.

Control Character Display permits the printing (or video display) of control characters. These characters reveal the author's commands regarding carrier returns, indentions of text, choice of character size, etc. Although normally not revealed on the text or printout, these characters can be of use to the author in editing a document.

Cursor Positioning (or Cursor Control) allows the user to place the cursor (the video indicator of the position of the character to be entered next) at any place on the display.

Default Format Statement gives information regarding those formatting rules (margin settings, tabulation settings, line spacing, etc.) which the system automatically implements unless otherwise instructed by the user.

Delete Capability allows the selective deletion of a character, a word, line of text, sentence, paragraph, page, or specified block of text.

Display Highlighting visually emphasizes a text segment which has been designated for some system activity (such as movement, copying, or deletion). Emphasis may be by means of intensifying the text, blinking the text, surrounding the text with a box, or shading the area behind the text. This aids in preventing accidental editing of the wrong block of text.

Document Assembly/Merging allows the insertion of stored text (such as *Boiler Plate)* with newly entered text.

Electronic Mail permits the storage, forwarding, and acknowledgment of the receipt of messages and documents within the system. (Usually most useful on networked systems, i.e., when several entry devices share a processor or a common storage device.)

End-of-Page Stop halts the printer at the end of a page to permit paper (forms or stationery) to be inserted.

First-Line-Forms Advance automatically spaces to the first line of a form.

Form Feed permits continuous feeding of paper for an automatic printout. Useful when printing grade reports, student schedules, individualized tests, etc.

Format Statement Display is similar to the *Default Format Statement* and reports the format choices made by the author.

Forms Data Entry automatically spaces from blank to blank as data is being entered in a prerecorded form such as a student permanent record form, class schedule, or grade report.

Global Search/Replace automatically locates all occurrences of a block of text (i.e., word or phrase) within a document. Allows the automatic replacement of that block by another block throughout the document. It is handy for changing the spelling of a word or for updating a document (e.g., replacing *Rhodesia* by *Zimbabwe).*

Graphics allow charts, graphs, or line drawings to be part of the document.

Hyphenation automatically makes decisions at the end of a line of type. The system may use a formula to make such hyphenation decisions or may store a dictionary of hyphenations. This feature would override *Automatic Word Wraparound.* It can itself be overridden by manual hyphenation.

Interword Spacing is the insertion of extra spaces between words in order to create a *Justified Printout.*

Justified Printout adjusts the text to create an even right-hand margin by using *Interword Spacing.* Gives newsletters, reports, handouts, and term papers a professional look by eliminating ragged right margins.

Line Justify/Spacing Display allows the video display (as opposed to the printout display) of right margin justification and selected line spacing (single, double, etc.).

Page Scrolling allows the author to flip forward and backward through the pages of a multipage document.

Spelling Check scans the document to locate (and flag) all words which do not match dictionary entries. Permits the entry of new words (proper names, technical terms, foreign phrases) into the dictionary to adjust to local misspelling habits.

Stored Form Recall/Display permits the recall and display of some form (e.g., a progress report form). The form then can be filled in with the help of the *Forms Data Entry* feature.

String Search locates the first use of a specified block of characters (string) within the document. Along with *Global Search,* the feature is useful in establishing an index for a document.

Subscript/Superscript permits characters to be typed one-half line above or below the main line of type. Most documents would make use of this feature in entering footnote numbers within the text. Mathematics and the sciences demand this feature in order to represent formulas and expressions such as H_2O or x^5 properly.

System Prompts/Menu engages the user in a dialogue which guides him/her through the use of a system by means of questions and answers. These prompts help train the new user. The system also may present a menu of the options available at any stage during the use of the word processor.

System Security controls access to the system by requiring a password or by locking the keyboard against unauthorized users. It prevents the unauthorized viewing or altering of tests, grade reports, or student data classified as nonpublic.

Temporary Margins permit the temporary establishment of a second set of margins. This is useful when typing a large block of indented text (such as an extended quotation) within the main body of the document.

Term Dictionary/Glossary allows the user to store the definitions of words or phrases. This feature is particularly attractive in fields which employ a great deal of technical vocabulary (mathematics, physics, medicine, law, psychology, semantics) or in research (where it is often necessary to propose working definitions for words or phrases). Definitions from the *Term Dictionary/Glossary* may then be used as *Boiler Plate* in writing a document.

Text Editing refers to a wide variety of attributes which allow the efficient manipulation of the text of a document. Among the *Text Editing* attributes mentioned elsewhere in this glossary are *Automatic Carrier Return, Automatic Centering, Automatic Decimal Tabulation, Automatic Margin Adjustment, Automatic Pagination/Repagination, Block Text Copying/Movement, Column Delete/Move, Cursor Positioning, Delete Capability,* and *Temporary Margins.*

Text-Imbedded Variables permit the preparation of text which contains variables. This text may be called up at any time and the variables replaced with words or numbers provided by a data base, a Term Dictionary/Glossary, or a person using the keyset. The feature could be used in test item generation (using an item template), in preparing periodic budgets or progress reports, or in generating individualized assignments.

Word Processing refers to the entire procedure by which a computer is used to create, store, modify, and print written materials.

Word Processor (or Word-Processing System) refers to a combination of hardware and software used to perform word processing tasks.

STUDY GUIDE: CHAPTER 12

1. Using the criterion *who's in control,* distinguish among the three principal instructional roles of the computer: teacher, instructional partner, aide.
2. The list of aide-de-camp applications has seven entries.
   a. In 25–50 words, give a capsule description of each. Each description should focus upon general characteristics of the applications and upon its function in the classroom.
   b. Develop an example of each—an example which is not given in the text.
3. With regard to *programming utility* applications, distinguish between program enhancement and program creation services.
4. The section of this chapter entitled "Aide Application 5: Word Processing" reports several errors that a teacher has made during the preparation of a paper on the use of word processors in the business world. For each error noted, identify by name the feature(s) of Super-Pen which would be employed to solve that problem.
5. Word-processing programs are said to have two kinds of features, editing and work-assist. Identify half a dozen of each among the features of Super-Pen.
6. Sketch floor plans for different types of computerized demonstration classrooms and describe the manner in which each type would be used by a teacher and students.

AGENDA FOR ACTION

University of Illinois
at Urbana-Champaign

Department of
Secondary Education

395 Education Building
1310 South Sixth Street
Champaign
Illinois 61820

College of Education

217 333-0227

MEMORANDUM

TO: Members of ICAC

FROM: Dick Dennis and Bob Kansky

DATE: April 15, 1983

RE: ICAC Paper 12

Although there are several ways in which the computer may serve as aide-de-camp in the classroom, we've chosen to present them all within a single paper. As we will explain in our discussion of the common characteristics of aide-de-camp programs, this area of application is much less stable than any of those discussed earlier. Generally speaking, aide-de-camp applications are the least well defined and the most subject to change.

Detecting that there are some real instructional computing zealots within ICAC, we have attached brochures describing summer instructional computing activities at the University of Illinois and the University of Wyoming. Note that several of the activities are multidisciplinary in design and that some require no previous experience with computers. Some are aimed at preparing the participant to teach an inservice course on instructional computing for his/her colleagues. Many universities are designing such summer programs for teachers, so you may wish to write to local institutions to find out what's available within driving distance.

DD:BK:glm

Attachments

AGENDA FOR ACTION

Obourn Senior High School

200 Woodbine Avenue
East Roachmont, New York

M. Jack Stivers
Principal

(716) 568-8840

ICAC Memo #12

TO: Members of ICAC

FROM: John Russell

DATE: April 28, 1983

REPORT OF ACTIVITIES

1. John and Donna have completed the Courseware Standards Guide. Several copies have been sent to Mr. Absher for use with the programming class at Sinclair High School.
2. Carrinne informs us that the school board has approved travel to professional meetings for up to four members of the committee. Given this limit, the board has agreed to pay the expense of travel, housing, and registration fees. The member will have to pay for food and incidentals. The offer is much appreciated; Carrinne has the committee's thanks.
3. It was agreed that the travel positions would be held for those meetings whose programs showed the greatest attention to computing. (Phil and Lolita report that programs have been requested from 14 organizations.)
4. Ted, Gerri, and Jeanne report that there are conspicuous "holes" in the software matrix that they've started (ICAC Memo #11). Committee contributions are welcomed.
5. Lolita and John provided the committee with bundles of brochures on computer hardware and software that they picked up at the NCTM meeting last month. Understandably, much of the software concerns the teaching of mathematics; surprisingly, many items deal with nonmathematical topics (particularly at the elementary school level). The materials will be used in preparing our purchasing proposal for the school board.

COMMITTEE ASSIGNMENTS

1. Ted will reprint the Software Selection Matrix (ICAC Memo #11) after subdividing the aide-de-camp application into the seven subcategories discussed in ICAC Paper 12.
2. The concept of a computerized demonstration classroom got high marks from the committee. Phil will seek information about video projectors. Carrinne and Ted will investigate possible locations for such classrooms by discussing the concept with school principals and the school board. (A prefab classroom module may be an answer.)
3. Two programming projects will be submitted to Sinclair High School.
   - A) Development of a problem solving program to explore the home finance questions raised in ICAC Paper 12.
   - B) Establishment of a local library of programming utility programs. The library would be comprised of modules which are recognized as common to several of the instructional programs written by the Sinclair High students. Future use of those program modules should increase the efficiency and consistency of program development.
4. Gerri will gather data on sample inventory, scheduling, and word processor programs. (He'll use Super-Pen as a guide in examining the attributes of potential word processors.) A word processor program will be on the "Christmas" list that we submit to the school board on June 10. (How's <u>that</u> for beating the Christmas rush?)

CHAPTER THIRTEEN

Profiles in Computing: Defining the Role of Computers in Your School

The smorgasbord of applications is spread before you. What unique combination of applications will define the instructional role of computers in your school(s)? In what ways will the importance of a given application (say, tutorials or simulations) differ across grade levels, student ability levels, or schools within the system? Who will guide the development of these applications within any given school? In short:

How will computers be applied to instruction in your school(s)?

Any answer to the question just posed must be expressed in the form of a specific instructional plan. That plan must detail both those actions to be taken early in the implementation of instructional computing and those actions reserved for future stages of the implementation. While the plan should look to the best of all possible worlds, it should have clearly stated priorities which will form the bases for sensible negotiation.

The key to success—immediate or long term—of the plan is the judicious selection and involvement of people. Who will make the first attempts at utilizing computers in instruction? What will they attempt to do? How will they acquire the training needed for these new ventures? How broad a faculty involvement is envisioned for the future? How will those who join later be enticed to do so? How will the vested interests of the early pioneers be protected from a possible flood of newcomers?

Sample Implementation Profiles

Our approach to the task of helping you to fashion an implementation plan for your school(s) will be to outline some plans that other schools have devised. In doing this, we realize that the computing plan for a particular school system will have the individuality of a thumbprint. Still, the study of a variety of plans should make you aware of the range of options and will allow you to select and modify elements that seem attractive. In this spirit we present the profiles of both typical and atypical schools which are already actively engaged in instructional computing. Neither the length of a profile nor its position within the list has any meaning with respect to its relative value. Each profile is simply an example. As examples, all are of equal merit.

Profile 1: Stemming the Tutorial Tide

A school district we know started investigating computers as a way to fill a large need for individual tutoring in the core subjects (language, mathematics, science). This need seemed to begin about grade 3 and continued on through to graduation. Having reviewed possible applications of technology to instruction, the district concluded that computers were a viable substitute for tutors for a majority of their needs.

Software recommendations were of three types: mastery materials in language and mathematics, problem-solving activities for mathematics and the sciences (activities that did not require students to engage in computer programming), and a small number of enrichment/motivational activities. The plan called for an all-out attack on both skills and problem solving beginning with the first year of implementation. In the self-contained classes of the lower grades, a microcomputer was placed in each classroom. In the upper grades, a computer classroom was established in each school and was monitored by an uncertified aide. Also, because students had some unscheduled time during the day, it was decided to put a small number of microcomputers in carrels in the library.

Teachers were concerned that the computer curriculum, especially that part directed at mastery, would soon "go stale." It was conjectured that students who had used a given set of materials to practice a particular procedure (e.g., computation of whole numbers) would be uninterested in using them again when review or refinement of that procedure was necessary. Such a student reaction might spring from boredom (at seeing the same old problem format) or discouragement (induced by earlier difficulty with the activity). Moreover, some students take offense at being asked to repeat an activity done at an earlier grade level since the activity was designed "for little kids." To minimize this anticipated effect, care was taken in the selection of all mastery materials so that particular activities or practice formats could be assigned to specific grades or ability levels. An important component of this selection plan was the purchase of two *cosmetically different* mastery packages in each subject area. That is, the two sets of mastery materials were to *look different* to the students but each set was to be compatible with the district's curricular design (scope, sequence, and general pedagogical approach) in the subject.

Teachers also were concerned that the computerized materials should attend to the needs of individual students. As a result, pursuit of software included the search for computerized instructional management systems in each subject. The features expected of a management system included automatic testing, placement of students within major categories of the curriculum, and prescription of assignments which would extend over more than one class session. It was of great importance that the system be able to generate printed student progress reports since students in the upper grades would likely be involved with independent study schedules.

A further demand was that the system permit a teacher to override its automatic decisions whenever his or her judgment (based, perhaps, on alternate forms of student evaluation) was in conflict with the system. Decisions by either the system or the teacher were held to be informed judgments. Since the teacher can make use of a greater variety of input than can the computer, the system must allow the teacher's judgment to take precedence. To accomplish this override, it was important that the system have a simple procedure by which the teacher could alter the computer's records regarding an individual student or a group of students.

Implementation of the district's instructional computing plan was supported by a two-phase teacher training component. The first phase preceded the opening of the school year in which the computerized materials were to be introduced and took the form of "computer comfort" sessions and activities aimed at familiarizing the teachers with the overall computerized curriculum.

During this intensive phase of training, each teacher learned about the daily care and feeding of the computers, practiced operation of the computerized instructional management systems, and explored those portions of each curriculum for which he or she would be responsible.

The second phase of teacher training began with the opening of school and continued over the next several years. During the first year, afternoon group sessions were held once a month, the composition of the groups being changed over time. While the therapeutic value of these sessions was a recognized component of their design, the meetings also included practical activities intended to carry forward the implementation plan. These activities provided teachers with opportunities not only to share problems and solutions which had presented themselves since the last meeting but also to look ahead at the materials to be used during the next several weeks.

At the conclusion of the first year, teachers met for a few days to "fine tune" planning for the second year based upon their experience to that date. Thus far, implementation had dealt only with the mastery materials; it was decided that this constraint would be continued through the second year. However, new materials (including problem solving and motivation/enrichment programs) were reviewed and recommended for adoption.

The third year of implementation was marked by expansion beyond the application of the mastery curricula. The district reconsidered its original decision to restrict its computerized problem-solving activities to those which did not require students to engage in programming. During the year, sixth-grade students were introduced to problem solving through the Logo computer language.[1] Problem solving in the introductory high-school mathematics courses and upper-level science courses made use of the language Pascal.[2] A selected group of teachers was given training in these languages prior to beginning the work with students; help from a nearby university was thereafter available.

Annual adjustment of the implementation plan continued to be guided by the experience gained. Implementation was judged to be complete when students who had experienced the use of computers in the delivery of instruction reached the level at which they employed the computers as problem-solving tools.

Profile 2: A Trickle-Down Implementation Plan

The plan of Profile 1 was characterized by a decision to introduce computers at several levels (grade 3 through high school) simultaneously. In Profile 2 we'll examine one of two other organizational schemes typically employed when implementing instructional uses of computers. (The second alternative appears as Profile 3.)

The plan to be described here was executed in a secondary school. Its designation as a "trickle-down" plan calls attention to the most distinctive feature of its organization: it was initiated with small audiences in specialized courses of the upper grades and then trickled downward to larger groups in courses of more general appeal.

The first year of the plan involved a single activity by a single teacher. An introductory unit in programming in the BASIC language was directed at problem solving within an eleventh-grade advanced mathematics course. Since the school was of such a size that one teacher taught all of the eleventh-grade mathematics, it was sufficient to equip one room with six microcomputers. The teacher's training in computer programming was comprised of a course taken at a nearby community college and a couple of short courses run by a local computer vendor.

During the second year, the mathematics teacher was joined by a twelfth-grade science teacher with a similar education in computer programming. Both had participated in an advanced programming class at the community college. The mathematics teacher worked on compacting the computer experience of the eleventh-grade students; applications and a few advanced topics were added. The science teacher introduced computer applications into his course. This was a natural step since all of the students who took advanced mathematics in grade 11 were enrolled in the grade 12 science course. (In planning, the teachers realized that a problem would arise if a student should move into the district and—lacking the programming instruction provided by the mathematics course—enroll in the science class. The science teacher was willing to deal with such a situation.) Owing to small class sizes and careful scheduling, no new equipment was necessary as a result of the science activity.

Additional equipment was purchased, however, to support a new and quite different movement which began during the second year. The school's only business teacher introduced a unit on computerized word processing and accounting into the grade 11 business education curriculum. By careful orchestration, the teacher was able to provide the intended experiences to all business classes, using four more microcomputers of the same kind as those used by the mathematics and science students. This was a happy accident, indeed, since the previous purchase had been made without any consideration of the availability of good word processing or accounting software! Were it not for this stroke of good fortune, the school might have been

[1] Logo is a simple but powerful language developed at the Massachusetts Institute of Technology under the leadership of Seymour Papert. A thorough description of the educational potential of Logo (including a brief introduction to the language) was the subject of a special focus issue of *Byte: The Small Systems Journal* 7, No. 8 (August 1982). A simpler, less detailed discussion of Logo appears in a special focus issue of *Classroom Computer News* 3, No. 5 (April 1983).

[2] Pascal was the choice of the College Entrance Examination Board for its 1984 advanced placement test in structured programming. A description of the advanced placement course in Pascal can be obtained by writing to College Board Publications, P.O. Box 2815, Princeton, NJ 08540.

faced with the prospect of purchasing technically incompatible systems.[3]

The application of computers within the business curriculum was unlike that in mathematics and science. In mathematics/science, both the teachers and students were *creators* of software—that is, each had to be able to program a computer. By contrast, the business teacher and students were *users* of software. Use required only an understanding of some task (word processing or accounting) and the manner in which the prepared computer programs could be used to handle that task. The business teacher, who already had expertise in dealing with the tasks by noncomputerized methods, needed only to become adept in the use of the computerized aids. This was accomplished through a combination of instruction by the vendor and self-study of the programs purchased.

Two years of courageous efforts by individual teachers paved the way for the bold steps of the third year in which computer literacy was the theme of an interdisciplinary effort at grade 9. Programming became part of the grade 9 mathematics curriculum. The grade 9 mathematics teachers received their instruction in BASIC from the grades 11–12 teachers; the latter also provided consulting assistance when the grade 9 programming courses got under way. Word processing was incorporated as a tool for teaching English composition. The social studies classes included the study of computers in society, citizens' rights and responsibilities in an information age, and careers in information processing. This expanded interaction with computers required more equipment; several classrooms were equipped with demonstration computers, and a computer laboratory was created. Utilization of the laboratory was optimized by a scheduling procedure based upon coordination of the literacy activities of the various departments. Coordination of course planning was necessary to guarantee that students' involvement in computer literacy would be spread out across the year. Not only did this control have an impact on the computer laboratory, but it also extended and reinforced the students' study of computers. All of the grade 9 students encountered most of the literacy experiences, and most grade 9 students encountered all of them. The trickle-down process had begun.

As interaction between computers and students was being planned for this larger population, teachers began to worry about the obvious: must all students be taught typing? Acting on the strength of observation of the students in the grade 11 and 12 classes in business, mathematics, and science, and of students working elsewhere with computers, the teachers opted for minimal student instruction in touch typing. They decided that the basic keyboard hand positions would be introduced but that any further typing skills would be derived individually from students' use of the computer in the activities planned or from their voluntary use of a set of computerized typing tutorials. In fact, this decision proved wise; typing skills developed adequately.

Year four saw the introduction of a complete, elective course in BASIC in grade 10 (taught by the grade 11 mathematics teacher). Programming problems completed by the students were selected from a broad range of computer applications to ensure that the students would experience several styles of programming.

By the fifth year, the literacy activities of grade 9 and the popularity of the grade 10 course in BASIC forced a revision of the program for grade 11. The Grade 11 teacher introduced Pascal. A new teacher, trained in a university summer course, took over the grade 10 course.

The fourth and fifth years of the plan were marked by constant but low-key efforts to involve all of the school's teachers in investigating appropriate computer-based activities and incorporating such activities into their curricula. In many cases, the first move was to encourage teachers to use word processing to improve the critique-rewrite aspect of theme writing. Also, the teacher in charge of the computing laboratory began building a collection of computerized review lessons in a variety of subject areas so that teachers encountering individual student weaknesses could prescribe such lessons as remedies.

Profile 3: A Bubble-Up Implementation Plan

Another secondary school developed its instructional computing program using a plan which, organizationally speaking, is the reverse of the strategy exhibited by Profile 2. Instead of trickling down from a select group to a general audience, this third plan displays a start-at-the-bottom-and-grow-with-the-students strategy. In the example to be discussed, "bottom" is grade 9; it could have been grade 7 . . . or grade 5 . . . or . . .

The plan was initiated through two grade 9 activities: a unit of programming (Pascal) in the mathematics classes and a unit of word-processing experiences in the English classes. During the second year, the grade 9 activities were intensified and expanded, and an extended programming experience (Pascal) was injected

[3] There *are* good reasons for the deliberate purchase of more than one brand of computer system. The pros and cons of mixed systems will be an issue for Chapter 14.

into the grade 10 mathematics classes. By the third year, the grade 9 activities were brought together into a complete course in computer topics (including programming, word processing, data-base uses, careers, and social implications of computer technology). Because the school had flexible scheduling, several teachers were able to share their expertise by teaching the course units on a revolving plan. Over a period of years, the application of computers continued to rise like bubbles through the curriculum. The strengthening of the activities in the lower grades effectively exerted pressure to create additional activities at higher levels. For instance, the computer topics of grade 9 eventually became part of the curriculum for all students. The process very soon resulted in several elective programming and computer applications courses.

Although the end products of the plans in Profiles 2 and 3 were similar, the needs which accompanied their developments were dissimilar. Three major differences are worth noting.

1. *Teacher Training.* The early stages of Profile 2 required the training of only a few teachers at a time; those trained had to maintain their missionary zeal. Profile 3 called for a massive training at the very outset, but had the advantages associated with sharing, consulting, and capitalizing on a misery-loves-company spirit. The teachers of Profile 2 understandably suffered doubts born of isolation.
2. *Equipment Acquisition.* Profile 2 broke the purchasing of equipment into as-you-need-it stages with little being purchased at any stage; Profile 3 began with a large acquisition. If one set of hardware purchased under Profile 2 had turned out to be a poor choice in terms of new applications (as the development trickled down), the error would be regrettable but not disabling. A purchasing misjudgment within Profile 3, however, would have left virtually no avenue of escape; the failure to anticipate future applications could have crippled overall implementation of computing activities for some time. In fact, total development of either plan may require the purchase of *more than one kind of computer system.* Good advanced planning involves the selection of the best combination of hardware for the kinds of applications to be developed.
3. *Student Morale.* Initial activities within Profile 2 seemed to ignore the undeniable computer interest of younger students. Moreover, it gave the impression that computers were to be reserved for an elite group, thus creating a new class of "disadvantaged" students. Conversely, the beginnings of the plan of Profile 3 made no provision for the older students who, closer to graduation, felt a special urgency to come to grips with computer technology. (A response to the latter problem could have been to organize an extracurricular computing club to serve older students during the first few years.)

Profile 4: Augmenting Instruction

Spurred on by the development of what we have referred to as "classroom demonstration courseware," some schools have introduced instructional computing through the simultaneous initiation of teacher-support activities in several subjects. The computer was employed to augment lectures, demonstrations, or problem-solving activities in such diverse fields of study as agriculture, business, consumer education, industrial education (e.g., construction, automotive repair), the social sciences, mathematics, and the natural sciences. Teachers focused on the identification and use of programs which would permit more dynamic presentations of key concepts or processes. Mathematics teachers employed programs which used graphs to illustrate dramatically the behavior of (and relationships between) functions without resorting to the tedium of point-by-point plotting. Science simulations were used to compress the time required for experimentally testing conjectures and/or to permit the low-cost and danger-free investigation of complex phenomena. Models of financial systems served to illustrate points of discussion and to test student decisions. Agri-business software allowed students to experiment with farm management variables in search of an efficient crop or animal production program. The industrial trades teacher could use problem-solving simulators to develop the diagnostic skills of student mechanics, to test the energy efficiency of a proposed building design, or to calculate the cost of construction using several alternate sets of building materials.

Schools using this plan placed a priority on the use of the computer to expand or refine classroom instruction. The teaching of programming as a first venture was rejected because (a) the available budget was insufficient for the purchase of the minimal equipment needed or (b) no teacher was willing to attempt instruction in programming without first undergoing extensive training. (That is, no one was comfortable with the prospect of trying to maintain a position which was one day ahead of the students.) By restricting the plan to the use of the computer in a demonstration mode, any given teacher could employ it effectively after a short self-study effort.

Equipment could be kept to a minimum. By carefully designing a computer demonstration classroom, it took only thoughtful scheduling and a mild dose of teacher cooperation to have a one-terminal system immediately serve the special instructional needs of several teachers.

Profile 5: Bridging the Education Gap

This venture into instructional computing arose as the proposed solution to local and national studies of a major educational problem—the inadequate mathematical and scientific preparation of first-year college students. Although the application took place at the university level, the curricula involved were based upon secondary-school syllabi. The goal of the plan was to use computers to help bridge the academic gap between the level of mathematical/scientific competence of secondary-school graduates and the level of competence required for successful participation in first-year college courses in mathematics, biology, chemistry, and physics.

The problem which caused the university to adopt the goal stated above first presented itself during the university's examination of the employment prospects of its graduates. It found that, nationally speaking, the business sector was unable to satisfy a growing demand for employees with strong mathematical/scientific educations. Business projections of growth in this demand pointed beyond the obvious need for more persons with traditional credentials in the sciences (e.g., engineers, professional mathematicians, research scientists, computer scientists, medical personnel, and teachers of mathematics or science) to three significant changes in the world of work. First, it noted the technological invasion of occupations which until recent times were thought of as havens for those who described themselves as having no interest or ability in mathematics or the sciences.[4] Second, there was intensification of the use of mathematical/scientific skills in what had been viewed as semitechnical fields (e.g., law, banking, business management, research in the humanities, accounting). Finally, there was the accelerated rate of obsolescence among existing occupations and the concomitant growing birthrate of new occupations. By contrast with the escalating scientific profile of the job market, the university found that very few of its graduates were in areas requiring mathematical/scientific coursework. Looking back over the previous ten years of its existence, the university discovered that it had graduated only 13 percent of its Bachelor's Degree candidates in science and mathematics. Of these, only 5 percent graduated in the time prescribed for the degree; some students took seven years to complete their work. The failure rate in first-year science courses had run as high as 83 percent. The study also revealed that a large number of the university's students suffered from a combination of poor extraclass study facilities and the lack of opportunity to take secondary-school courses in advanced science and mathematics.

Of the approximately 4000 students enrolled at the university, only about 800 could be housed in campus facilities; the remainder had to commute. Twenty percent of the commuters spent over two hours per day in transit. These characteristics of the student body identified the university as a "lunch pail" institution in which instruction was confined to the hours between 7:30 A.M. and 5 P.M.

The university examined several instructional alternatives by which it might provide compensatory instruction in mathematics and the sciences. The goals of that instruction were to reduce the failure rate in introductory courses in mathematics and the sciences and to shape the degree choices of graduates to match the employment needs of the nation. The constraints placed upon that instruction were many.

- It would have to be carried out within the normal academic programs of the students. That is, the compensatory work was to be accomplished in such a way that it would not delay students' progress through prescribed degree programs.
- It would have to be delivered in such a way that each student would be able to fit it into his or her usual work/study schedule.
- It would have to be efficient in the sense that it would focus upon the specific academic deficiencies of each individual student.
- It would accept the restriction that students came to campus on Monday through Friday only, arriving after 7:30 A.M. and leaving before 5 P.M.
- Its operation could not be dependent upon an increase in the number of faculty in mathematics and the sciences.[5]
- It would generate data for use in evaluating both the progress of individual students and the effectiveness of the total compensatory program.

Following a year of study and deliberation, the university decided to apply computers to its problems. The previously stated goals and constraints dictated that the instructional computing system selected would have to guarantee four features.

1. Immediate availability of a large amount of tested high-school level courseware in mathematics, biology, chemistry, and physics. (The courseware had to include appropriate tutorial, drill, practice, and simulation lessons.)

---

[4]Persons *once* found in such havens of nontechnical bliss would include secretaries, journalists, ranchers, farmers, auto mechanics, elementary-school teachers, graphic artists, musicians, librarians, law enforcement personnel, and athletes.

[5]There was a national shortage of such faculty. Moreover, the university was under a "hiring freeze" which forbade the creation of new faculty positions even if qualified persons and the necessary salary monies could be found.

2. A complete and flexible computerized instructional management package.
3. An inservice program to prepare the university faculty to make use of the system for compensatory instruction. (Such preparation was *not* to require the development of computer programming skills.)
4. The availability of courseware that would permit future expansion of the instructional computing program. (Expansion would be both to higher levels in mathematics/science and to other subject areas.)

During the second year of the plan, the university opted to contract for instructional computing services rather than to purchase a system (hardware and courseware) outright. It entered into an experimental year in which it made use of sixteen terminals which were linked by telephone lines to a large computer in a city 1500 kilometres away. The terminals were placed in a single room which was redesigned for the purpose by being carpeted, rewired, and furnished with sixteen custom-built study carrels, each equipped with two chairs. As part of the service contract, the university was provided with a full-time instructional computing consultant, whose duties were to conduct inservice courses for the faculty, to assist faculty in the establishment of instructional packages (under the control of the system's CMI software) for use with their classes, to train student monitors to maintain the computing laboratory, and to assist the university in developing long-range plans for the instructional application of computers.

Although the system was established to attack instructional problems in mathematics and the sciences, its use and the inservice training courses were immediately extended to all university faculty. By the end of the year, the facility was being used by approximately 1400 students; it was providing instruction in mathematics, biology, biochemistry, chemistry, law, physics, physiology, psychology, religion, sociology, statistics, and several languages. The laboratory was open (and staffed) from 8 A.M. to midnight on Monday through Friday and from 9 A.M. to 6 P.M. on Saturday. A simple log book was used to permit any student or faculty member to reserve a terminal for up to 45 minutes.

By the middle of the experimental year, two things were clear. First, the system not only met the university's expectations but also had been enthusiastically embraced by a significant number of students and faculty. Second, the phone line connection was unreliable and, hence, unacceptable. The university decided to borrow the money needed to purchase its own system. The price of purchase would include the salary of a full-time consultant for another year. The university began the immediate preparation of a room to house the mainframe computer and of two more instructional computing laboratories to accommodate another forty-eight terminals. The installation was completed early in the third year of the plan.

During the third year, use of the facility was expanded and refined. About one-third of the faculty completed an eight-session seminar on the use of the computer in classroom instruction; a subset of this group attended a second eight-session seminar dealing with the system's instructional management package. Each seminar required twenty-four clock-hours of work, sixteen of which were computerized lessons. The number of student users subsequently increased to over 2600.

The departments of mathematics, biology, chemistry, and physics executed a three-week pilot project to investigate the use of the system as a solution to their problems of compensatory instruction. All lectures were suspended during this period, and each student was scheduled for twenty-four clock-hours of computerized testing and instruction. The experience also included scheduled small-group discussion sessions, private sessions with the instructors involved, and group tours of laboratory and library facilities. Student performances on the computerized tests and lessons verified the need for an all-out effort in compensatory instruction. Student reactions obtained through a written survey revealed strong student support of the activity and indentified specific ways in which the content and procedures of the program could be improved. Following this experience, the departments worked with the instructional computing consultant to prepare a detailed proposal for a five-year compensatory curriculum effort in mathematics and the sciences. Annual evaluation and modification of the program's materials and procedures would be based upon the data gathered by a comprehensive research component designed to guide project development. By presenting the proposal to large business corporations, the university took only four months to secure the funds needed for the first year of the project.

The fourth year of the plan was marked by a major policy change: access to the computer was restricted to those students whose instructors had developed specific plans for incorporating computerized lessons, testing, or management into their total instructional program. Although another sixteen terminals were slated to be added during the year, it was clear that the system could not hope to keep pace with uncontrolled use. In the previous years, instructors had been permitted to send their students to study lessons from a large menu of materials available in the field. For the most part, the students' participation was voluntary, the lesson assignments were nonspecific, the instructors rarely reviewed the lessons before placing them on the menu, and instructors were not making use of the system's management package to monitor the progress of their students. This "casual" use of a valuable resource had been *deliberate*,[6] but now it was time to encourage thoughtful use which would protect the interests of those instructors who had invested their time and energies in curricular planning. In the future, an instructor would be assigned time and space on the system only after a Faculty Users Committee had reviewed and approved a written instructional plan submitted by the instructor. Growth and allocation of the resource would henceforth be directed by faculty who understood and valued the system's services.

The formation of the Faculty Users Committee was one of the events associated with the university's assumption of responsibility for the further development of the instructional computing program. In addition, the management of the facility, the further inservice training of faculty, the search for development funds, and the provision of support services for faculty users were placed in the hands of three persons hired for those purposes. The consultant, having trained these people during the previous year, was no longer required on a full-time basis. Henceforth, consultant services would be limited to short assignments on well-defined tasks.

Profile 6: One for Each . . . and All for Nought

This plan—and we use the word *plan* with some reservations—came to our attention through a national newspaper. The paper reported an interview with a school superintendent who asserted that within three years there would be a computer in every classroom in his district and that each of those computers *would be used*. To ensure that usage, the implementation plan included inservice education for every teacher. That inservice education was provided in the form of a single two-day workshop.

A proposal to provide a computer for every classroom, like a proposal to provide a chicken for every pot, certainly seems worthwhile. Still, the worth of either plan hinges on the assumptions that the receiver of the gift isn't allergic to it and is prepared to make use of it. The superintendent in this case appears to have given little consideration to these assumptions and, as a result, the implementation plan was confronted with many problems for which no preparation had been made. New to a school district in which computers were nowhere to be found, he had decided that some "motivation" was needed. However, his training efforts ignored all experience associated with introducing new technologies into developing environments. (Schools must be viewed as developing environments when they embark upon computer activities for the first time.) Teachers had played no part in the development of the proposal and, hence, had no ownership in it. Little, if any, thought had been given to probable classroom uses or to the software that would be needed to support those uses. Careful planning of computer uses would have revealed the magnitude of the implementation task. It also would have exposed the folly of placing the success of that implementation at the mercy of a two-day workshop.

The one-for-each plan reported above is neither unique nor financially untenable. With the decline in costs of microcomputers and the trend toward making popular microcomputers compatible with large mainframe systems, the proposed one-to-one correspondence may soon move from classrooms to students. In 1980, the president of a U.S. university announced a six-year plan under which the university would provide each incoming student with a personal computer terminal. The use of that terminal would by then be necessary for full participation in the institution's academic programs.

In Defense of Anonymity

The six profiles were selected with an eye to diversity. They vary in purpose, forethought, cost, breadth of application, and educational level (elementary, secondary, college) of implementation. One profile (Profile 4) is a composite.

In all presentations the names of the educational systems involved have been withheld and no final assessments of the projects have been given. The withholding of names allows us to present the profiles as generic examples, free of the apologies and qualifications that must accompany case histories. The absence of final reports is due to the fact that the projects are still evolving and are, after all, expressions of local conditions. While outlines of these projects raise issues which should be of interest to many other institutions, reports of the projects' intermediate successes and failures would be of only local relevance.

SELF-PORTRAIT

Profile 7 is your own. Unlike the first six, it must be presented with extreme attention to detail—and only you can do the job. The best we can do for you is to list a few guidelines that have been suggested by the experiences of other educators.

1. Prepare a statement of why instructional comput-

[6]The purposes were to entice both students and instructors to approach the computer, to create an awareness of the system's instructional potential, and to allow time for instructors to obtain inservice training.

ing is a necessary component of your educational system.
2. Decide what kinds of applications of computers are likely during the first two to five years. Set priorities for those applications.
3. Determine what specific actions must be taken at each stage of the implementation.
4. Determine who must support the actions; assess their willingness to make the necessary investments of time and money.
5. Attempt to secure a broad base of human involvement from the very outset. Capitalize upon the commitment of eager beavers by supporting their early efforts, *but avoid isolating anyone.*
6. Develop a multistage plan for training personnel. Consider a combination of the learning resources available from universities, community colleges, self-instruction packages, experienced teachers (perhaps from another school system), workshops offered as part of convention activities, and workshops presented by vendors. Investigate costs and clearly identify the source(s) of payment.
7. Identify the kinds of hardware and courseware needed to implement each stage of the plan. (More about this in chapter 14.)
8. Locate and evaluate the courseware required to execute the applications planned. Develop courseware evaluation checklists which focus upon the software attributes which are of greatest concern to local users.
9. Identify special personnel critical to the execution of any stage of the plan.
10. Develop a plan which recognizes the need for ongoing efforts to ensure that the instructional computing program does not falter. Attend to the coordinated selection, management, and maintenance of hardware and courseware.
11. Assume that the plan has flaws and that several things will go wrong. Be prepared to fall back, to cope with the failures, and to reset priorities without major violations of Guidelines 1 and 2.

AWARENESS: FOR WHOM AND WHY?

Guideline 5 reiterates the assertion we made at the beginning of this chapter. The key to success is in the judicious selection and involvement of people. Of course, it's unlikely that people will become involved with the implementation of instructional computing unless they are aware of what instructional computing is all about and what benefits it might offer to them. For this reason, persons interested in introducing an educational change will usually conduct an awareness campaign—that is, they will attempt to make the entire target community aware of what is planned.

Amateur agents of educational change are an endangered species. They almost became extinct during the "new math" era, but a few survived to find protection and sustenance within the ranks of computer educators. The reason that the amateur agents are endangered is that they have failed to observe that awareness, if it is to lead to involvement, is a two-way program. They are so eager to inform the public of their plans to change some situation that they fail (a) to find out what others in that public are already doing to change that situation, (b) to find out what changes others would like to see in that situation, or (c) to estimate what degree of change others are willing to support. In short, the amateur agent of change fails to develop public[7] ownership of the plans for change. This unwillingness to take the time to ask what the public knows or wants to do can produce militant public resistance under banners with slogans such as "Back to the Basics" or "Computers Are Dehumanizing."

There is another route to creating awareness and securing involvement in instructional computing. The first step is to ask members of the public what they are doing or wish to do with computers in the classroom, thus raising the awareness of both the agent and the public to the issues and the possible actions. The second step is to report back to others what you have learned from them. The third step is to *make honest use of the information gathered.* It is the third step, of course, that makes the difference. Not only does it convince those surveyed that you value their opinions and are sensitive to their concerns, but also it aids the plan by allowing you to begin work with those actions most likely to produce early successes, to hold off those actions that need time to gain acceptability, and to drop those actions that might be fatal to the overall plan.

An example of the efficacy of the gentle art of compromise as applied to instructional computing can be found in a statewide plan executed in Wyoming. In this example, awareness activities and implementation activities can be seen to continue side by side, each supporting the other.

In 1979, the University of Wyoming sought the assistance of the Wyoming State Department of Education and the public school teachers of Wyoming in developing a statewide plan for introducing instructional applications of computers in grades K–16. Work began in September of that year with a one-day invita-

---

[7]The word *public* refers to the group of persons which must consent to or support the proposed change. In some cases, the appropriate public may be a large community of both laypersons and educators; in other cases, the appropriate public may be the faculty of a single institution.

tional conference, the stated purpose of which was to engage leading classroom teachers in the formation of statewide policies and procedures regarding educational uses of computers. Of the sixty-one conference participants, only the fifty-four public-school educators (teachers and administrators) were permitted to introduce resolutions or to vote; the seven university and state department personnel served as facilitators. The teachers came from thirty-nine schools located in twenty-two of Wyoming's fifty school districts. They represented every level of grades K–12 and included instructors from seven secondary-school subject areas (business, counseling, English, mathematics, the natural sciences, social science, special education). Their deliberations were later published and distributed to every school in Wyoming.[8]

Participants in the 1979 invitational conference passed thirty-nine resolutions, eleven of which received unanimous approval. Among those eleven was Resolution 35 which proposed

> That a survey be conducted
> (a) to determine the current status of computer usage in Wyoming schools and
> (b) to obtain opinions from a representative sample of Wyoming educators regarding the potential instructional uses of computers.[9]

This study was subsequently executed by faculty of the University of Wyoming; the results were interpreted and recommendations were formulated by a panel of twelve of Wyoming's public-school teachers and administrators. The observations and recommendations of the panel, sent to every school in Wyoming, have guided the actions of the university, the Wyoming State Department of Education, and state professional organizations in the implementation of instructional computing.[10] A newsletter and special publications of the university provided the schools with periodic updates of actions taken with respect to both the resolutions of the 1979 conference and the recommendations of the panel that reviewed the survey data. One of the updates on the recommendations is attached to this paper (Appendix 1) to provide you with evidence of what the teachers of Wyoming thought about instructional computing when surveyed in 1980 and to give examples of some of the actions that were taken in response to the recommendations of the panel within twelve months of their publication.

While the Wyoming procedure may not be transferable to your situation, it does illustrate what we mean by creating awareness of and establishing teacher involvement in an instructional computing plan. With the hope that you will concur in our judgment of the importance of surveying the public that must give implicit or explicit endorsement to your plan, we have attached (Appendix 2) a modified version of the polling instrument used for the Wyoming survey.[11]

Appendix 1

Recommendations Regarding Statewide Development of Instructional Computing (A Twelve-Month Progress Report)

A statewide study of the status of instructional computing in Wyoming was published twelve months ago.[12] The report of that study was prepared under the supervision of the Wyoming Ad Hoc Advisory Committee on Instructional Applications of Computers. The Committee, appointed by the State Superintendent of Public Instruction and comprised of precollege public-school teachers and administrators, based these recommendations on data gathered by the study.

The complete report was distributed to every Wyoming teacher of mathematics or science, every public-school administrator, and every school counselor. A copy also was sent to the chief officer of each of Wyoming's professional organizations in education, to each subject matter consultant in the Wyoming State Department of Education, to selected faculty and administrators at the University of Wyoming, and to the presidents of several national professional organizations. At the request of the Association of State Supervisors of Mathematics, the report was sent to the mathematics consultant in each of the other 49 state departments of education.

The report concluded with 16 recommendations regarding the development of instructional computing in Wyoming. In the fall of 1981, the Committee extracted these (annotated) recommendations from the report and again brought them to the attention of (a) the chief officer of each of Wyo-

---

[8]Bob Kansky, *Conference Report: Wyoming Invitational Conference on Instructional Applications of Computers* (Laramie, WY: Center for Research Services and Publications of the University of Wyoming, 1979), ERIC Document ED 186 262.

[9]Kansky, p. 37.

[10]Bob Kansky, *Instructional Computing in Wyoming: Status and Recommendations* (Laramie, WY: Center for Research Services and Publications of the University of Wyoming, 1981), ERIC Document ED 202 675.

[11]Montana provides an example of statewide planning which builds upon the composite experience of teachers who have taken the initiative in introducing instructional applications of computers. Appointed to the Montana Task Force on Computer Education, these teachers compiled an excellent document which presents a step-by-step plan for starting a computer education program. It is a fine example of the type of planning which has been discussed in this chapter.

The Elements of Computer Education: A Complete Program (Montana Office of Public Instruction, Division of Public Information, State Capitol, Helena, MT 59620), 1983.

[12]January 1981.

ming's professional education organizations and (b) selected administrators at the University of Wyoming. The Committee invited comment by each of the organizations/individuals contacted. The comments received were discussed at the Committee's meeting in January 1982 and, by Committee action, resulted in some modification of the recommendations. With one exception, the modifications were directed at clarifying the recommendations; one recommendation was withdrawn.[13]

The following pages present the modified recommendations. Each recommendation is accompanied by explanatory comments which, it is hoped, will give the reader a better understanding of the Committee's intent with respect to that recommendation. For ten recommendations, an additional group of statements reports actions that have been taken or are being taken in response to the recommendation.

Recommendation 1:

A program of computer awareness for *all* students should be implemented in grades K–12 as soon as possible.

Explanatory Comments. Every student must learn about computers and their role in society. Instruction should include interaction with a computer, but that interaction need not be an experience in computer programming; in any case, instruction should not be *restricted* to computer programming. Experience at the secondary level should include opportunities to apply the computer as a tool within the student's area(s) of subject matter interest. Elementary-school experience should include work with a typewriter keyboard.

Recommendation 2:

Every student who is interested in learning how to program a computer should have the appropriate instruction and machinery available to him.

Explanatory Comments. The opportunity to study programming should not be a function of postsecondary plans, subject-area interest, or previous academic achievement. The extent of such experience should be limited only by the student's performance in this area.

Recommendation 3:

Planning for the instructional use of computers should include consideration of a wide variety of educational applications other than the teaching of computer programming.

Explanatory Comments. Careful planning must precede the purchase of computing equipment to ensure that the system acquired will support a broad range of uses by students and teachers. The teaching of computer programming should take its place as one application of computers. Planning also should consider such applications as problem solving, word processing, teacher-support services, test generation and analysis, instructional management, and career planning.

Recommendation 4:

In planning for educational computing, instructional applications should take priority over administrative applications. Separate computing facilities should be considered.

Explanatory Comments. Systems designed to perform a broad range of instructional computing tasks are, generally speaking, capable of performing administrative tasks as well. The assumption of administrative functions may require additional storage capability or higher printing speeds. The modification of administrative systems to meet instructional specifications is more complex because of the diversity of instructional applications.

Recommendation 5:

The State Department of Education and the University should cooperate in the development and execution of short workshops aimed at statewide "awareness" of the instructional uses of computers.

Explanatory Comments. There were large "No-Opinion" response rates on many items in the survey which support these recommendations. These rates suggest a general lack of understanding of the instructional possibilities offered by computers. The Committee feels that one-day or half-day workshops for teachers and administrators would go far in encouraging more detailed exploration of those possibilities, in preventing the purchase of inappropriate computer systems, and in helping schools identify sources of assistance within the State.

Current Actions. The Science and Mathematics Teaching Center of the University of Wyoming has assigned a full-time person to this task over the Academic Year 1981-82. This person conducted awareness workshops in over 20 Wyoming communities during September-December of 1981. The same person is conducting awareness programs in conjunction with professional meetings of teachers and administrators. This "awareness" activity is directed at *all* levels of instruction and *all* subject matter areas.

Recommendation 6:

The precertification educational programs of all teachers and administrators should include instruction aimed at producing a layman's knowledge of the nature of computers and their impact upon society.

Explanatory Comments. Instruction should lead to a layman's understanding of the capabilities and limitations of computers, the major components of a computer system and their functions, the *concept* of a computer program, applications (general) of computers in both education and in society as a whole, and criteria and procedures for evaluating computerized instructional materials. Interaction with a computer is a necessary component of such instruction.[14] A *brief* introduction to programming should be included.

---

[13]The deleted item recommended that "school districts should establish a formal policy of seeking to hire teachers who have coursework or experience in computer use." The explanatory comment on this proposal (which was to be applied to all grade levels) stated "In choosing among candidates whose academic and teaching/administrative experiences *are nearly equivalent,* hiring preference should go to candidates with computing knowledge."

[14]The Committee notes that many teachers are demanding inservice instruction in this area. It therefore feels that it is a serious error for any institution to continue to ignore the need for this component as a part of its preservice teacher education program.

Current Actions. Courses in this area are now offered by both the Computer Science Department and the Science and Mathematics Teaching Center of the University of Wyoming. At present neither course is required of preservice teacher education students.

Recommendation 7:

The preservice educational programs of all teachers and administrators should include instruction in the educational uses of computers.[15]

Explanatory Comments. The purpose of the instruction called for by Recommendation 6 is to develop a broad, non-technical knowledge about computers. The instruction called for in Recommendation 7 should focus upon concepts and skills employed in using a computer to teach in any of the curricular areas of Grades K–12. Without pursuing expertise in computer programming, educators must learn how to use the computer in the classroom as an instructional tool. The instructional modes of use to be explored by Recommendation 7 would include such applications as testing, instructional management, tutorial instruction, drill, practice, simulation, and problem solving.

Current Actions. A course in educational applications of computers has been designed and offered by the faculty of the Science and Mathematics Teaching Center of the University of Wyoming. At present it is not a required course for students in preservice teacher education.

Recommendation 8:

All teachers should be encouraged to develop skills in designing and evaluating instructional computer programs.

Explanatory Comments. While the actual writing of such programs might be an objective of such work, the focus should be upon program design and evaluation. The teacher must know how to specify program components in terms which take advantage of the computer's most advanced capabilities and to evaluate programs in terms of pedagogical expectations vis-a-vis computer technology. Supervision of actual program writing could be assigned to subject-area specialists.

Current Actions. A course in the design of instructional programs for computers is now offered by the Department of Educational Foundations and Instructional Technology of the University of Wyoming.

Recommendation 9:

All subject-area professional organizations should review their certification standards and propose changes that would comprise subject-related competence in instructional computing.

Explanatory Comments. The use of computers and their services is the right of every teacher. Qualification by field is necessary to ensure every teacher the access to computers and to an understanding of the use of computers relative to his teaching area.

Current Actions. The Committee has advised every Wyoming professional organization of this recommendation. The Wyoming State Department of Education is reviewing the entire procedure by which teacher certification is accomplished. The latter action may soon result in the need for professional organizations to participate in the examination of current standards; this, in turn, should lead to the consideration called for by Recommendation 9.

Recommendation 10:

Certification standards for teachers of computer science should be proposed only after careful review by public school personnel.

Explanatory Comments. Certification of computer science teachers must not affect the inclusion of computer use or programming instruction by qualified teachers with other certification specialties. Certification must serve to create teachers who can function as consultants in promoting computer usage by all educators; it must not create a privileged class which holds exclusive rights to instructional computing.

Current Actions. No certification standards are being proposed at this time. However, the Department of Computer Science and the Science and Mathematics Teaching Center of the University of Wyoming are preparing a *recommended* body of courses in this area. This will permit teachers to voluntarily pursue preservice or inservice programs which would equip them with the skills needed by a precollege teacher of computer science.

Recommendation 11:

The University should design courses in instructional computing which are appropriate for teachers and administrators from all grade levels and all certification areas.

Explanatory Comments. A variety of courses, open to preservice and inservice teachers, should provide instruction in three areas: computer literacy, computer programming, instructional applications of computers. A delivery system should be developed to take these courses to inservice educators.

Current Actions. In cooperation with the Department of Computer Science, the Science and Mathematics Teaching Center of the University of Wyoming now offers coursework in all three areas. A limited inservice offering in computer programming has been initiated. An extensive inservice program encompassing all three areas is being planned; implementation should begin no later than the fall of 1983. The Department of Computer Science will add programming courses (BASIC and Pascal) designed specifically for precollege educators.

Recommendation 12:

The College of Education of the University should evaluate its present teacher-education programs with the objective of replacing some of the current degree requirements with courses in instructional computing. It also should revise other course offerings to include the use of computers in instruction.

Explanatory Comments. The public schools are requested to look upon computer literacy as a basic skill and to use computers to improve instruction. It follows that future teachers should be educated in such a way that this request may be fulfilled.

[15]See footnote 14.

Current Actions. The Science and Mathematics Teaching Center and the College of Education are working together to introduce instructional computing into all teacher-education programs at the University of Wyoming. Tentative plans include the establishment of a centrally located microcomputer laboratory, the inservice instruction of College of Education faculty regarding the use of computers in instruction at all levels and in all subject areas, the revision of current course outlines of the College to make use of computers in teacher education courses, the development of new courses in the use of instructional technology, and the conduct of research in instructional computing.

Recommendation 13:

The leadership of the State's professional education organizations should cooperate in defining "computer literacy" as an object of study in Grades K-12.

Explanatory Comments. The Wyoming Council of Teachers of Mathematics (WCTM) is asked to prepare a draft of such a definition. To ensure its applicability across grade levels and subject areas, that draft must be refined by professionals from other areas of instruction.

Current Actions. At the request of the WCTM, the Science and Mathematics Teaching Center (SMTC) of the University of Wyoming has drafted a set of teacher resource materials which define "computer literacy" in terms of topics, textual resources, and suggested classroom activities. The materials will be refined during Academic Year 1981–82 and released in the fall of 1982. A copy will be sent to the president of each professional education association in Wyoming. Availability to teachers will be announced in the SMTC *Newsletter* and other professional publications.

Recommendation 14:

The state Department of Education, the University, and the public schools should cooperate in establishing a Wyoming Instructional Computing Exchange.

Explanatory Notes. While the detailed activities of the Exchange should be set by a task force which includes members from each of the educational agencies noted, the principal charge of the Exchange would be to promote communication among computer-using educators throughout Wyoming.

Current Actions. A group of Wyoming's teacher-leaders have established the Wyoming Educational Computing Council (WECC). With the aid of the Wyoming Council of Teachers of Mathematics and the Science and Mathematics Teaching Center, WECC has taken on the task of fostering communication among Wyoming's computer-using educators (current and potential). A newsletter has been published; a software exchange is being developed.

Recommendation 15:

The State Department of Education should urge and assist the Legislature to develop legislation providing for the adequate funding of instructional computing at all grade levels and all certification areas.

Explanatory Comments. Computers are instructional tools whose use should not be bounded by grade level or subject area. Neither should funding be a function of certification of computer science specialists.

Appendix 2

Computer-Usage Survey Form

General Instructions

The purpose of this survey is twofold: (1) to determine the nature and extent of computer usage in the State's schools and (2) to obtain the opinion of public-school educators regarding the potential uses of computers in the schools. To ensure that decision-makers have the best possible data from which to draw conclusions, your response is urgently needed WHETHER OR NOT YOUR SCHOOL USES COMPUTERS.

This survey is divided into three sections:

Section A: General information about your school
Section B: Opinions regarding instructional uses of the computer in the school
Section C: Current uses of computers by your school

Please adhere to the following guidelines in completing this questionnaire.

I. If your school does NOT use a computer (see definitions below), complete Sections A and B only.
II. If your school uses a computer for administrative or instructional purposes, complete all three sections (A–C).

Although this survey has been sent to you as the school's representative, you may wish to complete it by assigning each section to the staff member most knowledgeable of or interested in the area addressed. One person could then coordinate the completion of the questionnaire and be responsible for its return.

In responding to the items of this survey, feel free to write qualifying comments directly on the survey pages.

Definitions

1. *Computer.* For the purpose of this survey, a *computer* is a machine that operates under the control of a stored program. The term *computer* includes the central processing unit, auxiliary storage, communication links, and all peripheral equipment.
   Programmable desk top calculators and electronic accounting machines are specifically *excluded* from this definition.
2. *Computer access.* A school is said to have *computer access* if a computer is available to the school's faculty or administration in one or more of the following ways:
   - The computer is physically located in the school building.
   - The school has one or more terminals which are connected to a computer located outside the school building.
   - The computer is located near the school. Faculty/administration go to that location to use it.
   - Faculty/administrators do not personally interact with the computer, but computer services are provided by mail or phone by the school system, a bank, an industry, etc.

SECTION A: GENERAL INFORMATION

A.1 School name: ____________________

A.2 School telephone number: ____________________

A.3 County in which school is located: ____________________

A.4 Name of the person in your school who took the primary responsibility for completing this questionnaire:

____________________ ____________________

A.5 What grade levels are included in your school: ________ through ________

A.6 Number of full-time teachers in your school: ____________________

A.7 Current enrollment in your school:

____ Under 50	____ 400 – 599
____ 50 – 99	____ 600 – 999
____ 100 – 199	____ 1000 – 1499
____ 200 – 399	____ 1500+ (Specify number here:) ____

A.8 Does your school currently have access to a computer for either administrative or instructional purposes?

____ yes ____ no

A.9 If you responded "no" to Item A.8, is your school now planning to obtain access to a computer for administrative purposes?

____ yes ____ no

A.10 If you responded "no" to Item A.8, is your school now planning to obtain access to a computer for instructional purposes?

____ yes ____ no

Please go to SECTION B.

SECTION B: OPINIONS ABOUT INSTRUCTIONAL USE

NOTE: In completing this section you may wish to record the collective opinion of all (or some group) of the faculty in your school.

B.1 The opinions recorded below are those of

____ one person
____ the entire school faculty
____ a subgroup of faculty
(indicate number here:) ____

SECTION B: OPINIONS ABOUT INSTRUCTIONAL USE (continued)

B.2 Indicate your level of agreement with *each* of the following possible educational uses of computers in the school by circling the appropriate number. The opinion should be with respect to instructional uses of computers in general (and not just in your particular school).

Strongly Agree	Agree	No Opinion	Disagree	Strongly Disagree	
5	4	3	2	1	(a) To teach *every* student about computers and their role in society.
5	4	3	2	1	(b) To teach *every* student to program a computer.
5	4	3	2	1	(c) To provide computer experiences (including programming) for all potentially college-bound students (but to college-bound students only).
5	4	3	2	1	(d) To teach programming to only those potentially college-bound students who might enter programs in mathematics or the natural sciences.
5	4	3	2	1	(e) To allow any teacher who so wishes to utilize the computer as an instructional tool in teaching courses in his area.
5	4	3	2	1	(f) To permit any teacher to learn to program a computer.
5	4	3	2	1	(g) To provide instructional services (e.g., test grading, test analysis, record keeping, inventory management, objective-referenced test generation, form-letter generation, etc.) to any teacher requesting such services.
5	4	3	2	1	(h) As a special learning resource for handicapped students.
5	4	3	2	1	(i) As a special learning resource for gifted students (regardless of subject area of that giftedness).
5	4	3	2	1	(j) To permit each student to have experiences with computer applications (not necessarily programming) in his area of subject matter interest.
5	4	3	2	1	(k) To provide computer programming as a vocational/technical training skill for students who are not potentially college bound.

B.3 Indicate your opinion regarding the training of teachers with respect to computers and their uses.

5	4	3	2	1	(a) Inservice opportunities should be provided for *all* teachers to learn about computers and their uses, but no programming should be included in that inservice.
5	4	3	2	1	(b) Inservice opportunities should be provided for *all* teachers and should include an introduction to programming.
5	4	3	2	1	(c) Work with computers should be included in the preservice college education of all elementary-school teachers.
5	4	3	2	1	(d) Work with computers should be included in the preservice college training of all secondary-school teachers.
5	4	3	2	1	(e) Work with computers should be included in the preservice college training of all mathematics and science teachers.
5	4	3	2	1	(f) There is a need for secondary-school teachers who are qualified to teach computer science (i.e., computer literacy, computer programming, data processing, etc.).
5	4	3	2	1	(g) The State Department of Education should establish certification requirements in the area of computer science.

If your school now uses a computer, please go on to SECTION C.

If your school does not now use a computer (and you have completed SECTIONS A and B of this survey), please return this form using the envelope enclosed.

SECTION C: CURRENT USES OF COMPUTERS BY YOUR SCHOOL

C.1 If your school uses a computer for *administrative* applications, check each of the following which describes an administrative usage by your school.

_____ Student accounting (such as student scheduling, student records, attendance records, report cards, etc.)
_____ Research and evaluation of teaching methods, curriculum materials, etc.
_____ Resource management and planning (such as maintaining personnel and financial records, inventory control, projection of enrollments, transportation scheduling, payroll, etc.)
_____ Standardized test grading/reporting
_____ Word processing
_____ Other administrative uses (please specify) ____________________

C.2 If your school uses a computer for *instructional* applications, check each of the following which describes an instructional use of computers in your school.

_____ Tutorial (The student learns concepts through active involvement in a dialogue with the computer regarding content in some subject matter area.)
_____ Problem solving (The computer is used as a computational aid for solving complex problems in science, mathematics, business, social studies, etc.)
_____ Teaching computer programming (or data processing)
_____ Simulation (The instructional programs represent some real-life task such as decision-making in the social sciences, genetics experiments in biology, pest control, crop management, etc.)
_____ Career selection (The programs provide counseling in career selection and preparation.)
_____ Instructional games (The games have specific educational goals to develop, extend, or reinforce specific skills.)
_____ Drill or practice (The programs reinforce skills or concepts which were developed in earlier lessons.)
_____ Test construction (The computer constructs tailored tests from a stored file of objective-referenced items.)
_____ Instructional management (The computer provides students with individualized assignments and provides the teacher with a record of each student's progress on individualized contracts.)
_____ Word processing (The computer is used to improve writing skills by permitting the "massaging" of draft forms.)
_____ Teacher-aide services such as keeping inventories of resources, storing annotated bibliographies, generating individualized form letters to parents, etc.
_____ Other instructional uses (please specify) ____________________
____

STUDY GUIDE: CHAPTER 13

1. Chapter 13 presents six implementation profiles. In 75 or so words, distinguish between the trickle-down (Profile 2) and the bubble-up (Profile 3) profiles in terms of the following:
   a. effects upon teachers,
   b. effects upon students,
   c. hardware/software selection,
   d. the evolution of computer activity in the curriculum.
2. Of the six implementation profiles given in this chapter, Profile 4 is unique. What are the potential advantages and disadvantages of this plan?
3. Profile 5 is distinguished by its use of a mainframe. The collegiate level of application is a distinction which is more apparent than real since the initial subject matter of concern to the project was precollege. What are some characteristics of the project that separate it from the others? What changes mark its evolution over the four-year period reported?
4. Use an index such as *Microcomputer Index* to locate reports of other implementation plans. Review these plans in terms of the implementation guidelines suggested in Chapter 13.
5. How would you have voted on each of the recommendations of Appendix 1 (including the withdrawn item reported in Footnote 13 of Appendix 1)? Justify your decisions.
6. Design an instructional computing survey for a particular group.
   a. Describe the group. Tell why its opinions are important and how those opinions will be used.
   b. Construct the survey instrument and a cover letter.
   c. Propose a method of sampling and a method of administration.
   d. Tell how the data from the survey will be summarized, interpreted, and reported.
7. Working as a group, prepare an implementation plan which would account for the major issues raised in Chapter 13. (This planning would be preceded by developing a description of a real or imagined institution—school, school district, whatever—for which the plan is being prepared.)

AGENDA FOR ACTION

SCIENCE AND MATHEMATICS
TEACHING CENTER

ADDRESS REPLY TO WRITER

THE UNIVERSITY OF WYOMING
UNIVERSITY STATION, BOX 3992
LARAMIE, WYOMING, 82071

MEMORANDUM

TO: Members of ICAC

FROM: Bob Kansky and Dick Dennis

DATE: May 2, 1983

RE: ICAC Paper 13

The overall purpose of ICAC Papers 6-12 was to familiarize you with several significant ways in which computers can be applied to classroom instruction. Our theme has been the educator's role in teaching with computers (rather than that of teaching about computers). It's a role which is open to any teacher; it does not presuppose either experience or interest in computer programming.

Thus far we have called upon the members of ICAC to participate as scholars—that is, to study, discuss, experience, and evaluate the various applications which we've described. The remaining papers require that the committee members depart from the secure path of such scholarly pursuits and set out upon the hazardous road of decision making. To be specific, it's time for ICAC to answer three questions.

1. How will computers be applied to instruction in your school(s)?
2. Which computer system(s) should you buy in order to make those applications possible?
3. Where will you get the software needed for those applications?

The letters that ICAC received from Glena Harris (LaRamie Middle School) and Gretchen Potter (Plato Senior High School) might be worth rereading at this point. They report typical problems which beset school systems that address those three questions in the wrong order. Forewarned by those reports, we'll attend first to the task of having you define the role of computers in your school (ICAC Paper 13). Then, although software evaluation has been addressed continuously since ICAC Paper 4, we'll include further attention to software issues when considering hardware selection in Paper 14.

The style of presentation in ICAC Papers 13 and 14 will be quite unlike that of the earlier papers. Instead of presenting facts, analyses, and opinions on instructional computing issues, we'll be sharing examples which we hope will act as grist for your decision-making mill. We'll even offer some procedures and instruments which you might use to structure your search for answers to the three questions. However, we can go no further than to exemplify and suggest. The actual decisions must constitute responses to local educational conditions, and we foreign devils must not meddle at that level.

BK:DD:baa

AGENDA FOR ACTION

Obourn Senior High School

200 Woodbine Avenue
East Roachmont, New York

M. Jack Stivers
Principal

(716) 568-8840

ICAC Memo #13

TO: Members of ICAC

FROM: John Russell

DATE: May 11, 1983

REPORT OF ACTIVITIES

1. Ted has located a video projector, and Gerri has found a word-processing program worth recommending. Both items can be used with John's microcomputer. (See ASSIGNMENTS.)
2. Carrinne immediately contacted Superintendent Ennis regarding our request to conduct an Instructional Computing Opinions Survey in the district. The survey idea met with approval; details of its administration will be worked out with Superintendent Ennis by John.
3. In keeping with the committee's decision, our East Roachmont Instructional Computing Implementation Proposal will be organized under five main headings.

   —Computer Courseware
   —Computer Hardware
   —Laboratory/Classroom Space
   —Teacher Inservice Activities
   —Policy and Planning

   The request for inservice activities will be guided by the results of the opinions survey. The section on planning and policy will develop procedures for the future modification and execution of the implementation plan.

COMMITTEE ASSIGNMENTS

1. Donna and Jeanne will prepare the cover letter and survey instrument for an Instructional Computing Opinions Survey. They will use the document of Paper 13 as a model. John will clear all survey procedures with Dr. Ennis. Everyone will assist with the analysis of survey data.
2. Lolita has been asked to report ICAC activities to the faculty at Bird Elementary. She'll try to borrow the video projector discovered by Ted in order to make the presentation. This will allow her to display both commercial programs and some of the special programs developed by the students at Sinclair Senior High.
3. John has agreed to purchase the word-processor program out of his departmental budget. The program will be used to draft and "massage" the implementation plan. (John notes that the Obourn High School secretary is familiar with word processing and feels that she can quickly learn to use this particular program.)

JR:ms

CHAPTER FOURTEEN

WI$E BUY$: PURCHASE AS A FUNCTION OF PURPOSE

Government displeasure notwithstanding, you really should put a tap on our office phones. If you were to do so, you'd soon hear one of the reasons for this chapter:

> Hi. This is Hilary Tillery from Prosperity School District. Our district has just authorized $75,000 for the purchase of computers for our schools. In order to use these funds, we must turn in a detailed purchase order no later than next Tuesday. Which computer should we buy?

We've heard this opening dozens of times; only the names and the amount have differed. (In one case, the amount was $500,000!)

Since you're listening, note the surprise (disgust? disbelief? annoyance? suspicion?) that colors the tone of the caller's voice after we give the only response possible:

> I'm afraid that I really can't make a sensible recommendation. Your best choice of machine or machines depends upon a number of factors. Could we get together with you and some of the teachers for a few hours of discussion?

Were we able to sustain the conversation through a few penetrating questions, you'd soon learn that the typical decision to purchase has not been preceded by the development of an implementation plan. The caller may sound a bit chagrined by our request for a statement of the instructional purposes governing the purchase or by our queries regarding what funds have been set aside for the training of staff or the acquisition of appropriate courseware. It is with exasperation—and, perhaps, a hint of growing concern—that the caller admits that the funds can be spent on hardware only. In the long pause that follows, we suppress the impulse to suggest that this seemingly golden opportunity to purchase hardware be deferred—even refused—until an implementation plan is in place. The conversation concludes with an agreement to get together (before next Tuesday) or, should our persuasive powers fail us, with an apology for our being unable to be of service.

This chapter is addressed to a special caller. It is for the person like you who has already answered the question of how computers will be applied to instruction within a particular educational setting. It assumes that its response to the question "What kinds of hardware and courseware should be purchased?" is being made within the context of a multifaceted implementation plan for the instructional application of computers.

Putting the Cart Before the Horse

The purpose of this chapter is to help you select the computer system which best fits the goals proposed in your implementation plan. We begin by emphasizing that our search is for a computer system, and not just a computer. A computer system, like a hi-fi system, is a collection of components which fall into two major categories: hardware and software. In the case of a hi-fi system, the hardware components include such essentail elements as a receiver/amplifier, a turntable or tape deck, and speakers; hi-fi software is music recorded on records or tapes. In speaking of a computer system, the comparable hardware essentials would be a computer mainframe, an input device (such as a typewriter-like keyboard), an output device (such as a TV set), and a mass storage device (a tape cassette player/recorder or a disk drive); the software is comprised of computer programs that have been recorded on tapes or disks.[1]

In selecting a computer system, one is obligated to place the cart before the horse. That is, one must carefully consider what is to be delivered (i.e., computer courseware) before considering the machinery (i.e., computer hardware) with which to deliver it. Although Chapter 4 was devoted to the selection and evaluation of courseware, it describes procedures to be used *after the basic computer system has been adopted.* The courseware selection considerations of the present chapter are part of the initial implementation plan; they *precede* the selection of the basic computer hardware.

[1]This analogy between a hi-fi system and a computer system—specifically, a microcomputer system—is the subject of an article which Bob Kansky wrote for the February 1983 issue of the *Arithmetic Teacher.* Entitled "The CPU and You: Mastering the Microcomputer," the article is an elementary discussion of the components and operation of a microcomputer system.

Once the relevant courseware has been identified, the choice of equipment will have been narrowed considerably through the elimination of those models which do not have the software necessary to support the tasks specified in the implementation plan.

Filling the Cart

Every educational institution is on dozens of mailing lists. It regularly receives descriptive brochures as well as samples of textbooks, workbooks, reproducible materials, supplies, equipment, charts, and furniture. Vendors of such items have had a long time to develop procedures for presenting their wares via mail, conventions, and personal contacts. The market is well defined and carefully researched.

Vendors of electronic courseware are less well organized. Although some courseware is being offered by large, established educational firms, much is being done by small organizations with limited financial resources and little experience in dealing with schools. The large firms often suffer from having a sales force that has had little or no experience with computerized courseware. The young electronic publishing houses depend upon a sales force that is thoroughly versed in the product and the mechanisms for its delivery but may not be well informed of the educational needs of the schools, the attitudes of educators toward new curricula, or the procedures by which instructional materials are selected.

The developers of computerized courseware must also often serve as publishers and sales representatives. Since their principal task and talent is in the creation of courseware, one can appreciate why the members of such courseware cottage industries are not effective in disseminating information about their products. Recognizing this shortcoming, many courseware producers have turned to the use of specialized periodicals as their principal distribution mechanism.

There are several specialized publications which make a practice of periodically listing most sources of electronic courseware.[2] You can expedite your courseware search and selection process by making early and widespread contact with the sources listed in these resources. To ensure the best possible communication with the vendors, your contact should indicate the types of materials which you are seeking (that is, the types which are central to your instructional computing implementation plan). To help you in that task, the next six sections of this chapter suggest purchasing considerations specific to each of several instructional applications of the computer.

[2]Several are listed in Note 4 of Section 2 in Chapter 4.

Tutoring or Promoting Mastery Learning

Many instructional computing plans will include applications concerned with tutoring or with facilitating mastery learning of some subject. These applications, especially tutoring, are highly sensitive to local opinions regarding curricular content or presentation. There are key points in any curriculum at which teachers will disagree on selection, order, classification, vocabulary, or pedagogical approach. In English teaching, for example, some instructors will insist that *a, an,* and *the* be called *articles,* while others will classify them as *adjectives.* A teacher's analysis of the causes or consequences of the American Civil War is dependent upon the balance of factors (historic, economic, cultural, military, biographic) admitted. An arithmetic task as simple as subtracting two multidigit numbers can be performed in several ways, with each procedure having its own group of ardent supporters (while a few teachers argue for presenting more than one procedure). Some teachers of science approach their subject as a process; others present it as a product. The model(s) used to introduce fundamental concepts such as the origin of humankind can differ across teachers or schools. The selection of tutorial or mastery materials should, then, be preceded by the identification of such local points of academic dissidence.

The best tutorial or mastery materials will be individualized; each lesson will focus on a single objective. The use of instructional materials that assign students to a variety of tasks within a curriculum requires attention to instructional management—in particular, to record keeping and reporting. Hence, any school introducing tutorial or mastery applications will need well-designed classroom management software to support its use of computerized lessons.

Teachers usually will feel the need to augment or modify any collection of computerized lessons. No matter how insightful and careful the vendor may be, there are bound to be holes in the curricular package. It follows that the software selected must permit teachers to make changes or additions without having to write entire computer programs. Lesson authoring systems (Chapter 6) provide one solution to modification/expansion needs, while other software packages may permit a range of specific alterations by a user who has little or no programming skill. Contracting for the tailoring of software is another—if sometimes complicated—possibility.

Testing

Computerized testing services can make a significant contribution to instruction. Some software for testing operations is accompanied by banks of test items in one or more subjects, whereas other software provides only the support system by which teachers can enter and use their own sets of test items. The prepared question sets can be real time savers if they meet four basic conditions.

1. The objectives tested by the set match the objectives of your curriculum.
2. The items are carefully written.
3. The types of items (multiple choice, short answer, etc.) meet your curricular needs.
4. The courseware is designed to permit a nonprogrammer to revise items easily in the existing bank and to add new items to the bank.

Another desirable feature of computerized testing services is test and/or question analysis. Since such analysis requires inputting the responses of students, it follows either that testing must be done interactively or that student results must be recorded on forms which are easily processed by the computer system.[3] Not only can such software relieve the teacher of grading burdens and provide the students with rapid feedback on their performances, but also the analyses can lead to the systematic improvement of individual items and of test construction procedures. The extent to which test generation, test grading, item analysis, and question editing are integrated within the testing services system will determine the usefulness and efficiency of that system.

Programming Activities

In implementing the plans profiled in Chapter 10, some schools engage students in programming activities as part of their work in problem solving. Other schools teach programming as an activity in its own right. If the instructional applications that you plan include student or teacher programming activities, you must decide upon the programming languages which will be needed to support that work *at all levels throughout the implementation of the plan.*

Several languages are available even on microcomputers, but the version (or dialect) of the language used by a given computer system can be a function of the size of the computer or the brand of the system. For instance, although the American National Standards Institute has pursued the development of a standardized, structured BASIC language, many versions of BASIC have come and gone. The version of BASIC used by some computer manufacturers has evolved in

[3]A third (and gloomy) alternative is for the teacher to type in the responses of each student.

such a way that programs written in an earlier dialect cannot be executed on a system that uses the current version.

The choice of computer languages for instruction is an important issue. Computer languages were developed to serve different purposes and, consequently, have different characteristics and capabilities. Tasks which are handled with ease by one language may pose colossal programming problems in another language. Some languages cope nicely with textual input, whereas others are almost restricted to working with numbers. Any language involves a *choice* of advantages over disadvantages with respect to a range of anticipated uses. The principal uses a few languages (ALGOL, BASIC, COBOL, FORTRAN, Pascal) are noted in the Beginner's Glossary of Computerese which is the final section in this book.

In selecting a language to teach to students, both the purpose of instruction and the capability of the students must be considered. If the purpose is restricted to an awareness level or the programming activity is only a means to an end (such as in problem solving), the language should not be so complex as to present a barrier. In this regard, some important attributes of computer languages that affect selection would include syntactical rigidity, punctuation sensitivity, naturalness of vocabulary, and potential for organizing the logic of the language. Most people simply are not as meticulous about syntax and punctuation as some languages demand they be. Computer languages which are more forgiving (less rigid) in matters of syntax and punctuation will usually be considered "friendly" by the user. This perceived friendliness can, in turn, reduce the tension of programming experiences.

Other important items to consider when selecting a language are the editing features of the language—the features that help the user to create or change computer programs. Good editing capabilities reduce the time or number of machines needed to accomplish a group task. Some editing features are denoted by labels on keys of the keyboard, thus making it easier to do and to teach editing.

Managing Instruction

Individualized instruction does not imply that each student's curriculum will be reduced to independent study and, hence, academic isolation. At any given time, a student operating within an individualized environment may belong to several study groups within a class. The members of a group are bound together by a temporary dedication to common needs or interests; groups dissolve and reform into new groups as goals are reached. Many activities (field trips, guest speakers, project reporting, discussions) will call for the class to act as a single group.

Instructional management software must be flexible enough to serve both individuals and groups. If a decision to change an assignment or to reschedule events is one which has an impact on a group of students, the software should allow the teacher to change the record of one student in the group and, then, to automatically extend that change to all members of the group. If, on the other hand, the teacher wishes to tailor the assignment of a particular student, computerized intervention should be confined to the records of that student.

Changes in certain key information in the records of a group or individual may have hidden effects on the future actions of the entire management system. The system should be protected by warning messages which inform the teacher of the possible catastrophic results of manipulating such key items.

Teaching Decision Making

Computerized courseware designed to engage students in decision making or in the control of complex environments is among the most difficult to create. Such problems include not only simulations but also those instructional games which call for problem-solving behaviors. This style of computerized lesson has the potential to involve students in learning activities which would be inaccessible in any other form.

The search for software rich in motivational or decision-making aspects must be guided by considerations of the content involved and the manner in which the materials will be used. Simulations intended to develop high levels of decision-making skill with regard to performances in an environment have much more specific objectives than simulations intended to identify the need for or sources of information relevant to a problem or to create an awareness of the principles or variables at work within an environment. Also, simulations for supporting group presentations differ in format and performance from simulations designed for use by individual students.

The use of certain simulations requires special peripheral hardware. The special hardware could be something as simple as a printer, a graphics plotter which executes drawings in four colors of ink, a terminal with a touch-sensitive screen, or sound equipment which can produce the performance of a harpsichord or funky oboe. Other simulations employ instruments which can take continuous or timed samples of measures of temperature, heart rate, blood pressure, concentration of a particular compound within a solution, wind speed/direction, luminous intensity, or radioactivity. Computers—even microcomputers—may use the readings from such devices as data to drive the simulation activity. Teachers hoping to use activities involving such peripheral hardware must investigate the demands that these devices will make upon both computer hardware and computer software. To what models of computers can such devices be connected with relative ease? What special additional hardware or software will be needed to permit proper communication between the computer and the peripherals used in the simulation?

Aide-de-Camp Applications

The implications for hardware and software selection among aide-de-camp applications are as varied and changing as the list of uses itself. Let's think through a few specific examples of the situations described earlier.

Computerized demonstrations Classrooms designed for computerized demonstrations can be separated into two categories based upon student-to-terminal ratio in the classroom.

A. The classrooms of this category have a student-to-terminal ratio which does not exceed two to one. The teacher is able to temporarily reduce all of the student terminals to the status of "dumb" monitors whose displays are controlled by the teacher's terminal.
B. The classrooms of this category contain but a single terminal. The displays generated by that terminal are delivered to students over a chain of monitors or by projection on a single large screen.

A demonstration classroom of Category A demands more than a large number of terminals (which can also be used for interactive work by individual students). It requires special hardware and software through which the teacher can strip the terminals of their independence and place them under the complete control of the teacher's "master" terminal.

The classroom of Category B demands high quality monitors, with the student-to-monitor ratio depending upon the size of the monitor and the detail that must be visible to the students. If a Category B classroom employs a video projector, the room's ceiling must be high enough to elevate the screen (which may be over two metres on a side) to a position where the student's view will not be obstructed by the projector or terminal. (An alternative is to bolt the projector to the ceiling and project downwards.)

All demonstration classrooms also share common concerns. All require attention to the power demands of equipment, to the control of the room's lighting to avoid glare on the viewing screens or "washed out" images, and to a physical arrangement which allows the teacher to make eye contact with any student during a demonstration lesson.

Data-base utilization There are several problem-solving, informational, and instructional support applications that can involve the use of large data bases (sources of information) not internal to the computer system. Users form temporary links with these data bases by paying a subscription fee. The link is made over any telephone by simply dialing the number of the data service and then placing the phone's headset into a device called an *acoustic coupler* or *modem*. The user, having identified himself or herself by typing certain secret passwords, then has access to the information stored in the data base.

A very real problem associated with the activity just described is that the user is being charged by both the telephone company (if the call is long distance) and the data-base service for as long as the telephone link is in place. This problem can be minimized by having the user locate the information of interest (a task which calls for training in the efficient search of the data base) and then transferring that information to a local storage medium such as a floppy disk where it can be examined at leisure after the telephone link has been terminated. The trick, of course, is that the user's terminal has to be specially equipped in order to make that transfer. The compatibility between the user's system and the data-base service is something that must be checked in advance.

A data-base service can provide more than raw information. Some have an "electronic mail" feature which allows any user to send private, electronic correspondence to any other person using the system. Coast-to-coast delivery is instantaneous.

Some data services provide students with vocational counseling. Student responses to an instrument which assesses personal goals, job reward expectations, and attitudes toward a range of working conditions are used to identify probable vocational choices. The student can then examine any one of these choices at each of several levels of refinement with respect to such issues as job activities, salary variables, types of training required, methods of and possibilities for advancement, current employment demand, sources of training, and locations of employment. Again, on-line interaction is expensive. Hardware considerations for an institution planning to provide such vocational counseling services would include those previously noted with regard to transfer of information to a local storage medium. In addition, the system should allow students to complete the survey instrument (a time-consuming activity) before engaging the telephone link and then to quickly transmit their survey input for analysis. A printer also would be required to provide each student with a written summary of the relevant information received.

Since the information can be extensive, use of the system with a large number of students would dictate the purchase of a high-speed printer. (More about this a bit later.)

Inventories Inventories are an example of a popular type of instructional support application. They are, in fact, custom-built data bases. Designed to meet the needs of a particular user, they are small enough to be manipulated by the computer equipment available and are readily available for periodic alteration by the teacher. The generic software required to define and operate such customized inventories is often called a *modifiable data-base program.* It is a program which permits the user to establish (within certain constraints) the names of the categories within the inventory, the content of a particular entry in the inventory, and the dimensions along which the inventory may be searched.

Inventory applications are highly dependent upon the volume of information that can be made accessible to the computer at any given time. The size of the "on-board" memory of the computer determines the size of the program which can be used to establish or access the inventory. The type and size of the mass storage medium used by the computer will determine the total number of inventory entries with which the system can cope. The efficiency of the software used to search the inventory is all-important, since the time taken to make a search can increase dramatically as the number of inventory entries passes certain critical numbers. For instance, a computerized sorting procedure which takes 10 *seconds* to complete a search of 30 entries may take 15 *minutes* to complete a comparable search of 150 entries. The slow-down can be a function both of the sorting program and of the computer itself.

Estimating the mass storage requirements of an inventory application calls for a little arithmetic. Suppose, for example, that a social studies teacher wished to set up a "current events" inventory by which students would be able to locate annotated references to journal and newspaper articles specific to several major issues. The teacher also plans to have the students update the inventory by adding new entries each week. The documents to be used (journals and papers) will be selected from those available in the school library, the public library, and the library of the local community college. Finally, the teacher wishes to regularly "purge" the inventory of any newspaper entry which is over 12 months old and any journal entry which is over 24 months old.

Calculating the total mass storage space demands of such a current events inventory would begin with the estimation of the content and size of an individual entry. Let's suppose that the basic items contained in an entry are to be the following:

- name of the issue addressed by the article
- bibliographical data on the article:
  date of publication
  title of the article
  title of the source (i.e., the journal or newspaper)
  name of the author
- type of article (news, editorial, feature)
- annotation presenting the main points of the article
- name of the person making the inventory entry

To reserve sufficient space for a single entry, we must answer a number of questions. What is the longest name of an issue, the title of an article, the title of a journal or newspaper, or the name of a person (author or person making the entry)? Will the type of article be abbreviated, coded (i.e., indicated by a number), or entered in full? Will the date be numerical (e.g., 3–13–83) or alphanumerical (e.g., 13 March 1983)? What will be the maximum length of an annotation? With the exception of the annotation, all lengths will be estimates, so one must allow a margin as protection against, for example, a later entry with author surname "van der Beverheim-Donkerwyk III."

The estimate of the total number of keystrokes (including spaces) required for a single entry can then be used to estimate the total number of entries that can be held in the computer (during sorting) or on the mass storage medium (for long-term storage). If, for instance, your storage medium is a disk with a capacity of 160,000 keystrokes and the estimated size of a current events entry is 625 keystrokes (a modest estimate, by the way), the inventory is limited to 256 entries. Is this enough to cover all of the possible entries from all of the selected newspapers for 12 months and from all of the selected journals for 24 months? If not, can the capacity of the storage medium be expanded by going to more or larger disks? Can the length of the entry be reduced? Can you reduce the number of sources or the storage time of the entries without destroying the educational value of the inventory? When all is said and done, how long will it take the computer to complete a typical search task such as the locating of all of the news articles on ocean pollution that have appeared in *Time* magazine during the past 24 months? (If it takes 30 minutes, of what value is the inventory to a student population of 150?)

Word processing Examination of the instructional expectations of a word processing system in terms of the possible attributes of such a system will provide insight into the compromises that may be necessary when purchasing word processing software.[4]

---

[4]Recall that the appendix to Chapter 12 is a sample listing of word processor attributes.

Also, word processing activities can become cumbersome (if not wholly useless) if the visual display of the work is restricted to fewer than eighty characters per line. A shorter line prevents the user from seeing the text in a form which adequately resembles the printed version of the document to be generated later.

The success of word processing—and of many other aide-de-camp applications—is often at the mercy of the printing component of the computer system. There is no point buying computers to process student handouts, manuscripts, or other printed material when the quality of the print is in any way less than what can be achieved by other means. Check the type quality and style of the printing device. Can it produce graphics (screen images)? Does it adjust to varying widths of paper? Will it underline? Can it insert words typed in alternate type faces (e.g., italics or boldface type)?

Concern for printing speed leads us to another exercise in arithmetic. The task is to make sure the line-per-minute output of a printer is large enough to cope with the expected total line output of an application in a reasonable amount of time. Also, if the total printing output is large—perhaps requiring hours of uninterrupted printing—the sheer durability of the printing device becomes of paramount interest. The printer which performs faithfully and well on printing tasks which rarely reach thirty minutes in duration may soon collapse when faced with the daily generation of individualized study prescriptions for each of 550 students. The former task calls for a sprinter; the latter, a long-distance runner.

As an example of how to estimate printing demands, let's return to the class in which students are researching current events using an inventory. The system is to be designed to permit the students to print the relevant entries they locate. Let's say that, by experiment, we find that the average entry requries five lines of type, and that an average search will result in the printing of eight entries. Since there are 30 students in a class, this means that a maximum printing task of 40 lines per student will demand the generation of 1200 lines of type. Since an inexpensive printer can produce 60 lines per minute, the maximum task can be completed in 20 minutes on a single printer.

As a second example, let's examine the task of printing individualized study prescriptions for those 550 students. Suppose we find that an individual prescription has an average length of 17 lines and, hence, the daily printing task is 9350 lines. Generation of these prescriptions by our 60-line-per-minute printer would require over two and one-half hours of continuous printing. Even if this were done at night to resolve the time problem, an inexpensive printer really isn't up to that kind of daily grind. It's time to look for heavy duty equipment.

The Numbers Game

Thus far, Chapter 14 has dealt with the problem of matching the purposes of instructional computing—that is, the kinds of applications which are central to one's instructional computing implementation plan—with the general characteristics of the computer system to be used. The system might be comprised of several independent microcomputer units or of terminals served by a large mainframe computer. Whatever the configuration, a next important question is, How many computing units are necessary for the applications planned? (Here a "computing unit" is an individual microcomputer or terminal.)

As in the examples of Chapter 2, the arithmetic of estimating the minimum number of computer units needed calls for four basic figures:

1. the average number of minutes per day that each student will need to interact with the computer;
2. the average number of days that each student will be given to accomplish a computing task;
3. the number of students involved;
4. the number of minutes per day that a single unit will be available for student use.

The figures obtained will depend upon the flexibility in the schedules of the computer-using teachers and the overall flexibility of student scheduling. Do students have unscheduled time during a day? Can the computer units be made available to students during those times? Must all computing work for a given class be done during that class period? Can the availability of the computing facility be "extended" beyond the normal school day; could (would) students make use of that extended availability?

Once the four figures have been obtained, the product of the first three will give an estimate of the total number of computing contact minutes per day that will be required. When divided by the fourth figure (and rounded upwards to the next whole number), the result is a guess at the least number of computing units needed. Well . . . almost.

An Ounce of Prevention

A small dose of pessimism is highly recommended. Assume that something will go wrong, and you'll not be disappointed. Expressed in practical terms of responding to the how-many-computing-units issue, planned pessimism suggests the following rule.

The Backup Dictum

For each nine computing units needed to maintain the instructional computing program, purchase a tenth unit and hide it![5]

While the one-to-nine ratio is a rough one based upon the experiences of schools with which we've had contact, the basic principle is sound. The fact is, equipment will break down. If the day-to-day success of one's instructional computing program depends upon full utilization of every piece of equipment, disaster is but a matter of time. Adherence to The Backup Dictum is simply insurance against such disaster. However, that insurance remains in force only as long as the manager of the program's computing resource yields not to the pleas of teachers and students to remove those reserve units from their hidey-hole for "special" or "limited" uses. Uh-uh! Absolutely not! Once those units enter the operation, the program will expand to demand the upper limit of all units. Disaster is moved to a new level—and is just as certain.

The program security promised by The Backup Dictum is only as great as the intestinal fortitude of the person who guards the key to the hidey-hole. If you're that person, you'll have to defend that sanctuary with the resolve of the legendary Spartans. (Oh—and by the way—stay out of there yourself!)

The ounce of prevention principle should not be restricted to just the terminals or basic microcomputer units. It should, in fact, be extended to cover every item of hardware upon which your instructional computing program depends. Among those items would be such things as printers, disk drives, monitors, cassettes, and computer firmware. Insofar as your educational program is dependent on equipment, think like the National Aeronautics and Space Administration—always have a backup.

A Pound of Cure

Loving tender care notwithstanding, one must assume that the best of equipment will eventually fail. Every instructional computing program must prepare for this eventuality with a maintenance/repair plan.

The key to a good maintenance plan is the availability of service. Generally speaking, the more local and immediate the source of advice or service, the better you will be served. A higher purchase price to a local vendor may be more than balanced by the speed and reliability of service when things go awry. Local dealers may go so far as to promise a "loaner" to replace an ailing piece of equipment while repairs are undertaken. This could override The Backup Dictum and eliminate the need for a hidey-hole.

Many schools have opted for a do-it-yourself (as-far-as-reasonable) maintenance and repair program. Rather than contracting for a maintenance service (a service that can carry a monthly charge of 2 percent of the original value of the hardware) or relying wholly on the local repair shop (which may charge $50–$70 per hour), these schools have personnel who have developed a degree of hardware expertise. Specifically, they have negotiated with the manufacturer (or vendor) to send a teacher or other school employee to the manufacturer's maintenance school. At such a school, the educator can learn to diagnose and correct commonly occurring hardware problems which, while easy to repair, account for a major portion of repair costs and loss of hardware availability. For instance, the trainee can quickly learn to adjust the timing of disk drives (a simple procedure which cures many problems), to clean many of the system's components, or to test for faults in such system components as the memory. At the basic level, this work is performed by running special computer programs designed for repair purposes. The school person merely needs access to the programs and instruction in their use. Other things being relatively equal, willingness of a manufacturer or vendor to provide such maintenance school training might be the consideration which would swing the purchase contract to Brand X computing equipment.

In addition, all school personnel involved in instructional computing should be put through "Gremlin Detection School." The object of the school is to make instructors aware of a variety of *apparent* hardware problems--problems which are, in fact, the easily corrected pranks of student gremlins who have "adjustmented" the equipment in order to test the smarts of their mentors. For instance, a power plug which has been carefully removed part way from the receptacle can give the appearance of a total system's failure; the repair charge of the computer specialist who travels 80 kilometres to detect the problem will not be reduced by the simplicity of the solution. Similar kinds of fiddling with connecting cables, toggle switches, selector knobs, or other manually adjustable features can produce a rich array of apparent disasters. Even inadvertent gremlining (e.g., inserting a disk into the disk drive in the wrong position) can reduce the unaware instructor to a quivering mass of computer-allergic protoplasm and destroy the day's instructional plan.

---

[5] *The Backup Dictum* is exemplified by the following chart.

Units that must be operational at any given time	Backup Units
6–9	1
10–18	2
19–27	3

While gremlinitis is almost impossible to prevent, it is usually easy to control if one recognizes the symptoms. Education in recognizing those symptoms is accomplished by trying your own hand at being a gremlin. In the quiet of some morning or afternoon, creatively seek system havoc. Fiddle with the cords, switches, and knobs both singularly and in combinations; note the results. Make a notebook of bizarre states of the equipment and of their possible causes. Have a colleague randomly generate some of these gremlinesque situations in order to test your notes and deductive powers. A few sessions at the "Gremlin Detection School" will teach you a great deal about your computer system and will work miracles in developing your sense of power over the infernal machine.

If you're worried that you may induce some permanent malfunction by such creative twiddling, explain your plan to the vendor first. The vendor should be able to warn you of any potential problem. However, adjusting accessible controls *shouldn't* result in real damage; if it does, those controls *should not be accessible.* After all, most gremlins won't consult the vendor before making such adjustments.

Eena-Meena-Mina-Mo What Must Micro Buyers Know?

The search for a perfect computing system has taken us down many roads.

- We have explored the many forms in which the computer can enter the classroom as teacher, instructional partner, or aide.
- We have reviewed case studies of how specific groups of educators have implemented instructional computing.
- We have done our sums to estimate the number and performance capabilities of the computer units needed to support a given implementation plan.
- We have looked ahead to the tasks of staff training and hardware maintenance.
- We have examined software issues which must be resolved before purchasing a computer system.

The entire computer system selection process has now been reduced to the question "Which one(s)?"

At this point, most educational agencies will prepare a *specifications sheet* which details the minimal performance characteristics of the system(s) to be purchased. This sheet expresses the main points of the implementation plan in terms of the basic capabilities of the computing system needed to execute it. It is this document which will guide the bidding of vendors and which will guarantee that the successful bidder can deliver the fundamental materials and services required by that plan. A carefully prepared specifications sheet has the effect of eliminating many computing systems from further consideration.

Big Versus Appropriate

If your planning has resulted in the decision to investigate the purchase of a large, centralized computing system, you should seek professional help in preparing your specifications sheet. Such a system can mean the commitment of millions of dollars over a period of several years. Just because a system is "big" or "powerful" doesn't mean that it is suitable for the instructional applications that you have planned. In fact, many large systems are designed for business or administrative applications, and internal priorities can be set to give preference to the processing of such applications; students trying to access the system for instructional purposes can be subjected to long delays. Unless administrators are willing to schedule their processing for hours which lie outside the prime-time periods of an extended instructional day, your instructional computing plan can be destroyed.

Deliberations over the selection of a large, central system must be guided by an independent computing system consultant (i.e., one who is *not* a vendor for any manufacturer), who can assess the demands of all users and translate those demands into system specifications. An instructional computing plan and the interpretive input of teachers who developed that plan are invaluable components of these deliberations since it is reasonable to assume that (a) most computing consultants will know much less about educational applications than about business/administrative applications and (b) most large computing systems were not designed to accommodate instructional applications. If "delivery of instruction" is narrowly interpreted to be "teaching programming languages," you may find yourself burdened with an expensive system which has neither the software nor the specialized hardware required for tutorials, simulations, instructional management, or other educational applications.

General Specifications

Participation in the selection of any computing system will immediately cause you to think about some general constraints. Broad specifications regarding cost, computing power, memory size, and future expansion of the system will eliminate many systems from further consideration. That done, they lead to detailed specifications which will serve as a sieve through which to pass the claims of the remaining vendors.

Cost True, overall cost will be a primary constraint throughout the deliberations. The gross figure will set the upper limits of your "want list," but it must not be allowed to significantly alter the goals of your implementation plan. If your plan calls for twenty computing units with the ability to display high-resolution graphics, a "bargain" deal for thirty-five units with low graphics capability is no bargain. If your budget request of $62,000 is countered by a district offer of an $870,000 system with thirty terminals but no instructional software, the generous offer is a gold-plated bomb. (If these chapters have done nothing else, they should have convinced you that the programming of instructional software is not a spare-time activity for classroom teachers.)

The way to deal with the cost constraint is to set priorities within the instructional computing plan. Any good plan will look beyond what can be afforded at a particular moment, but it also will clearly direct the spending of limited funds *in a manner consistent with the long-range objectives of the plan.* Cost constraints may temporarily limit the extent of the implementation, but they must not alter its objectives. The planner must remain immune to bargains or generous gifts which do not serve those objectives. Contracting for fifty splendid new compact trucks rather than two heavy-duty vans won't serve a plan for the transcontinental relocation of an endangered herd of elephants. Introducing a revised plan to relocate warthogs could make excellent use of the compact trucks, but something basic will have been lost in the bargain.

Raw power There are several measures of power (speed) that can be applied to computers. Several computing journals regularly publish test results on computers and peripheral equipment of all types. These tests, called *benchmark* tests, are composed of a series of well-defined tasks a computer should be able to perform. Performance on the tests is usually rated in terms of speed. All other considerations being equal (a rare event), benchmark results could form a basis for deciding among competing machines. Realistically, however, speed is a consideration which is far back in the queue of selection criteria—a queue that is headed by questions of software availability and hardware reliability.

Memory size This gets a bit technical, so remember that there is a glossary attached to this book. The concepts to be discussed aren't all that difficult, but there is a need to employ a word or two of computerese.

The memory of a computer can be measured in electronic chunks called bytes. However, not all machines have the same size byte. The first popular microcomputers, for instance, ingested information in 8-bit bytes; currently, there seems to be a transition to a 16-bit byte. Some computer watchers predict that the 8-bit machines will soon be antiques. Maybe so, but the overriding concern for today's buyer remains whether software will be available to do the instructional tasks projected for the next five to seven years (which is the usual lifespan of a computer). A newer model, devoid of a variety of instructional software, will serve only those wishing to teach programming or problem solving. The model of the future is just that. Our purposes dictate that we confine our interests to models which can meet our instructional needs right now. The future will take care of itself.

A general rule with respect to memory is "More is better." Small memories, like small minds, won't support exciting applications. Many instructional applications on microcomputers will call for 48 kilobytes of memory. Programs that assume a 48-kilobyte memory simply will not run on a machine with a smaller memory. Sometimes the program can be rewritten (e.g., broken into smaller programs which can be chained together), but the cost of such rewriting could exceed the cost of purchasing the additional memory.

It is also important to distinguish among the mass storage memory, the resident memory, and the usable memory of a computing system. Mass storage memory can be large on even the smallest of microcomputers, with a capacity of 320 kilobytes being commonplace. This memory, comprised of information stored on tapes or disks, is external to the main computer. It serves as a library which the computer can search for facts or procedures needed for a particular computing job. The ease (speed) with which the computer can conduct that search depends upon the medium on which the information is stored (e.g., cassette tape or disk) and the manner in which the computer software conducts the search. Once the information is located, it must be transferred to the computer's resident memory before it can be used. How much can be transferred depends upon the total size of that resident memory and upon how much of that resident memory is already occupied by other information that may not be purged in order to make room for the material to be transferred. For instance, a microcomputer system with a total resident memory of 16 kilobytes may require 12.5 kilobytes for the storage of the language (BASIC) needed to execute the program. The usable memory of the system is thus a mere 3.5 kilobytes. There's little that one can do with such a small usable memory. From the standpoint of instructional computing, a machine with such a small usable memory would be unusable. When it comes to memory, remember to think big.

Expansion and compatibility In attending to the task of identifying a system that can deliver basic services here and now, don't lose sight of the need for expansion and change during the life of the system selected. Instructional applications will broaden and improve in keeping with the work of experts in the field and in keeping with the growth of our own ambitions, skills, and instructional computing sophistication. Desired changes may call for larger memories, increased storage capacities, or new peripheral equipment. What are the options, costs, and limitations associated with expanding the computing system(s) under consideration? Can the basic computer system make use of special peripherals produced by other manufacturers or is it essentially a "one brand" system? If the basic system can be adapted for addition of hardware from other sources, how much cost and system modification is required to permit those additions? Can the graphics capability be improved? Can voice or nonvoice audio be added? Is color available through the instructions of the programming language? Can color be displayed by the monitors and the printers? What computing languages are available and at what cost? How long does the company plan to make (and, by the way, service) this model?

A Sample Necessities/Niceties Specifications Procedure

A few years ago, the authors had the opportunity to purchase a single microcomputer system. Without involving you in a discussion of the tasks that the system was to serve, we think you might profit from learning about a technique employed during the final stage of the selection process.

Our review of the general specifications just discussed had reduced the field of choice to four microcomputer systems. (We'll refer to these systems as Brands W, X, Y, and Z.) Also, we had prepared a "want list" of detailed specifications and had divided the specifications of that list into two categories: *Necessities* and *Niceties*.

The *Necessities* category covered those features which were critical to accomplishing the instructional computing objectives to which the system was to be devoted. The list read as follows:

Necessities

a. 32 kilobytes of usable memory
b. black-and-white monitor
c. standard keyboard
d. printer port
e. printer interface
f. BASIC language
g. disk drive
h. disk interface
i. maintenance available locally[6]

[6]The cost of the maintenance was not a factor. Only its availability was important.

The cost of obtaining each of those Necessities on a Brand W (X, Y, or Z) computer system was to be used to compute the total cost of purchasing a computer system from the vendor of that brand.

Beyond the Necessities, we listed certain *Niceties* of the proposed systems. The Niceties were features which would simplify or enhance the use of the system but which were not absolute requirements for the task at hand:

Niceties

a. numerical keypad on the keyboard
b. color capability in the software
c. color monitor
d. graphics resolution finer than 128 by 128
e. may open for repair without losing warranty
f. single-unit construction
g. compatible with existing peripherals
h. extra memory included
i. dual-density disk drive

These two lists were combined into the sample Systems Evaluation Chart which appears as Appendix 1 to this chapter. The data (costs and comments) recorded in each column of the chart were obtained by visiting with vendors and by reading the brochures which they provided. Based upon that data, we opted for Brand W, although campus politics later necessitated a compromise (Brand X).

Politics aside, the procedure was a good one. It revealed that three of four systems could guarantee all of the Necessities. While Brands Y and Z had basic prices that were lower than Brands W and X, it was clear that the Niceties to be found in Brands W and X would more than outweigh the small differences in cost. Had basic cost or the Necessities been the only considerations in our search, we would not have made the best choice.

The lists of Necessities and Niceties in our Systems Evaluation chart were relatively short. Our budget was small, and our instructional computing task was both simple and well defined. Should you develop a Systems Evaluation Chart to guide your purchasing deliberations, be certain to make the lists as long and detailed as your implementation plan demands. In fact, leave some blanks at the bottom of the Niceties list so that you can later add those unanticipated but really nice Niceties that you discover during the evaluation procedure. Appendix 2 to this chapter mentions several items that you may wish to consider when constructing your list.

A Word in Defense of Diversity

An instructional computing system has been defined as a composite of many related items of hardware and software. These items constitute a system in that they work together to serve the goals of a unified plan for the instructional application of computers.

In the implementation profiles of Chapter 13 and in the sample list of Niceties just presented, we have lauded the use of single brand of computing equipment (or, at least, of electronically compatible equipment). We would be remiss in our duties as consultants if we failed to note also an argument against such uniformity.

The cardinal rule for selecting computing equipment is that the system(s) purchased be optimally suited to attaining the objectives of the implementation plan. If that plan extends over several grade levels, includes a variety of applications, and makes use of microcomputers, there is a good chance that no single type of microcomputer will serve all grade levels and applications equally well.

For instance, the problem-solving, simulation, and word-processing applications of a secondary school may require a system having excellent graphics capability and a mass storage system which is both large and easily searched. Such a system might constitute an extravagance (in terms of cost and/or performance) in elementary-school applications which focus on the delivery of short tutorial, drill, or practice lessons. Whereas the availability of color might be a frill in terms of the planned secondary-school applications in mathematics and science, it might be central to the models displayed in elementary-school mathematics lessons or to lessons in reading or writing music. The unique features of the business-oriented software of Brand M may make it the only sensible choice for the applications envisioned in that area; on the other hand, Brand M may be quite unacceptable for the proposed instructional management of the social studies curriculum.

Clearly, one doesn't want a different brand of equipment in every classroom. The staff training and hardware maintenance problems posed by such an arrangement could be overwhelming. On the other hand, it is equally foolish to insist that all aspects of an instructional computing plan must be met by a single type of computing equipment. The wise buy is still the purchase which matches the purpose.

APPENDIX 1

SAMPLE OF A SYSTEMS EVALUATION CHART

Necessities

Specification	*Brand W*	*Brand X*	*Brand Y*	*Brand Z*
basic cost with 32K usable memory	$1300	$1500	$2000	$1500
black-and-white monitor	150	200	included	included
standard keyboard	included	included	included	included
printer port	included	included	included	included
printer interface	150	200	included	included
BASIC language	included	included	included	included
disk drive	600	400	included	400
disk interface	200	200	included	200
local maintenance available	yes	yes	soon	yes
TOTAL COST OF SYSTEM	$2400	$2500	$2000	$2100

Niceties

Specification	*Brand W*	*Brand X*	*Brand Y*	*Brand Z*
numerical keypad on the keyboard	yes	no	yes	yes
color capability in the software	no	yes	yes	no
color monitor	no	yes	yes	no
graphics resolution finer than 128 X 128	yes (512x240)	no	no	no
can be opened for repair without losing warranty	yes	yes	?	no
single-unit construction	no	no	yes	yes
compatible with existing peripherals	yes	no	no	no
extra memory included	no	yes(16K)	no	no
dual-density disk drive	yes	no	no	no

APPENDIX 2

PURCHASING CONSIDERATIONS: ASSORTED HARDWARE FEATURES

This is a partial listing of hardware features to consider—either as necessities or as niceties—when you prepare to purchase. Which will be viewed as necessities or as niceties must, of course, be defined by the uses you propose for the hardware. The purpose of the list is to help get your intellectual juices flowing. The list employs many computing terms. Again, the Beginner's Glossary of Computerese should help break the code.

1. Documentation
   a. available now
   b. instructions written for the nonprogrammer
   c. details available for programmers or technicians
2. Adequate demonstration/instruction in use
   a. available at the vendor's establishment
   b. provided on-site for users
   c. consulting service available as needed
   d. overall ease of operation for nonprogrammer
3. Hardware source reliability
   a. established reputation of manufacturer
   b. established reputation of local dealer
4. Service
   a. provisions of the warranty
   b. local service available
   c. "loaners" available
   d. training in simple maintenance available
5. Mainframe
   a. compactness of unit
   b. expandability
   c. type of chip and bus
   d. byte size (8-bit, 16-bit, etc.)
   e. sensitivity to heat, movement, static, dust
   f. variable BAUD rates
6. Resident memory
   a. total bytes provided
   b. total bytes usable for program execution
   c. maximum memory size
   d. cost of additional memory
7. Mass storage
   a. cassette
   b. floppy diskette:
      number
      density (single, double, quad)
      total bytes per diskette
   c. hard disk
8. Terminal (keyboard and monitor)
   a. type: intelligent or dumb
   b. standard QWERTY keyset arrangement
   c. numeric pad
   d. special function keys
   e. screen resolution (40 x 40, 128 x 128, 240 x 512, etc.)
   f. monitor or television set
   g. black and white, color
   h. outlet for additional monitor (to daisy-chain)
9. Printer
   a. speed
   b. noise level
   c. type(s) of paper
   d. line width(s)
   e. graphics capability
10. Software available
    a. instructional courseware
    b. service/maintenance software
    c. networking software
    d. backup copy provided
    e. procedure for replacing or correcting faulty software (warranty)
    f. computing languages available; resident memory requirements of each; editor characteristics
11. Other accessories
    a. card reader: mark-sense or punch speed
    b. paddles or joy stick; external port
    c. sensory equipment (light sensor, temperature probe)
12. Continuing costs
    a. paper
    b. diskettes; tapes
    c. service contracts

STUDY GUIDE: CHAPTER 14

1. Simulate the process of preparing to purchase microcomputer systems with the following steps.
   a. Adopt some implementation plan.
   b. With the help of Appendix 2 to this chapter, develop a list of necessities and niceties relative to the system(s) to be purchased. Prepare a Systems Evaluation Chart like that in Appendix 1.
   c. Gather information on four or five microcomputer systems of possible interest. This information can come from periodicals, vendor literature, or visits to vendors.
   d. Fill in the cells of your Systems Evaluation Chart.
   e. Make a purchasing decision.
2. The 32 students in Journalism II at Very High School have access to a national newspaper data base through a dial-up service. The data base indexes news articles, feature articles, and editorials from three news services and 118 newspapers.

   Students conducting a data search on any topic will download the text of relevant items onto a disk and print hard copy of the items using a printer. Each student will make approximately 2 searches per week. Each search will locate an average of 12 items; each item will have a text summary of no more than 225 words.

   Recommend adequate printing equipment for this class.
3. In what basic way do the software considerations of Chapter 14 differ from those of Chapter 4?
4. What is the instructional significance of The Backup Dictum?
5. Working as a group, prepare an Instructional Computing Implementation Proposal having the five sections noted in ICAC Memo #13. You may be able to extract useful suggestions from the remarks made by Superintendent Ennis in her memorandum of June 24, 1983 (see the Epilogue to the Agenda for Action which follows this chapter).

AGENDA FOR ACTION

University of Illinois
at Urbana-Champaign

Department of Secondary Education

395 Education Building
1310 South Sixth Street
Champaign
Illinois 61820

College of Education

217 333-0227

MEMORANDUM

TO: Members of ICAC

FROM: Dick Dennis and Bob Kansky

RE: ICAC Paper 14

DATE: May 13, 1983

You've probably noticed that each issue of each instructional or personal computing journal is replete with announcements of whole new computing systems and of hundreds of new items of software and hardware to be used with "old" systems. Claims of computing excellence are couched in the peculiar language of computerese with its bits, bytes, disk drives, DOS, graphics tablets, high-level languages, interfaces, ports, RAM, ROM, and syntax. Somehow educators are supposed to cut through this jargon and electronic ballyhoo in order to purchase the computing system(s) that will support their instructional computing plans.

The goal of ICAC Paper 14 is to aid you in answering the questions "Which one(s) do we buy?" and "How many units do we need?" Since answering these questions will require that you read the documents of computer manufacturers and invade the dens of computer vendors, we again urge you to consult the glossary of computer-related terms. Written in what we hope you agree is understandable English, this "primer of computerese" could ease you through those first encounters with computing enthusiasts. To further condition you, we have employed many of the glossary's terms when writing ICAC Paper 14.

DD:BK:glm

AGENDA FOR ACTION

Obourn Senior High School

200 Woodbine Avenue
East Roachmont, New York

M. Jack Stivers
Principal

(716) 568-8840

ICAC Memo #14

TO: Members of ICAC

FROM: John Russell

DATE: May 27, 1983

REPORT OF ACTIVITIES

1. Lolita's presentation at Bird Elementary School was more than a success! She's had requests to repeat it at another school as well as at a luncheon meeting of one of East Roachmont's service clubs.
2. Phil, Lolita, and John have applied for summer institutes on instructional computing. The brochures suggest that the competition for positions in these institutes will be keen, so they've requested written support from Dr. Ennis.
3. All preparations for the opinions survey are complete. Data will be gathered on Tuesday and Wednesday of next week.
4. Carrinne used the May 20 meeting of the school board to alert board members to the fact that our purchasing proposal will be submitted in time for action at their June 17 meeting. She will inform John of any specific comments by the board that should be considered when drafting the proposal.
5. A draft of the implementation plan (prepared with the help of our word processor) will be distributed for committee discussion at our next—and final—meeting.

COMMITTEE ASSIGNMENTS

1. Phil, with the help of suggestions from Lolita, will prepare a demonstration program for the faculty at Morgan Junior High and for the Parent/Student/Teachers Association. Both have expressed interest. (Work with these new populations should provide direction for our inservice activities next year.)
2. Ted and Carrinne will design a 20-minute presentation of our implementation plan for the school board meeting on June 17. Both feel that the presentation should be made with the aid of the video projector.
3. John will prepare a Systems Evaluation Chart (as in Appendix 1 of Chapter 14) for inclusion in the implementation plan and will use the concepts of Necessities and Niceties to express ICAC's priorities. Although final bidding of the systems must be left to the district purchasing office, such a chart should go far in supporting our arguments within the plan and, hence, in assuring that the system(s) purchased will fit the plan.
4. Lolita, Gerri, Ted, and John will devote Saturday, June 4, to drafting the purchasing proposal. Copies of the draft will be circulated to the committee in preparation for the review meeting on June 7. This will allow enough time for revision before it is mailed to the school board members by Dr. Ennis on June 10.

JR:ms

EPILOGUE TO THE AGENDA FOR ACTION

THE ICAC EXPERIENCE CONCLUDED

EAST ROACHMONT INDEPENDENT SCHOOL DISTRICT
108 East Avenue
East Roachmont, New York

Dr. Josephine G. Ennis
Superintendent

(716) 568-8804

MEMORANDUM

TO: The Instructional Computing Advisory Committee
FROM: Dr. Josephine Ennis
RE: Board Action on Instructional Computing Purchasing Proposal
DATE: June 24, 1983

I am pleased to report that the East Roachmont School Board has taken favorable action with respect to all five sections of the Instructional Computing Implementation Proposal. Although the funds at hand are not sufficient to authorize purchase of all of the items requested, I assure you that the board was pleased by the quality of the proposal and treated it as generously as possible. I am confident that the board will be willing to consider additional purchases as monies become available.

A detailed list of the purchases authorized by the board is in preparation. John Russell will send a copy to each committee member. The purpose of this memorandum is to explain that detailed list by summarizing the board's actions with respect to each of the five sections of your proposal.

1. Computer Hardware
   a) Although the total budget was reduced by 37.4%, authorized items include all of those which you listed under Priority 1 and several of those listed under Priority 2. It is suggested that the items under Priorities 3 and 4 be held over for resubmission at some future date. The hardware purchased should be sufficient to equip three computerized learning laboratories and one computerized demonstration classroom.
   b) All equipment should be delivered within 45 days, thus allowing installation and testing before the schools reopen.
   c) The 12-month maintenance contracts guarantee service on most items within 48 hours of a reported failure.
2. Computer Courseware
   a) The board authorized the purchase of all items listed under Priority 1.
   b) Items under Priorities 2–4 have been referred to the Council of School Administrators with the board recommendation that such courseware be purchased with funds from individual school budgets. The programs to be purchased will be those selected by the various schools' faculties.
   c) The board endorsed the proposal that students be assigned instructional programming tasks as part of their course work in computer programming classes whenever appropriate.
   d) The board authorized school principals to make use of their part-time staffing monies to hire qualified student programmers to assist faculty members.

e) School principals have been advised of the availability of the Courseware Standards Guide developed by the ICAC. This is an excellent document. It will be suggested that courseware development throughout the district should conform to the Standards.

f) A District Courseware Clearinghouse (Grades K-12) will be established within the Obourn High School media center. The clearinghouse will be charged with the tasks of recording a description and evaluation of all courseware purchased or written by the district, gathering information regarding sources of courseware, and aiding teachers in obtaining courseware for evaluation purposes. Courseware will be catalogued using the committee's suggested Computerized Courseware Matrix.

3. Laboratory/Classroom Space

a) A classroom will be designated as a Computerized Learning Laboratory at each of the following schools:

   Bird Elementary School
   Morgan Junior High School
   Obourn Senior High School

The required electrical and security modifications will be made during the summer.

b) A Computerized Demonstration Classroom will be established at Obourn Senior High School.

4. Teacher Inservice Activities

a) Teachers will be offered the opportunity to participate in an Instructional Computing Awareness Seminar. Attendance will be voluntary; enrollment will be limited. The seminar should be designed to meet the teacher needs and interests as expressed through the Instructional Computing Opinion Survey conducted earlier by the committee. It will include hands-on experience with computing equipment.

b) Teachers will be offered the opportunity to participate in a Computer Programming Seminar which will make use of the equipment purchased by the district. Enrollment will be limited.

c) The board has authorized the purchase of such courseware as is needed for the seminars and the payment of salaries for instructors qualified to teach them.

d) University credit and/or district inservice credit will be attached to the seminars.

e) Presentations regarding the district's venture into instructional computing will be scheduled as part of the districtwide Fall Inservice Program which precedes the opening of the next school term.

5. Policy and Planning

a) The board authorized an operational budget (including travel) for a continuing Instructional Computing Policy Committee. The committee will be charged to advise the board regarding the development of instructional computing throughout the District.

b) The board authorized the allocation of two half-time teaching positions to the development of the district's instructional computing programs. As specified by the committee, these two positions would be devoted to the planning/executing of teacher inservice, the evaluation of the overall program of instructional computing throughout the district, the facilitation of communication among computer-using teachers, and the assisting/advising of teachers wishing to initiate instructional uses of computers. The persons in these two positions will be ex officio members of the Instructional Computing Policy Committee. (NOTE: The board here deviated from the ICAC suggestion that these persons be voting members of the policy committee. The board felt that the making of policy should be guided by but not determined by those persons charged with its implementation.)

JE:sn

EPILOGUE TO THE AGENDA FOR ACTION

Obourn Senior High School

200 Woodbine Avenue
East Roachmont, New York

M. Jack Stivers
Principal

(716) 568-8840

ICAC Memo #15

TO: Members of ICAC

FROM: John Russell

DATE: June 27, 1983

RE: Closing the Shop

The detailed list of instructional computing purchases authorized by the school board is on its way to you under separate cover. Modesty prevents my congratulating us for our cleverness in listing priorities in our proposal; nevertheless, it was a stroke of genius. As you will see, the cuts made by the board clearly followed our stated priorities and, as a result, the program came through intact.

Thanks to strong recommendations from Superintendent Ennis, three of us (Phil, Lolita, and I) will be attending instructional computing workshops during the latter part of this summer. Dr. Ennis submitted the ICAC purchasing proposal as an addendum to her letter of recommendation; she feels that this evidence of planning and commitment was a major factor in our being accepted in the workshops.

Finally, I want to thank you for making ICAC a success. We've learned a lot together, and we've helped Roachmont to move with confidence into the realm of instructional computing. It's going to be an exciting fall!

JR:ms

Enclosure

A Beginner's Glossary of Computerese

Even the friendliest computer salesperson is wont to use a few items of computer jargon when discussing a computer system. Far from wishing to befuddle or intimidate a potential customer, the salesperson is trying to give an accurate description of the hardware or software being marketed. Also, computer vendors spend much time in conversation with persons who are familiar with the vocabulary of the world of computing. Subsequent, honest attempts to answer the questions of an eager novice may leave the salesperson tongue-tied because he or she is not prepared to talk about computers using precomputer English.

This glossary is offered as a verbal survival kit. It should sustain you during brief visits to the Wonderful World of Computer Hardware, Software, and Assorted Electronic Doo-Dahs. For those who plan to take up extended residence in that World, greater fluency in Computerese is obligatory.[1]

Use of the glossary is aided by awareness of two features of its design. First, many of the glossary entries include words or phrases which are printed in italic letters. This printing convention is used to alert you to the fact that each such word or phrase is defined elsewhere in the glossary. Second, the space labeled *NOTES* has been provided for your entry of new items or of better wording of existing items.

---

[1]Two possible sources are *The Illustrated Computer Dictionary* by Donald D. Spencer (Columbus, OH: Charles E. Merrill Publishing Company, 1980) and the more comprehensive *Computer Dictionary*, 2nd ed., by Charles J. and Roger J. Sippl (Indianapolis, IN: Howard W. Sams & Company, Inc., 1980).

Acoustic Coupler: A device that allows a computer to "talk" to another computer (or some other piece of *hardware)* via an ordinary telephone set.

ALGOL: The acronym for ALGOrithmic Language. This *high-level language* was designed for application of the computer to scientific problems.

Algorithm (or **Algorism**): A step-by-step procedure that, precisely executed by a person or a machine, yields consistently correct and/or excellent results.

Alphanumeric Character: A keyboard character that is either a numeral or a letter of an alphabet.

Ancillary Materials: Noncomputerized materials (books, worksheets, charts, physical models, laboratory equipment) required for use with computerized *courseware.*

Array: An electronic set of numbered cubbyholes used to store information. The information in a particular cubbyhole is accessed by referring to the number of that cubbyhole.

ASCII (pronounced *as-key):* The acronym for American Standard Code for Information Interchange. This code represents an agreement to equate each symbol (such as a letter of the alphabet) with a particular number. Thus, a computer uses ASCII to associate the letter *A* with the number 65. (Why 65? Well . . .)

Author Language: A programming language designed specifically for the authoring of programs associated with instructional applications of computers. Some sample authoring languages have the names COURSEWRITER, PAL, PILOT, and PLANIT.

Backup: Duplicate *disk* of important *data* or *programs* stored as insurance from possible loss or destruction of an original disk copy.

Backup Memory: See *Mass Storage Memory.*

BASIC: The acronym for Beginner's All-purpose Symbolic Instruction Code. This is a *high-level language,* some dialect of which is available on almost any computer. It is a popular, easily learned language for persons who want to tell a computer what to do.

Baud Rate: A measure of the speed with which devices in a computer system exchange information. A typist can type at about 100 Baud (10 keyboard characters per second or about 75 words per minute). A microcomputer can command an inexpensive *printer* to type that material at 800 Baud (80 keyboard characters per second or about 600 words per minute). The same microcomputer can exchange textual information with its *disk drives* at 9600 Baud (960 keyboard characters per second or about 7200 words per minute).

NOTES

Binary: A system of numeration used by computers or by people with only two fingers. It can represent any number by using only *0*'s and *1*'s rather than using all ten digits of the decimal system (0, 1, 2, . . . 9). It's nice for computers, since it allows them to represent numbers using the two states of a circuit (*1* for open and *0* for closed). If you feel that you, too, must speak in binary, see your local *computernik.*

Bit: A single *0* or *1* stored in a computer. It is the smallest piece of information that the computer can store using *binary* representation. The word comes from 'BInary digiT' since a *0* or *1* is a single digit of a binary numeral.

Bit Pad: Sometimes called a *graphics tablet,* it is a piece of *hardware* that speeds up the programming of elaborate art work. Graphics drawn directly on the surface of this device can be immediately stored as parts of a computer program.

Boot: The use of a short *program* (bootstrap) to *load* a larger and more sophisticated program (e.g., DOS or a *high-level language*) into the *main memory* of the system.

Bug: The cause of a foul-up in the functioning of a computer system. It is most commonly used to refer to an error (in design or typing) by a programmer. It is less frequently used to refer to a *hardware* malfunction (see *Glitch*).

Bus (or Buss): The electronic means by which information moves about among the components of a computer system.

Byte: A bunch of *bits.* The number of *bits* in a byte may be 8, 16, or more depending upon the computer. Most microcomputers have 8-bit or 16-bit bytes. As a rule of thumb, you can think of a byte as corresponding to the *memory* space occupied by one *alphanumeric character.*

Cassette: Short for "cassette tape player/recorder," a common and inexpensive device used for the mass storage of *computer programs* and data on magnetic tapes. The device is less reliable and much slower than a *disk drive.*

Cassette Tape: The magnetic tape used by a *cassette.* The tape is housed in small, plastic cartridges for easy use and storage.

Central Processing Unit: See *CPU.*

Chaining: A feature of a computing language that allows the programmer to instruct the computer to terminate the execution of one *program* and begin the execution of another *program.*

Chaining-with-Variables: A variation on *chaining* that permits the programmer to store the information obtained while executing one program and then to use it after *chaining* to another program.

NOTES

Chip: A tiny wafer of silicon (about 5 millimetres on a side) etched with complex electronic circuitry. Some chips are wholly devoted to the storage of colossal amounts of information (memory chips); others combine memory with logic circuitry to form a complete computer-on-a-chip.

COBOL: The acronym for COmmon Business-Oriented Language. This is a *high-level language* designed specifically for folks who want to make business applications of computers.

Code: 1. Something written in a computer language. 2. An alternate way of representing textual input to a computer (e.g., *ASCII*). 3. The name of a common disease as pronounced by a sufferer.

Command: A request (such as *LOAD* or *RUN*) that is executed immediately when input by the user. The *command* should be distinguished from the *instruction* (or *statement*) which is a term used in writing a computer program.

Compiler: A *program* used by a computer to translate an entire program written in *high-level language* into a program written in *machine language*. Unlike an *interpreter*, a compiler does the whole translation job before executing a single instruction of the original program. After that, it can execute the program (via the machine language version) very efficiently without having to repeat the translation process.

Computer: A device that can manipulate either *text* or numbers under the control of a stored *program*, a program which may be altered. Many *microprocessors* do not permit the alteration of the stored program; programmable calculators can manipulate numbers but not text.

Computer Program: See *Program*.

Computerese: The mind-boggling jargon of the *computernik*. Reputed to have its origin in English.

Computernik: The generator/user of *computerese*. Reputed to have its origin in humankind.

Computer System: The composite of all of the *hardware* (the *computer* and its *peripherals*) and *software* which interact in a computing task.

Courseware: A set of computer *programs* with which a student has direct interaction during a learning sequence.

CPU: The abbreviation for Central Processing Unit. In the microcomputing world, the term is used to refer to that computer-on-a-chip which is the "brain" of the computer system.

CRT: The abbreviation for Cathode Ray Tube. Think of it as the screen of a television set and you'll be okay.

Cursor: A visible object (example: ■, +, ●, –, >) that moves around the face of the *CRT* to let you know where the next symbol that you type will appear.

NOTES

Data: Any kind of numbers, letters, sounds, electronic impulses, etc., which can be *input* or *output* by a *computer system.*

Data Base: A collection of *Data* that has been logically organized for efficient access and manipulation by a *computer.*

Data Base Management System (DBMS): An item of *software* that allows the user to easily manipulate and view the contents of a *data base.*

Debugging: The locating and eradicating of *bugs.*

Demonstration Program: A type of *software* designed for classroom discussions. Its use in instruction requires that it be executed by a teacher who understands its specific purpose and options. External *documentation* of the program must be provided for the teacher (see Chapter 12).

DIP: The acronym for Dual In-Line Package. It's a chunk of plastic that houses a *chip,* protecting that chip from dust and damp while connecting it electronically to other chips. (This relationship is one origin of the term chip-and-dip.)

Disk: An object which looks like a phonograph record. It is used by a computer as a medium on which to store masses of information.

Disk Drive: A *peripheral* that spins a *disk* at high speed while information is being stored on or retrieved from that disk by the computer.

Diskette: A *disk* made of relatively thin plastic and stored within a protective envelope.

Documentation: The written description of computer *software* or *hardware.*

DOS (pronounced *doss):* The acronym for Disk Operating System, the programs which facilitate use of the *disk drives.*

Drill Program: A type of *software* that aids the fixing of stimulus-response associations. For contrast, note the definition of *practice* (see Chapter 7).

Dumb Terminal: Something of a slur in computerese, the adjective *dumb* is used to describe a terminal which is limited to performing two jobs: it sends information to the computer to which it is connected, and it receives information from that computer (also see *Intelligent Terminal*).

Editing: The making of corrections in a computer *program* or in a collection of data used by that program.

Editor: A *program* which assists a person who is doing *editing.*

Execute: To *run* any portion of a *program.*

External Memory: See *Mass Storage Memory.*

Firmware: Items in the never-never land between *hardware* and *software.* They are, in fact, computer *programs* which are firmly locked into a *ROM.*

Notes

Floppy Disk: A flexible *diskette* used by most microcomputers.

Flow Chart: A diagram which presents a step-by-step solution to a problem.

FORTRAN: The abbreviation for FORmula TRANslation. Expressions in this widely-used *higher-level language* have a strong resemblance to algebraic expressions. It's not surprising, therefore, that the FORTRAN language is favored by those who are engaged in mathematical, scientific, or engineering applications of computers.

Glitch: A *bug* in *hardware* (rather than in *software*).

Graphics: Computer-created visual images.

Graphics Tablet: See *Bit Pad.*

Hardcopy: The printed form of a computer *program*, its output, or the data used by it.

Hardware: The tangible parts of a *computer system.*

High-Level Language: A human-oriented language used for communicating with a computer. Both the vocabulary and *syntax* of such a language are "natural" to the user. Since, in fact, the computer speaks only *machine language,* communication is delayed by the computer's need to translate the statements of the high-level language by means of *interpreter* or *compiler* programs.

Hi-Res Graphics: *Graphics* created by programs that draw by illuminating individual *pixels* on a video screen. Screens used for hi-res graphics will have from tens to hundreds of thousands of *pixels* depending upon the screen size and clarity of the image produced.

Information Generation Program: A type of *software* that is designed to generate data without any suggestion as to the use of that data. Use is determined by the person employing the *program;* the same data may, then, have many applications.

Initialize: A procedure by which the *DOS* prepares a *disk* for the task of storing information.

Input: Information entering a *computer system* through one of its ports.

Instruction: This commonly refers to the smallest piece of *code* (perhaps a single word or symbol) within a computer *program* which results in an action by the *computer system.*

Instructional Gaming Program: A type of *software* that uses a game environment (rules, randomness, competition) to promote a search for problem-solving strategies (see Chapter 11).

Instructional Management Program: A type of *software* that executes a number of supervisory tasks for the teacher. Acting upon curricular decisions and resource lists specified by a teacher, this type of *program* can make instructional diagnoses, prescribe assignments, evaluate student progress, evaluate resource effectiveness, keep student records, maintain student-student and student-teach-

NOTES

er communication, and manage the use of limited resources (see Chapter 9).

Instructional Support Program: A type of *software* designed to aid in the location of instructional resources, the dissemination and improvement of locally generated educational products, and the selection of instructional materials (see Chapter 12).

Intelligent Terminal: Something of an overstatement in computerese, the adjective *intelligent* is used to describe a *terminal* which can do something more than just send information to (or receive information from) the computer to which it is connected. Intelligent terminals often contain *microprocessors* that can do some data manipulation, thus reducing the workload of the main computer.

Interface Device: A piece of electronic wizardry that allows two parts of a *computer system* (e.g., the *CPU* and a *printer)* to communicate.

Interpreter: A *program* used by the computer to carry out a statement-by-statement translation of a *high-level language* into *machine language.* An interpreter program translates and executes one instruction at a time; it repeats this statement-by-statement, translate-and-execute procedure each time it is called upon to *run* the high-level language program.

I/O: Shorthand referring to an Input and/or Output device. Input devices include such objects as keyboards and mark-sense document readers; output devices include *printers* and *CRT*s.

Kilobyte (K): The term is used in measuring the number of *bytes* of information that can be stored in a computer's *resident memory* or on some mass storage medium such as a *disk.* A kilobyte is 1024 *bytes,* but most folks round off to 1000 *bytes* for ease of thinking. Thus, to say a computer has "64K of memory" means that it has about 64,000 *bytes* of memory—i.e., it can store about 64,000 *alphanumeric characters.*

Lesson Authoring System: A set of computer *programs* which, acting together, permit a nonprogrammer to create and refine instructional *courseware.* The subject matter content of the instructional program is provided by the teacher-author; the format and instructional options are provided by the system. Systems exist which will aid the teacher in preparing *drill, practice, tutorial,* or *simulation* programs (see Chapter 6).

Load: A *command* in the *basic* language that directs the computer to move a specified *program* from its *mass storage memory* to its *resident memory.*

Lo-Res Graphics: *Graphics* created by using rectangular clusters of *pixels.* Each cluster is about half the size of an *alphanumeric character.* Lo-res graphics divide the video screen into about 1600 such rectangles.

NOTES

Low-Level Language: A communication compromise between the computer and the programmer. Programmers who use a low-level language give up the natural vocabulary and syntax of a *high-level language* in order to communicate more efficiently with the computer. Computers find it much easier to translate *low-level language* into their native *machine language.*

Machine Language: The native language of the computer. Since the entire "alphabet" of machine language consists of *0* and *1,* it's not a very natural language for humans. Although some *computerniks* babble in machine language, most normal folks prefer a *high-level language.*

Mass Storage Memory: That part of a computer system that serves as a library for information (computer programs or data) which is in excess of the amount of information that can be held in the *resident memory* at any given time. The information of the mass storage memory is usually recorded on a *disk* or *cassette tape;* it is not "lost" when the computer system is turned off (also see *resident memory).*

Memory: That part of a computer that stores information (computer *program* or data); it comes in two basic forms (see both *mass storage memory* and *resident memory).*

Microcomputer: A computer that has a computer-on-a-chip as its "brain." Sometimes used to refer to a *personal computer.*

Microprocessor: Usually takes the form of a *chip* housed in a *DIP.* If the microprocessor is dedicated to performing an unalterable set of instructions, it does not qualify as a computer.

Modem: The term is an abbreviation for MOdulator-DEModulator. It refers to any device which allows a computer to "talk" over telephone lines (see *acoustic coupler).*

Monitor: An everyday TV set or one designed specifically for use with a computer or video recorder.

Output: Information leaving a *computer system.*

Pascal: This *high-level language* was named in honor of Blaise Pascal (1623–62), a French mathematician given to gambling and the invention of such devices as an adding/subtracting machine. It is a general-purpose language of growing popularity, and one that encourages organized thinking by the program writer.

Peripheral: A piece of *hardware* used by a computer. Examples include *disk drives, monitors, printers, Modems,* and *bit pads.*

Personal Computer: A small computer used for home, office, or educational tasks. Some of the better known names in this volatile market are Apple, Atari, Commodore, IBM, and Radio Shack.

Notes

Pixel: The smallest area that can be illuminated on a video screen or a single dot within the dot matrix used by a *printer*.

PL/1: The abbreviation for Programming Language 1. This *high-level language* is reputed to have combined some of the best features of *ALGOL, COBOL,* and *FORTRAN* to make it useful in both business and scientific applications.

Port: A physical point of entry through which a *peripheral* can communicate with a computer.

Practice Program: A type of *software* that is designed to reinforce, refine, or extend the use of a step-by-step process or procedure (see Chapter 7).

Printer: A device that is used by a computer to make *hardcopy*. Some printers are limited to reproducing keyboard symbols and using one size of type. Other printers can handle graphics and several sizes of type.

Problem-Solving Program: A type of *software* that is comprised of an *algorithm* that is useful in transforming problem data into the test of a conjecture about that problem (see Chapter 12).

Program: A sequence of instructions (written in some computer language) that cause a computer to carry out a given task.

Programming Utility Program: A type of *software* usually designed to aid a computer programmer in creating, testing, or enhancing a *program*. Some such programs, called *lesson authoring systems,* permit nonprogrammers to create and modify instructional programs (see Chapters 6 and 12).

RAM: The acronym for Random-Access-Memory. This is a form of computer memory *(resident* or *mass storage)* that can be equated with instant recall. Rather than having to search its memory sequentially beginning with the first item stored, a computer with RAM can go directly to a particular location to retrieve or store a piece of information. The contents of RAM can be altered by a program or programmer.

Resident Memory: That part of the computer that holds the information *(program* or *data)* currently being used by the computer. This memory is of much smaller size than the *mass storage memory* and, unlike the *mass storage memory,* is "lost" (erased) when the computer is turned off.

ROM: The acronym for Read-Only Memory. The contents of ROM are stored once and for all by a programmer with special privileges. (That person usually is the manufacturer.) While those contents can be instantly recalled by any user (as with RAM), they cannot be altered.

Run: A *command* in the BASIC language that directs the computer to execute the steps of a specified program which was previously *loaded* into its *resident memory*.

NOTES

Save: To place a computer program on some mass storage medium (outside the computer's *resident memory)* such as a *disk* or *cassette tape.*

Scroll: To move the display on a TV screen upwards or downwards.

Simulation: A type of *software* which presents a computerized surrogate of a "real life" environment; the user is called upon to play the role of a decision maker within that computerized environment (see Chapter 10).

Software: A *computer program.* (Use of the term sometimes also includes *documentation* or *ancillary materials* related to the program.)

Special Characters: Printable characters other than numerals or letters of an alphabet. These include such things as mathematical symbols or diacritical marks.

Statement: A complete sentence within the bounds set by the grammar, syntax, and punctuation of the programming language.

String: A collection of *alphanumeric* or *special characters.* The computer distinguishes between strings (symbols) and numbers.

Syntax: The rules of computer grammar that govern the way an *instruction* is written. Computer syntax is, generally speaking, much fussier (i.e., rigid) than the syntax of a spoken language such as English.

System-Error Message: A terse and usually cryptic comment displayed on the screen when a computer doesn't know what to do next.

Terminal: A *peripheral* comprised of a keyboard and either a TV-like screen or a *printer.*

Testing Operations Program: A type of *software* that assists a teacher in the creation, scoring, or evaluation of individual test items or complete tests (see Chapter 8).

Text: Printed stuff presented to the user as part of the *output* of a computer *program.*

Tutorial Program: A type of instructional *software* that, by means of a user-computer dialogue, is designed to introduce the user to a new concept (see Chapter 6).

User-Friendly Software: Software that anticipates the needs of the naive user.

Users' Group: An organization that is bound together by a common interest in a particular brand of computer *hardware,* a particular collection of computer applications, or a general zeal for computing. The organization's activities may include such things as the sharing of information (through a printed or electronic newsletter), the exchange of computer software or hardware, the holding of meetings devoted to the diagnosis and cure of hardware problems, or socializing for the purpose of ego building or moral support.

NOTES

VDT: The abbreviation for Video Display Terminal. A TV-like device with a keyboard designed for use with computers, it is essentially the same thing as a *CRT.*

Whistles-and-Bells Program: A program designed to demonstrate special features of the *hardware, software,* or *firmware* of a particular *computer system* (see Chapter 12).

Word Processing: The process of creating, modifying, deleting, and formatting *text.*

Word Processor: The *hardware* or *software* used in *word processing.*

NOTES

INDEX